PEARSON EDUCATION
AP* TEST PREP SERIES

AP* U.S. HISTORY

OUT OF MANY
A HISTORY OF THE AMERICAN PEOPLE
AP* EDITION

FARAGHER, BUHLE, CZITROM, ARMITAGE

PEARSON

Prentice
Hall

Upper Saddle River, New Jersey 07458

Printed in the United States of America

10 9 8 7 6 5 4

ISBN 0-13-198606-6

PEARSON PRENTICE HALL
Upper Saddle River, New Jersey 07458
A Pearson Education Company

Out of Many, AP* Test Prep Book

TABLE OF CONTENTS

CHAPTER 1

A Continent of Villages, to 1500 1
   Settling the Continent **1**
   New Ways of Living on the Land **1**
   The Development of Farming **1**
   Cultural Regions of North America on the
     Eve of Colonization **1**
     Multiple-Choice Questions **2**
     Document-Based Question **3**
     ANSWERS AND EXPLANATIONS **7**

CHAPTER 2

When Worlds Collide, 1492–1590 10
   The Expansion of Europe **10**
   The Spanish in the Americas **10**
   Northern Explorations and Encounters **10**
     Multiple-Choice Questions **11**
     Document-Based Question **12**
     ANSWERS AND EXPLANATIONS **16**

CHAPTER 3

Planting Colonies in North America, 1588–1701 19
   Spain and its Competitors in North
     America **19**
   England in the Chesapeake **19**
   The New England Colonies **19**
   The Proprietary Colonies **19**
   Conflict and War **20**
     Multiple-Choice Questions **20**
     Document-Based Question **21**
     ANSWERS AND EXPLANATIONS **25**

CHAPTER 4

Slavery and Empire, 1441–1770 28
   The Beginnings of African Slavery **28**
   The African Slave Trade **28**
   The Development of North American Slave
     Societies **28**
   African to African American **28**
   Slavery and Empire **28**
   Slavery and Freedom **28**
     Multiple-Choice Questions **29**
     Document-Based Question **30**
     ANSWERS AND EXPLANATIONS **33**

CHAPTER 5

The Cultures of Colonial North America, 1700–1780 35
   North American Regions **35**
   Diverging Social and Political Patterns **35**
   The Cultural Transformation of British North
     America **35**
     Multiple-Choice Questions **35**
     Document-Based Question **36**
     ANSWERS AND EXPLANATIONS **41**

CHAPTER 6

From Empire to Independence, 1750–1776 44
   The Seven Years' War in America **44**
   The Imperial Crisis in British North
     America **44**
   "Save Your Money and Save Your
     Country" **44**
   From Resistance to Rebellion **44**
   Deciding for Independence **44**
     Multiple-Choice Questions **45**
     Document-Based Question **46**
     ANSWERS AND EXPLANATIONS **50**

CHAPTER 7

The American Revolution, 1776–1786   53

The War for Independence   53
The United States in Congress
   Assembled   53
Revolutionary Politics in the States   53
   Multiple-Choice Questions   54
   Document-Based Question   55
ANSWERS AND EXPLANATIONS   59

CHAPTER 8

The New Nation, 1786–1800   62

The Crisis of the 1780s   62
The New Constitution   62
The First Administration   62
Federalists and Jeffersonian
   Republicans   62
"The Rising Glory of America"   62
   Multiple-Choice Questions   63
   Document-Based Question   64
ANSWERS AND EXPLANATIONS   67

CHAPTER 9

An Agrarian Republic, 1790–1824   70

North American Communities from Coast
   to Coast   70
A National Economy   70
The Jefferson Presidency   70
Renewed Imperial Rivalry in North
   America   70
The War of 1812   70
Defining the Boundaries   70
   Multiple-Choice Questions   71
   Document-Based Question   72
ANSWERS AND EXPLANATIONS   75

CHAPTER 10

The South and Slavery, 1790s–1850s   78

King Cotton and Southern Expansion   78
To Be a Slave   78
The African American Community   78
The White Majority   78
Planters   78
The Defense of Slavery   79
   Multiple-Choice Questions   79
   Document-Based Question   80
ANSWERS AND EXPLANATIONS   83

CHAPTER 11

The Growth of Democracy, 1824–1840   85

The New Democratic Politics in North
   America   85
The Jackson Presidency   85
Changing the Course of Government   85
The Second American Party System   85
American Arts and Letters   85
   Multiple-Choice Questions   86
   Document-Based Question   87
ANSWERS AND EXPLANATIONS   91

CHAPTER 12

Industry and the North, 1790s–1840s   94

Preindustrial Ways of Working   94
The Transportation Revolution   94
The Market Revolution   94
From Artisan to Worker   94
A New Social Order   94
   Multiple-Choice Questions   95
   Document-Based Question   96
ANSWERS AND EXPLANATIONS   101

CHAPTER 13

**Coming to Terms with the New Age,
1820s–1850s**   103

Immigration and Ethnicity   103
Urban America   103
The Labor Movement and Urban
   Politics   103
Social Reform Movements   103
Antislavery and Abolitionism   103
The Women's Rights Movement   103
   Multiple-Choice Questions   104
   Document-Based Question   105
ANSWERS AND EXPLANATIONS   108

CHAPTER 14

**The Territorial Expansion of the United States,
1830s–1850s**   111

Exploring the West   111
The Politics of Expansion   111
The Mexican-American War   111
California and the Gold Rush   111
The Politics of Manifest Destiny   111
   Multiple-Choice Questions   112
   Document-Based Question   113
ANSWERS AND EXPLANATIONS   117

CHAPTER 15

The Coming Crisis, the 1850s 119

America in 1850 **119**
The Compromise of 1850 **119**
The Crisis of the National Party
   System **119**
The Differences Deepen **119**
The South Secedes **120**
   Multiple-Choice Questions **120**
   Document-Based Question **121**
ANSWERS AND EXPLANATIONS **126**

CHAPTER 16

The Civil War, 1861–1865 129

Communities Mobilize for War **129**
Governments Organize for War **129**
The Fighting Through 1862 **129**
The Death of Slavery **129**
The Front Lines and the Home Front **129**
The Tide Turns **130**
   Multiple-Choice Questions **130**
   Document-Based Question **131**
ANSWERS AND EXPLANATIONS **134**

CHAPTER 17

Reconstruction, 1863–1877 137

The Politics of Reconstruction **137**
The Meaning of Freedom **137**
Southern Politics and Society **137**
Reconstructing the North **138**
   Multiple-Choice Questions **138**
   Document-Based Question **139**
ANSWERS AND EXPLANATIONS **143**

CHAPTER 18

Conquest and Survival: The Trans-Mississippi West, 1860–1900 146

Indian Peoples Under Siege **146**
The Internal Empire **146**
The Open Range **146**
Farming Communities on the Plains **146**
The World's Breadbasket **146**
The Western Landscape **147**
The Transformation of Indian
   Societies **147**
   Multiple-Choice Questions **147**
   Document-Based Question **148**
ANSWERS AND EXPLANATIONS **153**

CHAPTER 19

The Incorporation of America, 1865–1900 155

The Rise of Industry, The Triumph of
   Business **155**
Labor in the Age of Big Business **155**
The New South **155**
The Industrial City **155**
The Rise of Consumer Society **155**
Cultures in Conflict, Culture in
   Common **156**
   Multiple-Choice Questions **156**
   Document-Based Question **157**
ANSWERS AND EXPLANATIONS **162**

CHAPTER 20

Commonwealth and Empire, 1870–1900 165

Toward a National Governing Class **165**
Farmers and Workers Organize Their
   Communities **165**
The Crisis of the 1890s **165**
The Age of Segregation **165**
"Imperialism of Righteousness" **165**
The Spanish-American War **166**
   Multiple-Choice Questions **166**
   Document-Based Question **167**
ANSWERS AND EXPLANATIONS **171**

CHAPTER 21

Urban America and the Progressive Era, 1900–1917 174

The Currents of Progressivism **174**
Social Control and Its Limits **174**
Working-class Communities and
   Protest **174**
Women's Movements and Black
   Awakening **174**
National Progressivism **175**
   Multiple-Choice Questions **175**
   Document-Based Question **176**
ANSWERS AND EXPLANATIONS **180**

CHAPTER 22

World War I, 1914–1920   183
    Becoming a World Power   183
    The Great War   183
    American Mobilization   183
    Over Here   183
    Repression and Reaction   184
    An Uneasy Peace   184
        Multiple-Choice Questions   184
        Document-Based Question   185
    ANSWERS AND EXPLANATIONS   188

CHAPTER 23

The Twenties, 1920–1929   191
    Postwar Prosperity and its Price   191
    The New Mass Culture   191
    Resistance to Modernity   191
    The State, the Economy, and
        Business   191
    Promises Postponed   192
        Multiple-Choice Questions   192
        Document-Based Question   193
    ANSWERS AND EXPLANATIONS   197

CHAPTER 24

**The Great Depression and the New Deal,
1929–1940**   199
    Hard Times   199
    FDR and the First New Deal   199
    Left Turn and the Second New Deal   199
    The New Deal in the South and the
        West   199
    Depression-Era Culture   200
    The Limits of Reform   200
        Multiple-Choice Questions   200
        Document-Based Question   201
    ANSWERS AND EXPLANATIONS   205

CHAPTER 25

World War II, 1941–1945   208
    The Coming of World War II   208
    Arsenal of Democracy   208
    The Home Front   208
    Men and Women in Uniform   209
    The World at War   209
    The Last Stages of War   209
        Multiple-Choice Questions   209
        Document-Based Question   210
    ANSWERS AND EXPLANATIONS   214

CHAPTER 26

The Cold War, 1945–1952   217
    Global Insecurities at War's End   217
    The Policy of Containment   217
    Cold War Liberalism   217
    The Cold War at Home   217
    Cold War Culture   218
    Stalemate for the Democrats   218
        Multiple-Choice Questions   218
        Document-Based Question   219
    ANSWERS AND EXPLANATIONS   223

CHAPTER 27

America at Midcentury, 1952–1963   226
    American Society at Midcentury   226
    Youth Culture   226
    Mass Culture and Its Discontents   226
    The Cold War Continued   226
    John F. Kennedy and the New
        Frontier   227
        Multiple-Choice Questions   227
        Document-Based Question   228
    ANSWERS AND EXPLANATIONS   232

CHAPTER 28

The Civil Rights Movement, 1945–1966   234
    Origins of the Movement   234
    No Easy Road to Freedom,
        1957–1962   234
    The Movement at High Tide,
        1963–1965   234
    Civil Rights Beyond Black and White   234
        Multiple-Choice Questions   235
        Document-Based Question   236
    ANSWERS AND EXPLANATIONS   240

CHAPTER 29

War Abroad, War at Home, 1965–1974   242
    Vietnam: America's Longest War   242
    A Generation in Conflict   242
    Wars on Poverty   242
    1968   243
    The Politics of Identity   243
    The Nixon Presidency   243
    Watergate   243
        Multiple-Choice Questions   243
        Document-Based Question   244
    ANSWERS AND EXPLANATIONS   248

CHAPTER 30

**The Conservative Ascendancy,
1974–1991** 250

    The Overextended Society **250**
    The New Conservatism **250**
    Adjusting to a New World **250**
    Reagan Revolution **251**
    Best of Times, Worst of Times **251**
    Reagan's Foreign Policy **251**
        Multiple-Choice Questions **251**
        Document-Based Question **252**
    ANSWERS AND EXPLANATIONS **256**

CHAPTER 31

**Toward a Transnational America,
since 1988** 259

    "A Kinder, Gentler Nation" **259**
    The Clinton Presidency **259**
    Changing American Communities **259**
    A New Age of Anxiety **260**
    The New Millennium **260**
        Multiple-Choice Questions **260**
        Document-Based Question **261**
    ANSWERS AND EXPLANATIONS **265**

**AP United States History
Sample Practice Test 1** 267

**AP United States History
Sample Practice Test 2** 288

Introduction

The Advanced Placement Program*

The AP program offers thirty-five college-level courses to qualified high school students. If you receive a grade of 3 or higher on an AP exam, you may be eligible for college credit, depending on the policies of the institution you plan to attend. Approximately 3,000 college and universities around the world grant credit to students who have performed well on AP exams. If you are taking several AP courses and if you score well on multiple AP exams, you may even be eligible to enter college as a sophomore. Some institutions grant sophomore status to incoming first-year students who have demonstrated mastery of many AP subjects. In addition, the College Board confers a number of AP Scholar Awards on students who score 3 or higher on three or more AP exams. Additional awards are available to students who receive very high grades on four or five AP exams.

Why Take an AP Course?

You may be taking one or more AP courses simply because you are thirsty for knowledge. Of course, the fact that colleges look favorably on applicants who have AP courses on their secondary school transcripts is another powerful incentive! Because AP classes usually involve rigorous lessons, a great deal of homework, and many tests, they signal to college admissions officers that AP students are willing to work hard to get the most from their education. Because AP course work is more difficult than average high school work, many admissions officers evaluate AP grades on a kind of curve—if you receive a *B* in an AP class, for example, it might carry the same weight as an *A* in a regular high school class.

Your AP U.S. History course prepares you for many of the skills you will need in college. For example, your teacher may assign research papers and encourage you to use resources outside the scope of your textbook. Some of these resources may be primary sources that permit you to analyze events as a historian would. Other class assignments may require you to write longer-than-usual essays on historical subjects. The AP U.S. History course will challenge you to gather and consider information in new—and sometimes unfamiliar—ways. You can feel good knowing that your ability to use these methods and skills will give you a leg up as you enter college.

Each college or university decides whether or not to grant college credit for an AP course, and each bases this decision on what it considers satisfactory grades on AP exams. Depending on what college you attend and what area of study you pursue, your decision to take the AP U.S. History Exam could end up saving you tuition money. You can contact schools directly to find out their guidelines for accepting AP credits.

Taking an AP Examination

Your AP teacher or school guidance counselor can give you information on how to sign up for an AP exam. Remember, the deadline to sign up and pay the fees for the exam is usually in January, four months before the actual date of the exam in May. If, after taking the exam, you want to have your score report sent to additional schools besides those you named on your registration—or if you want to withhold or cancel your score—you will need to notify the College Board by June 15. Your exam grades will be sent to you by mail in early-mid July. However, for an additional fee, Educational Testing Service (the organization that develops and scores tests for the College Board) will release your score to you over the phone around July 1st. If your school does not administer the AP exam, your teacher or guidance counselor can help you find a nearby school that does. If you continue to have difficulty determining what schools in your region offer the exam, you can always visit the College Board's website (*www.collegeboard.com*) for more information. The cost of the exam frequently changes and can differ depending on the number of exams taken.. If you feel that you cannot afford this fee, you may apply to the College Board for a fee reduction based on your financial need.

Test-Taking Strategies for the AP U.S. History Examination

Below is a brief list of basic tips and strategies to think about *before* you arrive at the exam site.

- It's a good idea to arrive at the exam site thirty minutes before the start time. This saves you additional worry about arriving late. You should plan your schedule so that you get *two* very good nights of sleep before exam day. On the day of the exam, make sure that you eat good, nutritious meals. These tips may sound corny or obvious, but your body must be in peak form in order for your brain to perform well.

- It's a good idea to have a photo I.D. with you when you arrive at the exam site. (It is essential if you are taking the exam at a school other than your own.) Carrying a driver's license or a student I.D. card will allow you to prove your identity, if anyone needs such proof.

- You should bring at least two pencils for the multiple-choice section, as well as two black or dark blue pens for the free-response section of the exam. Take a moment to make sure that your pencils are labeled #2 and that they have good erasers. After all, the machine that scores Section I of the exam cannot recognize marks made by other types of pencils. Also, it cannot read a correct answer if a previous answer has not been erased completely.

- If possible, it's helpful to have a watch with you at the exam. It's true that most testing rooms will have clocks and that most test administrators will give you periodic reminders of how much time you have remaining. Still, having your own watch makes it easy to keep close track of your own pace. The watch cannot have a calculator or an alarm, however, as these are not permitted in the exam room.

- There are a few other things that are not allowed in the exam room. Do not bring books of any kind, laptop computers, wireless instant-messaging devices, cameras, or portable radios. If you must bring a cellular phone with you, prepare to turn it off and give it to the test proctor until you are finished with your exam.

  Educational Testing Service prohibits the objects listed above in the interest of fairness to all test-takers. Similarly, the test administrators are very clear and very serious about what types of conduct are not allowed during the examination. Below is a list of actions to avoid at all costs, since each is grounds for your immediate dismissal from the exam room.

- Do not consult any outside materials during the three hours and five minutes of the exam period. Remember, the break is technically part of the exam—you are not free to review any materials at that time either.

- Do not speak during the exam, unless you have a question for the test proctor. Raise your hand to get the proctor's attention.

- When you are told to stop working on a section of the exam, you must stop *immediately*.

- Do not open your exam booklet before the test begins.

- Never tear a page out of your test booklet or try to remove the exam from the test room.

- Do not behave disruptively—even if you're distressed about a difficult test question or because you've run out of time. Stay calm and make no unnecessary noise. Remember, too, the worst-case scenario: if you are displeased with your performance on test day, you can always cancel your exam scores.

Section I: Strategies for Multiple-Choice Questions

Having a firm grasp of U.S. history is, of course, the key to your doing well on the AP U.S. History Examination. In addition, being well-informed about the exam itself increases your chances of achieving a high score. Below is a list of strategies that you can use to increase your comfort, your confidence, and your chances of excelling on the multiple-choice section of the exam.

- Pace yourself and keep track of the remaining time as you complete the multiple-choice section of the exam. Remember, you have fifty-five minutes to answer all eighty questions. It's important that you don't get stuck on one question for too long.

- Make a light mark in your test booklet next to any questions you can't answer. Return to them after you reach the end of Section I. Sometimes questions that appear later in the test will refresh your memory of a particular period, and you will be able to answer one of those earlier questions.

- Always read the entire question carefully, and underline key words or ideas. You might wish to double underline words such as *NOT* or *EXCEPT* in that type of multiple-choice question.

- Read each and every one of the answer choices carefully before you make your final selection.

- Trust your first instinct. Since it has been proven statistically that your first choice is more likely to be correct, you should replace it only if you are completely certain that your second choice is correct.

- Use the process of elimination to help you home in on a correct answer. Even if you are quite sure of an answer, cross out the letters of incorrect choices in your test booklet as you eliminate them. This cuts down on distraction and allows you to narrow the remaining choices even further.
- If you are able to eliminate two or more answer choices, it is better to make an educated guess at the correct answer than to leave the answer blank.
- Remember that the multiple-choice section of the AP U.S. History Exam is designed so that easier questions appear at the start of the test. Try to answer the easy questions as quickly as you can without sacrificing care and thoroughness. If you are able to rack up many correct answers at the start of the section, you will conserve time (and mental energy) for the more difficult questions toward the end of the test.
- About a month prior to the test date, you should begin doing drills to prepare for the multiple-choice section of the test. Ask your teacher for copies of old AP U.S. History Exams, and answer the multiple-choice questions. Answer the sample questions in Part II of this book, and take the sample tests in Part III. After you've answered the questions, check your answers and use the answer explanations to determine any content areas that you need to study or review more thoroughly.
- Make yourself completely familiar with the instructions for the multiple-choice questions *before* you take the exam. You'll find the instructions in this book. By knowing the instructions cold, you'll save yourself the time of reading them carefully on the day of the test.
- In the week before the exam, do a comprehensive review of the history you've studied. However, don't dwell on obscure details. Focus on the larger issues that you might confront in the exam. It's a good idea to revisit with your teacher any major themes that you have found confusing or that you feel you don't know as well as you should. You can review using information in the Part I correlation chart and in Part II of this book, as well as in your textbook.
- Try to grow as familiar as you can with the format of Section I. The more comfortable you are with the multiple-choice format and with the kinds of questions you'll encounter, the easier the exam will be. Remember, Part II and Part III of this book provide you with invaluable practice on the kinds of multiple-choice questions you will encounter on the AP U.S. History Exam.

In addition to these strategies, be on the lookout for the six types of questions:
  - Identification questions;
  - "NOT/EXCEPT" questions;
  - Reading/quotation questions;
  - Analysis questions;
  - Skill-based questions;
  - Illustration-based questions.

Section II: Strategies for Free-Response Questions

Below is a list of strategies that you can use to increase your chances of excelling on the free-response section of the exam.

- Since you have just two hours and ten minutes to outline and write three essays in the free-response section of the AP U.S. History Exam, you must manage your time carefully.
- Be careful not to stray from the focus of the question being asked. As you read a question, underline any directive words that indicate how you should address and focus the material in your essay. Some of the most frequently used directives on the AP U.S. History Exam are listed below, along with descriptions of what you need to do in your writing to answer the question.
  - *Analyze* (show relationships between events; explain)
  - *Assess/Evaluate* (give an opinion of; appraise; discuss advantages and disadvantages)
  - *Compare* (address similarities and differences between two or more things)
  - *Contrast* (examine to illustrate points of difference or divergence)
  - *Defend/Refute* (argue for or against a specific statement or position, using factual support to back up your argument)
  - *Describe* (give a detailed account)
  - *Discuss* (consider or examine; debate)

> - *Explain* (clarify; tell the meaning)
> - *To what extent and in what ways* (tell how much and how)
- As you formulate your thesis, always consider whether or not it will answer the essay question directly.

Part A: The Document-Based Question

The following strategies will help you conceive, organize, and write your response to the DBQ.

- During the fifteen-minute reading period, begin by reading carefully the DBQ and the historical background provided along with it.
- Underline key words and make a note of any outside information you might be able to connect to the question or to the historical background material.
- Then read each of the historical documents in order, reviewing some for more in-depth analysis, and flagging any phrases or words that connect that document to the main theme of the DBQ.
- Although some documents will be more crucial to an understanding of the topic than others, each document is relevant to the question. Make a mark next to those documents that you feel are the most pertinent and that you will use most extensively to support your argument.
- Take note of the date of each source and identify the author's position or point-of-view (including any potential bias).
- If the reading period allows, decide on a thesis statement and plan an outline that will enable you to analyze and interpret as many of the documents as possible into a cohesive essay.
- Keep in mind that successful DBQ responses incorporate analysis of the majority of documents. However, you do not need to cite every document to get a high score. Specific mention of individual documents should always occur in the context of the overall topic and should help to illustrate or organize arguments made in your essay. In short, documents should *never* be cited or summarized without analysis. One key to your success on the DBQ portion of the exam is a seamless integration of the documents into the body of your essay.
- Whenever you make use of documents in your DBQ response, ask yourself how they function with respect to your thesis and to the DBQ question itself. It is important also to address any documents that directly refute your thesis. Readers will be as interested to see how you handle material that contradicts your main argument as they will be to see your use of documents that support your thesis.
- Remember to refer to individual documents by author name and/or by the document number. If time allows, you may want to write a conclusion to your DBQ essay that reflects on how the documentary evidence illustrates your thesis.
- If you have time, try to proofread your essays for any inconsistencies or weaknesses.

Here is an abbreviated version of the kind of DBQ you will encounter on your AP U.S. History Exam. In this sample DBQ, you will have just four historical documents to consider and integrate into your response. A sample analysis of the documents and the manner in which you should proceed to write your essay follows.

> 1. *To what extent and in what ways did sixteenth-century Spanish attitudes toward the lands and people conquered in the New World affect government policy?*

Background History: The fifteenth century witnessed the beginning of western Europe's expansion into unknown lands. A quest for gold and spices dominated these initial adventures at sea. Christopher Columbus's voyage of 1492 marked the beginning of the Spanish dominance of a vast American territory. Subsequently, Spaniards set up satellite governments in North America and South America, and they recruited and enslaved native Indians to assist them in mining, agriculture, and other endeavors aimed at creating a New World economy to profit Spain.

DOCUMENT 1 Source: Hernán Cortés, Spanish conqueror, second letter to Charles V, 1520

In the place of these I put images of Our Lady and the Saints, which excited not a little feeling in Montezuma and the inhabitants, who at first remonstrated, declaring that if my proceedings were known throughout the country, the people would rise against me; for they believed that their idols bestowed on them all temporal good, and if they permitted them to be ill-treated, they would be angry and without their gifts, and by this means the people would be deprived of the fruits of the earth and perish with famine. I answered, through the interpreters, that they were deceived in expecting any favors from idols, the work of their own hands, formed of unclean things; and that they must learn there was but one God, the universal Lord of all, who had created the heavens and earth, and all things else, and had made them and us …

DOCUMENT 2   Source: Bartolomé de las Casas (1474–1566), Dominican missionary, "A Brief Account of the Destruction of the Indies," ca. 1542

That which led the Spaniards to these unsanctified impieties was the desire of Gold, to make themselves suddenly rich … In a word, their covetousness, their ambition, which could not be more in any people under heaven, the riches of the Country, and the patience of the people gave occasion to this their devilish barbarism. For the Spaniards so condemned them … that they used them not like beasts, for that would have been tolerable, but looked upon them as if they had been but the dung and filth of the earth, and so little they regarded the health of their souls, that they suffered this great multitude to die without the least light of Religion …

DOCUMENT 3 Source: "The New Laws of the Indies," laws and ordinances made by Charles V for the government of the Indies and treatment of the Indians, 1542

As we have ordered provision to be made that from henceforward the Indians in no way be made slaves, including those who until now have been enslaved against all reason and right and contrary to the provisions and instructions thereupon, We ordain and command that the Audiencias having first summoned the parties to their presence, without any further judicial form, but in a summary way, so that the truth may be ascertained, speedily set the said Indians at liberty unless the persons who hold them for slaves show title why they should hold and possess them legitimately. And in order that in default of persons to solicit the aforesaid, the Indians may not remain in slavery unjustly, We command that the Audiencias appoint persons who may pursue this cause for the Indians and be paid out of the Exchequer fines, provided they be men of trust and diligence.

DOCUMENT 4 Source: Anonymous, "The Gold of the Indies," from the Court of Philip II of Spain, 1559

[G]reat quantities of gold and silver are no longer found upon the surface of the earth, as they have been in past years; and to penetrate into the bowels of the earth requires greater effort, skill and outlay, and the Spaniards are not willing to do the work themselves, and the natives cannot be forced to do so, because the Emperor has freed them from all obligation of service as soon as they accept the Christian religion. Wherefore it is necessary to acquire negro slaves, who are brought from the coasts of Africa, both within and without the Straits, and these are selling dearer every day, because on account of their natural lack of strength and the change of climate, added to the lack of discretion upon the part of their masters in making them work too hard and giving them too little to eat, they fall sick and the greater part of them die.

This sample DBQ question asks you to consider *how* Spanish attitudes toward lands and peoples in the New World contributed to government policy and *how much* they contributed. By narrowing the focus to Spanish attitudes in the sixteenth century, and by relying on documents exclusively from that period, this question provides you with much of the equipment that you will use in formulating your response.

As you read through each of the documents, pay attention to the author of each work. You should recognize Hernán Cortés, the author of **DOCUMENT 1**, the Spanish conquistador who brutally defeated the Aztecs of Mexico in 1521 and reclaimed the region as New Spain. Here Cortés relates his efforts to convert the Aztecs to Christian worship, and he characterizes their worship of idols as wrong. It is worth noting that Cortés' primary objective in his dealing with the Aztecs was not religious conversion, but the vast quantities of gold held by the Aztec ruler, Montezuma. Cortés and his soldiers brutally conquered the city of Tenochtitlán, killing thousands of Aztecs and asserting Spanish control of the region. Any analysis of this document (and its benevolent but paternalistic attitude toward the Indians) must take into account Cortés's brutality against the Aztecs.

You may be familiar with Bartolomé de las Casas, the author of **DOCUMENT 2**, the Dominican missionary who waged a campaign against the exploitative aspects of conquest in the Americas. You may also recall that the ideas of Las Casas led to new royal regulations of conquest. In this excerpt, you should detect Las Casas' anger at the greed of the Spanish, as well as his frustration at their debasing treatment of the Indians. His emphasis on religion is clear in his condemnation of the Spanish massacre of Indian societies and of the failure to offer Native Americans religious enlightenment.

The third document reflects new royal laws about the treatment of Indians, and it demands their liberty from slavery. The authorship of this officia document from the court of Charles V is unclear, but the sentiments expressed reflect a significant departure from the conditions described by Las Casas (**DOCUMENT 2**) and call for freedom for the Indians under Spanish control.

The fourth document, from the court of Philip II of Spain, alludes to the problem of carrying out some of the labor-intensive mining of gold and silver that has been done in the past by Indians. The author contends that Indians were freed from forced labor as soon as they converted to Christianity, and that African slaves will be necessary to carry out the difficult work. It is worth noting that though the Indians were released from forced servitude, they gained their liberty only by converting to a new faith—hardly the liberty and freedom described in **DOCUMENT 3**.

As you develop a strong thesis that answers the question and enables you to discuss these works in detail, you will want to respond to the "To what extent and in what ways," portion of the question. If you don't know much about this period in history, you can rely on some of the details provided in the documents. You should make use of most of the documents in your response, and you should explain authorial bias whenever you detect it. You should glean the following basic ideas from the documents and keep them in mind as you compose your thesis:

■ Christianity was important to sixteenth-century Spaniards, many of whom were concerned that the natives in the lands they conquered were not believers.

■ Natives experienced significant bloodshed and brutality at the hands of the Spanish. Many of the natives were treated by the Spanish as if they were worthless creatures who had no basic rights as human beings.

■ In the sixteenth century, new laws released natives from enslavement, but these laws were conditional on the natives' conversion to Christianity.

■ Among the primary motives of sixteenth-century explorers and discoverers was the acquisition of gold and other riches in the New World. This ambition to gain access to more minerals and wealth, coupled with new laws prohibiting native slavery, led Spaniards to seek other unrestricted labor markets, such as those in Africa.

One way to address the question in thesis form would be as follows:

Spanish greed to acquire the riches of the New World at any cost competed with a desire to convert to Christianity the peoples it conquered; the result of these conflicting desires was sixteenth-century legislation that sought to protect the rights of natives but that led ultimately to the exploitation of natives in Africa.

In your first paragraph, you might want to back up your thesis statement by discussing the Spanish quest for riches of the New World. You could cite passages from Bartolomé de Las Casas and from **DOCUMENT 4**, and you could describe the quest of Hernán Cortés to find the gold of the Aztecs. This would be an excellent place in the essay to demonstrate your outside knowledge on the subject, as you could refer to other explorers whose conquests you recall. Using details, you should develop the idea that this quest for wealth led to tremendous exploitation of the natives.

In your second paragraph, you could address the Spanish desire to impart Christian faith in the lands they conquered, and you could cite the Cortés passage. You would want to acknowledge the bias implicit in this document—that is, that Cortés was a brutal conquistador who could liken himself to the Indians and make claims of their being made by the same God, but who could then go on to destroy their civilization. You could also refer to Las Casas' concern that the natives were killed without the benefit of religious enlightenment, and you could allude to the fact (noted in **DOCUMENT 4**) that natives who converted were granted freedom from slavery. You could assert that the campaign of Las Casas and other reformers persuaded Emperor Charles V that Spanish exploitation of natives was wrong, and that the campaign resulted in the legislation (indicated in **DOCUMENT 3**) that granted natives their freedom from slavery. You might feel that it is worth acknowledging that by 1542, much damage had already been done to these native civilizations, as Columbus had arrived in the New World fully fifty years earlier.

You might close the essay by saying that while Spanish concern for the religious faith of the peoples they conquered was significant, it was overwhelmed by their desire for the wealth of the New World. As **DOCUMENT 4** suggests, though new legislation protected the natives (provided that they agreed to convert—in itself a kind of enslavement, one might argue), it did not compel the Spanish to check their desire to seize the region's riches. The policies of the Spanish government had changed over time as a result of demands from religious organizations seeking human rights assurances, and exploitation of the natives had slowed by the middle of the sixteenth century. However, greedy Spanish colonials sought new labor markets in other continents and displayed a similar disregard for the rights of natives on the African continent.

A response that has a strong thesis statement, develops its ideas clearly, integrates information from most of the documents, identifies and explains any bias demonstrated by those documents, and directly answers the actual Document-Based Question will earn a high score.

Part B: Thematic Questions

The following strategies will help you conceive, organize, and write your response to two thematic questions.

■ Read all three questions in each group and note any facts that are relevant to each question. It is best to answer the thematic question for which you have the most information. Decide which question this is. (Sometimes, but not always, this will be a question concerning a subject you have studied extensively in class.)

■ As in the DBQ, you should underline key directive words and phrases such as *Analyze, Assess, Evaluate, Compare, Contrast, Defend, Refute, Describe, Discuss, Explain,* and *To what extent and in what ways.*

■ Because the time you have to complete these essays is short, you should focus your energy on defending a simple thesis that answers the question and discussing as much relevant historical information as possible.

■ Each of your essays should include an introductory paragraph that asserts a thesis, paragraphs that support your argument, and a concluding paragraph that summarizes your argument. As you consider which two thematic questions to answer, think about how you would argue the essay. Do you have a lot to say about the topic? Create a graphic organizer or write an outline to help you organize your ideas.

■ Always use concrete historical ideas and examples to substantiate your thesis, and avoid including any information that you are not certain is correct.

■ If time allows, proofread both of your essays. Don't worry about crossing out material—readers understand that your responses are first drafts and that you are writing down ideas under the pressure of time. Your answers should be legible, but they do not need to reflect perfect penmanship. Focus your efforts on making the essays strong by backing up your thesis with a clear organization and plenty of historical detail.

Much as in your response to the DBQ, the success of your two thematic essays will depend a great deal on how clearly and extensively you address the question being posed. In Part B of Section II, of course, you don't have any documents to back up your argument. Thus, it is even more essential that you identify a thesis that responds directly to the thematic question. The structure of your thematic essay depends entirely on your knowledge of a subject. In the introduction of your essay, you should indicate how you will respond to the question.

CHAPTER 1

A Continent of Villages, to 1500

This chapter covers the first settlement of the Western Hemisphere by immigrants from Asia. Over the centuries these immigrants developed a variety of technologies, and these communities adapted to their physical environments. Europeans coming to the Americas would find not an empty land but instead a populated continent of many villages. Native Americans had a great deal of diversity in culture, community organization, language, and technology. European colonists would profit from these technologies and regional adaptations.

Settling the Continent

The origins of the American Indians, their migration to the Americas, and early cultural development are covered. Scientific research indicates that the first Americans migrated from Asia over a land bridge to North America during the last Ice Age beginning approximately 30,000 years ago. Over time, new technology and methods of hunting were developed that spread throughout the continent.

New Ways of Living on the Land

The warming of the climate contributed to the transformation of plant and animal life, causing regional climate and cultural regions to develop in the Great Plains, the Southwest, and east of the Mississippi River.

The Development of Farming

The development of farming helped transform many Indian cultures, though some hunting groups resisted farming. Farming of maize originated in Mexico about 5,000 years ago and led to the development of large, complex, urban communities. Farming stimulated increased social complexity in terms of political organization, economic systems of production and distribution, and gender-related division of labor. Religious traditions arose to reflect means of securing food. In different regions, farming led to the creation of large, urban, socially stratified societies. Competition for land fostered conflict among Indian peoples.

Cultural Regions of North America on the Eve of Colonization

Regional cultures influenced by regional environments had developed in North America on the eve of European colonization. The Indian population numbered in the millions by 1500.

Multiple-Choice Questions

1. Early Spanish observers of New World Indians
   (A) rarely thought about the origins of these people.
   (B) believed they must have originated in some part of the New World.
   (C) proposed a migration hypothesis that suggested the Indians had come from Asia.
   (D) asserted the superiority of Indian lifestyles and culture compared to those of Europeans.
   (E) were only interested in non-migratory theory.

2. The center of the development of the practice of farming in North America among Indian peoples was the
   (A) Great Basin.
   (B) Great Plains.
   (C) highlands of Mexico.
   (D) desert of Arizona.
   (E) plains of Peru.

3. These carbohydrate sources contributed much to the Indian food supply and still contribute the most to the world's supply of staple foods:
   (A) maize and potatoes.
   (B) rice and beans.
   (C) yams and beans.
   (D) maize and beans.
   (E) wheat and rice.

4. A consequence of Native Americans' increasing reliance on agriculture was
   (A) a decrease in the need for military forces.
   (B) a new division of labor and, ultimately, the emergence of classes.
   (C) increased reliance on weather patterns.
   (D) higher levels of disease.
   (E) a lesser role for religion in their lives.

5. The first Europeans arriving in North America found
   (A) a few dominant native societies and a common Native American language.
   (B) no areas densely settled by Indians.
   (C) abundant evidence of the influence of the native societies of Mexico and Central America.
   (D) a homogeneous native society.
   (E) hundreds of native societies speaking nearly as many distinct languages.

6. Desert farmers like the Pima and Yuma
   (A) exported high quality flint hoes.
   (B) were highly communal apartment dwellers.
   (C) were the first to plow using animals.
   (D) remained semi-nomadic in the Southwest.
   (E) lived in dispersed settlements called rancherias.

7. The combined effects of warmer climate and increased hunting in America led to
   (A) Clovis technology.
   (B) increased Asian migration.
   (C) settled villages.
   (D) increased glacial activity.
   (E) Pleistocene Overkill.

8. The culture of Indian peoples was shaped primarily by these two traditions:
   (A) the practices of farming and intertribal warfare.
   (B) intertribal warfare and the development of clans.
   (C) the practices of foraging and farming.
   (D) farming and warfare.
   (E) Folsom and Plano.

9. The people generally recognized as the first to develop a settled farming way of life in the Southwest were the
   (A) Hohokam.
   (B) Pimas and Papagos.
   (C) Skoaquik.
   (D) Mogollon.
   (E) Arawaks.

10. A major achievement of the Hohokams involved
   (A) the building of communities of cliff dwellings.
   (B) the development of the first system of irrigation in America.
   (C) the importation of grains like maize into North America.
   (D) the development of crops that needed no water.
   (E) their refusal to engage in religious practice.

Document-Based Question

Defend or refute the following statement: Native American peoples that European explorers encountered in North America prior to 1500 were highly civilized and coordinated tribes.

DOCUMENT 1

DOCUMENT 2

DOCUMENT 3

DOCUMENT 4

DOCUMENT 5

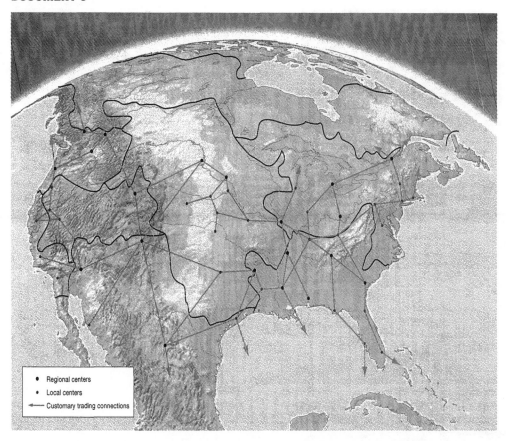

- Regional centers
- Local centers
- Customary trading connections

DOCUMENT 6

DOCUMENT 7

DOCUMENT 8

DOCUMENT 9

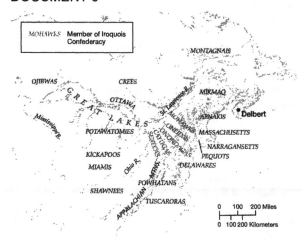

DOCUMENT 10

Source: Thomas Harriot (1560–1621)

> They are a people clothes with loffe mantles made of Deere skins, & aprons of the same rounde about their middles; all els naked; of such a difference of statures only as wee in England; having no edge tooles or wewapons of yron or steele to offend us...by the experience we have had in some places, the turning up of the heels against us in running away was their best defence.

ANSWERS AND EXPLANATIONS

Multiple-Choice Questions

1. (C) is correct. A number of Spanish scholars thought deeply about the question of Indian origins. In 1590, the Spanish Jesuit missionary Joseph de Acosta reasoned that because Old World animals were present in the Americas, they must have crossed by a land bridge that could have been used by humans as well.

2. (C) is correct. Archaeological evidence suggests that plant cultivation in the highlands of Mexico began about 5,000 years ago. Ancient Mexicans developed crops that responded well to human care and produced large quanities of food in a limited space. Over time such practices adapted to a wide range of American climates, and farming spread throughout the temperate regions of North America.

3. (A) is correct. Today the two American staples—maize and potatoes—contribute more to the world's food supply than do any other carbohydrates, including wheat and rice.

4. (B) is correct. As farming became increasingly important, it radically reshaped social life. Where a foraging society might require 100 square miles to support 100 people, a farming society required only one square mile. The division of labor increased with the appearance of specialists like toolmakers, craftworkers, administrators, priests, and rulers as well as farmers and food processors. Ultimately, unequal access to wealth and power resulted in the emergence of classes.

5. (E) is correct. At the time of their first contacts with Europeans at the beginning of the sixteenth century, the native inhabitants of the Western Hemisphere represented over 2,000 separate cultures, spoke several hundred different languages, and made their livings in scores of fundamentally different environments.

6. (E) is correct. On the eve of European colonization, Indian farmers in the Southwest had been cultivating fields for nearly 3,000 years. In the floodplain of the Gila and Salt Rivers lived the Pimas and Papagos. Working small irrigated fields along the Colorado River and even on the floor of the Grand Canyon were the Yuman peoples. These desert farmers cultivated their produce and traded throughout the Southwest. They lived in dispersed settlements the Spanish called *rancherias*, which were separated by as much as a mile.

7. (E) is correct. About 15,000 years ago a global warming trend began to alter the North American climate. One of the most important effects of this massive climatological shift was the stress it placed on the big-game animals best suited to an Ice Age environment. It seems likely that the lowered reproduction and survival rates of large animals forced hunting bands to intensify their efforts, and the combined effects of warmer climate and increased hunting eventually led to what some archaeologists have called the "Pleistocene Overkill."

8. (C) is correct. Descriptions of the culture of the modern Shoshones suggest that their emphasis on sharing and gift giving, their condemnation of hoarding, and their limitations on the accumulation of material goods, fostered by a nomadic lifestyle, prevented individuals or families from acquiring excessive wealth and forged a strong sense of community among these people of the desert. Desert communities were characterized by a kind of social equality in which decisions were made by consensus among the adults and leadership tended to be informal, based on achievement and reputation.

9. (D) is correct. Farming communities began to emerge in the arid Southwest during the first millennium B.C.E. Among the first to develop a settled farming way of life were the Mogollon people, who lived along what is today the southern Arizona-New Mexico border during the first millennium B.C.E.

10. (B) is correct. From about C.E. 300 to 1500 the people of the Hohokam culture flourished in the region along the floodplain of the Salt and Gila rivers in southern Arizona. The Hohokams, who lived in agricultural villages, built and maintained the first irrigation system in America north of Mexico, channeling river water through 500 miles of canals to to water desert fields of maize, beans, squash, tobacco, and cotton.

Document-Based Question

Defend or refute the following statement: The Native American peoples that European explorers encountered in North America prior to 1500 were highly civilized and coordinated tribes.

Native American societies were highly structured and ceremonial ones that European explorers often did not understand. This lack of understanding often led Europeans to disparage Native American culture as "uncivilized," or in other words, non-European.

Native American cultures were highly adadptable, as is evident by the transformation of their societies based upon the abundence or scarcity of natural resources. Some tribes were nomadic; others were more tied to the land and began farming. New technology and innovations resulted from the presence or absence of these natural resources (**DOCUMENT 1**).

Mesoamerican maize cultivation exemplifies the most highly developed variety of cultivated crops in the world at the time, and Native American agricultural productivity helped sustain one of the world's greatest and most populous civilizations. Trade routes were formed to spread science, technology, craft specialization, and other products. As tribes participated in these trade routes, communication and cultural identity also traveled the routes. Although the degree of conclusions about trade by examining the origin of artifcts found at ancient sites and thus drawing up a conjectural map of Indian trade networks (**DOCUMENT 5**).

As trade evolved, Native American civilizations flourished with ideas and innovation. Cities spread as new farming techniques allowed more food production, a better quality of life, and trade specialization (**DOCUMENT 3**). With better health and food allocations, especially due to irrigation systems, cities and population grew (**DOCUMENT 6**). The Hohokams, located on the floodplain of the Gila River near present-day Phoeniz, Arizona, were the first irrigation farmers of North America (**DOCUMENT 2**). More job and trade specialization allowed public works and other nonessential survival skills, such as the creation of religious monuments, to occur. (**DOCUMENT 4**).

Family life and art is depicted in artifacts found throughout Native American culture. Men, women, and children had specific roles in their societies (**DOCUMENT 7**). Beyond gender and family roles, hierarchical communities with classes emerged (**DOCUMENT 8**). These hierarchies were not necessarily patriarchial; women were sometimes community leaders and could hold the title of chief. Regardless of gender, leadership often recognized the need to gain a sense of alliance and assistance against common enemies or threats. The Indians of the Northeast were mostly village peoples. In the fifteenth century, five Iroquois groups—the Mohawks, Oneidas, Onondagas, Cayugas, and Senecas—joined together to form the Iroqouis Five Nation Confederacy (**DOCUMENT 9**).

Native American civilization was often questioned by the European immigrants to North America (**DOCUMENT 10**). The interpretation of cultural differences is often subjective, and the Europeans' technological superiority in terms of weaponry and other equipment often led to a feeling of overarching cultural superiority based on science and resources.

CHAPTER 2

When Worlds Collide, 1492–1590

The impact of European expansion—first by the Spanish and French and later by the English—is discussed in this chapter. Following the Portuguese tradition of seafaring exploration, the Spanish began the exploration of the New World in search of new lands to conquer and precious metals. Ultimately, the Spanish New World empire took root in what is now the West Indies, Central America, and Mexico, later extending northward to the American south and southwest. While both the explorer and the sponsoring nation often reaped the benefits of endless resources of the New World such as gold, silver, corn, and tobacco, they also introduced uniquely European commodities—wheat, domesticated animals, and disease, some of which proved disastrous for the Native peoples. Fish and fur played a far more significant role in French interests than silver and gold and, unlike the Spanish and English, their early relationships with natives were rarely based on conquest. Eventually, the English entered the game, seeking to punish their enemy, Spain, and break the Spanish trade monopoly with tropical America.

The Expansion of Europe

The political, economic, social, and cultural transformation of Europe, including technological advances, paved the way for European expansion overseas. Voyages of exploration aimed at reaching Asia first by moving south and east and later going west across the Atlantic. The European mastery of the seas set the stage for American colonization.

The Spanish in the Americas

In the sixteenth century, the Spanish constructed an empire in the Americas that stretched from Florida and the Southwest of present-day United States down through most of Central and South America. Their success was aided by a variety of political, military, technological, and natural factors. A consequence of this meeting of two worlds was the intercontinental exchange of people, animals, plants, disease, and cultures.

Northern Explorations and Encounters

Following the Spanish success in the Americas, other European nations launched exploration and colonization efforts with mixed results. Religious turmoil in Europe, as well as social and political changes, influenced these early efforts, which soon afterward generated more substantial and successful colonization endeavors.

Multiple-Choice Questions

1. A principal cause of the Spanish success in conquering the Aztecs in the early sixteenth century was
   (A) the superiority of Spanish arms.
   (B) the Spaniards' ability to take advantage of native peoples' hostility to Aztec rule.
   (C) the absence of an Aztec military "bureaucracy" that could launch a counterattack.
   (D) the availability of horses to the Spanish.
   (E) the military genius of Hernando Cortes.

2. Which of the following was the <u>MOST</u> important reason for the population decline that occurred in native populations in the wake of the Spanish conquest?
   (A) starvation
   (B) declining birth rates
   (C) disease
   (D) immigration
   (E) warfare

3. By establishing a "frontier of inclusion," the Spanish developed communities
   (A) of large mixed-ancestry groups.
   (B) of equals with native peoples.
   (C) with other European peoples.
   (D) that were more rural than urban.
   (E) of strict racial separation.

4. Beginning with Cartier's failed settlements on the St. Lawrence, relationships among the French and the Indians were based on
   (A) conquest.
   (B) missionary work.
   (C) common culture.
   (D) hostility.
   (E) trade.

5. Chief Wingina saw the early Roanoke colonists as
   (A) carriers of diseases killing his people.
   (B) certain military enemies.
   (C) protectors of the Grand Banks from the Iroquois.
   (D) useful trading partners.
   (E) potential allies to increase his power.

6. Which of the following was an Indian emissary who distrusted the intentions of the English settlers?
   (A) Manteo.
   (B) Wingina.
   (C) Hatteras.
   (D) Wanchese.
   (E) Croatoan.

7. Among the <u>MOST</u> important contributions that the Spanish made to the New World in the continental exchange was/were
   (A) Old World foodstuffs.
   (B) sugar.
   (C) tobacco.
   (D) spices and silk.
   (E) domesticated animals and livestock.

8. England's first ventures into the New World were motivated by
   (A) fear of the French.
   (B) a desire for colonization.
   (C) missionary zeal.
   (D) animosity toward Spain.
   (E) animosity toward the Indians.

9. Which one of the following was NOT part of Walter Raleigh's vision of his English colony at Roanoke?
   (A) an English community
   (B) making the Indians serfs of the English masters
   (C) exploring for precious metals
   (D) a tobacco producing center
   (E) establishing a thriving fur trade

10. The Renaissance was based in the belief that
    (A) the authority of the Roman Catholic Church should be obeyed in all instances.
    (B) learning was the domain of the upper class.
    (C) concern for the afterlife must always be the primary focus of human beings.
    (D) ancient classical beliefs and forms must be rejected.
    (E) human potential is important and should be celebrated.

Document-Based Question

Defend or refute the following statement: The colonization of North America was primarily a religious endeavor.

DOCUMENT 1

Christopher Columbus, Letter to Ferdinand and Isabella of Spain (1494)
Source: AmDocs Website, University of Kansas,
http://www.ukans.edu/carrie/docs/texts/columlet.html

1. That in the said island there shall be founded three or four towns, situated in the most convenient places, and that the settlers who are there be assigned to the aforesaid places and towns.

2. That for the better and more speedy colonization of the said island, no one shall have liberty to collect gold in it except those who have taken out colonists' papers, and have built houses for their abode, in the town in which they are, that they may live united and in greater safety.

3. That each town shall have its alcalde [Mayor] . . . and its notary public, as is the use and custom in Castile.

4. That there shall be a church, and parish priests or friars to administer the sacraments, to perform divine worship, and for the conversion of the Indians.

5. That none of the colonists shall go to seek gold without a license from the governor or alcalde of the town where he lives; and that he must first take oath to return to the place whence he sets out, for the purpose of registering faithfully all the gold he may have found, and to return once a month, or once a week, as the time may have been set for him, to render account and show the quantity of said gold; and that this shall be written down by the notary before the alcalde, or, if it seems better, that a friar or priest, deputed for the purpose, shall be also present.

6. That all the gold thus brought in shall be smelted immediately, and stamped with some mark that shall distinguish each town; and that the portion which belongs to your Highnesses shall be weighed, and given and consigned to each alcalde in his own town, and registered by the above-mentioned priest or friar, so that it shall not pass through the hands of only one person, and there shall be no opportunity to conceal the truth.

7. That all gold that may be found without the mark of one of the said towns in the possession of any one who has once registered in accordance with the above order shall be taken as forfeited, and that the accuser shall have one portion of it and your Highnesses the other.

8. That one per centum of all the gold that may be found shall be set aside for building churches and adorning the same, and for the support of the priests or friars belonging to them; and, if it should be thought proper to pay any thing to the alcaldes or notaries for their services, or for ensuring the faithful perforce of their duties, that this amount shall be sent to the governor or treasurer who may be appointed there by your Highnesses.

DOCUMENT 2

Jacques Cartier: First Contact with the Indians (1534)
Source: "The First Relation of Jacques Cartier of S. Malo," in Henry S. Burrage, ed., Early English and French Voyages, Chiefly from Hakluyt, Original Narratives of Early American History (New York: Charles Scribner's Sons, 1906).

How our men set up a great Crosse upon the poynt of the sayd Porte, and the Captaine of those wild men, after a long Oration, was by our Captain appeased, and contented that two of his Children should goe with him. Upon the 25 of the moneth, wee caused a faire high Crosse to be made of the height of thirty foote, which was made in the presence of many of them, upon the point of the entrance of the sayd haven, (6) in the middest whereof we hanged up a Shield with three Floure de Luces in it, and in the top was carved in the wood with Anticke letters this posie, Vive le Roy de France. Then before them all we set it upon the sayd point. They with great heed beheld both the making and setting of it up So soone as it was up, we altogether kneeled downe before them, with our hands toward Heaven, yeelding God thankes: and we made signes unto them, shewing them the Heavens, and that all our salvation dependeth onely on him which in them dwelleth: whereat they shewed a great admiration, looking first one at another, and then upon the Crosse. And after wee were returned to our ships, their Captaine clad with an old Beares skin, with three of his sonnes, and a brother of his with him, came unto us in one of their boates, but they came not so neere us as they were wont to doe: there he made a long Oration unto us, shewing us the crosse we had set up, and making a crosse with two fingers, then did he shew us all the Countrey about us, as if he would say that all was his, and that wee should not set up any crosse without his leave.

DOCUMENT 3

Reasons for the Plantation in New England (1629)
Source: The Winthrop Society, 1996–2001, http://www.winthropsociety.org/document.htm

Reasons to be considered for justifying the undertakers of the intended Plantation in New England, and for encouraging such whose hearts God shall move to join with them in it.
1. It will be a service to the Church of great consequence to carry the Gospel into those parts of the world, to help on the fullness of the coming of the Gentiles, and to raise a bulwark against the kingdom of AnteChrist, which the Jesuits labor to rear up in those parts.
2. All other Churches of Europe are brought to desolation, and our sins, for which the Lord begins already to frown upon us and to cut us short, do threaten evil times to be coming upon us, and who knows, but that God hath provided this place to be a refuge for many whom he means to save out of the general calamity, and seeing the Church hath no place left to fly into but the wilderness, what better work can there be, than to go and provide tabernacles and food for her when she be restored.
3. This England grows weary of her inhabitants, so as Man, who is the most precious of all creatures, is here more vile and base than the earth we tread upon, and of less price among us than a horse or a sheep. Masters are forced by authority to entertain servants, parents to maintain their own children, all towns complain of their burden to maintain their poor, though we have taken up many unnecessary, yea unlawful, trades to maintain them. We use the authority of the Law to hinder the increase of our people, as by urging the statute against cottages and inmates—and thus it is come to pass, that children, servants and neighbors, especially if they be poor, are counted the greatest burdens, which if things were right would be the chiefest earthly blessings.
4. The whole earth is the Lord's garden, and He hath given it to mankind with a general commission (Gen. 1:28) to increase and multiply and replenish the earth and subdue it, which was again renewed to Noah. The end is double and natural, that Mankind might enjoy the fruits of the earth, and God might have His due Glory from His creatures. Why then should one strive here for places of habitation, at such a cost as would obtain better land in another country, and at the same time suffer a whole continent as fruitful and convenient for the use of man to lie waste without any improvement?
5. We are grown to that height of intemperance in all excess of riot that as no man's estate, almost, will suffice to keep sail with his equals. He who fails herein must live in scorn and contempt. Hence it comes that all arts and trades are carried on in that deceitful and unrighteous course, so that it is almost impossible for a good and upright man to maintain his charge and live comfortably in any of them.
6. The fountains of learning and religion are so corrupted that most children (besides the unsupportable charge of their education) are perverted, corrupted, and utterly overthrown by the multitude of evil examples and the licentious government of those seminaries, where men strain at gnats and swallow camels, and use all severity for maintenance of caps and like accomplishments, but suffer all ruffianlike fashions and disorder in manners to pass uncontrolled.
7. What can be a better work, and more honorable and worthy of a Christian than to help rise and support a particular church while it is in its infancy, and to join his forces with

such a company of faithful people, as by a timely assistance may grow strong and prosper, when for want of such help may be put to great hazard, if not wholly ruined.

DOCUMENT 4

DOCUMENT 5

The Trial of Anne Hutchinson (1638)
Source: The American Colonist's Library, Primary Source Documents Pertaining to Early American History, http://personal.pitnet.net/primarysources/hutchinson.html

MR. NOWEL [ASSISTANT TO THE COURT]: How do you know that was the spirit?

MRS. H.: How did Abraham know that it was God that bid him offer his son, being a breach of the sixth commandment?

DEP. GOV.: By an immediate voice.

MRS. H.: So to me by an immediate revelation.

DEP. GOV.: How! an immediate revelation.

MRS. H.: By the voice of his own spirit to my soul. I will give you another scripture, Jer[emiah] 46: 27–28—out of which the Lord showed me what he would do for me and the rest of his servants. But after he was pleased to reveal himself to me I did presently, like Abraham, run to Hagar. And after that he did let me see the atheism of my own heart, for which I begged of the Lord that it might not remain in my heart, and being thus, he did show me this (a twelvemonth after) which I told you of before.. . . Therefore, I desire you to look to it, for you see this scripture fulfilled this day and therefore I desire you as you tender the Lord and the church and commonwealth to consider and look what you do. You have power over my body but the Lord Jesus hath power over my body and soul; and assure yourselves thus much, you do as much as in you lies to put the Lord Jesus Christ from you, and if you go on in this course you begin, you will bring a curse upon you and your posterity, and the mouth of the Lord hath spoken it.

DEP. GOV.: What is the scripture she brings?

MR. STOUGHTON [ASSISTANT TO THE COURT]: Behold I turn away from you.

MRS. H.: But now having seen him which is invisible I fear not what man can do unto me.

GOV.: Daniel was delivered by miracle; do you think to be deliver'd so too?

MRS. H.: I do here speak it before the court. I look that the Lord kshould deliver me by his providence.. . . [because God had said to her] though I should meet with affliction, yet I am the same God that delivered Daniel out of the lion's den, I will also deliver thee.

MR. HARLAKENDEN [ASSISTANT TO THE COURT]: I may read scripture and the most glorious hypocrite may read them and yet go down to hell.

MRS. H.: It may be so.. . .

GOV.: I am persuaded that the revelation she brings forth is delusion.

[The trial text here reads:] All the court but some two or three ministers cry out, we all believe it—we all believe it. [Mrs. Hutchinson was found guilty]

DOCUMENT 6

A Jesuit Priest Describes New Amsterdam (1642)
Source: New Netherlands in 1644, by Rev. Isaac Jogues, S.J. http://www.lihistory.com/

The river, which is very straight and runs due north and south, is at least a league broad before the fort. Ships lie at anchor in a bay which forms the other side of the island and can be defended from the fort. Shortly before I arrived there three large vessels of 300 tons each had come to load wheat; two had found cargoes, the third could not be loaded because the savages had burnt a part of their grain. These ships came from the West Indies where the West India Company usually keeps up seventeen ships of war. No religion is publicly exercised but the Calvinist, and orders are to admit none but Calvinists, but this is not observed, for there are, besides Calvinists, in the Colony Catholics, English Puritans, Lutherans, Anabaptists, here called Muistes &c.When any one comes to settle in the country, they lend him horses, cows &c, they give him provisions, all which he repays as soon as he is at ease, and as to the land he pays in to the West India Company after ten years the tenth of the produce which he reaps. This country is bounded on the New England side by a river they call the Fresche river, which serves as a boundary between them and the English. The English however come very near to them preferring to hold lands under the Dutch who ask nothing from them rather than to be dependent on English Lords who exact rents and would fain be absolute. On the other side southward towards Virginia, its limits are the river which they call the South river on which there is also a Dutch settlement, but the Swedes have at its mouth another extremely well provided with men and cannon. It is believed that these Swedes are maintained by some merchants of Amsterdam, who are not satisfied that the West India Company should alone enjoy all the commerce of these parts. It is near this river that a gold mine is reported to have been found.

DOCUMENT 7

George Alsop, The Importance of Tobacco (1660)
Source: George Alsop, A Character of the Province of Maryland (Baltimore: Maryland Historical Society Fund, Publication No. 15, 1880), pp. 475–477

The three main Commodities this Country affords for Trafique, are Tobacco, Furrs, and Flesh. Furrs and Skins, as Beavers, Otters, Musk-Rats, Rackoons, Wild-Cats, and Elke or Buffeloe, with divers others, which were first made vendible by the Indians of the Country, and sold to the Inhabitant, and by them to the Merchant, and so transported into England and other places where it becomes most commodious.

Tobacco is the only solid Staple Commodity of this Province: The use of it was first found out by the Indians many Ages agoe, and transferr'd into Christendom by that great Discoverer of America Columbus. It's generally made byall the Inhabitants of this Province, and between the months of March and April they sow the seed (which is much smaller then Mustard-seed) in small beds and patches digg'd up and made so by art, and about May the Plants commonly appear green in those beds: In June they are transplanted from their beds, and set in little hillocks in distant rowes, dug up for the same purpose; some twice or thrice they are weeded, and succoured from their illegitimate Leaves that would be peeping out from the body of the Stalk. They top the several Plants, as they find occasion in their predominating rankness: About the middle of September they cut the Tobacco down, and carry it into houses, (made for that purpose) to bring it to its purity: And after it has attained, by a convenient attendance upon time, to its perfection, it is then tyed up in bundles, and packt into Hogs-heads, and then laid by for the Trade. Between November and January there arrives in this Province Shipping to the number of twenty sail and upwards, all Merchant-men loaden with Commodities to Trafique and dispose of, trucking with the Planter for Silks, Hollands, Serges, and Broad-clothes, with other necessary Goods, priz'd at such and such rates as shall be judg'd on is fair and legal, for Tobacco at so much the pound, and advantage on both sides considered; the Planter for his work, and the Merchant for adventuring himself and his Commodity into so far a Country: Thus is the Trade on both sides drove on with a fair and honest Decorum. The Inhabitants of this Province are seldom or never put to the affrightment of being robb'd of their money, nor to dirty their Fingers by telling of vast sums: They have more bags to carry Corn, then Coyn; and though they want, but why should I call that a want which is only a necessary miss? the very effects of the dirt of this Province affords as great a profit to the general Inhabitant, as the Gold of Peru doth to the straight-breecht Commonalty of the Spaniard. Our Shops and Exchanges of Mary-Land, are the Merchants Store-houses, where with few words and protestations Goods are bought and delivered; not like those Shop-keepers Boys in London, that continually cry, What do ye lack Sir? What d'ye buy? yelping with so wide a mouth, as if some Apothecary had hired their mouths to stand open to catch Gnats and Vagabond Flyes in.

Tobacco is the currant Coyn of Mary-Land, and will sooner purchase Commodities from the Merchant, then money. I must confess the New-England men that trade into this Province, had rather have fat Pork for their Goods, than Tobacco or Furrs, which I conceive is, because their bodies being fast bound up with the cords of restringent Zeal, they are fain to make use of the lineaments of this Non-Canaanite creature physically to loosen them; for a bit of a pound upon a two-peny Rye loaf, according to the original Receipt, will bring the cos tiv'st red-ear'd Zealot in some three hours time to a fine stool, if methodically observed. Medera-Wines, Sugars, Salt, Wickar-Chairs, and Tin Candlesticks, is the most of the Commodities they bring in They arrive in Mary-Land about September, being most of them Ketches and Barkes, and such Small Vessels, and these dispersing themselves into several small Creeks of this Province, to sell and dispose of their Commodities, where they know the Market is most fit for their small Adventures. ...

ANSWERS AND EXPLANATIONS

Multiple-Choice Questions

■ **1. (B) is correct.** Cortés brilliantly exploited the resentment of the many peoples who lived under Aztec domination, forging Spanish-Indian alliances that became a model for the subsequent European colonization of the Americas.

■ **2. (C) is correct.** The primary cause of drastic reduction in native populations was epidemic disease—influenza, plague, smallpox, measles, typhus. Although preconquest America was by no means disease free—skeletal evidence suggests that natives suffered from arthritis, hepatitis, polio, and tuberculoisis—there were no diseases of epidemic potential.

■ **3. (A) is correct.** Spanish women came to America as early as Columbus's second expedition, but over the course of the sixteenth century they made up only about 10 percent of the immigrants. Most male colonists married or cohabited with Indian or African women, and the result was the growth of large mixed-ancestry groups known as mestizos and mulattoes, respectively.

3. (A) is correct. Spanish women came to America as early as Columbus's second expedition, but over the course of the sixteenth century they made up only about 10 percent of the immigrants. Most male colonists married or cohabited with Indian or African women, and the result was the growth of large mixed-ancestry groups known as mestizos and mulattoes, respectively.

4. (E) is correct. Cartier's attempts to plant settlements on the St. Lawrence failed, but he established France's imperial claim to the lands of Canada. The French and other northern Europeans thus discovered the Indian people of the northern woodlands, and the Indians in turn discovered them. The contacts between Europeans and natives here took a different form than in the tropics; they were based on commerce rather than conquest.

5. (E) is correct. At an island the Indians called Roanoke, the English had been "entertained with all love and kindness" by a chief name Wingina. The leader of several surrounding villages, Wingina welcomed the English as potential allies in his struggle to extend his authority over still others.

6. (D) is correct. Wanchese described the disturbing inequalities of English society and warned Chief Wingina of brutality. Wanchese rightly suspected English intentions, for Raleigh's plans were not based on the expectation that Indians would be treated as equals, but as serfs to be exploited.

7. (E) is correct. Columbus introduced domesticated animals into Hispaniola and Cuba, and livestock were later transported to Mexico. The movement of Spanish settlement into northern Mexico was greatly aided by an advancing livestock, for grazing animals invaded native fields and forests, undercutting the ability of communities to support themselves. Horses, used by Spanish stockmen to tend their cattle, also spread northward. In the seventeenth century, horses reached the Great Plains of North America, where they eventually transformed the lives of the nomadic hunting Indians.

8. (D) is correct. England's first ventures in the New World were made against the backdrop of its conflict with Spain. A consensus soon developed among Elizabeth's closest adviors that the time had come to enter the competition for American colonies. In a state paper written for the queen, the scholar Richard Hakluyt summarized the advantages that would come from the colonies, such as the opportunity to provide bases from which to raid the Spanish in the Caribbean.

9. (A) is correct. Walter Raleigh, a wealthy adventurer who sought profit and prestige by organizing an English colony to compete with Spain's power empire in the New World, had sponsored the Roanoke settlement. Raleigh did intend to make the Indians serfs of the English master, as Wanchese warned Indian Chief Wingina. Raleigh also anticipated that his colony would return profits through the lucrative trade in furs, a flourishing plantation culture, or gold and silver mines with the Indians supplying the labor. An English community was not in Raleigh's plan for the Roanoke colony.

10. (E) is correct. The Renaissance celebrated human possibility. This human-centered perspective was evident in many endeavors, such as architecture, painting, and sculpture.

Document-Based Question

Defend or refute the following statement: The colonization of the Americas was primarily a religious endeavor.

Religion was a powerful factor in the colonization of the Americas, but it was not the primary motivation of most colonists. The majority of those who came to the Americas did so for economic reasons, in order to export the wealth of the New World back to the old. Another significant minority came for nationalist reasons.

The primary intention of early Spanish colonies in the New World was the mining and exportion of gold, which they believed was easily found there. The earliest colonies were to be organized in such a way as maximized profit to the Crown and the colonists. While there were

The Southern British colonies were no exception to this pattern. Maryland's main exports were tobacco, fur, and slaves, with tobacco being the most significant of the three. Its internal economy worked for the most part on a barter system. (**DOCUMENT 7**).

In new France there was a somewhat more complicated situation in the early stages of colonial development. While it is clear that there was a powerful religious motivation (**DOCUMENT 2**), there were also clear nationalist and economic reasons for exploring the New World (**DOCUMENT 4**).

The only colonists primarily motivated by religion were the British Puritan settlers of New England. They viewed themselves as spreading the Gospel to the untainted New World, as they left behind the corrupt Old World, full of sinners and temptations (**DOCUMENT 3**). As they built their colony, they did so not on the model of their Calvinist bretheren in New Amsterdam, who ignored the religious restrictions on settlement. Instead, they strictly enforced doctrinal purity, banishing those who did not conform to their relgious dogma (**DOCUMENT 5**).

The primary motivation of most colonial efforts was economic, though not purely so. The colonists, with the exception of the British Puritans, saw themselves as exporting the goods of the New World back to the Old.

CHAPTER 3

Planting Colonies in North America, 1588–1701

This chapter emphasizes the European settlement of North America. The Spanish, French, and English established settlements that would later be sections of the United States. French and Spanish settlers mixed with the Indian population when building communities more than the British did. Differences in economies, ideological outlooks, and events in England also accounted for differences between the British colonies in the Chesapeake, New England, and the South. The colonists of New England built the most vital communities. Various self-government systems were set up, but they were not democratic. Conflicting views in England, as well as rivalry with France, brought an attempt at tighter centralization of control under royal authority. Native Americans tried to use differences and rivalries to keep their cultures intact and limit their rivals. A series of wars weakened Indian control east of the Appalachians.

Spain and its Competitors in North America

The initial planting of colonies in North America outside of Mexico set up competition among European nations for land and trade with the Indians cultures. Several different nations were involved in such diverse areas as Canada and the present-day southwestern United States. Unlike earlier efforts, these colonies proved more substantial and long term.

England in the Chesapeake

The planting of English colonies in the Chesapeake demonstrated how difficult and expensive it was to maintain such settlements. The influence of regional conditions on colonial development was also illustrated.

The New England Colonies

A combination of human and natural factors placed the New England colonies on a path distinct from those in the Chesapeake. In addition to the geography and climate, the New England colonists had different backgrounds, motivations, and aims from the Chesapeake colonists.

The Proprietary Colonies

Following the restoration of the English monarchy, several new colonies were established that cemented the English presence down much of the Atlantic coast and stretching west over the Appalachian Mountains. These new colonies were all founded under the same type of charter but followed different paths of development.

Conflict and War

The last quarter of the seventeenth century experienced much violence as warfare raged from Santa Fe in New Mexico to the Atlantic coast. It involved conflicts between Indians and colonists, between Indian tribes, and between colonists.

Multiple-Choice Questions

1. The Spanish forts along the Florida coast were designed to protect
   (A) against a French invasion.
   (B) their fur trade.
   (C) potential gold in the interior.
   (D) rich fishing grounds.
   (E) Gulf Stream sea lanes.

2. After he led a successful revolt against the Spanish, Pueblo leader Popé was deposed ten years later by this people because he
   (A) allowed Christian practices to continue.
   (B) allied himself with their Navajo and Apache enemies.
   (C) ordered them to destroy everything Spanish.
   (D) continued to enslave Indians for his own advantage.
   (E) forbade animal sacrifice practiced by the Aztecs.

3. French interest in the Indians was based primarily in
   (A) commercial concerns.
   (B) their belief that the Indians should be converted to Christianity.
   (C) their need for heavy labor from the Indians.
   (D) their desire for Indian land.
   (E) their need to populate New France.

4. The cultivation of tobacco by the English colonists
   (A) encouraged trade between the settlers and the Indians.
   (B) prompted the English to seek a community of inclusion.
   (C) created pressure for more expansion into Indian territory
   (D) made Indian slave labor profitable.
   (E) was ultimately banned by the King of England.

5. Which one of the following is <u>LEAST</u> true of community life in the Chesapeake of the 1600s?
   (A) The scarcity of women gave them some advantages in bargaining.
   (B) Houses and settlements were generally crude.
   (C) Colonists were developing a distinctive American culture.
   (D) Few schools and churches existed.
   (E) Family sizes were large in hopes of populating the colony.

6. The primary reason for the establishment of the colony at Plymouth was the settlers' desire to
   (A) convert local Indian populations to Christianity.
   (B) establish their own church independent of the Anglican Church.
   (C) profit from the great commercial potential evident in New England.
   (D) compete with Virginia in the production of tobacco.
   (E) to reform the practices of the Church of England.

7. The Plymouth colony was
   (A) the best financial success of the English in the New World.
   (B) known for its established Anglican Church.
   (C) very hostile to the Indian peoples.
   (D) a successful and strong community.
   (E) the least self-governing of the English colonies.

8. By 1634, Massachusetts Bay freemen would
   (A) select town representatives to draft laws of their colony.
   (B) establish churches of their choice in the company towns.
   (C) complete their service as indentured servants early.
   (D) write a new compact for their colonial government.
   (E) expand their holdings into New York and Pennsylvania.

9. Maryland was the only English colony in North America with a substantial <u>MINORITY</u> of
   - (A) Puritans.
   - (B) Jews.
   - (C) Spaniards.
   - (D) Dutch.
   - (E) Catholics.

10. The Puritans were unique in the seventeenth century colonies of North America because of their
   - (A) religious toleration.
   - (B) peaceful relations with the Indians.
   - (C) more equal sex roles.
   - (D) impressive educational system
   - (E) requirement that no work be performed on the Sabbath.

Document-Based Question

Analyze the the relationship between the British North American colonies and the government back in England in light of the following documents.

DOCUMENT 1

Navigation Act of September 13, 1660
Source: http://www.founding.com/library/lbody.cfm?id=83&parent=17

For the increase of shipping and encouragement of the navigation of this nation wherein, under the good providence and protection of God, the wealth, safety, and strength of this kingdom is so much concerned; (2) be it enacted by the king's most excellent Majesty, and by the Lords and Commons in this present Parliament assembled, and by the authority thereof, that from and after the first day of December, one thousand six hundred and sixty, and from thence forward, no goods or commodities whatsoever shall be imported into or exported out of any lands, islands, plantations, or territories to his Majesty belonging or in his possession, or which may hereafter belong unto or be in the possession of his Majesty, his heirs, and successors, in Asia, Africa, or America, in any other ship or ships, vessel or vessels whatsoever, but in such ships or vessels as do truly and without fraud belong only to the people of England or Ireland, dominion of Wales or town of Berwick upon Tweed, or are of the built of and belonging to any the said lands, islands, plantations, or territories, as the proprietors and right owners thereof, and whereof the master and three fourths of the mariners at least are English; (3) under the penalty of the forfeiture and loss of all the goods and commodities which shall be imported into or exported out of any the aforesaid places in any other ship or vessel, as also of the ship or vessel, with all its guns, furniture,tackle, ammunition, and apparel; one third part thereof to his Majesty, his heirs and successors; one third part to thegovernor of such land, plantation, island, or territory where such default shall be committed, in case the said ship or goods be there seized, or otherwise that third part also to his Majesty, his heirs and successors; and the other third part to him or them who shall seize, inform, or sue for the same in any court of record, by bill, information, plaint, or other action, wherein no essoin, protection, or wager of law shall be allowed; (4) and all admirals and other commanders at sea of any the ships of war or other ship having commission from his Majesty or from his heirs or successors, are hereby authorized and strictly required to seize and bring in as prize all such ships or vessels as shall have offended contrary hereunto, and deliver them to the court of admiralty, there to be proceeded against; and in case of condensation, one moiety of such forfeitures shall be to the use of such admirals or commanders and their companies, to be divided and proportioned amongst them according to the rules and orders of the sea in case of ships taken prize; and the other moiety to the use of his Majesty, his heirs and successors XVIII. And it is further enacted by the authority aforesaid, that from and after the first day of April, which shall be in the year of our Lord one thousand six hundred sixty-one, no sugars, tobacco, cotton-wool, indigoes, ginger, rustic, or other dyeing wood, of the growth, production, or manufacture by the authority aforesaid, that from and after the first day of April, which shall be in the year of our Lord one thousand six hundred sixty-one, no sugars, tobacco, cotton-wool, indigoes, ginger, rustic, or other dyeing wood, of the growth, production, or manufacture of any English plantations in America, Asia, or Africa, shall be shipped, carried, conveyed, or transported from any of the said English plantations to any land, island, territory, dominion, port, or place whatsoever, other than to such other English plantations as do belong to his Majesty, his heirs and successors, or to the kingdom of England or Ireland, or principality of Wales, or town of Berwick upon Tweed, there to be laid on shore; (2) under the penalty of the forfeiture of the said goods, or the full value thereof, as also of the ship, with all her guns, tackle, apparel, ammunition, and furniture; the one moiety to the king's Majesty, his heirs and successors, and the other moiety to him or them that shall seize, inform, or sue for the same in any court of record, by bill, plaint, or information, wherein no ession, protection, or wager of law shall be allowed.

DOCUMENT 2

Nathaniel Bacon's Challenge to William Berkeley (1676)
Source: A Hypertext on American History From the Colonial Period Until Modern Times,
http://odur.let.rug.nl/~usa/D/1651-1700/bacon_rebel/bacon_i.htm

The Declaracion of the People.
1. For haveing upon specious pretences of publiqe works raised greate unjust taxes upon the Comonality for the advancement of private favorites and other sinister ends, but noe visible effects in any measure adequate, For not haveing dureing this long time of his Gouvernement in any measure advanced this hopefull Colony either by fortificacons Townes or Trade.
2. For haveing abused and rendred contemptable the Magistrates of Justice, by advanceing to places of Judicature, scandalous and Ignorant favorites....
4. For haveing, protected, favoured, and Imboldned the Indians against his Majesties loyall subjects, never contriveing, requireing, or appointing any due or proper meanes of sattisfaction for theire many Invasions, robberies, and murthers comitted upon us.
5. For haveing when the Army of English, was just upon the track of those Indians, who now in all places burne, spoyle, murther and when we might with ease have destroyed them: who then were in open hostillity, for then haveing expressly countermanded, and sent back our Army, by passing his word for the peaceable demeanour of the said Indians, who imediately prosecuted theire evill intentions, comitting horred murthers and robberies in all places, being protected by the said engagement and word past of him the said Sir William Berkeley, haveing ruined and laid desolate a greate part of his Majesties Country, and have now drawne themselves into such obscure and remote places, and are by theire success soe imboldned and confirmed, by theire confederacy soe strengthned that the cryes of blood are in all places, and the terror, and constimation of the people soe greate, are now become, not onely a difficult, but a very formidable enimy, who might att first with ease have beene destroyed.
6. And lately when upon the loud outcryes of blood the Assembly had with all care raised and framed an Army for the preventing of further mischeife and safeguard of this his Majesties Colony....
These are therefore in his majesties name to command you forthwith to seize the persons above mentioned as Trayters to the King and Country and them to bring to Midle plantacon, and there to secure them untill further order, and in case of opposition, if you want any further assistance you are forthwith to demand itt in the name of the people in all the Counties of Virginia.
Nathaniel Bacon
Generall by Consent of the people.

DOCUMENT 3

William Berkeley's Response to Nathaniel Bacon (1676)
Source: A Hypertext on American History From the Colonial Period Until Modern Times,
http://odur.let.rug.nl/~usa/D/1651-1700/bacon_rebel/berke.htm

The declaration and Remonstrance of Sir William Berkeley his most sacred Majesties Governor and Captain Generall of Virginia...

And now I will state the Question betwixt me as a Governor and Mr. Bacon, and say that if any enimies should invade England, any Councellor Justice of peace or other inferiour officer, might raise what forces they could to protect his Majesties subjects, But I say againe, if after the Kings knowledge of this invasion, any the greatest peere of England, should raise forces against the kings prohibition this would be now, and ever was in all ages and Nations accompted treason. Nay I will goe further, that though this peere was truly zealous for the preservation of his King, and subjects, and had better and greater abibitys then all the rest of his fellow subjects, doe his King and Country service, yett if the King (though by false information) should suspect the contrary, itt were treason in this Noble peere to proceed after the King's prohibition, and for the truth of this I appeale to all the laws of England, and the Laws and constitutions of all other Nations in the world, And yett further itt is declared by this Parliament that the takeing up Armes for the King and Parliament is treason, for the event shewed that what ever the pretence was to seduce ignorant and well affected people, yett the end was ruinous both to King and people, as this will be if not prevented, I doe therefore againe declair that Bacon proceedeing against all Laws of all Nations modern and ancient, is Rebell to his sacred Majesty and this Country, nor will I insist upon the sweareing of men to live and dye togeather, which is treason by the very words of the Law.

To conclude, I have don what was possible both to friend and enimy, have granted Mr. Bacon three pardons, which he hath scornefully rejected, suppoaseing himselfe stronger to subvert then I and you to maineteyne the Laws, by which onely and Gods assisting grace and mercy, all men mwt hope for peace and safety. I will add noe more though much more is still remaineing to Justifie me and condenme Mr. Bacon, but to desier that this declaration may be read in every County Court in the Country, and that a Court be presently called to doe itt, before the Assembly meet, That your approbation or dissattisfaction of this declaration may be knowne to all the Country, and the Kings Councell to whose most revered Judgments itt is submitted, Given the xxixth day of May, a happy day in the xxv"ith yeare of his most sacred Majesties Reigne, Charles the second, who God grant long and prosperously to Reigne, and lett all his good subjects say
Amen.
Sir William Berkeley
Governor

DOCUMENT 4

Edward Randolph Describes King Philip's War (1685)
Source: The American Colonist's Library, A Treasury of Primary Documents,
http://www.swarthmore.edu/SocSci/bdorsey/docs/45-ran.html

That notwithstanding the ancient law of the country, made in the year 1633, that no person should sell any armes or ammunition to any Indian upon penalty of £10 for every gun, £5 for a pound of powder, and 40s. for a pound of shot, yet the government of the Massachusets in the year 1657, upon designe to monopolize the whole Indian trade did publish and declare that the trade of furrs and peltry with the Indians in their jurisdiction did solely and properly belong to their commonwealth and not to every indifferent person, and did enact that no person should trade with the Indians for any sort of peltry, except such as were authorized by that court, under the penalty of £100 for every offence, giving liberty to all such as should have licence from them to sell, unto any Indian, guns, swords, powder and shot, paying to the treasurer 3d. for each gun and for each dozen of swords; 6d. for a pound of powder and for every ten pounds of shot, by which means the

Indians have been abundantly furnished with great store of armes and ammunition to the utter ruin and undoing of many families in the neighbouring colonies to enrich some few of their relations and church members.

DOCUMENT 5

William Penn's Charter of Privileges (1701)
Source: The Avalon Project at the Yale Law School: Documents in Law, History and Diplomacy.
http://www.yale.edu/lawweb/avalon/states/pa07.htm

WILLIAM PENN, Proprietary and Governor of the Province of Pensilvania and Territories thereunto belonging, To all to whom these Presents shall come, sendeth Greeting. WHEREAS King CHARLES the Second, by His Letters Patents, under the Great Seal of England, bearing Date the Fourth Day of March in the Year One Thousand Six Hundred and Eighty-one, was graciously pleased to give and grant unto me, and my Heirs and Assigns for ever, this Province of Pennsilvania, with divers great Powers and Jurisdictions for the well Government thereof. AND WHEREAS the King's dearest Brother, JAMES Duke of YORK and ALBANY, &c. by his Deeds of Feoffment, under his Hand and Seal duly perfected, bearing Date the Twenty-Fourth Day of August, One Thousand Six Hundred Eighty and Two, did grant unto me, my Heirs and Assigns, all that Tract of Land, now called the Territories of Pensilvania, together with Powers and Jurisdictions for the good Government thereof. AND WHEREAS for the Encouragement of all the Freemen and Planters, that might be concerned in the said Province and Territories, and for the good Government thereof, I the said WILLIAM PENN, in the Year One Thousand Six Hundred Eighty and Three, for me, my Heirs and Assigns, did grant and confirm unto all the Freemen Planters and Adventurers therein, divers Liberties, Franchises and Properties, as by the said Grant, entitled, The FRAME of the Government of the Province of Pensilvania, and Territories thereunto belonging, in America, may appear; which Charter or Frame being found in some Parts of it, not so suitable to the present Circumstances of the Inhabitants, was in the Third Month, in the Year One Thousand Seven Hundred, delivered up to me, by Six Parts of Seven of the Freemen of this Province and Territories, in General Assembly met, Provision being made in the said Charter, for that End and Purpose. AND WHEREAS I was then pleased to promise, That I would restore the said Charter to them again, with necessary Alterations, or in lieu thereof, give them another, better adapted to answer the present Circumstances and Conditions of the said Inhabitants; which they have now, by their Representatives in General Assembly met at Philadelphia, requested me to grant. KNOW YE THEREFORE, That for the further Well-being and good Government of the said Province, and Territories; and in Pursuance of the Rights and Powers before mentioned, I the said William Penn do declare, grant and confirm, unto all the Freemen, Planters and Adventurers, and other Inhabitants of this Province and Territories, these following Liberties, Franchises and Privileges, so far as in kme lieth, to be held, enjoyed and kept, by the Freemen, Planters and Adventurers, and other Inhabitants of and in the said Province and Territories "hereunto annexed, for ever.

DOCUMENT 6

The Closing of the Frontier (1763)
Source: The Solon Law Archive
http://www. solon.org/Constitutions/Canada/English/PreConfederation/rp_1763. html
also in Henry Steele Commager, ed., Documents of American History (New York: Appleton Century-Crofts, 1949), 47–50.

October 7, 1763
BY THE KING. A PROCLAMATION
Whereas We have taken into Our Royal Consideration the extensive and valuable Acquisitions in America, secured to our Crown by the late Definitive Treaty of Peace, concluded at Paris the 10th Day of February last; and being desirous that all Our loving Subjects, as well of our Kingdom as of our Colonies in America, may avail themselves

concluded at Paris the 10th Day of February last; and being desirous that all Our loving Subjects, as well of our Kingdom as of our Colonies in America, may avail themselves with all convenient Speed, of the great Benefits and Advantages which must accrue therefrom to their Commerce, Manufactures, and Navigation, We have thought fit, with the Advice of our Privy Council, to issue this our Royal Proclamation, hereby to publish and declare to all our loving Subjects, that we have, with the Advice of our Said Privy Council, granted our Letters Patent, under our Great Seal of Great Britain, to erect, within the Countries and Islands ceded and confirmed to Us by the said Treaty, Four distinct and separate Governments, styled and called by the names of Quebec, East Florida, West Florida and Grenada, and limited and bounded as follows, viz....

We have also thought fit, with the advice of our Privy Council as aforesaid, to give unto the Governors and Councils of our said Three new Colonies, upon the Continent full Power and Authority to settle and agree with the Inhabitants of our said new Colonies or with any other Persons who shall resort thereto, for such Lands, Tenements and Hereditaments, as are now or hereafter shall be in our Power to dispose of; and them to grant to any such Person or Persons upon such Terms, and under such moderate Quit-Rents, Services and Acknowledgments, as have been appointed and settled in our other Colonies, and under such other Conditions as shall appear to us to be necessary and expedient for the Advantage of the Grantees, and the Improvement and settlement of our said Colonies.

DOCUMENT 7

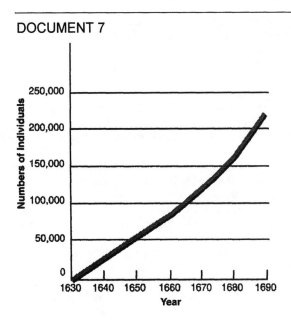

ANSWERS AND EXPLANATIONS

Multiple-Choice Questions

1. (E) is correct. At the beginning of the seventeenth century, the Spanish controlled the only colonial outposts on the mainland, a series of forts along the Florida coast to protect the Gulf Stream sea lanes used by convoys carrying wealth from their New World to Spain.

2. (C) is correct. Popé forced Christian Indians "to plunge into the rivers" to wash away the taint of baptism, and ordered the destruction of everything Spanish.

3. (A) is correct. In the early seventeenth century, the French devised a strategy to monopolize the northern fur trade. The French did not have the manpower to bully, dispossess, or enslave native peoples, but instead attempted to build an empire through alliances with independent Indian nations, which included commercial relations with Indian hunters.

4. (C) is correct. Tobacco cultivation required a great deal of hand labor and quicky exhausted the soil. Questions of land and labor began to dominate the history of the Virginia colony, especially when word of available land spread to England. Massive immigration began due to headright grants and with more people, more land to cultivate was needed. The English colonists began to push the Indians to the periphery, creating a "frontier of exclusion." Indian land would soon be taken, through multiple measures, for the English colonists.

5. (C) is correct. In contrast to the colonists of New France, who were developing a distinctive American identity because of their commercial and political connections to native peoples, the population of the Chesapeake maintained close emotional ties to England. In the disease-ridden environment of the early Chesapeake, Englihs men apparently suffered a higher rate of mortality than women. Their scarcity provided women with certain advantages. English visitors remarked on the crude conditions of community life. Propserous planters lived in rough wooden dwellings. On the western edge of settlements, former servants lived with their families in shacks, huts, even caves. Before 1650, there wre few community institutions such as schools and churches. Due to high mortality rates, family size was smaller and kinship bonds were weaker than in England.

6. (B) is correct. The first English colony in New England, Plymouth, was founded by a group of religious dissenters known to later generations as the Pilgrims. At the time they were called Separatists, because they believe the English Anglican church to be so corrupt that they had to establish their own independent congregations.

7. (D) is correct. The Pilgrims succeeded during the first two or three decades, establishing the self-sufficient community for which they had hoped.

8. (A) is correct. In 1632, Governor Winthrop and his advisors declared that all the male heads of households in Massachusetts who were also church members were freemen. Two years later, the freemen secured their right to select delegates to represent the towns in drafting the laws of the colony.

9. (E) is correct. In 1632, King Charles I granted 10 million acres at the northern end of the Chesapeake Bay to the Calvert family, the Lords of Baltimore, important Catholic supporters of the English monarchy. Because the proprietors were Catholics, they encouraged settlement by their coreligionists, a presecuted minority in seventeenth-century England. Maryland became the only English colony in North America with a substantial Catholic minority.

10. (D) is correct. A large source of New England's strength was the impressive system the Puritans built to educate their young. In 1647, Massachusetts required that towns with 50 families or more support a public school; those with 100 familes were to establish a grammar school that taught Latin, knowledge of which was required for admission to Harvard College, founded in 1636.

Document-Based Question

Analyze the the relationship between the British North American colonies and the government back in England in the light of the following documents.

The seventeenth century saw many changes in British religion and government. The death of Queen Elizabeth in 1603 saw the rise of the Stuarts to the British throne. They were deposed by Oliver Cromwell in 1649, but restored to the throne in 1660, only to lose it again to William of Orange in 1688. It was during this period of civil unrest that the British colonial project in North America was born and matured, such that by The Glorious Revolution they had a population of 225,000 people (**DOCUMENT 7**). This population, though distinctly British in character, was not always obedient to the British crown.

By the 1670s there was substantial dissatisfaction with the royally appointed colonial governments. Nathanial Bacon led a revolt in Virginia, charging the governor with unjustly taxing the people and not protecting them sufficiently. The seeds of popular sovereignty were already sown, as he signed his declaration "Generall by Consent of the people" (**DOCUMENT 2**). The fundamental disagreement about the roots of authority between Bacon, the colonist, and Berkeley, the Royal governor, is a stark one, which would have echoes in later colonial history. Bacon derived his authority from the people, Berkeley from his appointment by the King (**DOCUMENT 3**).

In New England there were also clear signs that the King's authority was losing its grip. A law against selling weapons to Indians had passed Parliament in 1633. In 1657, the Commonwealth of Massachusetts had passed a law permitting them to be sold by licensed dealers (**DOCUMENT 4**).

In 1701 William Penn issued his charter for Pennsylvania, granting various rights to its inhabitants. His effort was less subversive than those of Massachusetts, or of Nathaniel Bacon. Penn appealed to the King's authority, and was very clear that he had the land only through that authority. However, the very existence of the charter, granting rights to Englishman above those given by the crown, is subversive to royal power (**DOCUMENT 5**).

By 1763, at the end of the French and Indian War, the King was through with this disobedience. He issued a declaration that reaffirmed the power of the Royal governors in the colonies, as well as establishing governors in the newly acquired colonies (**DOCUMENT 6**).

The British North American colonies took advantage of the varying states of governmental disarray over the course of the seventeenth century to pull away from Royal control. By the mid-eighteenth century the Crown would no longer tolerate this, which would soon lead to a conflict.

CHAPTER 4

Slavery and Empire, 1441–1770

This chapter illustrates how the success of European empires was based on a system of slavery, and particularly how the English benefited from that system in the Americas and at home. Just as the English gained knowledge and skills from the Indians, colonists also were aided by the skills and agricultural knowledge of African slaves. The hardship and suffering of slavery was buffered by the development of African-American communities among people drawn from many different West African cultures, as well as from positive, if unintended, cultural exchanges between Europeans and enslaved peoples.

The Beginnings of African Slavery

African slavery evolved out of an existing Mediterranean tradition. It was adapted to the rise of changing modes of agricultural production. The slave trade focused on African societies familiar with slavery and farming.

The African Slave Trade

Various European nations participated in the African slave trade. The trade was an exercise in brutality that profoundly affected African societies.

The Development of North American Slave Societies

Slavery was an acceptable labor system throughout colonial America. Slave societies developed in different regions in different European settlements and were quite diverse. The presence of slavery did not necessarily mean a slave society developed.

African to African American

Building upon their African heritage, the people wrenched from their homelands across the Atlantic Ocean constructed a community that was adapted to their situations. Family life, culture, methods of accommodation and resistance, and acculturation created the African Americans and their communities. In the process, African influences became integrated into the life, culture, and society of the South.

Slavery and Empire

Slavery was the mainspring of colonial economic development and a major force behind the rise of European empires in the Americas. The competition for wealth among European nations stimulated wars and attempts by England to regulate the economy of its colonies.

Slavery and Freedom

Slavery created a stratified society with a small planter elite that controlled most of the wealth and power. In most cases, wealth was connected to owning land, but wealth was not the only determinant of status. Skin color played as large a role.

Multiple-Choice Questions

1. The African American song "Quow" illustrates
   - (A) the refitting of religion to New World circumstances.
   - (B) need for kinship in their culture.
   - (C) problems of the middle passage.
   - (D) powerful awareness of their oppression.
   - (E) plans to organize slave revolts.

2. Locations such as Madeira, Barbados, Jamaica, and Haiti illustrate the commercial connection between slavery and
   - (A) tobacco.
   - (B) cotton.
   - (C) sugar.
   - (D) rice.
   - (E) indigo.

3. About half of the slaves imported to the New World between 1701 and 1810 were delivered to
   - (A) Brazil.
   - (B) Hudson's Bay.
   - (C) the British colonies of North America
   - (D) Mexico.
   - (E) the Caribbean Basin.

4. Among the worst of the horrors confronting slaves during the Middle Passage was
   - (A) seasickness.
   - (B) poor food quality.
   - (C) stories told describing what lay ahead in America.
   - (D) inadequate sanitation and related deadly diseases.
   - (E) slaves were thrown overboard when they became unruly.

5. Before the 1730s, the most profitable activity of the early Carolina economy was
   - (A) the growing of rice.
   - (B) the Indian slave trade.
   - (C) the export of indigo and tobacco.
   - (D) the importation and sale of slaves from the Caribbean.
   - (E) the growing of timber and naval stores.

6. One of the first written antislavery sentiments was "Considerations on The Keeping of Negroes" (1754) by
   - (A) Elizabeth Lucas Pinckney.
   - (B) Olaudah Equiano.
   - (C) James Edward Oglethorpe.
   - (D) John Woolman.
   - (E) William Byrd, II.

7. Eighteenth century slave masters were reluctant to allow their slaves to become Christians because
   - (A) they believed slaves could not understand Christian teachings.
   - (B) they feared that Christian teachings would foster violence among the slaves.
   - (C) they did not want to see Christianity influenced by African religions.
   - (D) they feared Christianity would give the slaves dangerous ideas about freedom and equality.
   - (E) they believed that Christianity was incompatible with African populations.

8. With the many ethnic groups present, this may have first formed the foundation of a common African American culture:
   - (A) conversion to Christianity.
   - (B) learning English.
   - (C) music and dance.
   - (D) fictive kinship.
   - (E) interest in commerce.

9. The Navigation Acts passed between 1660 and 1696
   - (A) opened trade within the future British empire to any nation.
   - (B) encouraged colonial manufacturing.
   - (C) consolidated the English colonies into one centralized trading unit.
   - (D) defined the role colonies would play within the future British empire.
   - (E) forbade customs collectors from going into warehouses to look for smuggled goods.

10. Which one of the following is NOT an area of Africa from which most enslaved people came?
    - (A) West Africa
    - (B) Congo and Angola
    - (C) Lower Niger River
    - (D) Gold Coast
    - (E) South Africa

Document-Based Question

Explain the process by which slavery was created in North America.

DOCUMENT 1

DOCUMENT 2

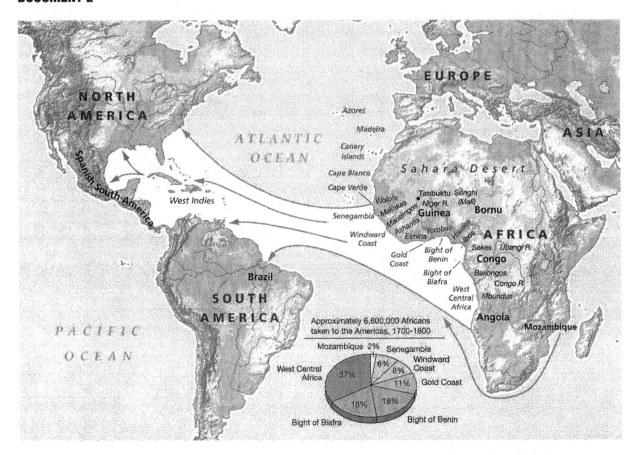

DOCUMENT 3

Source: Alexander Falconbridge, The African Slave Trade (1788)

. . . About eight o'clock in the morning the Negroes are generally brought upon deck. Their irons being examined, a long chain, which is locked to a ring-bolt, fixed in the deck, is run through the rings of the shackles of the men, and then locked to another ring-bolt, fixed also in the deck. By this means fifty or sixty, and sometimes more, are fastened to one chain, in order to prevent them from rising, or endeavoring to escape. If the weather proves favorable, they are permitted to remain in that situation till four or five in the afternoon, when they are disengaged from the chain, and sent down. . . . Upon the Negroes refusing to take sustenance, I have seen coals of fire, glowing hot, put on a shovel, and placed so near their lips, as to scorch and burn them. And this has been accompanied with threats, of forcing them to swallow the coals, if they any longer persisted in refusing to eat. These means have generally had the desired effect. I have also been credibly informed that a certain captain in the slave trade poured melted lead on such of the Negroes as obstinately refused their food. Exercise being deemed necessary for the preservation of their health, they are sometimes obligated to dance, when the weather will permit their coming on deck. If they go about it reluctantly, or do not move with agility, they are flogged; a person standing by them all the time with at cat-o'-nine-tails in his hand for that purpose.

DOCUMENT 4

Source: Olaudah Equiano, The Middle Passage (1788)

. . . I and some few more slaves, that were not saleable amongst the rest, from very much fretting, were shipped off in a sloop for North America. . . . While I was in this plantation [in Virginia] the gentleman, to whom I suppose the estate belonged, being unwell, I was one day sent for to his dwelling house to fan him; when I came into the room where he was I was very much affrighted at some things I saw, and the more so as I had seen a black woman slave as I came through the house, who was cooking the dinner, and the poor creature was cruelly loaded with various kinds of iron machines; she had one particularly on her head, which locked her mouth so fast that she could scarcely speak; and could not eat nor drink. I was much astonished and shocked at this contrivance, which I afterwards learned was called the iron muzzle . . .

DOCUMENT 5

An Act Concerning Servants and Slaves
Source: William Waller Hening, The Statutes at Large; Being a Collection of all the Laws of Virginia, from the First Session of the Legislature in the Year 1619, (New York: R & W & G. Bartow, 1823). Vol. I. http://www.law.du.edu/russell/lh/alh/docs/virginiaslaverystatutes.html

IV. And also be it enacted, by the authority aforesaid, and it is hereby enacted, That all servants imported and brought into this country, by sea or land, who were not Christians in their native country, (except Turks and Moors in amity with her majesty, and others that can make due proof of their being free in England, or any other Christian country, before they were shipped, in order to transportation hither) shall be accounted and be slaves, and as such be here bought and sold notwithstanding a conversion to Christianity afterwards.

V. And be it enacted, by the authority aforesaid, and it is hereby enacted, That if any person or persons shall hereafter import into this colony, and here sell as a slave, any person or persons that shall have been a freeman in any Christian country, island, or plantation, such importer and seller as aforesaid, shall forfeit and pay, to the party from whom the said freeman shall recover his freedom, double the sum for which the said freeman was sold. To be recovered, in any court of record within this colony, according to the course of the common law, wherein the defendant shall not be admitted to plead in bar, any act or statute for limitation of actions.

VI. Provided always, That a slave's being in England, shall not be sufficient to discharge him of his slavery, without other proof of his being manumitted there.

DOCUMENT 6

James Oglethorpe: The Stono Rebellion (1739)
Source: James Oglethorpe: The Stono Rebellion (1739), Allen Chandler, ed., The Colonial Records of the State of Georgia, vol. 22 (Atlanta: Chas. P. Byrd Press, 1913), pp. 232–236.

Sometime since there was a Proclamation published at Augustine, in which the King of Spain (then at Peace with Great Britain) promised Protection and Freedom to all Negroes Slaves that would resort thither. Certain Negroes belonging to Captain Davis escaped to Augustine, and were received there. They were demanded by General Oglethorpe who sent Lieutenant Demere to Augustine, and the Governour assured the General of his sincere Friendship, but at the same time showed his Orders from the Court of Spain, by which he was to receive all Run away Negroes... On the 9th day of September last being Sunday which is the day the Planters allow them to work for themselves, Some Angola Negroes assembled, to the number of Twenty; and one who was called Jemmy was their Captain, they suprized a Warehouse belonging to Mr. Hutchenson at a place called Stonehow [sicÑ]; they there killed Mr. Robert Bathurst, and Mr. Gibbs, plundered the House and took a pretty many small Arms and Powder, which were there for Sale. Next they plundered and burnt Mr. Godfrey's house, and killed him, his Daughter and Son. They then turned back and marched Southward along Pons Pons, which is the Road through Georgia to Augustine, they passed Mr. Wallace's Taxern towards day break, and said they would not hurt him, for he was a good Man and kind to his Slaves, but they broke open and plundered Mr. Lemy's House, and killed him, his wife and Child. They marched on towards Mr. Rose's resolving to kill him; but he was saved by a Negroe, who having hid him went out and pacified the others. Several Negroes joyned them, they calling out Liberty, marched on with Colours displayed, and two Drums beating, pursuing all the white people they met with, and killing Man Woman and Child when they could come up to them...The Lieutenant Governour sent an account of this to General Oglethorpe, who met the advices on his return form the Indian Nation He immediately ordered a Troop of Rangers to be ranged, to patrole through Georgia, placed some Men in the Garrison at Palichocolas, which was before abandoned, and near which the Negroes formerly passed, being the only place where Horses can come to swim over the River Savannah for near 100 miles, ordered out the Indians in pursuit, and a Detachment of the Garrison at Port Royal to assist the Planters on any Occasion, and published a Proclamation ordering all the Constables &c. of Georgia to pursue and seize all Negroes, with a Reward for any that should be taken. It is hoped these measures will prevent any Negroes from getting down to the Spaniards.

DOCUMENT 7

Jefferson the Slaveowner
Source: Thomas Jefferson, advertisement, *Virginia Gazette*, September 14, 1769.

Run away from the subscriber in Albemarle, a Mulatto slave called Sandy, about 35 years of age, his stature is rather low, inclining to corpulence, and his complexion light; he is a shoemaker by trade, in which he uses his left hand principally, can do coarse carpenters work, and is something of a horse jockey; he is greatly addicted to drink, and when drunk is insolent and disorderly, in his conversation he swears much, and in his behavior is artful and knavish. He took with him a white horse, much scarred with traces, of which it is expected he will endeavor to dispose; he also carried his shoemakers tools, and will probably endeavor to get employment that way. Whoever conveys the said slave to me, in Albemarle, shall have 40 s. reward, if taken up within the county, 4 l. if elsewhere within the colony, and 10 l. if in any other colony, from Thomas Jefferson.

ANSWERS AND EXPLANATIONS

Multiple-Choice Questions

1. (D) is correct. The African song "Quow" is the story of an oppressed slave. The song includes the lyrics, "The white man's wronged you, "Brother Quow."
Slaves often wrote or sang tales about their common oppression.

2. (C) is correct. Sugar and slaves had gone together since Italian merchants imported the first cane sugar from the Middle Eat and set up the first modern sugar plantations on the islands of the Mediterranean. Columbus brought sugar cane to Hispaniola, and soon sugar plantations were in operation. African slaves came to the Americas with the introduction of sugar production.

3. (E) is correct. Seventy-six percent of 10 to 12 million slaves were brought to the New World between the years 1701–1810. Out of this number more than half ended up on Dutch, French, or British sugar plantations in the Caribbean.

4. (D) is correct. On the slave ships, the sanitation conditions were awful, especially below deck. There slaves, chained together lay in their own waste. Among the diseases that slaves contracted and died from included; dysentery, smallpox, measles, and yellow fever. According to one Atlantic seaman, "you could smell a slaver five miles down wind."

5. (B) is correct. The Carolinas were a slave society from the very beginning of the slave industry. Practicing a strategy of divide and conquer, the Carolina settlers used the Native American tribes to fight one another. The Caroliniains then enslaved tens of thousands of Native Americans shipping many to the Carribean and keeping others for the cattle and timber industries.

6. (D) is correct. John Woolman, was a Quaker, who wanted people to imagine themselves in the position of an African slave. Woolman, imagining himself as a slave wrote: "we have been exposed to constant servitude in the more servile and inferior employments of life….."

7. (D) is correct. The slaveowners especially did not want slaves to become baptized, fearing it would give slaves ideas of freedom, universal brotherhood, and equality with their owners. One plantation owner remarked a slave was, "ten times worse when a Christian then in their form of paganism."

8. (B) is correct. Universal forms of music and dance often came before even a common language in slave societies. Future President and plantation owner Thomas Jefferson wrote that blacks,"are more generally gifted than the whites, with accurate ears for tune and time."

9. (D) is correct. The series of laws known as the Navigation Acts passed between 1660 and 1696 created both the legal and institutional structure of the colonies. The acts defined the colonies as both suppliers of raw materials and as markets for English manufactured products. The acts forbade other European nations from trading with the colonies and specified a list of "enumerated commodities" that could be shipped only to England. These products included; sugar, molasses, rum, furs, skins, timber, and a variety of other products exported everywhere from the manufacturing colonies of the north to the slave plantations of the south.

10. (E) is correct. Slave traders shipped slaves from all parts of Western Africa. These areas included West Africa, Angola, Congo, Ghana, and the lower Niger River.

Document-Based Question

Explain the process by which slavery was created in North America.

Though the presence of household slaves had existed in Mediterranean Europe prior to colonial expansion, slavery in North America developed over time and was influenced by a variety

Though the presence of household slaves had existed in Mediterranean Europe prior to colonial expansion, slavery in North America developed over time and was influenced by a variety of factors. Through colonial expansion, Europeans had developed economies in North America that were dependent on an ever-increasing need for labor. At first, they filled this need with indentured servants and slaves purchased from African traders, who captured Africans, forced them on brutal marches to the west coast of Africa, and sold them to Europeans in exchange for European goods (**DOCUMENT 1**). These captured men, women, and children were then shipped to North America via the Middle Passage of the trade pattern between Europe, Africa, and America called Triangular Trade (**DOCUMENT 2**). Conditions on the slave ships that traveled the Middle Passage were abysmal, and though Africans often rebelled in a variety of ways against such treatment, they were abused, starved, and susceptible to serious illness on the long journey (**DOCUMENT 3**). The shock of enslavement and the savage treatment of the slaves on their forced migration to America did not end upon arrival; slavery was early characterized by various forms of oppression and brutality that were employed as a way to maintain control over slaves (**DOCUMENT 4**). Slavery soon became encoded in laws that defined the difference between indentured servants and slaves and outlined the process by which such a system would be upheld (**DOCUMENT 5**). Nonetheless, there were many ways in which slaves rebelled and tried to achieve freedom from an increasingly institutionalized system. Large-scale group attempts at retaliation and escape, such as the Stono Rebellion, are clear evidence that slavery was not established without rebellion and struggle, though most attempts to achieve freedom were met with harsh reprisals designed to quell future rebellions (**DOCUMENT 6**). This was true even for those who attempted individual acts of rebellion as slavery became increasingly institutionalized as part of the American system. Escaped slaves could expect that they would be pursued in order to maintain the system (**DOCUMENT 7**).

CHAPTER 5

The Cultures of Colonial North America, 1700–1780

This chapter emphasizes the number of distinct European colonial regions and new Native American ones that had developed by the 1700s. These regions (Spanish, French, English, and Indian) created distinct forms of community life that would continue to shape American history. The maturing of the European colonies, particularly those held by Britain, brought many social and religious tensions in the 1700s. These tensions produced much public discussion in the British colonies, which may have encouraged more political involvement on the part of ordinary people.

North American Regions

The development of regional cultures was a multicultural enterprise. Relations between Indian peoples and European colonists followed differing patterns. The same was true of colonial development. The resulting colonial societies reflected the meeting of peoples and cultures.

Diverging Social and Political Patterns

Immigration fueled population growth in the British colonies. Both in terms of status and mobility, the development of classes in the colonies differed from the social structure in England, and it also varied by region. British policy influenced colonial development.

The Cultural Transformation of British North America

New ideas from Europe combined with trends in development helped transform the British colonies in the eighteenth century. The interplay between the traditional and the new stimulated strong movements in response to the ongoing changes.

Multiple-Choice Questions

1. The Deerfield raid illustrates the population conflict between the
   (A) English, French and Spanish.
   (B) French and the Iroquois.
   (C) French, Spanish and English.
   (D) African Americans and Spanish.
   (E) English, French and Indians.

2. A significant characteristic of Spanish colonial communities was
   (A) their close association with religious missions.
   (B) the religious equality between the colonizers and the natives.
   (C) the rigid segregation practiced between Indians and Europeans.
   (D) the close contact maintained with the administrators of New Spain.
   (E) the great prosperity most of them experienced.

3. During the eighteenth century the middle colonies exhibited certain characteristics that distinguished them from New England. Among these was (were)
   (A) the settlement of planned communities.
   (B) high rates of mobility.
   (C) relative equality of the sexes.
   (D) religious uniformity.
   (E) communal land distribution.

4. English authorities made the Church of England the official state religion in
   (A) New England.
   (B) Rhode Island.
   (C) Pennsylvania.
   (D) the Chesapeake colonies.
   (E) New Jersey.

5. The majority of farmers of eighteenth century North America were interested in
   (A) commercial farming.
   (B) breaking free from farming.
   (C) communal agriculture.
   (D) little diversity of activities.
   (E) small self-sufficient communities.

6. Which one of the following BEST describes English immigration policy?
   (A) They wanted to keep colonies Catholic.
   (B) They limited migration because they did not want to lose population.
   (C) They had a liberal policy for both English and foreign nationals.
   (D) Encouraged women to immigrate more than men.
   (E) They allowed only English-speaking Protestant settlers.

7. An Enlightenment thinker would emphasize that
   (A) the natural world imposed restriction on humans that they could not overcome.
   (B) the rhythms of life and nature guide human behavior.
   (C) humans were capable of understanding natural laws and using them to improve their condition.
   (D) philosopher kings could best rule the nation.
   (E) progress occurred through the natural working of God's laws.

8. In Poor Richard's Almanac, Ben Franklin tried to promote this to ordinary folk:
   (A) enlightenment thought.
   (B) the Great Awakening.
   (C) scientific progress.
   (D) representative government.
   (E) colonial unity.

9. In establishing the half-way covenant, the Puritans
   (A) denied church membership to most second generation Puritans in colonial America.
   (B) required a conversion experience for acceptance into church membership.
   (C) allowed the children of church members all the privileges of church membership.
   (D) managed rather than resolved the problem of compulsory church attendance and requirements for church membership.
   (E) mediated between Calvinism and Arminianism.

10. The Great Awakening had its deepest effects on
    (A) the young people.
    (B) the elderly.
    (C) persons who had little previous association with a church.
    (D) the wealthy.
    (E) the native population.

Document-Based Question

Defend or refute the following statement: Differing patterns of immigration and migration created different social and political climates in the various regions of the Americas.

DOCUMENT 1

Source: J. Hector St. John Crèvecoeur, "What Is an American?" (1782)

The next wish of this traveller will be to know whence came all these people? They are a mixture of English, Scotch, Irish, French, Dutch, Germans, and Swedes. From this promiscuous breed, that race now called Americans have arisen. The eastern provinces must indeed be excepted, as being the unmixed descendants of Englishmen. I have heard many wish that they had been more intermixed also: for my part, I am no wisher, and think it much better as it has happened. They exhibit a most conspicuous figure in this great and variegated picture; they too enter for a great share in the pleasing perspective displayed in these thirteen provinces. I know it is fashionable to reflect on them, but I respect them for what they have done, for the accuracy and wisdom with which they have settled their territory; for the decency of their manners; for their early love of letters; their ancient college, the first in this hemisphere; for their industry; which to me who am but a farmer, is the criterion of everything. There never was a people, situated as they are, who with so ungrateful a soil have done more in so short a time. Do you think that the monarchical ingredients which are more prevalent in other governments, have purged them from all foul stains? Their histories assert the contrary.

DOCUMENT 2

Source: Benjamin Franklin, "Observations Concerning the Increase of Mankind, Peopling of Countries, &c." (1751)

There is in short, no Bound to the prolific Nature of Plants or Animals, but what is made by their crowding and interfering with each others Means of Subsistence. Was the Face of the Earth vacant of other Plants, it might be gradually sowed and overspread with one Kind only; as, for Instance, with Fennel; and were it empty of other Inhabitants, it might in a few Ages be replenish'd from one Nation only; as, for Instance, with Englishmen. Thus there are suppos'd to be now upwards of One Million English Souls in North-America, (tho' 'tis thought scarce 80,000 have been brought over Sea) and yet perhaps there is not one the fewer in Britain, but rather many more, on Account of the Employment the Colonies afford to Manufacturers at Home. This Million doubling, suppose but once in 25 Years, will in another Century be more than the People of England, and the greatest Number of Englishmen will be on this Side the Water. What an Accession of Power to the British Empire by Sea as well as Land! What Increase of Trade and Navigation! What Number of Ships and Seamen! We have been here but little more than 100 Years, and yet the Force of our Privateers in the late War, united, was greater, both in Men and Guns, than that of the whole British Navy in Queen Elizabeth's Time. . . .

And since Detachments of English from Britain sent to America, will have their Places at Home so soon supply'd and increase so largely here; why should the Palatine Boors be suffered to swarm into our Settlements, and by herding together establish their Language and Manners to the Exclusion of ours? Why should Pennsylvania, founded by the English, become a Colony of Aliens, who will shortly be so numerous as to Germanize us instead of our Anglifying them, and will never adopt our Language or Customs, any more than they can acquire our Complexion.

DOCUMENT 4

1700

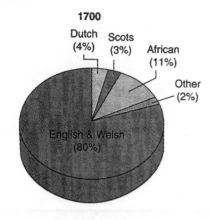

Dutch (4%) Scots (3%) African (11%) Other (2%) English & Welsh (80%)

1790

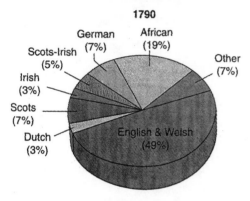

German (7%) Scots-Irish (5%) Irish (3%) Scots (7%) Dutch (3%) African (19%) Other (7%) English & Welsh (49%)

DOCUMENT 5

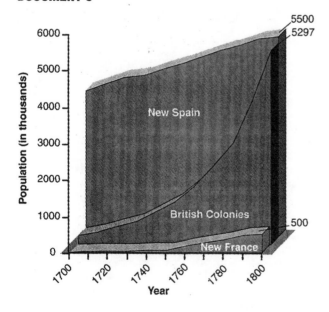

New Spain British Colonies New France

5500
5297
500

Population (in thousands)
6000 5000 4000 3000 2000 1000 0
Year
1700 1720 1740 1760 1780 1800

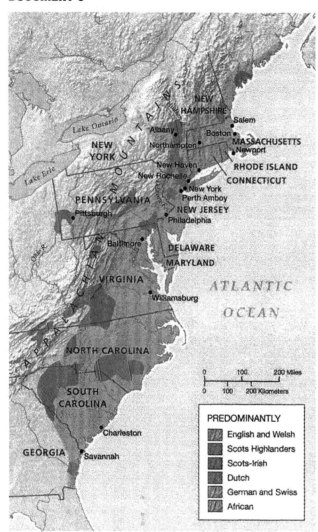

DOCUMENT 7

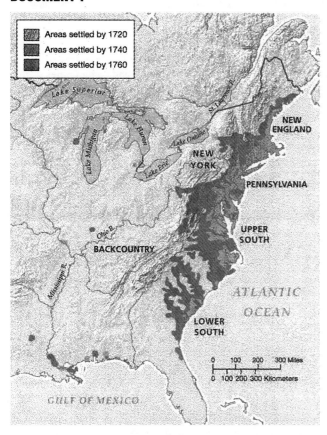

Areas settled by 1720
Areas settled by 1740
Areas settled by 1760

ANSWERS AND EXPLANATIONS

Multiple-Choice Questions

1. **(E) is correct.** The Deerfield raids became one of the most infamous events in a long series of attacks and counterattacks between English and French colonists and their Indian allies. After the raid the governor of Massachusetts ordered a day of fasting, raised the bounty on Indian scalps from £10 to £100, and organized bloody raids on French and Indian settlements to the north in reprisal.

2. **(A) is correct.** Spanish colonial communities had close association with religious missions. A string of Franciscan missions were constructed among the Indian peoples of Texas in 1716. In the 1690s, Jesuit missionaries, led by Father Eusebio Kino, built missions among the desert Indians of the lower Colorado River and Gila River Valleys. In the eighteenth century, the Spanish also established missions in arid Baja California.

3. **(B) is correct.** The middle colonies were more loosely bound than those of New England. Rates of mobility were considerably higher, with about half the population moving in any given decade. Because land was sold in individual lots rather than in communal parcels, farmers tended to disperse themselves at will over the open countryside. Villages gradually developed at crossroads and ferries but with little forethought or planning.

4. **(D) is correct.** English authorities made the Church of England the state religion in the Chesapeake colonies. Residents paid taxes to support the Church and were required to

4. (D) is correct. English authorities made the Church of England the state religion in the Chesapeake colonies. Residents paid taxes to support the Church and were required to attend services. No other churches were allowed into Virginia and Maryland (despite the role of Catholics in its founding) and dissenters were excluded or exiled.

5. (E) is correct. The majority of eighteenth-century North American farmers grew crops and raised livestock for their own needs or for local barter, and communities were largely self-sufficient. Rather than specializing in the production of one or two crops for sale, most farmers attempted to remain as independent of the market as possible, diversifying their activities.

6. (C) is correct. The British colonies grew far more rapidly than those of France or Spain. It was immigration that made the difference. Fearful of depleting their population at home, the Spanish severely limited the migration of their own subjects, and absolutely forbade the immigration of foreigners. The French, dedicated to keeping their colonies exclusively Catholic, ignored the desire of Protestant Huguenots to immigrate. The British were the only imperial power to encourage the immigration of foreign nationals to the colonies. In the 1680s, William Penn was the first colonial official to promote the immigration of Western Europeans, sending agents to recruit settlers in Holland, France, and the German principalities along the Rhine River.

7. (C) is correct. Drawing from the discoveries of Galileo, Copernicus, and the seventeenth-century scientists René Descartes and Issac Newton, Enlightenment thinkers in Britain and in Europe argued that the universe was governed by natural laws that people could understand and apply to their own advantage.

8. (A) is correct. The best remembered almanac is *Poor Richard's Almanac*, published by Philadelphia publisher Benjamin Franklin, but it was preceded and outlived by many others. What was so innovative about Franklin's alamanac, and what made it so important, was the manner in which the author used this traditional literary form to promote the new Enlightenment emphasis on useful and practical knowledge.

9. (D) is correct. The Puritan churches of New England suffered a declining membership and falling attendance at services, and many ministers began to warn of Puritanism's "declension," pointing to the "dangerous" trend toward the "evil of toleration." When Puritanism became an established church, attendance was expected of all townspeople, and conflicts inevitably arose over the requirement of a conversion experience. An agreement of 1662, known as the Half-Way Covenant, offered a practical solution: members' children who had not experienced conversion themselves could join as "half-way" members, restricted only from participation in communion. Thus the Puritans chose to manage rather than resolve the conflicts involved in becoming an established religion.

10. (A) is correct. The Great Awakening had its deepest effects on the young people. Before the Great Awakening, attendance at church had been mostly an adult affair, but throughout the colonies the revival of religion ha dits deepest effects on young people, who flocked to church in greater numbers than ever before.

Document-Based Question

Defend or refute the following statement: Differing patterns of immigration and migration created different social and political climates in the various regions of the Americas.

Each region in the North American colonies had its own pattern of settlement, which was a component in its cultural development. The colonies of the French Crescent differed from those of Puritan New England, which differed from the Spanish colonies of New Mexico or the British Mid-Atlantic colonies. Each was shaped by its own particular settlers. However, no colony was identical in culture to the mother country of its settlers, but each one had its own American culture.

Many of the colonies were peopled by immigrants from different countries, as opposed to a homogenous group of settlers. The primary exception, were the eastern colonies, which were the British Colonies were not exclusively English. Farther south and west they had, German, Scottish, Dutch, Swiss and Irish settlers, as well as a significant number of Africans, brought over as slaves (**DOCUMENT 6**). Over the course of the eighteenth century the population of British North America had gone from being 80 percent English to being barely half English. This large demographic switch was partially due to an influx of African slaves (they increased from 11 to 19 percent of the population), but also to a large amount of European immigration. (**DOCUMENT 4**).

Benjamin Franklin was of the belief that despite this non-English immigration, the English population was so large that they would dominate North America, politically and culturally (**DOCUMENT 2**). While he turned out to be largely correct, he was basing his hypothesis on false data. At the time, the largest population group in North America was in New Spain (**DOCUMENT 5**). It was not only large, it was also diverse. The particular character of New Spain, where ethnic mixing was frequent, led to a highly stratified society, in a way that was very distinct from the British and French colonies (**DOCUMENT 3**).

At the same time that the population of the colonies was growing, it was also moving. Over the course of the middle of the eighteenth century, there was a steady stream of expansion from the east coast westwards, into the backcountry. By the 1760's there was settlement as far west as the Ohio river (**DOCUMENT 7**).

The demographic shifts over the course of the eighteenth century changed the characters of the North American colonies, but they did so in different ways. Each colony had its own demographics, consequently they differed culturally.

CHAPTER 6

From Empire to Independence, 1750–1776

This chapter covers the development of hostility between Britain and its colonies. While Britain became the dominant European power in North America, its very success and subsequent attempts to centralize power brought resistance from British colonists. Through many types of organization, the colonies developed an "American" identity. This new community of interest was often encouraged by inept British actions. The outcome of this unhealthy dynamic was that thirteen colonies decided to leave the empire and declare themselves independent.

The Seven Years' War in America

Colonial expansion created tensions between European nations, colonists, and Indian peoples. Events in Europe, combined with competition for land and resources in the Americas, culminated in the Seven Years' War. The end of the war eliminated one source of conflict but stimulated several others.

The Imperial Crisis in British North America

Attempts by the British government to tighten regulation and increase taxation of the colonies triggered a series of crises. American colonists began questioning their relationship with Great Britain as they resisted efforts at more rigorous regulation.

"Save Your Money and Save Your Country"

British attempts to raise revenue from the colonies generated more widespread resistance. Greater colonial unity and violence characterized British colonial relations.

From Resistance to Rebellion

Colonial resistance became more unified as Great Britain again tried to tighten its rule of the colonies and raise revenues. Violence became more common. Eventually, the protest movement convened a national legislature. War broke out as resistance became rebellion.

Deciding for Independence

The expanding conflict between Great Britain and the rebellious colonists created a unified front in the colonies that approximated a national Congress. Other North American colonies, especially British colonies, were affected by the coming war. The outbreak of fighting stimulated the creation of a colonial military and eventually led to the Declaration of Independence, which established the United States.

Multiple-Choice Questions

1. In the Treaty of Paris, ending the French and Indian War
   (A) the French lost their North American empire to the British.
   (B) the French gained a new foothold on the North American continent.
   (C) the Iroquois Confederacy ceded to the British title to all lands east of the Mississippi River.
   (D) the Spanish acquired New Orleans and Florida.
   (E) France retained only Canadian Quebec in its empire in North America.

2. The Royal Proclamation of 1763
   (A) established and expanded the province of Quebec.
   (B) encouraged British land speculation.
   (C) forbade any Indian confederacies.
   (D) created an alliance between the colonists and the Iroquois confederacy.
   (E) set aside an area west of the Appalachians as "Indian Country."

3. The primary weapon that colonial opponents of the various revenue acts used to force their repeal was
   (A) nonviolent civil disobedience.
   (B) petitions to the crown.
   (C) nonimportation and nonconsumption.
   (D) guerrilla tactics.
   (E) meetings of colonial congresses.

4. The law that provoked the Boston Tea Party
   (A) placed a heavy tax on any tea not imported by the East India Company.
   (B) actually lowered the price of tea.
   (C) closed the port of Boston to further foreign trade.
   (D) was the harshest measure yet taken by the British against the colonies.
   (E) received little attention in other port cities.

5. The Declaration and Resolves passed at the Continental Congress in 1774 committed the colonies to
   (A) the creation of a grand council to legislate for all the colonies in cooperation with Parliament.
   (B) a declaration of independence and military action against the British.
   (C) economic sanctions prohibiting importation and consumption of British goods and export of colonial goods to other parts of the empire.
   (D) capitulate to the British.
   (E) improving their relationship with the mother country.

6. In his work *Common Sense*, Thomas Paine assisted the movement for independence by damning Parliament while
   (A) treating King George with respect.
   (B) appealing to the Americans' sense of special purpose.
   (C) advocating a socialist republic.
   (D) frightening the Americans with accounts of retribution against rebels in other parts of the empire.
   (E) pointing out that no foreign assistance would be forthcoming with a declaration of independence.

7. As a result of the fighting at Breed's Hill and Bunker Hill
   (A) King George rebuked his commanders in North America.
   (B) the colonists almost gave up hope of a military solution.
   (C) the British offered the Olive Branch Petition seeking peace.
   (D) the colonists won two major victories.
   (E) British casualties ended the possibility of reconciliation.

8. Which one of the following was NOT one of the first military engagements of the war that took place in or around Boston?
   (A) Breed's Hill
   (B) Lexington
   (C) Moore's Creek Bridge
   (D) Concord
   (E) Bunker Hill

9. In recognition of its significance to them, the French begin building forts here in 1753:
   (A) Minnesota and Michigan.
   (B) St. Louis to New Orleans.
   (C) Acadia.
   (D) Caribbean Sea.
   (E) from Lake Erie to the Ohio.

10. The Quebec Act covered an area that extended as far South as
   (A) the Mississippi River.
   (B) British West Florida.
   (C) the Ohio River.
   (D) Maine and New Hampshire.
   (E) Tennessee and Kentucky.

Document-Based Question

Explain and assess the underlying cause or causes of the American Revolution. Which, if any, was the most significant and why?

DOCUMENT 1

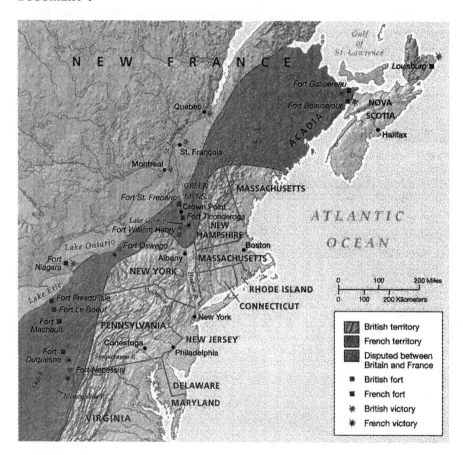

DOCUMENT 2

Source: Benjamin Franklin, Testimony Against the Stamp Act (1766)

Q. For what purposes are those taxes laid?

A. For the support of the civil and military establishments of the country, and to discharge the heavy debt contracted in the last [Seven Years'] war. . . .

Q. Are not all the people very able to pay those taxes?

A. No. The frontier counties, all along the continent, have been frequently ravaged by the enemy and greatly impoverished, are able to pay very little tax. . . .

Q. Are not the colonies, from their circumstances, very able to pay the stamp duty?

A. In my opinion there is not gold and silver enough in the colonies to pay the stamp duty for one year.

Q. Don't you know that the money arising from the stamps was all to be laid out in America?

A. I know it is appropriated by the act to the American service; but it will be spent in the conquered colonies, where the soldiers are, not in the colonies that pay it. . . .

Q. Do you think it right that America should be protected by this country and pay no part of the expense?

A. That is not the case. The colonies raised, clothed, and paid, during the last war, near 25,000 men, and spent many millions.

Q. Where you not reimbursed by Parliament?

A. We were only reimbursed what, in your opinion, we had advanced beyond our proportion, or beyond what might reasonably be expected from us; and it was a very small part of what we spent. Pennsylvania, in particular, disbursed about 500,000 pounds, and the reimbursements, in the whole, did not exceed 60,000 pounds. . . .

Q. Do you think the people of America would submit to pay the stamp duty, if it was moderated?

A. No, never, unless compelled by force of arms. . . .

Q. What was the temper of America towards Great Britain before the year 1763?

A. The best in the world. They submitted willingly to the government of the Crown, and paid, in all their courts, obedience to acts of Parliament. . . .

Q. What is your opinion of a future tax, imposed on the same principle with that of the Stamp Act? How would the Americans receive it?

A. Just as they do this. They would not pay it.

Q. Have not you heard of the resolutions of this House, and of the House of Lords, asserting the right of Parliament relating to America, including a power to tax the people there?

A. Yes, I have heard of such resolutions.

Q. What will be the opinion of the Americans on those resolutions?

A. They will think them unconstitutional and unjust.

Q. Was it an opinion in America before 1763 that the Parliament had no right to lay taxes and duties there?

A. I never heard any objection to the right of laying duties to regulate commerce; but a right to lay internal taxes was never supposed to be in Parliament, as we are not represented there. . . .

DOCUMENT 3

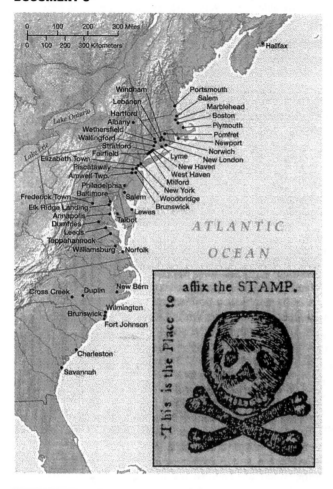

DOCUMENT 4

Source: The Boston "Massacre" or Victims of Circumstance? (1770)

Thirty or forty persons, mostly lads, being by this means gathered in King Street, Capt. Preston with a party of men with charged bayonets, came from the main guard to the commissioner's house, the soldiers pushing their bayonets, crying, make way! They took place by the custom house and, continuing to push to drive the people off, pricked some in several places, on which they were clamorous and, it is said, threw snow balls. On this, the Captain commanded them to fire; and more snow balls coming, he again said, damn you, fire, be the consequence what it will! One soldier then fired, and a townsman with a cudgel struck him over the hands with such force that he dropped his firelock; and, rushing forward, aimed a blow at the Captain's head which grazed his hat and fell pretty heavy upon his arm. However, the soldiers continued the fire successively till seven or eight or, as some say, eleven guns were discharged.

DOCUMENT 5

Source: John Andrews to William Barrell, Letter Regarding the Boston Tea Party (1773)

They muster'd I'm told, upon Fort Hill, to the number of about two hundred, and procceded, two by two, to Griffin's wharf, where Hall, Bruce, and Coffin lay, each with 114 chests of the ill fated article on board; the two former with only that article, but ye latter arriv'd at ye wharf only ye day before, was freighted with a large quantity of other goods, which they took the greatest care not to injure in the least, and before nine o'clock in ye evening, every chest from on board the three vessels was knock'd to pieces and flung over ye sides.

They say the actors were Indians from Narragansett. Whether they were or not, to a transient observer they appear'd as such, being cloath'd in Blankets with the heads muffled, and copper color'd countenances, being, each arm'd with a hatchet or axe, and pair pistols, nor was their dialect different from what I conceive these geniusses to speak, as their jargon was unintelligible to all but themselves. Not the least insult was offer'd to any person, save one Captain Conner, a letter of horses in this place, not many years since remov'd from dear Ireland, who had ript up the lining of his coat and waistcoat under the arms, and watch-ing, his opportunity had nearly fill'd them with tea, but being detected, was handled pretty roughly. They not only stripp'd him of his cloaths, but gave him a coat of mud, with a severe bruising into the bargain; and nothing but their utter aversion to make any disturbance pre-vented his being tar'd and feather'd.

DOCUMENT 6

Source: The Daughters of Liberty Urge Americans to Boycott British Goods.

> Young ladies in town, and those that live
> round,
> Let a friend at this season advise you:
> Since money's so scarce, and times
> growing worse,
> Strange things may soon hap and
> surprise you;
> First then, throw aside your high top
> knots of pride,
> Wear none but your own country linen,
> Of Economy boast, let your pride be
> the most
> To show clothes of your own make and
> spinning.

DOCUMENT 7

Source: James Otis, The Rights of the British Colonies Asserted and Proved (1763)

> The form of government is by nature and by right so far left to the individuals of each society that they may alter it from a simple democracy or government of all over all to any other form they please. Such alteration may and ought to be made by express compact. But how seldom this right has been asserted, history will abundantly show. For once that it has been fairly settled by compact, fraud, force, or accident have determined it an hundred times. As the people have gained upon tyrants, these have been obliged to relax only till a fairer opportunity has put it in their power to encroach again...
>
> Now can there be any liberty where property is taken away without consent? Can it with any color of truth, justice, or equity be affirmed that the northern colonies are represented in Parliament? Has this whole continent of near three thousand miles in length, and in which and his other American dominions His Majesty has or very soon will have some millions of as good, loyal, and useful subjects, white and black, as any in the three king-doms, the election of one member of the House of Commons?

DOCUMENT 8

Source: The Crisis Comes to a Head: April 19, 1775

> It is hoped however that this large Reinforcement to your Army will enable you to take a more active & determined part, & that you will have Strength enough, not only to keep Possession of Boston, but to give Protection in to Salem & the friends of Government at

that Place, & that you may without Hazard of Insult return thither if you think fit, & exercise Your Functions there, conformable to His Majesty's Instructions.

I have already said, in more Letters than one, that the Authority of this Kingdom must be supported, & the Execution of its Laws inforced, & you will have seen in His Maty's Speech to both Houses of Parliament, & in the Addresses which they have presented to His Majesty, the firm Resolution of His Majesty and Parliament to act upon those Principles; and as there is a strong Appearance that the Body of the People in at least three of the New England Governments are determined to cast off their Dependence upon the Government of this Kingdom, the only Consideration that remains is, in what manner the Force under your Command may be exerted to defend the Constitution & to restore the Vigour of Government.

DOCUMENT 9

Source: A Freelance Writer Urges His Readers To Use Common Sense (1776)

To the evil of monarchy we have added that of hereditary succession; and as the first is a degradation and lessening of ourselves, so the second, claimed as a matter of right, is an insult and an imposition on posterity. For all men being originally equals, no one by birth could have a right to set up his own family in perpetual preference to all others for ever, and though himself might deserve some decent degree of honors of his contemporaries, yet his descendants might be far too unworthy to inherit them. One of the strongest natural proofs of the folly of hereditary right in kings, is, that nature disapproves it, otherwise she would not so frequently turn it into ridicule by giving mankind an ass for a lion. Secondly, as no man at first could possess any other public honors than were bestowed upon him, so the givers of those honors could have no power to give away the right of posterity, and though they might say 'We choose you for our head,' they could not, without manifest injustice to their children, say 'that your children and your children's children shall reign over ours for ever.' Because such an unwise, unjust, unnatural compact might (perhaps) in the next succession put them under the government of a rogue or a fool. Most wise men, in their private sentiments, have ever treated hereditary right with contempt; yet it is one of those evils, which when once established is not easily removed; many submit from fear, others from superstition, and the more powerful part shares with the king the plunder of the rest.

DOCUMENT 10

Source: Thomas Jefferson, "Original Rough Draught" of the Declaration of Independence (1776)

We hold these truths to be sacred & undeniable that all men are created equal & independant, that from that equal creation they derive rights inherent & inalienable, among which are the preservation of life, & liberty, & the pursuit of happiness; that to secure these ends, governments are instituted among men, deriving their just powers from the consent of the governed; that whenever any form of government shall become destructive of these ends, it is the right of the people to alter or to abolish it, & to institute new government, laying its foundation on such principles & organising it's powers in such form, as to them shall seem most likely to effect their safety & happiness.

ANSWERS AND EXPLANATIONS

Multiple-Choice Questions

1. **(A) is correct.** France in the Treaty of Paris ceded all their North American territorial possessions east of the Mississippi River, other than the city of New Orleans. The British

1. **(A) is correct.** France in the Treaty of Paris ceded all their North American territorial possessions east of the Mississippi River, other than the city of New Orleans. The imperial rivalry in eastern North America that had begun in the sixteenth century now came to an end with complete victory for the British empire.

2. **(E) is correct.** The Royal or British Proclamation of 1763 set off much conflict between white settlers and the Native Americans. The settlers could not understand why the British would give land to a group of people who had fought against them in the French and Indian War. The Paxton Boys' Massacre was a direct result with the killing of Native American men, women, and children. A settlement helped reached by Benjamin Franklin ended further hostilities for the time being.

3. **(C) is correct.** An example of nonconsumption and nonimportation occurred in Boston, where in a town meeting, colonists decided to boycott British goods as a response to the Sugar Act. Many other colonial ports followed Boston's lead.

4. **(B) is correct.** The British figured that by actually lowering tea prices, colonists would stop boycotting the product and help the East India Company. In actuality, colonists looked at the Tea Act as a scheme by the British to make the unconstitutional payment of taxes look more palatable. The colonists rebelled leading to the Boston Tea Party.

5. **(C) is correct.** The delegates of the first Continental Congress passed a Declaration and Resolves that established a boycott of all British goods, would not be lifted, until all thirteen acts passed by Parliament in relation to the colonies were repealed. The colonists considered these acts to be a direct violation of, "the immutable laws of nature, the principles of the English constitution and several charters or compacts" of their provinces.

6. **(B) is correct.** In *Common Sense*, Paine argued that British rule under King George III was based on two tyrannies: aristocracy and monarchy. Paine appealed to the millennial spirit of the American Protestant culture by writing "We have it in our power to start the world over again."

7. **(E) is correct.** In June 1775, the Battle of Bunker Hill, which actually occurred mostly at Breed's Hill, cost the Brtish dearly despite an overall victory. The British suffered over a thousand causalties including 226 dead. These heavy losses led King George to reject the Olive Petition in August and declared the colonists to be in an "open and avowed rebellion."

8. **(C) is correct.** Lexington and Concord were and still are communities just outside Boston. Bunker and neighboring Breed's Hill are directly in Boston. Moore's Creek Bridge however is in North Carolina.

9. **(E) is correct.** The French started building numerous forts between Lake Erie and the Ohio River because they were fearful of British frontiersmen taking over the area. This area was disputed between the British and the French and was one of the main reasons for the outbreak of the Seven Years' War.

10. **(B) is correct.** With the Quebec Act of 1774, Britain created a permanent government for the territory taken from France during the Seven Years' War. This government was both authoritarian and anti-republican, with a royal government and an appointed council. Furthermore, the act confirmed the feudal system of land tenure along the St. Lawrence. It also granted religious toleration to the Roman Catholic Church and upheld the church's traditional right to collect tithes, thus, in effect, establishing Catholicism as the state religion in Quebec. To the American colonists, the Quebec Act was a frightening preview of what imperial authorities might have in store for them, Many colonists saw this Act as a threat to American liberty.

Document-Based Question

Explain and assess the underlying cause or causes of the American Revolution. Which, if any, was the most significant and why?

common political and economic interests, the colonies also opposed the empire's power to levy taxes outside of trade and at first expressed their concerns through established legal channels (**DOCUMENT 2**). This opposition blossomed into open acts of rebellion following the passage of the Stamp Act, an official duty leveled on all colonial documents (**DOCUMENT 3**). Though Great Britain attempted to control the growing rebellion in its colonies through the imposition of new regulations, most colonists bristled over what they felt were violations of their rights as English citizens. The most notorious conflict over the new laws occurred in Boston after young Bostonians and British troops quartered there confronted one another at what was soon labeled the Boston Massacre (**DOCUMENT 4**). The violence brought new British regulations and reprisals, which in turn led to increased acts of disobedience, including the infamous Boston Tea Party (**DOCUMENT 5**). Soon, many different sectors of colonial society began to make their voices heard and utilize every weapon at their disposal, including their own economic power, as part of the growing opposition to British law (**DOCUMENT 6**). It was soon clear that what had begun as an economic conflict between Great Britain and its profitable colonies had led to larger discussions about the philosophical foundations of power and the absence of actual, as opposed to virtual, parliamentary representation for the British citizens of the colonies (**DOCUMENT 7**). Recognizing this new new controversy over representation and power as a potential threat to their holdings in North America, the British increased their military strength there and adopted a more forceful policy against the rebellion (**DOCUMENT 8**). However, a growing segment of the colonial population was increasingly swayed toward independence rather than revolution, particularly through persuasive public arguments against the institution of monarchy (**DOCUMENT 9**). The final decision to declare independence was therefore a result of many different economic and political conflicts, each rooted in a concern over the philosophical nature of power and its practical applications (**DOCUMENT 10**).

CHAPTER 7

The American Revolution, 1776–1786

This chapter covers the struggle for independence from the British as well as a struggle for national identity. Americans had traditions of local autonomy and power competing against the new and much more fragile concept of nationhood. Various groups based on class, sex, and ethnic identity also made demands upon the new state governments and Congress. Economic dislocation added to the volatile mix. The national government under the Articles of Confederation managed successfully to gain independence and make certain reforms. Its inability to solve economic problems and resulting internal rebellions led to a desire to strengthen the national government and create a more centralized United States.

The War for Independence

The world's best-equipped and most disciplined army supported and a strong navy faced a newly formed, ill-trained, and poorly equipped American military. Still, the war seesawed back and forth as fighting took place in the North, South, and West. A variety of military, geographic, diplomatic, and psychological factors contributed to the American victory.

The United States in Congress Assembled

During and after the war for independence, the United States faced the task of creating a government while dealing with numerous crises. The Articles of Confederation created the first national government that successfully coped with paying for the war. It also addressed diplomatic initiatives including the peace treaties with Britain and France, and issues over land.

Revolutionary Politics in the States

Newly formed states established their own constitutions across a wide political spectrum. The broadened base of politics and concerns over the appropriate structure of government created a strong debate that led to important political and social reforms. Economic turmoil produced problems that led to political unrest, but also raised questions about the role of government.

Multiple-Choice Questions

1. Which of the following is <u>NOT</u> true of American men who fought in the Revolution?
   (A) More soldiers died of disease than of battle wounds.
   (B) Continental Army regiments had the highest casualties.
   (C) The casualty ratio was higher than in any other American conflict except the Civil War.
   (D) Patriot militia were the most important group in winning battles.
   (E) Over 200,000 saw some action.

2. Encounters between the British Army and Continental Army at Trenton and Princeton, New Jersey in late 1776
   (A) pushed the British south into Delaware.
   (B) enabled the Americans to control New York.
   (C) convinced Washington that the Americans had to pursue an aggressive offensive policy to defeat the British.
   (D) turned the tide in favor of the Americans.
   (E) gave the Americans small victories needed to help morale.

3. The biggest British defeat before Yorktown occurred at
   (A) Trenton, New Jersey.
   (B) Saratoga, New York.
   (C) Fort Ticonderoga.
   (D) Brandywine Creek.
   (E) Harlem Heights.

4. When the Revolutionary War moved to the South, the British shifted to a strategy of
   (A) military conquest and occupation of territory.
   (B) turning the military conflict over to German mercenaries.
   (C) taking territory and turning it over to Loyalists.
   (D) guerilla warfare.
   (E) relying on the use of naval force to cut off supplies.

5. Which one of the following was <u>NOT</u> significant to the American victory at Yorktown?
   (A) Rochambeau's Army
   (B) French Caribbean fleet
   (C) Washington's Continentals
   (D) French and American heavy artillery
   (E) Cherokee Warriors

6. The Congress under the Articles of Confederation did not have the authority to
   (A) conduct war and foreign affairs.
   (B) establish a monetary system.
   (C) tax citizens directly.
   (D) maintain the armed forces.
   (E) obtain loans.

7. Which one of the following is <u>NOT</u> one of the provisions of the Treaty of Paris of 1783?
   (A) the right to fish in northern waters
   (B) Britain would withdraw from all forts within American territory.
   (C) Britain acknowledged the United States as "free, sovereign, and independent."
   (D) the western boundary of the Mississippi
   (E) Loyalists would not be compensated for property.

8. The type of state governments established in New York, Maryland, and Pennsylvania after the Revolution indicated
   (A) power of the conservatives throughout the fourteen states that existed at the time.
   (B) amount of control the radical element had seized.
   (C) reluctance to blend conservative and democratic elements.
   (D) balance of political power between conservative Whigs and radical democrats.
   (E) a complete repudiation of conservative ideas.

9. In their emphasis on the need for a "balanced government," conservatives were expressing their
   (A) support for strong local governments.
   (B) desire to expand political participation to the masses.
   (C) fear of tyranny by a majority of "the unthinking."
   (D) love for the church.
   (E) support for universal manhood suffrage.

10. In taking the position he did in the wake of the issuance of the Newburgh address, George Washington
   (A) officially declared himself a candidate for the presidency.
   (B) established the principle of separation of church and state.
   (C) set a precedent for the subordination of the military to civil authority.
   (D) took a step towards assuming political control of the colonies.
   (E) revealed his hostility toward the British.

Document-Based Question

What goals did the colonists have in waging the Revolutionary War and how did these goals shape their emergent political system?

DOCUMENT 1

A Freelance Writer Urges His Readers To Use Common Sense (1776)
Source: A Hypertext on American History From the Colonial Period Until Modern Times,
http://odur.let.rug.nl/~usa/D/1776-1800/paine/CM/sense03.htm

The nearer any government approaches to a republic the less business there is for a king. It is somewhat difficult to find a proper name for the government of England. Sir William Meredith calls it a republic; but in its present state it is unworthy of the name, because the corrupt influencè If the crown, by having all the places in its disposal, hath so effectually swallowed up the power, and eaten out the virtue of the house of commons (the republican part in the constitution) that the government of England is nearly as monarchical as that of France or Spain. Men fall out with names without understanding them. For it is the republican and not the monarchical part of the constitution of England which Englishmen glory in, viz. the liberty of choosing an house of commons from out of their own body and it is easy to see that when the republican virtue fails, slavery ensues. My is the constitution of England sickly, but because monarchy hath poisoned the republic, the crown hath engrossed the commons?

DOCUMENT 2

Source: Thomas Jefferson, "Original Rough Draught" of the Declaration of Independence (1776)

We therefore the representatives of the United States of America in General Congress assembled do, in the name & by authority of the good people of these states, reject and renounce all allegiance & subject to the kings of Great Britain & all others who may hereafter claim by, through, or under them; we utterly dissolve & break off all political connection which may have heretofore subsisted between us & the people or parliament of Great Britain; and finally we do assert and declare these colonies to be free and independent states, and that as free & independent states they shall hereafter have power to levy war, conclude peace, contract alliances, establish commerce, & to do all other acts and things which independent states may of right do. And for the support of this declaration we mutually pledge to each other our lives, our fortunes, & our sacred honour.

DOCUMENT 3

The TORY'S Day of JUDGMENT.

DOCUMENT 4

Source: Rights of Women in an Independent Republic
Abigail Adams to John Adams, Braintree, 31 March 1776

I long to hear that you have declared an independancy-and by the way in the new Code of Laws which I suppose it will be necessary for you to make I desire you would Remember the Ladies, and be more generous and favourable to them than your ancestors. Do not put such umlimited power into the hands of the Husbands. Remember all Men would be tyrants if they could. If perticuliar care and attention is not paid to the Laidies we are determined to foment a Rebelion, and will not hold ourselves bound by any Laws in which we have no voice, or Representation.

That your Sex are Naturally Tyrannical is a Truth so thoroughly established as to admit of no dispute, but such of you as wish to be happy willingly give up the harsh title of Master for the more tender and endearing one of Friend. Why then, not put it out of the power of the vicious and the Lawless to use us with cruelty and indignity with impunity. Men of Sense in all Ages abhor those customs which treat us only as the vassals of your Sex. Regard us then as Beings placed by providence under your protection and in immitation of the Supreem Being make use of that power only for our happiness.

DOCUMENT 5

Source: African Americans and the Revolution

In this excerpt, Cato and his family, slaves freed because their owner failed to comply with slave registration laws, wrote the following to the legislature to uphold the law and their freedom:

We esteem in a particular blessing granted to us, that we are enabled this day to add one more step to universal civilization by removing as much as possible the sorrows of those who have lived in "undeserved" bondage, and from which by the assumed authority of the kings of Great Britain, no effectual legal relief could be obtained.

Extending his writing to a political scene, in this excerpt Benjamin Banneker addresses Thomas Jefferson regarding slavery:

Sir, Suffer me to recall to your mind that time in which the Arms and tyranny of the British Crown were exerted with powerful effort, in order to reduce you to a State of Servitude . . . You cannot but acknowledge, that the present freedom and tranquility which you enjoy you have mercifully received, and that is the peculiar blessing of Heaven.

DOCUMENT 6

Source: Constitution of Pennsylvania (1776)

A Declaration of the Rights of the Inhabitants of the Commonwealth, or State of Pennsylvania

I. That all men are born equally free and independent, and have certain natural inherent and inalienable rights, amongst which are the enjoying and defending life and liberty, acquiring, possessing and protecting property, and pursuing and obtaining happiness and safety.

II. That all men have a natural and unalienable right to worship Almighty God according to the dictates of their own consciences and understanding: And that no man ought or of right can be compelled to attend any religious worship, or erect or support any place of worship, or maintain any ministry, contrary to, or against, his own free will and consent: Nor can any man, who acknowledges the being of a God, be justly deprived or abridged of any civil right as a citizen, on account of his religious sentiments or peculiar mode of religious worship: And that no authority can or ought to be vested in, or assumed by any power whatever, that shall in any case interfere with, or in any manner controul, the right of conscience in the free exercise of religious worship.

III. That the people of this State have the sole, exclusive and inherent right of governing and regulating the internal police of the same.

IV. That all power being originally inherent in, and consequently derived from, the people; therefore all officers of government, whether legislative or executive, are their trustees and servants, and at all times accountable to them.

V. That government is, or ought to be, instituted for the common benefit, protection and security of the people, nation or community; and not for the particular emolument or advantage of any single man, family or set of men, who are a part only of that community; And that the community hath an indubitable, unalienable and indefeasible right to reform, alter, or abolish government in such a manner as shall be by that community judged most conducive to the public weal.

VI. That those who are employed in the legislative and executive business of the State, may be restrained from oppression, the people have a right, at such periods as they may think proper, to reduce their public officers to a private station, and supply the vacancies by certain and regular elections.

VII. That all elections ought to be free; and that all free men having a sufficient evident common interest with, and attachment to the community, have a right to elect officers, or to be elected into office.

A Declaration of the Rights of the Inhabitants of the Commonwealth of Massachusetts (1780)
Source: Francis N. Thorpe, ed., The Federal and State Constitutions, 7 vols. (Washington, D.C., Government Printing Office, 1909), vol. III, pp. 1888–1895.

ARTICLE IV. The people of this commonwealth have the sole and exclusive right of governing themselves, as a free, sovereign, and independent state; and do, and forever hereafter shall, exercise and enjoy every power, jurisdiction, and right, which is not, or may not hereafter be, by them expressly delegated to the United States of America, in Congress assembled.

ARTICLE V. All power residing originally in the people, and being derived from them, the several magistrates and officers of government, vested with authority, whether legislative, executive, or judicial, are their substitutes and agents, and are at all times accountable to them.

ARTICLE VI. No man, nor corporation, or association of men, have any other title to obtain advantages, or particular and exclusive privileges, distinct from those of the community, than what arises from the consideration of services rendered to the public; and this title being in nature neither hereditary, nor transmissible to children, or descendants, or relations by blood, the idea of a man born a magistrate, lawgiver, or judge, is absurd and unnatural.

ARTICLE VII. Government is instituted for the common good; for the protection, safety, prosperity, and happiness of the people; and not for the profit, honor, or private interest of any one man, family, or class of men: Therefore the people alone have an incontestible unalienable, and indefeasible right to institute government; and to reform, alter, or totally change the same, when their protection, safety, prosperity, and happiness require it.

ARTICLE VIII. In order to prevent those who are vested with authority from becoming oppressors, the people have a right at such periods and in such manner as they shall establish by their frame of government, to cause their public officers to return to private life; and to fill up vacant places by certain and regular elections and appointments.

ARTICLE IX. All elections ought to be free; and all the inhabitants of this commonwealth having such qualifications as they shall establish by their frame of government, have an equal right to elect officers, and to be elected, for public employments.

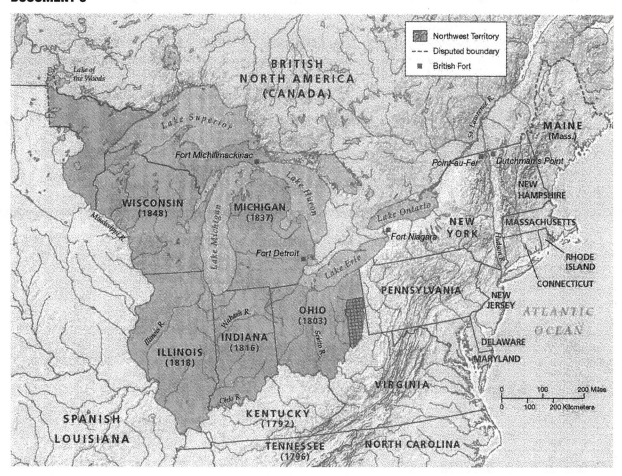

ANSWERS AND EXPLANATIONS

Multiple-Choice Questions

1. **(D) is correct.** Militias proved important in the defense of their own areas, for they had homes as well as local reputations to protect. In the face of battle, however, militia companies often demonstrated appalling rates of desertion. The final victory, rather, resulted primarily from the steady struggle of the Continental Army.

2. **(E) is correct.** Before the encounters with the British morale was desperately low: whole militia companies deserted; others, announcing the end of their terms of enlistment, left for home. American resistance seemed to be collapsing around Washington. On Christmas night 1776, Washington led 2,400 troops back across the Delaware, and the next morning defeated the Hessian forces in a surprise attack on their headquarters at Trenton, New Jersey. The Americans inflicted further heavy losses on the British at Princeton. Although these small victories had little strategic importance, they salvaged American morale.

3. **(B) is correct.** The forces of American general Horatio Gates surrounded the forces of General John Burgoyne at Saratoga, New York. Lacking alternatives, he surrendered his nearly 6,000 men. It would be the biggest British defeat until Yorktown, decisive because

it forced the nations of Europe to recognize that the Americans had a fighting chance to wit their Revolution.

- 4. **(C) is correct.** In the South, British policy involved a fundamental change from a strategy of military conquest to one of pacification. Territory would be retaken step by step, then handed over to Loyalists, who would reassert colonial authority loyal to the crown.
- 5. **(E) is correct.** The forces of Washington and Rochambeau marched south to join the French Caribbean fleet and surrounded Cornwallis and the British at Yorktown. French and American heavy artillery hammered the British unmercifully until the middle of October. Cherokee warriors did not aid in the effort.
- 6. **(C) is correct.** Lacking the power to tax citizens directly, the national government was to apportion its financial burdens among the states according to the extent of their surveyed land. The Congress was invested with the ability to conduct war and foreign affairs, establish a monetary system, maintain the armed forces, and obtain loans.
- 7. **(E) is correct.** One of the provisions of the treaty was that the national government would cease confiscating Loyalist property and try to persuade the states to fairly compensate Loyalist exiles.
- 8. **(D) is correct.** The constitutions of these three states typified the political range of the times. Pennsylvania instituted a radical democracy. Maryland created a conservative set of institutions designed to keep citizens and rulers as far apart as possible, and New York adopted a system somewhere in the middle.
- 9. **(C) is correct.** Conservative Americans took up the Whig argument on the need for a balanced government. The "unthinking many," wrote a conservative pamphleteer, should be checked by a strong executive and an upper house. The greatest danger, according to conservatives, was the possibility of majority tyranny, which might lead to the violation of property rights and to dictatorship.
- 10. **(C) is correct.** At Newburgh, Washington denounced any resort to force. In December 1783, he resigned his commission as general of the army despite calls for him to remain. There is little doubt that he could have assumed the role of an American dictator. Instead, by his actions and example, the principle of military subordination to civil authority was firmly established.

Document-Based Question

What goals did the colonists have in waging the Revolutionary War and how did these goals shape their emergent political system?

Unhappy with Great Britain's new economic policies following the Seven Years' War, the loyal dissent of colonists who criticized and rebelled against new taxes quickly became a larger argument about the legitimacy of imperial rule and the institution of monarchy itself (**DOCUMENT 1**). The adoption of the Declaration of Independence formally established the alienation of colonists from the monarchy, and rejected the empire's authority over the colonies themselves, plunging the colonists into open rebellion and initiating the full onset of the War for Independence (**DOCUMENT 2**). This was not a completely unified struggle, as many colonists remained loyal to Great Britain. But the goal of independence was seen by many colonists as inherently tied to a unified North American people, and such Loyalists, called Tories, were often subjected to harsh reprisals from revolutionaries, as they tried to instill a republican unity among the colonists and maintain their own control over the North American territories (**DOCUMENT 3**).

The struggle between Tories and Patriots was not the only evidence of division over the goal of independence from the control of imperial Britain. The practical meaning of liberty during the revolution also became a subject of controversy, for the American Revolutionary War was not only a military struggle. It was also an arena in which various groups interpreted the idea of liberty and independence in unexpected ways. Gender issues, the contradiction of the continued existence of slavery within a society struggling for liberty, and concerns over the definition of state power all grew from the ideologies of the revolution and helped shape the political and social structure of the newly forming nation. Women, who played an active role in revolutionary activities, took the ideas and rhetoric of liberty to heart, and questioned how the new nation would determine its laws and women's status, threatening to employ the revolutionary tactics in their own struggle to achieve liberties that had not existed under the British Empire (**DOCUMENT 4**). Similarly, African Americans, who often fought on the side of the empire in exchange for their freedom from slavery, were concerned that the idea of liberty so championed by the American rebels would not be extended to them and seized upon the new ideologies of liberty and representation as a way to point out the persistent inequities of slavery (**DOCUMENT 5**). The concern for liberty and the limitation of power extended to the colonies, which incorporated specific rights within their new state constitutions. Upholding the larger goals of the Revolution, including the elimination of monarchy and hereditary power, freedom of religion, and the creation of self-government, the new states created constitutions that included provisions for the removal of representatives from power (**DOCUMENTS 6 and 7**). Finally, the desire to create a strong and independent nation from the formerly disparate colonies resulted in the expansion of the North American territories under the control of the newly independent nation, established through a new system of land organization (**DOCUMENT 8**). The Revolutionary War, therefore, was more than a colonial movement for independence, as it unleashed a series of new issues and concerns for the new nation.

CHAPTER 8

The New Nation, 1786–1800

This chapter covers the challenge of blending local community sentiments with national ones once the unifying factor of a common enemy was eliminated by victory in the Revolution. A new Constitution was developed that was stronger than the old Articles of the Confederation. Washington as the first president set many precedents for the government of the new nation. Thomas Jefferson and Alexander Hamilton debated the future of the nation in their efforts at interpreting the real meaning of the new Constitution. Under pressure of external events such as the French Revolution and the Napoleonic Wars, political factions developed into the Federalist and Democratic-Republican parties. Writers and artists helped to develop a national culture.

The Crisis of the 1780s

As depression struck in the mid-1780s, and a country rose up in protest, spawning a strong nationalist sentiment among the American elite. The depression also forced many to reassess the role of the federal government. Many conservatives believed that the answer to economic woes would lie in a stronger national government. Most radicals believed it was up to the states to relieve the financial burden of their people. This question of relative integrality would remain a topic of debate throughout American history.

The New Constitution

Rising nationalist sentiment fostered a movement for a new constitution. The resulting convention transformed the political structure of the nation. The strength of the new government was countered by constitutional guarantees of certain rights.

The First Administration

The new government faced the task of establishing its role and organization under the leadership of George Washington. Legislation and plans set the course of the new nation. The government also instituted a policy on Indian relations and swiftly dealt with domestic and international crises.

Federalists and Jeffersonian Republicans

Political differences stimulated the creation of political parties. A variety of issues and conflicting responses to the French Revolution led to questionable practices by the Federalists led by President John Adams. The election of 1800 was a revolution because it produced a peaceful transfer of power. During this period, a vibrant democratic political culture emerged.

"The Rising Glory of America"

The 1790s witnessed the rise of an American culture. American artists achieved recognition while architecture reflected growing nationalism. High literacy rates contributed to the expansion of the press and a distinctive American literature in which women played a role.

Multiple-Choice Questions

1. Approval of the Great Compromise at the Philadelphia constitutional convention guaranteed
   - (A) an immediate end to the international slave trade.
   - (B) slaves would count as full human beings in determining representation.
   - (C) elimination of slaves from the count to determine representation in Congress.
   - (D) that the instution of slavery would be gradually eliminated in 100 years.
   - (E) representation based on population in the House and by state in the Senate.

2. The first ten amendments were quickly added to the newly-ratified Constitution to
   - (A) expand the power of the federal government over its citizens.
   - (B) fulfill the promise made to Federalists who had opposed ratification.
   - (C) limit the expressed rights of citizens in the face of national governmental power.
   - (D) reassure those who feared the power of the national government to restrict citizens' rights.
   - (E) prove that the new constitution was changeable.

3. Under the provisions of the Virginia Plan
   - (A) the Articles of Confederation would have been amended to give Congress the power to levy taxes.
   - (B) a bicameral legislature would be organized according to state population.
   - (C) an independent judiciary would have final control.
   - (D) an independent chief executive elected by popular vote would check legislative power.
   - (E) a single house legislature would equally represent all states.

4. Under the impact of the Hamilton economic program
   - (A) the United States teetered on the brink of economic disaster.
   - (B) foreign investment in government securities dramatically declined.
   - (C) the health of the United States' economy improved significantly.
   - (D) america emerged in the forefront of New Mercantilism.
   - (E) a heavily industrializad economy appeared in the United States.

5. Washington established the precedent of executive privilege when he refused to
   - (A) testify before Congress about his role in subduing Pennsylvania farmers protesting taxes in 1794.
   - (B) allow House members to review the diplomatic correspondence related to the signing of Jay's Treaty.
   - (C) be a witness before the Supreme Court.
   - (D) permit Congress to investigate the president's role in negotiating the Treaty of Greenville.
   - (E) answer the Supreme Court's request to review presidential correspondence with the French government during the Genet incident.

6. Which one of the following was NOT opposed by Washington in his Farewell Address?
   - (A) sectional loyalty
   - (B) party politics
   - (C) American disinterst in Europe
   - (D) political ties to England
   - (E) American economic ties to England

7. Political supporters of Thomas Jefferson used the name Republicans to emphasize that the Federalists were
   - (A) pro-French.
   - (B) pro-Monarchy.
   - (C) localists.
   - (D) for European political ties.
   - (E) unclear of their politics.

8. Pasage of the Naturalization Act, the Alien Act, the Alien Enemies Act, and the Sedition Act by Federalists in 1798 reflected their primary intent to
   (A) eliminate British Loyalist influence in the United States once and for all.
   (B) limit foreign immigration to the United States.
   (C) force John Adams to take a stand on the issue of French-American relations.
   (D) defeat the Republican opposition in Congress.
   (E) join forces with the Jeffersonian wing of the party.

9. Susana Haswell Rowson's book, *Charlotte Temple*, illustrated
   (A) the rise of feminist views in the Revolution of 1800.
   (B) the rise in demand for books appealing to women.
   (C) the rise of the American novel as an art form.
   (D) the ideas of "republican motherhood."
   (E) federalist viewpoints embedded in novels.

10. A response to the problem that emerged in the election of 1800, the Twelfth Amendment
    (A) created separate ballots for the president and vice president.
    (B) limited the terms of the president and vice president.
    (C) limited campaign spending.
    (D) created an electoral college for the election of president and vice president.
    (E) listed candidates on the ballot according to party affiliation.

Document-Based Question

What were some of the issues involved in the debate surrounding the composition and ratification of the Constitution?

DOCUMENT 1

Source: Constitution of Pennsylvania (1776)

I. That all men are born equally free and independent, and have certain natural inherent and inalienable rights, amongst which are the enjoying and defending life and liberty, acquiring, possessing and protecting property, and pursuing and obtaining happiness and safety.

II. That all men have a natural and unalienable right to worship Almighty God according to the dictates of their own consciences and understanding: And that no man ought or of right can be compelled to attend any religious worship, or erect or support any place of worship, or maintain any ministry, contrary to, or against, his own free will and consent: Nor can any man, who acknowledges the being of a God, be justly deprived or abridged of any civil right as a citizen, on account of his religious sentiments or peculiar mode of religious worship: And that no authority can or ought to be vested in, or assumed by any power whatever, that shall in any case interfere with, or in any manner controul, the right of consciencein the free exercise of religious worship...

XI. That in controversies respecting property, and in suits between man and man, the parties have a right to trial by jury, which ought to be held sacred.

XII. That the people have a right to freedom of speech, and of writing, and publishing their sentiments; therefore the freedom of the press ought not to be restrained.

XIII. That the people have a right to bear arms for the defence of themselves and the state; and as standing armies in the time of peace are dangerous to liberty, they ought not to be kept up; And that the military should be kept under strict subordination to, and governed by, the civil power.

DOCUMENT 2

Source: A Declaration of the Rights of the Inhabitants of the Commonwealth of Massachusetts (1780)

CHAPTER I
THE LEGISLATIVE POWER SECTION I. THE GENERAL COURT
ARTICLE I. The department of legislation shall be formed by two branches, a Senate and House of Representatives; each of which shall have a negative on the other.
The legislative body shall assemble every year [on the last Wednesday in May, and at such other times as they shall judge necessary; and shall dissolve and be dissolved on the day next preceding the said last Wednesday in May;] and shall be styled, THE GENERAL COURT OF MASSACHUSETTS.

DOCUMENT 3

Source: Henry Knox, Letter to George Washington (1786)

Our political machine, composed of thirteen independent sovereignties, have been perpetually operating against each other and against the federal head ever since the peace. The powers of Congress are totally inadequate to preserve the balance between the respective States, and oblige them to do those things which are essential for their own welfare or for the general good. The frame of mind in the local legislatures seems to be exerted to prevent the federal constitution from having any good effect. The machine works inversely to the public good in all its parts: not only is State against State, and all against the federal head, but the States within themselves possess the name only without having the essential concomitant of government, the power of preserving the peace, the protection of the liberty and property of the citizens. On the very first impression of faction and licentiousness, the fine theoretic government of Massachusetts has given way, and its laws [are] trampled under foot. Men at a distance, who have admired our systems of government unfounded in nature, are apt to accuse the rulers, and say that taxes have been assessed too high and collected too rigidly. This is a deception equal to any that has been hitherto entertained. That taxes may be the ostensible cause is true, but that they are the true cause is as far remote from truth as light from darkness. The people who are the insurgents have never paid any or but very little taxes. But they see the weakness of government: they feel at once their own poverty compared with the opulent, and their own force, and they are determined to make use of the latter in order to remedy the former.

DOCUMENT 4

Source: Marquis de Chastellux, Travels in North America (1786)

The government [of Virginia] may become democratic, as it is at the present moment; but the national character, the very spirit of the government, will always be aristocratic. Nor can this be doubted when one considers that another cause is still operating to produce the same result. I am referring to slavery, not because it is a mark of distinction or special privilege to possess Negroes, but because the sway held over them nourishes vanity and sloth, two vices which accord wonderfully with established prejudices. It will doubtless be asked how these prejudices have been reconciled with the present revolution, founded on such different principles. I shall answer that they have perhaps contributed to it; that while New England revolted through reason and calculation, Virginia revolted through pride. . . .

DOCUMENT 5

Source: Thomas Jefferson to James Madison

Paris, January 30th, 1787

Dear Sir,

...Societies exist under three forms, sufficiently distinguishable: (1) without government, as among our Indians; (2) under governments, wherein the will of everyone has a just influence, as is the case in England, in a slight degree, and in our states, in a great one; (3) under governments of force, as is the case in all other monarchies, and in most of the other republics.

To have an idea of the curse of existence under these last, they must be seen. It is a government of wolves over sheep. It is a problem, not clear in my mind, that the first condition is not the best. But I believe it to be inconsistent with any great degree of population. The second state has a great deal of good in it. The mass of mankind under that enjoys a precious degree of liberty and happiness. It has its evils, too, the principal of which is the turbulence to which it is subject. But weigh this against the oppressions of monarchy, and it becomes nothing. Malo periculosam libertatem quam quietam servitutem. Even this evil is productive of good. It prevents the degeneracy of government and nourishes a general attention to the public affairs.

I hold it that a little rebellion now and then is a good thing, and as necessary in the political world as storms in the physical. Unsuccessful rebellions, indeed, generally establish the encroachments on the rights of the people which have produced them. An observation of this truth should render honest republican governors so mild in their punishment of rebellions as not to discourage them too much. It is a medicine necessary for the sound health of government. . . .

Yours affectionately,

Th. Jefferson

DOCUMENT 6

The "Distracting Question" in Philadelphia (1787)
Source: The Avalon Project at the Yale Law School
http://www.yale.edu/lawweb/avalon/debates/711.htm

Wednesday July 11, 1787

IN CONVENTION

...Mr. WILLIAMSON was for making it the duty of the Legislature to do what was right & not leaving it at liberty to do or not do it. He moved that Mr. Randolph's proposition be postponed. in order to consider the following "that in order to ascertain the alterations that may happen in the population & wealth of the several States, a census shall be taken of the free white inhabitants and 3/5 ths. of those of other descriptions on the 1st. year after this Government shall have been adopted and every year thereafter; and that the Representation be regulated accordingly."

DOCUMENT 7

Patrick Henry Speaks Against Ratification of the Constitution (1788)
Source: Jonathan Elliot, ed., The Debates in the Several State Conventions on the Adoption of the Federal Constitution 2nd ed., 5 vols. (Philadelphia: J. B. Lippincott Company, 1907).

...And here I would make this inquiry of those worthy characters who composed a part of the late federal Convention. I am sure they were fully impressed with the necessity of forming a great consolidated government, instead of a confederation. That this is a consolidated government is demonstrably clear; and the danger of such a government is, to my mind, very striking I have the highest veneration for those gentlemen; but, sir, give me leave to demand, What right had they to say, We, the people? My political curiosity, exclusive of my anxious solicitude for the public welfare, leads me to ask, Who authorized them to speak the language of, We, the people,instead of, We, the states?

States are the characteristics and the soul of a confederation. If the states be not the agents of this compact, it must be one great, consolidated, national government, of the people of all the states. . .. It is not mere curiosity that actuates me: I wish to hear the real, actual, existing danger, which should lead us to take those steps, so dangerous in my conception.

DOCUMENT 8

James Madison Defends the Constitution (1788)
Source: Jonathan Elliot, ed., The Debates in the Several State Conventions on the Adoption of the Federal Constitution. 2nd ed., 5 vols. (Philadelphia: J. B. Lippincott Company, 1907).

...Give me leave to say something of the nature of the government, and to show that it is safe and just to vest it with the power of taxation. There are a number of opinions; but the principal question is, whether it be a federal or consolidated government. In order to judge properly of the question before us, we must consider it minutely in its principal parts. I conceive myself that it is of a mixed nature; it is in a manner unprecedented; we cannot find one express example in the experience of the world. It stands by itself. In some respects it is a government of a federal nature; in others, it is of a consolidated nature. Even if we attend to the manner in which the Constitution is investigated, ratified, and made the act of the people of America, I can say, notwithstanding what the honorable gentleman has alleged, that this government is not completely consolidated, nor is it entirely federal. Who are parties to it? The people but not the people as composing one great body; but the people as composing thirteen sovereignties. Were it, as the gentleman asserts, a consolidated government, the assent of a majority of the people would be sufficient for its establishment; and, as a majority have adopted it already, the remaining states would be bound by the act of the majority, even if they unanimously reprobated it. Were it such a government as is suggested, it would be now binding on the people of this state, without having had the privilege of deliberating upon it. But, sir, no state is bound by it, as it is, without its own consent. Should all the states adopt it, it will be then a government established by the thirteen states of America, not through the intervention of the legislatures, but by the people at large. In this particular respect, the distinction between the existing and proposed governments is very material. The existing system has been derived from the dependent derivative authority of the legislatures of the states; whereas this is derived from the superior power of the people.

ANSWERS AND EXPLANATIONS

Multiple-Choice Questions

1. **(E) is correct.** After much debate and a series of votes that split the convention down the middle, the delegates finally agreed to what has been termed the Great Compromise: representation proportional to population in the House and equal representation by states in the Senate. The compromise allowed the creation of a strong national government while still providing an important role for the states.

2. **(D) is correct.** Anti-Federalist delegates in numerous state ratification conventions proposed a grab bag of over 200 potential amendments protecting the power of the people against the power of the central government. James Madison set about transforming them into a coherent series of proposals. Congress passed twelve and sent them to the states, and ten survived the ratification process to become the Bill of Rights in 1791.

3. **(B) is correct.** The Virginia plan would have reduced the states to little more than administrative institutions, something like counties. According to its terms, representation in the bicameral national legislature would be based on population districts. The members of the House of Representatives would be elected by popular vote, but senators were chosen indirectly by state legislators so they might be insulated from democratic pressure.

3. (B) is correct. The Virginia plan would have reduced the states to little more than administrative institutions, something like counties. According to its terms, representation in the bicameral national legislature would be based on population districts. The members of the House of Representatives would be elected by popular vote, but senators were chosen indirectly by state legislators so they might be insulated from democratic pressure.

4. (C) is correct. Hamilton's financial plan had three components. He recommended that the federal government assume the obligations accumulated by the states during the previous fifteen years and redeem the national debt by agreeing to a new issue of interest-bearing bonds. Next, he proposed the establishment of a Bank of the United States to be funded by private capital and serve as the depository of government funds and the fiscal agent of the Treasury. Finally, he proposed using government securities as investment capital for "infant industries" and high protective tariffs to encourage the development of an industrial economy.

5. (B) is correct. In the House, a coalition of Southerners, Westerners, and friends of France attempted to stall Jay's treaty by threatening to withhold the appropriations necessary for its implementation. They demanded that they be allowed to examine the diplomatic correspondence regarding the whole affair, but President Washington refused, establishing the precedent of "executive privilege" in matters of state.

6. (C) is correct. During the final months of his term, Washington published his Farewell Address to the nation. He argued not for American isolation, but rather for American disinterest in the affairs of Europe.

7. (B) is correct. Supporters of Jefferson used the name Republicans to emphasize that the Federalists were monarchs at heart. It became the majority party after 1800.

8. (D) is correct. The Federalists intended these repressive laws as weapons to defeat the Jeffersonian Republicans. The more effective Jeffersonian Republicans became in contesting the legislation, the more treasonous they appeared in the eyes of the Federalists. The Federalists pursued the prosecution of dissent, indicting leading Republican newspaper editors and writers.

9. (B) is correct. One of the most interesting literary trends of the 1790s was the growing demand for books that appealed to women readers. Rowson's book, a tale of seduction and abandonment, ran up tremendous sales and remained in print for more than a century. Although women's literacy rates continued to be lower than men's, they rose steadily as girls joined boys in common schools.

10. (A) is correct. According to the constitution, the presidential candidate receiving a majority of electoral votes became president and the runner-up became vice president. Jeffersonian Republican electors unintentionally created a tie between Jefferson and Burr by casting all their ballots for the pair and forced the election into the House. Jefferson was elected on the thirty-fifth ballot by the exhausted and unhappy Federalist majority. The Twelfth Amendment, creating separate ballots for president and vice president, was ratified in time for the next presidential election.

Document-Based Question

What were some of the issues involved in the debate surrounding the composition and ratification of the Constitution?

The ratification of the U.S. Constitution was not a universally celebrated measure, and its composition was a controversial process. There were powerful concerns, determined both by regional politics and larger ideological issues, that shaped the document. Even once those had been resolved, its ratification was not guaranteed.

In the 1780s a number of problems forced the governments of the United States to reassess the Articles of Confederation. There was a feeling that the federal government was too weak, and that the states were pulling away from each other. Congress seemed unable to maintain the balance between the states (**DOCUMENT 3**). It was in this context that the Constitutional convention was called. However, not everybody believe that these problems were worth address.

There were a few early models on which the convention was able to base its discussion. For example, Pennsylvania had a constitution that guaranteed the basic rights of free speech, freedom of religion, and the right to a fair trial (**DOCUMENT 1**), which were eventually adopted as the first amendments to the Consitution. Massachusetts had a bicameral legislature (**DOCUMENT 2**), a feature that became part of the US constitution.

It was not easy for the members of the convention to come to an agreement on how to organize the government. For example, the question of how slaves were to be counted in the population for the purposes of representation was controversial. Southern states wanted them to count as full citizens, though they did not vote, as this would give them greater representation in Congress, due to the large number of slaves in the South. The Northern states, with far fewer slaves, did not want them to count. Eventually, a compromise was proposed, that they should count as three fifths of a citizen (**DOCUMENT 6**).

Even once this and other compromises were reached, the Constitution's ratification was not certain. There were those who argued against it, saying that it was creating a central government that was too powerful, and was illegitimate (**DOCUMENT 7**). Others defended the Constitution, arguing that it balanced central power with federal concerns (**DOCUMENT 8**).

Though the Constitution was ratified, this tension continued to be a part of American discourse. The tug-of-war between artistocracy and democracy, nowhere as sharply embodied as in the slave Virginia's arguments for liberty (**DOCUMENT 4**), is an essential part of the American national heritage, as enshrined in the U.S. Constitution.

CHAPTER 9

An Agrarian Republic, 1790–1824

This chapter covers the growth of a mostly agrarian United States in terms of a developing economy, territorial expansion, and reassertion of national unity in the War of 1812. In each case, however, regional conflicts appeared. In spite of an "Era of Good Feelings" and successful diplomatic settlements, the slavery issue reasserted itself as a crucial divisive issue in American politics, but conflict was temporarily averted with the Missouri Compromise of 1820.

North American Communities from Coast to Coast

In 1800, European countries and the United States had established territorial claims and communities that spanned the North American continent. Each European colony developed along different paths and was subject to potential conflict arising from imperial rivalries. Though the United States experienced substantial growth, political and economic dominance remained in traditional centers.

A National Economy

In 1800, the United States was a producer of raw materials with an economy that was divided between self-sufficiency and market production. Events in Europe stimulated international trade that fueled development of other industries.

The Jefferson Presidency

As president, Thomas Jefferson attempted to implement his philosophy of democratic government. Events overseas offered Jefferson the opportunity to expand the nation's territory dramatically.

Renewed Imperial Rivalry in North America

The continuing conflict between England and France eventually created tensions and disputes with the United States. Jefferson's Indian policy and western expansion stimulated Indian revitalization and resistance movements.

The War of 1812

Grievances against the British led to the War of 1812. Military campaigns often involved British-Indian alliances against American forces allied with other Indian peoples and produced mixed results. Though the British captured Washington, D.C., they eventually sought peace. In New England, opposition to the war produced strong protests.

Defining the Boundaries

Following the War of 1812, the United States turned its attention to national development and expansion. Migration surged into the trans-Appalachian West. Diplomacy secured and expanded American borders as well as signaled America's stronger role as a diplomatic leader. An economic downturn and a crisis over the expansion of slavery signaled that the United States faced serious issues.

Multiple-Choice Questions

1. The Mandans welcomed Lewis and Clark because the Indians hoped for
   (A) economic help since they were in poverty.
   (B) a buffer between them and the Cherokee.
   (C) an alliance against the Russians and British.
   (D) a group to play against British fur traders.
   (E) expanded trade and support against the Sioux.

2. The period between 1800 and 1850 in the United States was characterized by
   (A) a decline in the overall population.
   (B) a dramatic expansion of population to the west.
   (C) declining westward expansion due to fear of Indian attacks.
   (D) the tremendous growth of Atlantic seaboard cities.
   (E) a decrease in the birthrate across the nation as a whole.

3. The first trans-Appalachian states admitted to the Union were
   (A) Ohio and Indiana.
   (B) Louisiana and Mississippi.
   (C) Kentucky and Illinois.
   (D) Maine and Vermont.
   (E) Kentucky and Tennessee.

4. The fortunes of cities like Cincinnati were connected to
   (A) easier land purchasing.
   (B) slave trading.
   (C) control of New Orleans.
   (D) the fur trade.
   (E) military bases.

5. In pursuing the purchase of Louisiana, Jefferson violated this principle that he had rigidly insisted on earlier:
   (A) nullification.
   (B) "millions for defense but not one cent for tribute."
   (C) "no manifest destiny."
   (D) rights for Native Americans.
   (E) limited interpretation of the Constitution.

6. Americans found British actions with regard to naturalization and impressment particularly objectionable because they
   (A) seemed too favorable to the Spanish, Canadians, and Indians.
   (B) resulted in disruptions, which lessened profits in shipping.
   (C) demonstrated Great Britain's failure to recognize American citizenship.
   (D) violated civil rights.
   (E) hoped their objections would please Napoleon.

7. The hardest hit under the Embargo Act were the
   (A) French.
   (B) Indians.
   (C) British.
   (D) Southern states.
   (E) New Englanders.

8. Jefferson advocated a policy of removal to the trans-Mississippi region for Indians because he believed that
   (A) they were "noble savages" whose ways of life must be preserved.
   (B) it would temporarily placate them and white settlement would push them out soon enough.
   (C) British emissaries could not influence them as easily in more remote areas.
   (D) those unreconciled to assimilation would be able to live there undisturbed.
   (E) French efforts to ally themselves with the Indians could prove dangerous to the republic.

9. The battle at Tippecanoe
   (A) was a victory for William Henry Harrison and the Northwest Territory.
   (B) resulted in the death of Tecumseh.
   (C) was a victory for the Northwest Confederation tribes.
   (D) was a defeat for Andrew Jackson.
   (E) resulted in further conflict and Tecumseh's alliance with the British.

10. At the Hartford Convention, representatives from five New England states
    (A) insisted states could nullify unconstitutional federal actions.
    (B) sought a revision of the Constitution.
    (C) passed a secession resolution to go into effect by 1815.
    (D) condemned the terms of the Treaty of Ghent.
    (E) criticized American Indian policy.

Document-Based Question

Analyze the circumstances leading up to the Missouri Compromise.

DOCUMENT 1

An African American Calls for an End to Slavery (1791)
Source: The History Net: African American History,
http://afroamhistory.about.com/library/blbanneker_letter.htm

> Maryland, Baltimore County, August 19, 1791.
> SIR,
> ...Sir, if these are sentiments of which you are fully persuaded, I hope you cannot but acknowledge, that it is the indispensable duty of those, who maintain for themselves the rights of human nature, and who possess the obligations of Christianity, to extend their power and influence to the relief of every part of the human race, from whatever burden or oppression they may unjustly labor under; and this, I apprehend, a full conviction of the truth and obligation of these principles should lead all to. Sir, I have long been convinced, that if your love for yourselves, and for those inestimable laws, which preserved to you the rights of human nature, was founded on sincerity, you could not but be solicitous, that every individual, of whatever rank or distinction, might with you equally enjoy the blessings thereof; neither could you rest satisfied short of the most active effusion of your exertions, in order to their promotion from any state of degradation, to which the unjustifiable cruelty and barbarism of men may have reduced them...
> And now, Sir, I shall conclude, and subscribe myself, with the most profound respect,
> Your most obedient humble
> servant,
> BENJAMIN BANNEKER.

DOCUMENT 2

An African American Calls for an End to Slavery (1791)
Source: The History Net: African American History
http://afroamhistory.about.com/library/blbanneker_letter.htm

> To Mr. BENJAMIN BANNEKER.
> Philadelphia, August 30, 1791.
> SIR,
> I THANK you, sincerely, for your letter of the 19th instant, and for the Almanac it contained. No body wishes more than I do, to see such proofs as you exhibit, that nature has given to our black brethren talents equal to those of the other colors of men; and that the appearance of the want of them, is owing merely to the degraded condition of their existence, both in Africa and America. I can add with truth, that no body wishes more ardently to see a good system commenced, for raising the condition, both of their body and mind, to what it ought to be, as far as the imbecility of their present existence, and other circumstances, which cannot be neglected, will admit.

I have taken the liberty of sending your Almanac to Monsieur de Condozett, Secretary of the Academy of Sciences at Paris, and Member of the Philanthropic Society, because I considered it as a document, to which your whole color had a right for their justification, against the doubts which have been entertained of them.

I am with great esteem, Sir, Your most obedient Humble Servant,

THOMAS JEFFERSON.

DOCUMENT 3

Thomas Jefferson Reacts to the "Missouri Question" (1820)
Source: Library of Congress, Thomas Jefferson Papers, Series 1. General Correspondence. 1651–1827,
Thomas Jefferson to John Holmes, April 22, 1820,
http://memory.loc.gov

Monticello, April 22, 1820
…The cession of that kind of property, for so it is misnamed, is a bagatelle which would not cost me a second thought, if, in that way, a general emancipation and expatriationcould be effected; and gradually, and with due sacrifices, I think it might be. But as it is, we have the wolf by the ears, and we can neither hold him, nor safely let him go. Justice is in one scale, and self-preservation in the other. Of one thing I am certain, that as the passage of slaves from one state to another would not make a slave of a single human being who would not be so without it, so their diffusion over a greater surface would make them individually happier, and proportionally facilitate the accomplishment of their emancipation, by dividing the burden on a greater number of coadjutors. An abstinence too, from this act of power, would remove the jealousy excited by the undertaking of Congress to regulate the condition of the different descriptions of men composing a state. This certainly is the exclusive right of every state, which nothing in the Constitution has taken from them and given to the general government. Could Congress, for example, say that the non-freemen of Connecticut shall be freemen, or that they shall not emigrate into any other state?

DOCUMENT 4

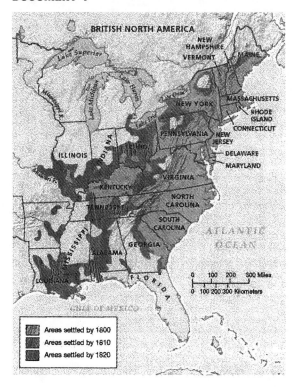

Areas settled by 1800
Areas settled by 1810
Areas settled by 1820

DOCUMENT 5

Source: "Memoirs of a Monticello Slave, as Dictated to Charles Campbell by Isaac" (1847)

... Mr. Jefferson had a clock in his kitchen at Monticello; never went into the kitchen except to wind up the clock.

He never would have less than eight covers at dinner if nobody at table but himself. Had from eight to thirty-two covers for dinner. Plenty of wine, best old Antigua rum and cider; very fond of wine and water. Isaac never heard of his being disguised in drink. He kept three fiddles; played in the arternoons and sometimes arter supper. This was in his early time. When he begin to git so old, he didn't play. Kept a spinnet made mostly in shape of a harpsichord; his daughter played on it. Mr. Fauble, a Frenchman that lived at Mr. Walker's, a music man, used to come to Monticello and tune it. There was a fortepiano and a guitar there. Never seed anybody play on them but the French people. Isaac never could git acquainted with them; could hardly larn their names. Mr. Jefferson always singing when ridin' or walkin'; hardly see him anywhar outdoors but what he was a-singin'. Had a fine clear voice, sung minnits (minuets) and sich; fiddled in the parlor. Old Master very kind to servants.

DOCUMENT 6

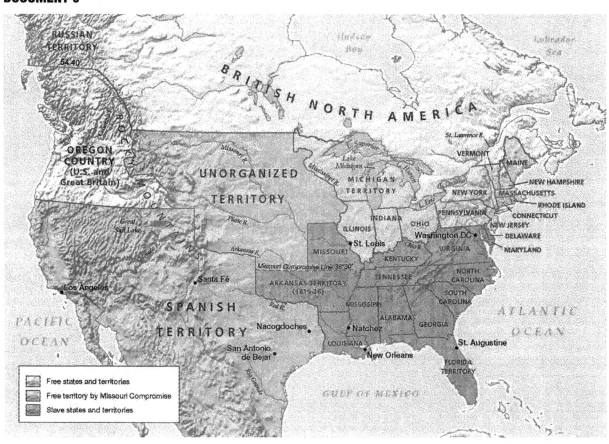

DOCUMENT 7

Source: Constitutionality of the Louisiana Purchase (1803)

Thomas Jefferson to John C. Breckinridge
Monticello, Aug. 12, 1803
DEAR SIR,-
...Our information as to the country is very incompleat; we have taken measures to obtain it in full as to the settled part, which I hope to receive in time for Congress. The boundaries, which I deem not admitting question, are the high lands on the western side of the Mississippi enclosing all it's waters, the Missouri of course, and terminating in the line drawn from the northwestern point of the Lake of the Woods to the nearest source of the Missipi, as lately settled between Gr Britain and the U S. We have some claims to extend on the sea coast Westwardly to the Rio Norte or Bravo, and better, to go Eastwardly to the Rio Perdido, between Mobile & Pensacola, the antient boundary of Louisiana. These claims will be a subject of negociation with Spain, and if, as soon as she is at war, we push them strongly with one hand, holding out price in the other, we shall certainly obtain the Floridas, and all in good time. In the meanwhile, without waiting for permission, we shall enter into the exercise of the natural right we have always insisted on with Spain, to wit, that of a nation holding the upper part of streams, having a right of innocent passage thro' them to the ocean. We shall prepare her to see us practise on this, & she will not oppose it by force.

DOCUMENT 8

Source: "The Western Country," Extracts from Letters Published in Niles' Weekly Register (1816)

The western country continues to rise in population and importance with unabated rapidity. This town has been, since the war, full to overflowing; many being obliged to leave it after coming from the Eastern states, not being able to get a room to dwell in. More houses will be built this summer than during the last three years together. Manufactories of several important kinds are establishing, among which is a steam grist and saw mill. The surveyor general is making arrangements for laying out, agreeably to late acts of Congress, towns at the Lower Rapids of Sandusky, and at the Rapids of the Miami of the Lakes. The local situation of the latter cannot but render it a most important place. It will be situated at some point within the reservation of twelve miles square, to which vessels of a small tonnage can ascend, and as near the foot of the rapids as may be. I believe the time not very distant when the wealth and resources of the western country will be brought almost to your doors, by means of an extensive inland navigation through the lakes and the grand canal proposed to be made in New York. It will be an easy matter to connect the Miami of the Lakes and the Miami of the Ohio by a canal, the face of the country between the head of the navigation of each of those rivers being quite level. What an extensive inland navigation would then be opened!-from New Orleans to the Hudson!

ANSWERS AND EXPLANATIONS

Multiple-Choice Questions

■ **1. (E) is correct.** In mid-October 1804, news arrived at the Mandan villages that an American military party led by Meriwether Lewis and William Clark was coming up the river. The principal chiefs, hoping for expanded trade and support against their enemies the Sioux, welcomed these first American visitors with gifts of food and dance.

■ **2. (B) is correct.** Growth by migration was greatest in the trans-Appalachian West, a reigion that was already home to approximately 100,000 Indians. From 1800 to 1850, in an extraordinary burst of territorial expansion, Americans surged westward all the way to the Pacific. In 1800, few people would have predicted that within fifty years the nation would encompass the entire continent.

3. (E) is correct. By 1800, about 500,000 people had found rich and fertile land along the Ohio River system. Soon there was enough population for statehood. Kentucky (1792) and Tennessee (1796) were the first trans-Appalachian states admitted to the Union.

4. (B) is correct. River traffic increased yearly and the control of New Orleans became a key concern of western farmers and merchants. If New Orleans refused to accept American goods, Cincinnati merchants and many thousands of trans-Appalachian farmers would be ruined.

5. (E) is correct. Jefferson suffered brief qualms about acquiring the Lousiana Purchase. The Constitution did not authorize the president to purchase territory, and Jefferson had always rigidly insisted on limited intereperetation of executive rights.

6. (C) is correct. At least 6,000 innocent American citizens suffered forced impressments into the British navy from 1803 to 1812. In 1807, impresssment turned bloody when the British ship *Leopard* stopped the American ship *Chesapeake* in American territorial waters and demanded to search for deserters. When the Amreican captain refused, the *Leopard* opened fire, killing three men, wounding eighteen, and removing four deserters (three with American naturalization papers) from the damaged ship. An indignant public protested British interference, the death of innocent sailors, and the Great Britan's failure to recognize American citizenship.

7. (E) is correct. Under the Embargo Act the commerce of the new nation came to a standstill. Exports fell from $108 million in 1807 to $22 million in 1808, and the nation was driving into a deep depression. There was a widespread evasion of the embargo and smuggling flourished. Pointing out that the American navy's weakness was due to the deep cuts Jefferson had inflicted on it, the Federalists sprang to life with the campaign of outspoken opposition to Jefferson's policy, and they found they had a ready in the area hardest hit by the embargo, New England.

8. (D) is correct. Thomas Jefferson was deeply concerned with the fate of the western Indian peoples. Convinced that Indians had to give up hunting in favor of the yeoman farmer lifestyle he so favored for all Americans, Jefferson directed the governors of the Northwest Territories to "promote energetically" his vision for civilizing the Indians. Many Indian peoples actively restisted these efforts at conversion. After the Louisiana Purchase, as an alternative to assimilation, Jefferson offered traditionalist Indian groups new lands west of the Mississippi River, where they could live undisturbed by white settlers.

9. (E) is correct. In November 1811, while Tecumseh was still recruiting among the southern tribes, Harrison marched to the pan-Indian village of Tippecanoe with 1,000 soldiers. The 600 to 700 Indian warriors at the town attacked Harrison's forces before dawn on November 7, hoping to surprise them. The attack failed, and in the battle that followed, the Americans inflicted about 150 casualities, while sustaining about as many themselves. Although Harrison claimed victory, the truth was far different. Dispersed from Tippecanoe, Tecumseh's angery followers fell on American settlements in Indiana and southern Michigan, killing many pioneers and forcing the rest to flee to fortified towns. Tecumseh himself entered into a formal alliance with the British. For western settlers, the Indian threat was greater than ever.

10. (A) is correct. America's occasional successes failed to diminish the angry opposition of New England Federalists to the War of 1812. Opposition to the war culminated in the Hartford Convention of 1814, where Federalist representatives from the five New England states met to discuss their grievances. The convention insisted that a state had the right "to interpose its authority" to protect its citizens against unconstitutional federal laws. Though in the end the nullification threat from Hartford was ignored, for peace with Britain was announced as delegates from the convention made their way to Washington to deliver their message to Congress.

2. (B) is correct. Growth by migration was greatest in the trans-Appalachian West, a reigion that was already home to approximately 100,000 Indians. From 1800 to 1850, in an extraordinary burst of territorial expansion, Americans surged westward all the way to the Pacific. In 1800, few people would have predicted that within fifty years the nation would encompass the entire continent.

3. (E) is correct. By 1800, about 500,000 people had found rich and fertile land along the Ohio River system. Soon there was enough population for statehood. Kentucky (1792) and Tennessee (1796) were the first trans-Appalachian states admitted to the Union.

4. (C) is correct. River traffic increased yearly and the control of New Orleans became a key concern of western farmers and merchants. If New Orleans refused to accept American goods, Cincinnati merchants and many thousands of trans-Appalachian farmers would be ruined.

5. (E) is correct. Jefferson suffered brief qualms about acquiring the Lousiana Purchase. The Constitution did not authorize the president to purchase territory, and Jefferson had always rigidly insisted on limited interepretation of executive rights.

6. (C) is correct. The British refusal to recognize genuine naturalization papers (on the principle "once a British subject, always a British subject") was particularly insulting to the new American sense of nationhood. At least 6,000 innocent American citizens suffered forced impressments into the British navy from 1803 to 1812. In 1807, impresssment turned bloody when the British ship *Leopard* stopped the American ship *Chesapeake* in American territorial waters and demanded to search for deserters. When the Amreican captain refused, the *Leopard* opened fire, killing three men, wounding eighteen, and removing four deserters (three with American naturalization papers) from the damaged ship. An indignant public protested British interference, the death of innocent sailors, and the Great Britan's failure to recognize American citizenship.

7. (E) is correct. Under the Embargo Act the commerce of the new nation came to a standstill. Exports fell from $108 million in 1807 to $22 million in 1808, and the nation was driving into a deep depression. There was a widespread evasion of the embargo and smuggling flourished. Pointing out that the American navy's weakness was due to the deep cuts Jefferson had inflicted on it, the Federalists sprang to life with the campaign of outspoken opposition to Jefferson's policy, and they found they had a ready in the area hardest hit by the embargo, New England.

8. (D) is correct. Thomas Jefferson was deeply concerned with the fate of the western Indian peoples. Convinced that Indians had to give up hunting in favor of the yeoman farmer lifestyle he so favored for all Americans, Jefferson directed the governors of the Northwest Territories to "promote energetically" his vision for civilizing the Indians. Many Indian peoples actively restisted these efforts at conversion. After the Louisiana Purchase, as an alternative to assimilation, Jefferson offered traditionalist Indian groups new lands west of the Mississippi River, where they could live undisturbed by white settlers.

9. (E) is correct. In November 1811, while Tecumseh was still recruiting among the southern tribes, Harrison marched to the pan-Indian village of Tippecanoe with 1,000 soldiers. The 600 to 700 Indian warriors at the town attacked Harrison's forces before dawn on November 7, hoping to surprise them. The attack failed, and in the battle that followed, the Americans inflicted about 150 casualities, while sustaining about as many themselves. Although Harrison claimed victory, the truth was far different. Dispersed from Tippecanoe, Tecumseh's angery followers fell on American settlements in Indiana and southern Michigan, killing many pioneers and forcing the rest to flee to fortified towns. Tecumseh himself entered into a formal alliance with the British. For western settlers, the Indian threat was greater than ever.

10. (A) is correct. America's occasional successes failed to diminish the angry opposition of New England Federalists to the War of 1812. Opposition to the war culminated in the Hartford Convention of 1814, where Federalist representatives from the five New England states met to discuss their grievances. The convention insisted that a state had the right "to interpose its authority" to protect its citizens against unconstitutional federal laws. Though in the end the nullification threat from Hartford

CHAPTER 10

The South and Slavery, 1790s–1850s

This chapter covers the first settlement of the Western Hemisphere by immigrants from Asia. Over the centuries these immigrants developed a variety of technologies, and these communities adapted to their physical environments. Europeans coming to the Americas would find not an empty land but instead a populated continent of many villages. Native Americans had a great deal of diversity in culture, community organization, language, and technology. European colonists would profit from these technologies and regional adaptations.

King Cotton and Southern Expansion

The growing profitability of cotton stimulated western expansion and increased support for slavery. As cotton became the dynamic force in the American economy, plantation-oriented production strongly influenced the development of southern society and culture along different lines from the North.

To Be a Slave

In the age of King Cotton, slavery and the African American community matured. Cotton concentrated slaves on large plantations where they faced harsh conditions and lifelong labor. Distinct divisions emerged among slaves who worked in the house, as skilled labor, or in the fields. But all faced the potential of moving or being sold to plantations in the southwest.

The African American Community

Despite the harshness of slavery, African Americans developed a strong, enduring culture based on family, religion, and resistance to slavery. Families offered a sense of continuity in an uncertain environment, performing essential survival skill functions. African Americans also adapted Christianity to their needs and condition. In addition, they practiced numerous forms of resistance. Free African Americans, meanwhile, lived a precarious existence.

The White Majority

Most white southerners did not own slaves. The white majority lived in cities and in rural areas. A class structure developed based on wealth and landownership. Rural whites espoused attitudes and values in tune with Andrew Jackson and the ideal of the common man.

Planters

The planters were an elite class. They developed a way of life and ideology that combined "benevolent" and harsh treatment of slaves.

The Defense of Slavery

Drawing from several sources, southerners defended slavery. Slave owners became more unified after 1830. Still, changes in the South led to attacks on slavery.

Multiple-Choice Questions

1. Which one of the following is the <u>MOST</u> true of the South in regard to industrialization?
   (A) Urban growth kept pace with the North.
   (B) It failed to recognize industrial and transportation potential.
   (C) Southerners chose to concentrate on cotton.
   (D) It hoped technology could replace slavery.
   (E) It had 75 percent of the nation's railroads to transport cotton.

2. Both enslaved and free blacks had more opportunity to obtain skilled occupations in the South than in the North because
   (A) the South failed to attract much immigrant labor.
   (B) they were seen as an alternative to a technological society.
   (C) southerners felt blacks were more intelligent than northerners did.
   (D) southern whites wouldn't do them.
   (E) southerners preferred their loyalty compared to white laborers.

3. A common defense of the institution of slavery by slave owners was that
   (A) slaves were treated better than northern industrial workers.
   (B) slaves were becoming Christianized and thus their souls would be saved.
   (C) slave children played with white children.
   (D) slaves lived better on southern plantations than the natives in Africa.
   (E) slaves lived much longer than whites.

4. Slave marriages
   (A) were expressly forbidden by most slave owners.
   (B) were considered legal in most southern states.
   (C) encouraged many slaves to rebel.
   (D) had little chance to survive.
   (E) were encouraged by most owners.

5. The Evangelical religion that spread after the Second Great Awakening
   (A) was used by whites as a means of social control over the slaves.
   (B) had no impact on slaves or slavery.
   (C) was accepted wholeheartedly by the slaves.
   (D) was totally rejected by the slaves.
   (E) encouraged many blacks to rebel.

6. The most successful slave revolt was led by
   (A) Hinton Helper.
   (B) Nat Turner.
   (C) Sojourner Truth.
   (D) Denmark Vesey.
   (E) Gabriel Prosser.

7. Prior to the Civil War, only this fraction of white families owned slaves:
   (A) 1/10.
   (B) 1/3.
   (C) 2/5.
   (D) 2/3.
   (E) 3/4.

8. The word "yeoman" was often applied to
   (A) slaves who had families.
   (B) large slave brokers.
   (C) large plantation owners.
   (D) slaves who worked on the riverboats.
   (E) independent farmers who lived on family-size farms.

9. In 1831, the South began to close ranks in defense of slavery for all of the following reasons <u>EXCEPT</u>
   (A) hysteria over the Nat Turner rebellion.
   (B) the publication of William Lloyd Garrison's *The Liberator*.
   (C) the British abolition of slavery in the West Indies.
   (D) the Portuguese abolition of slavery in Brazil.
   (E) "outside" slavery propaganda.

10. By 1860, America's largest single export was
   (A) tobacco.
   (B) rum.
   (C) cotton.
   (D) slaves.
   (E) rice.

Document-Based Question

Discuss the role of paternalism in the southern slave system.

DOCUMENT 1

Source: State v. Boon (1801)

> JOHNSTON, J. The murder of a slave, appears to me, a crime of the most atrocious and barbarous nature; much more so than killing a person who is free, and on an equal footing. It is an evidence of a most depraved and cruel disposition, to murder one, so much in your power, that he is incapable of making resistance, even in his own defence ...and had there been nothing in our acts of Assembly, I should not hesitate on this occasion to have pronounced sentence of death on the prisoner.

A Black Abolitionist Speaks Out (1829)
Source: PBS Online, Africans in America.
http://cgi.pbs.org/wgbh/aia/part4/4h2931t.html

> My dearly beloved Brethren and Fellow Citizens:
> . . . to my no ordinary astonishment, [a] Reverend gentleman got up and told us (coloured people) that slaves must be obedient to their masters—must do their duty to their masters or be whipped—the whip was made for the backs of fools, &c. Here I pause for a moment, to give the world time to consider what was my surprise, to hear such preaching from a minister of my Master, whose very gospel is that of peace and not of blood and whips, as this pretended preacher tried to make us believe. What the American preachers can think of us, I aver this day before my God, I have never been able to define.

Nat Turner, Confession (1831)
Source: From Thomas R. Gray, The Confessions of Nat Turner, The Leader of the Late Insurrection in Southamton Virginia (Baltimore,. 1831).

> Several years rolled round, in which many events occurred to strengthen me in this my belief. At this time I reverted in my mind to the remarks made of me in my childhood, and the things that had been shewn me-and as it had been said of me in my childhood by those by whom I had been taught to pray, both white and black, and in whom I had the greatest confidence, that I had too much sense to be raised, and if I was, I would never be of any use to any one as a slave. Now finding I had arrived to man's estate, and was a slave, and these revelations being made known to me, I began to direct my attention to this great object, to fulfill the purpose for which, by this time, I felt assured I was intended.

DOCUMENT 4

An Abolitionist Defends the Amistad Mutineers (1839)
Source: Exploring Amistadat Mystic Seaport,
http://amistad.mysticseaport.org/library/news/journal.of.commerce.html

> Sabbath evening. The Rev. H. G. Ludlow prayed for the poor Africans this forenoon, very feelingly, at the service in his church. The outer door of the jail was closed today, and visitors generally were not admitted. I distributed some religious tracts, in the morning, to the convicts, and attempted to instruct the African prisoners, especially the children. They pronounce words in English very distinctly, and have already nearly the numerals. In showing them some books containing pictures of tropical animals, birds, &c., they seemed much pleased to recognize those with whose appearance they were acquainted, endeavoring to imitate their voices and actions. With suitable instruction these intelligent and docile Africans would soon learn to read and speak our language, and I cannot but hope that some of the benevolent inhabitants of this city will diligently continue to improve the opportunity to impart instruction to these pagans, brought by the providence of God to their very doors.

DOCUMENT 5

Source: De Bow's Review, "The Stability of the Union," (1850)

> In this undisturbed progress, the condition of the black race is being elevated on the swelling tide of white progress. Inasmuch as that the first slaves imported were, under their new masters, vastly superior in condition to the nude cannibals by whom they were sold, only because avarice triumphed over appetite so is the condition of the slave of the present day far above that of his progenitor a few generations back. The black race, in its servitude to the whites, has undergone an improvement, which the same race, in its state of African freedom, has failed to manifest. By whatever degree, physically and morally, the blacks of the United States are superior to the nude cannibals of Africa, are they indebted to the white race for its active, though not disinterested agency. That process of improvement has not ceased, but is ever progressive in the train of white advancement.

DOCUMENT 6

Source: Benjamin Drew, Narratives of Escaped Slaves (1855)

> [Mrs. James Steward]
> I am from the eastern shore of Maryland. I never belonged but to one master; he was very bad indeed. I was never sent to school, nor allowed to go to church. They were afraid we would have more sense than they. I have a father there, three sisters, and a brother. My father is quite an old man, and he is used very badly. Many a time he has been kept at work whole long summer day without sufficient food. A sister of mine has been punished by his taking away her clothes and locking them up, because she used to run when master whipped her. He kept her at work with only what she could pick up to tie on her for decency. He took away her child which had just begun to walk, and gave it to another woman-but she went and got it afterward. He had a large farm eight miles from home. Four servants were kept at the house. My master could not manage to whip my sister when she was strong. He waited until she was confined, and the second week after her confinement he said, "Now I can handle you, now you are weak." She ran from him, however, and had to go through water, and was sick in consequence.

DOCUMENT 7

DOCUMENT 8

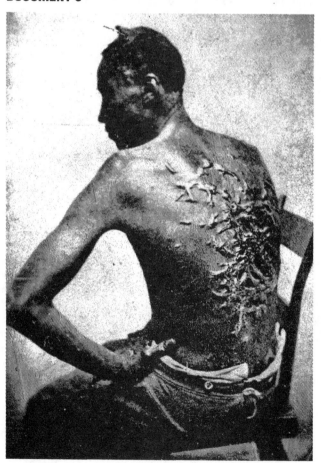

ANSWERS AND EXPLANATIONS

Multiple-Choice Questions

⬛ **1. (C) is correct.** There was no question that concentration on plantation agriculture diverted energy and resources from the South's cities. The agrarian ideal, bolstered by the cotton boom, encouraged the antiurban and anticommercial sentiments of many white Southerners. Southern capital was tied up in land and slaves, and Southerners, buoyed by the world's insatiable demand for cotton saw no reason to invest in economically risky railroads, canals, and factories. Nor were they eager to introduce the disruptive factor of free wage labor into the tightly controlled slave system.

⬛ **2. (A) is correct.** In the North, the laboring class was made up of white workers. In part, because the South failed to attract as much immigrant labor as the North, southern cities offered both enslaved and free black people opportunities in skilled occupations such as blacksmithing and carpentering that free African Americans in the North were denied.

⬛ **3. (A) is correct.** Slavery was a lifelong labor system, and the constant and inescapable issue between master and slave was how much work the slave would—or could be forced—to do. Southern white slave owners claimed that by housing, feeding, and clothing their slaves from infancy to death they were acting more humanely than northern industrialists who employed people only during their working years. But in spite of occasional instances of manumission—the freeing of a slave—the child born of a slave was destined to remain a slave.

⬛ **4. (E) is correct.** Although no southern state recognized state marriage in law, most owners not only recognized but encouraged them, sometimes even performing a kind of wedding ceremony for the couple. Masters encouraged marriage among their slaves, believing it made the men less rebellious, and for economic reasons they were eager for the slave women to have children.

⬛ **5. (A) is correct.** Many slave owners expected Christianity to make their slaves obedient and peaceful. Forbidding their slaves to hold religious gatherings, owners insisted that their slaves attend white church services. On many plantations, slaves attended religious services with their masters every Sunday as the minister preached messages justifying slavery and urging obedience. But at night, away from white eyes, they held their own prayer meetings.

⬛ **6. (B) is correct.** Turner was a lay preacher who killed his master in 1831 and started a slave rebellion. By morning, their band numbered sixty people and they had killed fifty-five white people. Nat Turner's rebellion greatly magnified southern fears of slave uprisings.

⬛ **7. (B) is correct.** The pervasive influence of the slave system in the South is reflected in the startling contrast of two facts: two-thirds of all Southerners did not own slaves, yet slave owners dominated the social and political life of the region.

⬛ **8. (E) is correct.** The word "yeoman" is often applied to independent farmers of the South, most of whom lived on family-sized farms. Although yeoman farmers sometimes owned a few slaves, in general they and their families worked their land by themselves. This land ranged from adequate to poor. The yeoman farmer community grew enough vegetables to feed its families and raised enough cotton every year to bring in a little cash.

⬛ **9. (D) is correct.** Several factors contributed to this regional solidarity. Nat Turner's rebellion was important, linked as it was in the minds of many Southerners with antislavery agitation from the North. Militant abolitionist William Lloyd Garrison began publishing the *Liberator*, the newspaper that was to become the leading antislavery organ, in 1831. The British gave notice that they would soon abolish slavery on the sugar plantations of the West Indies.

⬛ **10. (C) is correct.** By the time of the Civil War, cotton accounted for almost sixty percent of American exports, representing a total value of nearly $200 million a year.

Cotton's central place in the national economy and its international importance led Senator James Henry Hammond of South Carolina to boast "Cotton is King."

Document-Based Question

Discuss the role of paternalism in the southern slave system.

Southern slave owners saw themselves in a paternal relationship with their slaves. Their self image as enlightened, racially superior caretakers of their slaves, who raised the slaves from their natural state as near animals, was an important means of justifying the structure of southern society. However, their actions towards their slaves were rarely as benevolent as the plantation owners would have liked to believe, and they were consequently more often hated as oppressors than beloved as patrons.

Many whites viewed slavery as beneficial not only to the white slave owners, but to the slaves as well. The country was viewed as moving forward, the north expanding its industry, and the south finding more and larger markets for its agriculture. The slaves were viewed as gaining something from this progress as well. The fact that they were transplanted to America and were able to take part in western civilization was perceived as greatly to their benefit, almost as a favor done for them by their owners (**DOCUMENT 5**).

Black slaves were presented as being better treated than white northern and British factory workers, being watched by their benevolent masters, as opposed to the "wage slaves" who were being overseen by cruel taskmasters (**DOCUMENT 7**). Even when whites spoke up to defend slaves, they were patronized. When a punishment was demanded for the murder of a slave, it was due to the slaves' inferior nature, his inability to defend himself. Had the victim been free, the crime would not have been so terrible (**DOCUMENT 1**). Abolitionists also believed in the inferiority of blacks, intending to convert them from what was perceived to be a lowly, pagan religion (**DOCUMENT 4**).

The excuses of the white slave owners were both far off the mark and hypocritical. Slaves could be the equals of their masters, in intelligence, if not education (**DOCUMENT 3**). The system was also not at all benevolent in most cases. Severe whippings were common (**DOCUMENT 8**). Not only were they whipped, but slaves often were subject to even more severe forms of torture, malnourishment, rape and other harsh treatment (**DOCUMENT 6**). This naturally enraged the slave community, which saw through the obvious hypocrisy with which it was treated. The claims of benevolence in the face of obvious maltreatment were often more than they could stand (**DOCUMENT 2**).

CHAPTER 11

The Growth of Democracy, 1824–1840

This chapter covers the development of a number of factors that helped build national unity. A strong national party system and mass participation in politics developed. As president, Andrew Jackson advanced the powers of the presidency through national appeals. Economic growth, especially in transportation, created unifying forces. Writers, artists, and builders all promoted national themes in their works. Sectional differences, however, did not disappear as a force.

The New Democratic Politics in North America

The issue of popular rights arose throughout North America. In the United States, political developments revolved around expansion of suffrage, though not universally. The party system also began the process of reorganization.

The Jackson Presidency

Andrew Jackson's election ushered in a new era in American politics. An extremely popular leader, Jackson brought to the office a strong vision of what the president should be. Practicing this vision created tensions with other political leaders.

Changing the Course of Government

Despite his popularity, Andrew Jackson's stand on several issues provoked strong opposition that helped change the political culture of the nation. The disagreements raised important constitutional issues and solidified political opposition to Jackson.

The Second American Party System

The second party system set the pattern for American politics. The national parties developed strategies and techniques designed to appeal to as many people as possible.

American Arts and Letters

During the Age of Jackson, a national American culture emerged. American artists and writers discovered national themes to produce the first distinctive American literature and art.

Multiple-Choice Questions

1. Jackson's "negative activism" as president resulted in
   (A) his use of the veto more times than all of his predecessors combined.
   (B) a loss of political idealism in the country.
   (C) the strengthening of the power of the legislative branch of government.
   (D) the development of a class of government office holders.
   (E) allowing less power to remain in state hands.

2. Jackson vetoed the Maysville Road Bill of 1830 because he
   (A) disapproved of any federal funding for internal improvements.
   (B) felt it infringed on state powers.
   (C) felt that corrupt government contractors would destroy the project.
   (D) objected to it being funded by the Second Bank of the United States.
   (E) knew it was unpopular with western voters.

3. The Supreme Court's decision in *Gibbons* v. *Ogden* and *Dartmouth College* v. *Woodward*
   (A) asserted the broad power of the federal government over interstate commerce.
   (B) said that the federal government must stay out of interstate commerce.
   (C) questioned the constitutionality of federal law limit to the expansion of slavery.
   (D) strengthened the power of state governments in commercial matters.
   (E) denied the states the right to tax branches of the Second Bank of the United States.

4. Which one of the following was NOT part of Jackson's veto message on the renewal of the Nation's Bank?
   (A) It was dangerous to the liberties of the people.
   (B) It was a treasonous enterprise.
   (C) It was unconstitutional.
   (D) Only the rich benefited from it.
   (E) The bank would lead to a socialist economy.

5. Which one of the following has the LEAST in common with the other four?
   (A) Panic of 1837
   (B) Specie Circular
   (C) Bank War
   (D) Tariff of 1832
   (E) the widespread use of paper money

6. The Whigs were most closely identified with the
   (A) Jeffersonian tradition.
   (B) Federalists.
   (C) South.
   (D) anti-Masons.
   (E) anti-federalists.

7. The Whigs were a short-lived national party because they
   (A) were too aristocratic.
   (B) had no western appeal.
   (C) refused to use mass rallying types of politics.
   (D) were too diverse and fragmented.
   (E) couldn't bridge the North-South sectionalism.

8. In his lecture, "The American Scholar," this intellectual urged Americans to write about their own culture:
   (A) Benjamin Franklin.
   (B) Washington Irving.
   (C) James Fenimore Cooper.
   (D) Ralph Waldo Emerson.
   (E) A. Bronson Alcott.

9. Most of the cities that nurtured American culture and provided intellectual leadership were
   (A) in the West.
   (B) along the National Road.
   (C) on the northern half of the eastern seaboard.
   (D) in the South along the eastern seaboard.
   (E) on both sides of the Erie Canal.

10. The Virginia and Kentucky Resolves and the Hartford Convention had considered this issue, which came up again in tariff debates:
    (A) the tariff.
    (B) presidential veto power.
    (C) universal manhood suffrage.
    (D) slavery.
    (E) nullification.

Document-Based Question

The Jacksonian Era is often described as a time when the United States experienced the "democratization of politics." Is this accurate? How was democracy defined in this era?

DOCUMENT 1

DOCUMENT 2

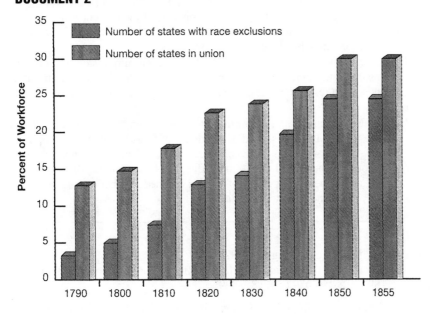

DOCUMENT 3

A "Corrupt Bargain" or Politics as Usual? (1824)
Source: Charles Francis Adams, ed. Memoirs of John Quincy Adams, 12 Volumes (Philadelphia: J. B. Lippincott & Co., 1875).

9th. . . . Mr. Clay came at six, and spent the evening with me in a long conversation explanatory of the past and prospective of the future. He said that the time was drawing near when the choice must be made in the House of Representatives of a President from the three candidates presented by the electoral colleges; that he had been much urged and solicited with regard to the part in that transaction that he should take, and had not been five minutes landed at his lodgings before he had been applied to by a friend of Mr. Crawford's, in a manner so gross that it had disgusted him; that some of my friends also, disclaiming, indeed, to have any authority from me, had repeatedly applied to him, directly or indirectly, urging considerations personal to himself as motives to his cause. He had thought it best to reserve for sometime his determination to himself: first, to give a decent time for his own funeral solemnities as a candidate; and, secondly, to prepare and predispose all his friends to a state of neutrality between the three candidates who would be before the House, so that they might be free ultimately to take that course which might be most conducive to the public interest. The time had now come at which he might be explicit in his communication with me, and he had for that purpose asked this confidential interview. He wished me, as far as I might think proper, to satisfy him with regard to some principles of great public importance, but without any personal considerations for himself. In the question to come before the House between General Jackson, Mr. Crawford, and myself, he had no hesitation in saying that his preference would be for me.

18th. (…) Mr. S. L. Southard came, to ask for the papers he had left with me yesterday, of which Mr. Kirkpatrick wishes to take copies. I gave them to him. He then asked me some questions respecting the election, upon which I spoke to him with entire confidence. I asked him if he wished me so to speak to him, and he said he did. I told him of the present state of things, so far as it is known to myself; of the present prospect, that a majority of the friends of Mr. Clay and Mr. Crawford would finally vote for me, but that the whole of the aspect may be changed from day to day.

Feb. 4. . . . I delivered to the President the letter I had written him yesterday upon the subject of the nominations to the foreign missions, and told him that I wished to put it as a deposit in his hands, for a testimonial that I had not used those missions to promote any purpose of my own.

Feb. 12. . . . General Brown entered this morning into an argument to convince me that it would not be expedient that Mr. Clay should be Secretary of State. He had a high opinion of Mr. Clay, but if I should offer him the Department he hoped he would not accept it, and he believed it would be better if I should not offer it to him. General Brown wished that De Witt Clinton should be the Secretary of State. I listened to what he said, and then told him I had already made the offer to Mr. Clay…

DOCUMENT 4

Andrew Jackson, First Annual Message to Congress (1829)
Source: From Messages and Papers of the Presidents, ed. J. D. Richardson, National Archives and Records Administration, (1896), II, 456-459 (Dec. 8, 1829).

The condition and ulterior destiny of the Indian tribes within the limits of some of our states have become objects of much interest and importance. It has long been the policy of government to introduce among them the arts of civilization, in the hope of gradually reclaiming them from a wandering life. This policy has, however, been coupled with another wholly incompatible with its success. Professing a desire to civilize and settle them, we have at the same time lost no opportunity to purchase their lands and thrust them farther into the wilderness. By this means they have not only been kept in a wandering state, but been led to look upon us as unjust and indifferent to their fate....

Our conduct toward these people is deeply interesting to our national character. Their present condition, contrasted with what they once were, makes a most powerful appeal to our sympathies. Our ancestors found them the uncontrolled possessors of these vast regions. By persuasion and force they have been made to retire from river to river and from mountain to mountain, until some of the tribes have become extinct and others have left but remnants to preserve for awhile their once terrible names...I suggest for our consideration the propriety of setting apart an ample district west of the Mississippi, and without [outside] the limits of any state or territory now formed, to be guaranteed to the Indian tribes as long as they shall occupy it, each tribe having a distinct control over the portion designated for its use. There they may be secured in the enjoyment of governments of their own choice, subject to no other control from the United States than such as may be necessary to preserve peace on the frontier and between the several tribes...This emigration should be voluntary, for it would be as cruel as unjust to compel the aborigines to abandon the graves of their fathers and seek a home in a distant land. But they should be distinctly informed that if they remain within the limits of the states they must be subject to their laws.

DOCUMENT 5

Source: "Memorial of the Cherokee Nation" (1830)

We are aware that some persons suppose it will be for our advantage to remove beyond the Mississippi. We think otherwise. Our people universally think otherwise. Thinking that it would be fatal to their interests, they have almost to a man sent their memorial to Congress, deprecating the necessity of a removal. . . . It is incredible that Georgia should ever have enacted the oppressive laws to which reference is here made, unless she had supposed that something extremely terrific in its character was necessary in order to make the Cherokees willing to remove. We are not willing to remove; and if we could be brought to this extremity, it would be not by argument, nor because our judgment was satisfied, not because our condition will be improved; but only because we cannot endure to be deprived of our national and individual rights and subjected to a process of intolerable oppression.

We wish to remain on the land of our fathers. We have a perfect and original right to remain without interruption or molestation. The treaties with us, and laws of the United States made in pursuance of treaties, guaranty our residence and our privileges, and secure us against intruders. Our only request is, that these treaties may be fulfilled, and these laws executed.

DOCUMENT 6

Source: Andrew Jackson, Veto of the Bank Bill (1832)

To the Senate:

The bill "to modify and continue" the act entitled "An act to incorporate the subscribers to the Bank of the United States" was presented to me on the 4th July instant. Having considered it with that solemn regard to the principles of the Constitution which the day was calculated to inspire, and come to the conclusion that it ought not to become a law, I herewith return it to the Senate, in which it originated, with my objections...

I sincerely regret that in the act before me I can perceive none of those modifications of the bank charter which are necessary, in my opinion, to make it compatible with justice, with sound policy, or with the Constitution of our country.

The present corporate body, denominated the president, directors, and company of the Bank of the United States, will have existed at the time this act is intended to take effect twenty years. It enjoys an exclusive privilege of banking under the authority of the General Government, a monopoly of its favor and support, and, as a necessary consequence, almost a monopoly of the foreign and domestic exchange. The powers, privileges, and favors bestowed upon it in the original character, by increasing the value of the stock far above its par value, operated as a gratuity of many millions to the stockholders. . . .

It is not conceivable how the present stockholders can have any claim to the special favor of the Government. The present corporation has enjoyed its monopoly during the period stipulated in the original contract. If we must have such a corporation, why should not the Government sell out the whole stock and thus secure to the people the full market value of the privileges granted? Why should not Congress create and sell twenty-eight millions of stock, incorporating the purchasers with all the powers and privileges secured in this act and putting the premium upon the sales into the Treasury?

But this act does not permit competition in the purchase of this monopoly. It seems to be predicated on the erroneous idea that the present stockholders have a prescriptive right not only to the favor but to the bounty of Govenrment. It appears that more than a fourth part of the stock is held by foreigners and the residue is held by a few hundred of our own citizens, chiefly of the richest class. For their benefit does this act exclude the whole American people from competition in the purchase of this monopoly and dispose of it for many millions less than it is worth. This seems the less excusable because some of our citizens not now stockholders petitioned that the door of competition might be opened, and offered to take a charter on terms much more favorable to the Government and country. . . .

It is to be regretted that the rich and powerful too often bend the acts of government to their selfish purposes. Distinctions in society will always exist under every just government. Equality of talents, of education, or of wealth can not be produced by human institutions. In the full enjoyment of the gifts of Heaven and the fruits of superior industry, economy, and virtue, every man is equally entitled to protection by law; but when the laws undertake to add to these natural and just advantages artificial distinctions, to grant titles, gratuities, and exclusive privileges, to make the rich richer and the potent more powerful, the humble members of society-the farmers, mechanics, and laborers-who have neither the time nor the means of securing like favors to themselves, have a right to complain of the injustice of their Government.

DOCUMENT 7

Source: The Force Bill (1833)

SEC. 5. And be it further enacted, That whenever the President of the United States shall be officially informed, by the authorities of any state, or by a judge of any circuit or district court of the United States, in the state, that, within the limits of such state, any law or laws of the United States, or the execution thereof, or of any process from the courts of the United States, is obstructed by the employment of military force, or by any other unlawful means, too great to be overcome by the ordinary course of judicial proceeding, or by the powers vested in the marshal by existing laws, it shall be lawful for him, the President of the United States, forthwith to issue his proclamation, declaring such fact or information, and requiring all such military and other force forthwith to disperse; and if at any time after issuing such proclamation, any such opposition or obstruction shall be made, in the manner or by the means aforesaid, the President shall be, and hereby is, authorized, promptly to employ such means to suppress the same, and to cause the said laws or process to be duly executed . . .

A French Traveler Reports on American Society (1835)
Source: Alexis de Tocqueville, Democracy in America, Volume 2 (American Studies at the University of Virginia, Hypertexts) http://xroads.virginia.edu/~HYPER/DETOC/ch2_05.htm

The political associations that exist in the United States are only a single feature in the midst of the immense assemblage of associations in that country. Americans of all ages, all conditions, and all dispositions constantly form associations. They have not only commercial and manufacturing companies, in which all take part, but associations of a thousand other kinds, religious, moral, serious, futile, general or restricted, enormous or diminutive. The Americans make associations to give entertainments, to found seminaries, to build inns, to construct churches, to diffuse books, to send missionaries to the antipodes; in this manner they found hospitals, prisons, and schools. If it is proposed to inculcate some truth or to foster some feeling by the encouragement of a great example, they form a society. Wherever at the head of some new undertaking you see the government in France, or a man of rank in England, in the United States you will be sure to find an association...Thus the most democratic country on the face of the earth is that in which men have, in our time, carried to the highest perfection the art of pursuing in common the object of their common desires and have applied this new science to the greatest number of purposes. Is this the result of accident, or is there in reality any necessary connection between the principle of association and that of equality?

(...)

Nothing, in my opinion, is more deserving of our attention than the intellectual and moral associations of America. The political and industrial associations of that country strike us forcibly; but the others elude our observation, or if we discover them, we understand them imperfectly because we have hardly ever seen anything of the kind. It must be acknowledged, however, that they are as necessary to the American people as the former, and perhaps more so. In democratic countries the science of association is the mother of science; the progress of all the rest depends upon the progress it has made.

Among the laws that rule human societies there is one which seems to be more precise and clear than all others. If men are to remain civilized or to become so, the art of associating together must grow and improve in the same ratio in which the equality of conditions is increased.

ANSWERS AND EXPLANATIONS

Multiple-Choice Questions

1. **(A) is correct.** Jackson freely used the tools of his office to strengthen the executive branch of government at the expense of the legislature and judiciary. By using the veto more frequently than all previous presidents combined, Jackson forced Congress to constantly consider his opinions. Even more important, Jackson's "negative activism" restricted federal activity, in sharp contrast to the nationalizing tendencies of previous governments.

2. **(A) is correct.** Because Jackson was a Westerner, his supporters expected him to recognize the nation's urgent need for better transportation and to provide federal funding for internal improvements, especially in the West. Jackson's veto of the Maysville Road Bill of 1830 was therefore one of his most unexpected actions. Jackson refused to allow federal funding of a southern spur of the National Road in Kentucky, claiming it should be paid for by the state. Jackson argued that federal funding for extensive and expensive transportation measures was unconstitutional, because it infringed on the "reserved power" the Constitution left to the states.

3. **(A) is correct.** These two key decisions were handed down by Chief Justice John Marshall and asserted broad federal powers over interstate commerce. In *Dartmouth College* v. *Woodward* (1819), the Supreme Court prevented states from interfering in contracts, and in *Gibbons* v. *Ogden* (1824), it enjoined the state of New York from giving a monopoly over a steamboat line to Robert Fulton, inventor of the vessel. Although Fulton's invention was protected by federal patent, its commercial application was not. Patenting thus encouraged technology, but not at the expense of competition.

4. **(B) is correct.** Jackson wrote one of the strongest veto messages in American history denouncing the Bank as unconstitutional, harmful to states' rights, and "dangerous to the liberties of the people." Jackson presented himself as the spokesman for the majority of ordinary people and the enemy of special privilege.

5. **(D) is correct.** Consequences of the Bank War continued as inflation pressures worsened. Jackson became alarmed at the use of paper money (which he blamed for the inflation), and in July 1836, he issued the Specie Circular, announcing the government would only accept payment for public lands in hard currency. In 1837, in what is commonly known as the Panic of 1837, the banking system collapsed, unemployment spiked, and businesses around the country closed.

6. **(B) is correct.** The Whigs were often the initiators and beneficiaries of economic change and were more receptive to it. Heirs of the Federalist belief in the importance of a strong federal role in the national economy, they supported Henry Clay's American System: a strong central government, the Bank of the United States, a protective tariff, and internal improvements. Religion was an important element in political affiliation, and many Whigs were members of evangelical reforming denominations.

7. **(E) is correct.** After the death of William Henry Harrison, John Tyler became president. The Whigs had sought him primarily for his sectional appeal and had not inquired too closely into his political opinions, which turned out to be anti-Whit as well as anti-Jackson. After a series of vetoes, exasperated Whigs forced Tyler out of the party and his entire cabinet resigned. Tyler appointed former Democrats to replace them. Thus, the Whig triumph of 1840 was negated by the stalemate between Tyler and the Whig majority in Congress.

8. **(D) is correct.** Emerson proclaimed "Our day of dependence, our long apprenticeship to the learning of other lands, comes to a close. He went on to encourage American writers to find inspiration in the ordinary details of daily life.

9. **(C) is correct.** In the early years of the nineteenth century, eastern seaboard cities actively built the cultural foundation that would nurture American art and literature. Philadelphia's American Philosophical Society boasted a distinguished roster of scientists and Boston ran a close second to Philadelphia.

10. **(E) is correct.** The doctrine of nullification upheld the right of a state to declare a federal law null and void and to refuse to enforce it within the state. South Carolinian John C. Calhoun wrote a widely circulated defense of the doctrine, the *Exposition and Protest*, in 1828. Although the Nullification Crisis was about the tariff, it was also about the greatest of sectional issues, slavery. In like manner, the Virginia and Kentucky Resolves and the Hartford Convention were also about sectional issues.

Document-Based Question

The Jacksonian Era is often described as a time when the United States experienced the "democratization of politics." Is this accurate? How was democracy defined in this era?

When Andrew Jackson came to the presidency in 1828, the United States was a significantly different nation than it had been when first created in the aftermath of the triumphant War for Independence. Westward expansion had created new states and increased population, unsettling the old balance between the original northern and southern states and introducing a new form of popular participation in which universal white manhood suffrage exercised a decisive shift in the location of power in the nation (**DOCUMENT 1**). However, the extension of the right to vote did not necessarily guarantee a wholesale re-evaluation of democracy, as slavery continued to exist and free male African Americans were denied the right to vote, as were American women (**DOCUMENT 2**). In addition, the demise of the First Party System and the emergence of sectional differences that had always simmered, resulted in the controversial Election of 1824, when the increased number of presidential candidates and reflected the different goals of the various regions of the country. Some, including candidate Andrew Jackson, even suspected that the winner of that election, John Quincy Adams, secured his presidency only through a "corrupt bargain" with candidate Henry Clay of Kentucky (**DOCUMENT 3**). Nonetheless, increasing sectionalism benefited Jackson, who emerged as the winner of the 1828 election following a huge increase in voter turnout and the creation of new political parties. Jackson, a lawyer, military hero and slaveowner, had little political experience but took pride in his pioneer's spirit of independence and presented himself as a man of the people, many of whom also identified with Jackson's frontier experience and rallied around "Old Hickory."

But another aspect of Jackson's frontier experience was a long reputation as a fierce opponent of Native American claims to land, and when his presidency was confronted with conflicts between settlers and Native tribes along the frontier, he took quick action to establish the supremacy of American claims over formerly native lands (**DOCUMENT 4**). The resulting loss of land and the tragedy of removal deeply affected the status and culture of Native peoples, including the Cherokee, who were forced in 1838 to migrate west from Georgia on the brutal Trail of Tears (**DOCUMENT 5**). The status of Native Americans in the United States can be viewed as another aspect of the ongoing definition of democracy in the United States.

Jackson continued to strengthen federal power, especially executive power, in other areas of policy as well. The Market Revolution had expanded the economy, making the United States a larger power in the global economy as foreign investment in American business grew. This redefined the relationship between business and politics. In a series of court cases, the courts similarly agreed that the federal government should exercise control over the rapidly mushrooming American economy, establishing the rights of the federal government to regulate interstate commerce. However, Jackson drew the line at the extension of the Second Bank of the United States; when Congress approved the bill, he vetoed it in the name of the people's liberties (**DOCUMENT 6**). Jackson similarly exercised executive and federal power, this time over state power, in his handling of the Nullification Crisis that emerged over national protective tariffs (**DOCUMENT 7**). Sectional difference arose again, underscoring the observations of foreign visitors that Americans tended to form associations in order to achieve political, economic, and social aims (**DOCUMENT 8**). The definition of democracy, then, may have been a subject of contention in the era known as the "Age of the Common Man."

CHAPTER 12

Industry and the North, 1790s–1840s

This chapter covers the way in which the North was affected by the commercialization and industrialization that defined the Market Revolution. The preindustrial ways of work and trade gave way to industrial and commercial methods. The Market Revolution transformed the North into an urbanized, industrializing society of workers connected to expanded commercial markets. As new social classes emerged in urban areas, an equally new social order developed to cope with the deep-rooted, substantial changes in patterns of work and daily living.

Preindustrial Ways of Working

Preindustrial society followed patterns of work and living that showed signs of change by the 1790s. In rural areas, the transformation from traditional to commercial agriculture had begun. Among urban artisans and workers, changes in traditional modes of work and living were also evident.

The Transportation Revolution

Expansion created the need for better movement of goods and people. A transportation revolution resulted that was fueled by hard work and invention. The transportation revolution also influenced the legal and economic development of the nation.

The Market Revolution

The Market revolution was the most fundamental change American communities experienced. A variety of innovations and inventions helped place the production and distribution of goods on an industrial, commercial footing. In the process, methods of manufacturing drastically changed.

From Artisan to Worker

Industrialization transformed the nature and status of work, destroying or weakening traditional methods and systems of production. At the same time, the market revolution dramatically altered the way people bought, traded, and sold goods. The ongoing changes led to collective action by workers.

A New Social Order

The market revolution transformed the social order, creating the social classes we have today. During the late eighteenth and early nineteenth centuries, evangelical religion spread rapidly. Family roles were also substantially altered, as were child-rearing methods. Culturally, sentimentalism, transcendentalism, and self-reliance were major intellectual trends.

Multiple-Choice Questions

1. The history of Lowell epitomizes this transition:
   (A) effect of the Erie Canal on manufacturing.
   (B) industrial town to ghost town
   (C) working class to middle class.
   (D) slave to non-slave labor.
   (E) self-sufficient farm families to urban wageworkers.

2. A crucial aspect of the new putting-out system was
   (A) uniform parts.
   (B) assembly lines.
   (C) apprenticing.
   (D) lack of family ties.
   (E) division of labor.

3. Francis Cabot Lowell and Paul Moody changed textile manufacturing with their invention of a/an
   (A) power loom.
   (B) assembly line.
   (C) carding machine.
   (D) power sewing machine.
   (E) uniform part assembly machine.

4. Many of the first strikes in American labor history were led by
   (A) apprentices.
   (B) Irish immigrants.
   (C) middle class reformers.
   (D) rural women workers.
   (E) Socialists.

5. Due to the market revolution, male children of artisans and farmers were more likely to be
   (A) white collar workers.
   (B) Brahmins.
   (C) manufacturers.
   (D) factory workers.
   (E) skilled craftsmen.

6. The religion that captured the attention of the new middle class in the early 1800s
   (A) emphasized an intellectual as opposed to emotional experience.
   (B) convinced its converts that original sin doomed all but an elite to damnation.
   (C) had its greatest impact on young males.
   (D) incorporated an enthusiastic evangelistic approach to religious practice.
   (E) promoted a narrow path to salvation.

7. Catharine Beecher's book *Treatise on Domestic Economy* illustrated the need for
   (A) helping middle-class women modernize their tasks and family role.
   (B) suffrage for women.
   (C) scientifically explained methods of birth control.
   (D) occupational training for working class and immigrant women.
   (E) new attitudes on sexuality and child-bearing for middle-class women.

8. The core of sentimentalism of the urban middle class developed from
   (A) romantic love.
   (B) nostalgia for imagined preindustrial village security.
   (C) the advertising culture of the day.
   (D) Evangelicalism.
   (E) proper social codes.

9. In his *Walden*, Henry David Thoreau
   (A) reassured middle-class businessmen on self-interest.
   (B) criticized society for wasting women's potential.
   (C) humanized the factory system.
   (D) argued for the development of the nation's natural resources.
   (E) questioned the spiritual cost of the market revolution.

10. The first productive tariff in the United States was passed in
    (A) 1798.
    (B) 1807.
    (C) 1816.
    (D) 1824.
    (E) 1833.

Document-Based Question

Defend or refute the following statement: The market revolution was an unmitigated good for the American People.

DOCUMENT 1

The Case for the Erie Canal
Source: David Hosack, Memoir of De Witt Clinton(New York: J. Seymour, 1829),
http://www.history.rochester.edu/canal/bib/hosack/APPOT.html

...When completed, this would afford a course of navigation from New-York, by sloop navigation to Albany, 160 miles—from Albany to Buffalo, by boat navigation, 300 miles—from Buffalo to Chicago by sloop navigation, 1200 miles; making a distance of 1600 miles of inland navigation up stream, where the cargo has to be shifted but three times.

The probable charges of freight would be—from New-York to Albany (the present price on small packages of merchandise up freight is about) five dollars per ton, from thence to Buffalo (full large enough, including no charge for lockage) fifty dollars a ton, from thence to Chicago, say large fifty dollars per ton—is equal to 105 dollars per ton, or five cents per pound nearly. From Chicago harbour it might be continued up its river, by portage, into and down the Illinois, and up the Mississippi; and into, as yet, almost unknown regions.

The navigation of the four largest lakes in the known world, together with all their tributary streams—the agricultural products and the commerce of all the surrounding country, would pass through this canal—and even the fifth (Ontario) would become its tributary.—The additional duty on the Canadian trade alone would defray the annual repairs of the canal.

The vast extension of and facility to commerce, together with the additional spur to industry which this canal would give, would in twenty years redeem the principal and interest of their expenditure, at the rate of their present imposts, by its additional increase.

Its invitation to the culture of the fertile soil surrounding these extensive navigable waters, would be such, that in a few generations the exhibition of their improvements and the display of their wealth, would even scarcely be equaled by the old world.

DOCUMENT 2

Source: Henry Clay, "Defense of the American System" (1832)

I have now to perform the more pleasing task of exhibiting an imperfect sketch of the existing state of the unparalleled prosperity of the country. On a general survey, we behold cultivation extended, the arts flourishing, the face of the country improved; our people fully and profitably employed, and the public countenance exhibiting tranquility, contentment and happiness. And if we descend into particulars, we have the agreeable contemplation of a people out of debt, land rising slowly in value, but in a secure and salutary degree; a ready though not extravagant market for all the surplus productions of our industry; innumerable flocks and herds browsing and gamboling on ten thousand hills and plains, covered with rich and verdant grasses; our cities expanded, and whole villages springing up, as it were, by enchantment; our exports and imports increased and increasing; our tonnage, foreign and coastwise, swelling and fully occupied; the rivers of our interior animated by the perpetual thunder and lightning of countless steam-boats; the currency sound and abundant; the public debt of two wars nearly redeemed; and, to crown all, the public treasury overflowing, embarrassing Congress, not to find subjects of taxation, but to select the objects which shall be liberated from the impost. If the term of seven years were to be selected, of the greatest prosperity which this people have enjoyed since the establishment of their present constitution, it would be exactly that period of seven years which immediately followed the passage of the tariff of 1824.

DOCUMENT 3

Source: The Harbinger, Female Workers of Lowell (1836)

In Lowell live between seven and eight thousand young women, who are generally daughters of farmers of the different states of New England. Some of them are members of families that were rich in the generation before. . . .

The operatives work thirteen hours a day in the summer time, and from daylight to dark in the winter. At half past four in the morning the factory bell rings, and at five the girls must be in the mills. A clerk, placed as a watch, observes those who are a few minutes behind the time, and effectual means are taken to stimulate to punctuality. This is the morning commencement of the industrial discipline (should we not rather say industrial tyranny?) which is established in these associations of this moral and Christian community.

At seven the girls are allowed thirty minutes for breakfast, and at noon thirty minutes more for dinner, except during the first quarter of the year, when the time is extended to forty-five minutes. But within this time they must hurry to their boardinghouses and return to the factory, and that through the hot sun or the rain or the cold. A meal eaten under such circumstances must be quite unfavorable to digestion and health, as any medical man will inform us. After seven o'clock in the evening the factory bell sounds the close of the day's work.

Thus thirteen hours per day of close attention and monotonous labor are extracted from the young women in these manufactories. . . . So fatigued-we should say, exhausted and worn out, but we wish to speak of the system in the simplest language-are numbers of girls that they go to bed soon after their evening meal, and endeavor by a comparatively long sleep to resuscitate their weakened frames for the toil of the coming day.

DOCUMENT 4

Source: James F. Cooper, Notions of the Americans (1840)

The construction of canals, on a practical scale, the mining for coal, the exportation of cotton goods, and numberless other improvements, which argue an advancing state of society, have all sprung into existence within the last dozen years. It is a knowledge of these facts, with a clear and sagacious understanding of their immense results, coupled with the exciting moral causes, that render the American sanguine, aspiring, and confident in his anticipations. He sees that his nation lives centuries in an age, and he feels no disposition to consider himself a child, because other people, in their dotage, choose to remember the hour of his birth.

DOCUMENT 5

DOCUMENT 6

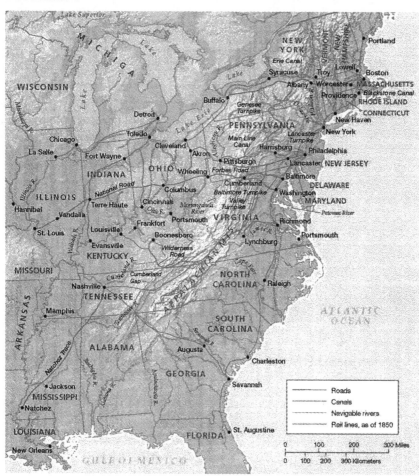

DOCUMENT 7

DOCUMENT 8

TIME TABLE OF THE LOWELL MILLS,

To take effect on and after Oct. 21st, 1851.

The Standard time being that of the meridian of Lowell, as shown by the regulator clock of JOSEPH RAYNES, 43 Central Street

	From 1st to 10th inclusive.				From 11th to 20th inclusive.				From 21st to last day of month.			
	1st Bell	2d Bell	3d Bell	Eve.Bell	1st Bell	2d Bell	3d Bell	Eve.Bell	1st Bell	2d Bell	3d Bell	Eve.Bell.
January,	5.00	6.00	6.50	*7.30	5.00	6 00	6.50	*7.30	5.00	6.00	6.50	*7.30
February,	4.30	5.30	6.40	*7.30	4.30	5.30	6.25	*7.30	4.30	5.30	6.15	*7.30
March,	5.40	6.00		*7.30	5.20	5.40		*7.30	5.05	5.25		6.35
April,	4.45	5.05		6.45	4.30	4.50		6.55	4.30	4.50		7.00
May,	4.30	4.50		7.00	4.30	4.50		7.00	4.30	4.50		7 00
June,	"	"		"	"	"		"	"	"		"
July,	"	"		"	"	"		"	"	"		"
August,	"	"		"	"	"		"	"	"		"
September,	4.40	5.00		6.45	4.50	5.10		6.30	5.00	5.20		*7.30
October,	5.10	5.30		*7.30	5.20	5.40		*7.30	5.35	5.55		*7.30
November,	4.30	5.30	6.10	*7.30	4.30	5.30	6.20	*7.30	5.00	6.00	6.25	*7.30
December,	5.00	6.00	6.45	*7.30	5.00	6.00	6.50	*7.30	5.00	6.00	6.50	*7.30

* Excepting on Saturdays from Sept. 21st to March 20th inclusive, when it is rung at 20 minutes after sunset.

YARD GATES,

Will be opened at ringing of last morning bell, of meal bells, and of evening bells; and kept open Ten minutes.

MILL GATES.

Commence hoisting Mill Gates, Two minutes before commencing work.

WORK COMMENCES,

At Ten minutes after last morning bell, and at Ten minutes after bell which "rings in" from Meals.

BREAKFAST BELLS.

During March "Ring out"........at....7.30 a. m........."Ring in" at 8:05 a. m.
April 1st to Sept. 20th inclusive.....at....7 00 " " .... " " at 7.35 " "
Sept. 21st to Oct. 31st inclusive.....at....7.30 " " .... " " at 8.05 " "
Remainder of year work commences after Breakfast.

DINNER BELLS.

"Ring out" ....12.30 p. m........."Ring in".... 1.05 p. m.

In all cases, the *first* stroke of the bell is considered as marking the time.

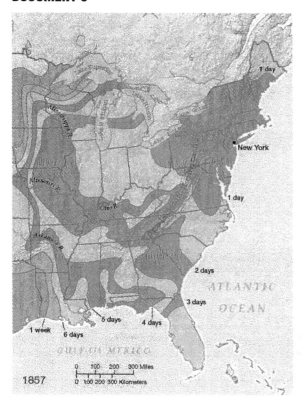

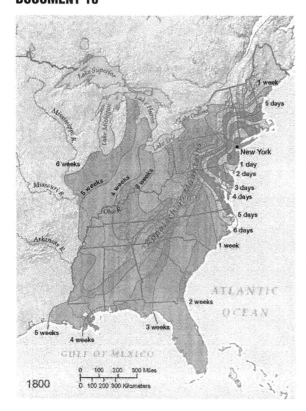

ANSWERS AND EXPLANATIONS

Multiple-Choice Questions

1. (E) is correct. The history of Lowell epitomized the growing trend in the New England and the Mid-Atlantic states from self-sufficient farming communities to manufacturing. This was an ongoing process and large factories were not common until the 1880s. Still, changes in people's life and work styles could be seen long before that.

2. (E) is correct. Division of labor was the most crucial part of the putting-out system. Before industrialization, a laborer would make the entire product. Now a worker was expected to only make one part of the product with the raw materials he was given.

3. (A) is correct. The power loom was a great advancement for the entire textile industry. The power loom made the process much easier; from the initial cleaning and combing to the production of finished lengths of cloth. The loom made it possible to do the entire textile process all in one factory. However, only owners with large capital could afford an item as expensive as the loom.

4. (D) is correct. Early strikes were led by women protesting wage cuts and longer hours. The owners considered the women on strike to be unfeminine and ungrateful. In most cases, the strikes were unsuccessful and in many instances women left the factories in disgust and returned to the family farm.

5. (A) is correct. The market revolution changed the lives, especially of the male children of artisans and farmers. These children went into white-collar jobs such as accountants, clerks, bank tellers, book keepers and insurance salesmen. With these jobs came new responsibilities such as hard work, sobriety, responsibility, and steadiness.

6. (D) is correct. The new evangelistic approach to religion that came out of the Great Awakening was more enthusiastic than religion in the past. The concept of original sin was replaced by the notion that anybody who had the willingness to be saved could find salvation. Conversion and repentance now took place at large revival meetings that focused on the sinners and their salvation.

7. (A) is correct. Beecher's book, *Treatise on Domestic Economy*, became the housekeeping guide for a generation of middle-class women. The book included ideas for the kitchen, recipes, child-rearing, and moral advice. It became the only book other than the Bible that women traveled west with.

8. (B) is correct. The new middle class put extra emphasis on on sincerity and feeling. These feelings came from the nostalgia of the face to face life of the pre-industrial village. Sermons and documents warned young middle class men of the dangers and deceit of urban life, including women who were not what they seemed.

9. (E) is correct. In *Walden*, Henry David Thoreau expresses discontent with the market system. In the book, Thoreau denounces materialism, as what led to "the mass of men to lead lives of quiet desperation." Thoreau felt that a life of subsistence was more beneficial because it left time for spiritual thought.

10. (C) is correct. The first protective tariff passed in 1816 was passed largely in response to complaints of New England mill workers, who believed that they needed protection for their young industry from British cotton textiles.

Document-Based Question

Defend or refute the following statement: The market revolution was an unmitigated good for the American People.

The market revolution was far from an unmitigated good for the American people. However, they did benefit substantially from it. Though many workers were mistreated, it helped make the United States one of the more important commercial nations. It also improved the quality of life of many Americans.

Pre-industrial society was often idealized by the residents of industrial America. Harkening back to Jeffersonian ideas of an agrarian republic, they viewed the past as an agricultural Eden (**DOCUMENT 5**), a marked contrast to the smoke filled industrial world. There is some truth to their critique. Workers were often driven to work up to thirteen hour days, while living in over crowded quarters (**DOCUMENT 3**). They were required to follow precise timetables, living on a clock run schedule (**DOCUMENT 8**), which was different from the daylight driven schedule they had been used to while living on farms.

However, despite these hardships, there was a great deal of good that accrued to the nation due to the new conditions. Agricultural work was made easier, and yields higher, by new technology (**DOCUMENT 7**). In the period of the transportation revolution, it was predicted that the building of new canals, particularly the Erie Canal, would vastly increase travel times, as well as create revenue (**DOCUMENT 1**). These high hopes turned out to be true, connecting the country's centers of commerce (**DOCUMENT 6**) and speeding up travel thought the countryside tremendously (**COMPARE DOCUMENTS 9 & 10**). Writing in defense of the American System, a program of legislation designed to encourage the change to a market economy, Henry Clay presented the various benefits of the changes: sound currency, reduced public debt, and improved transportation (**DOCUMENT 2**).

Aside from the various material improvements, the changes helped to spark the national spirit to be one of innovation, and strengthened the national character (**DOCUMENT 4**). The market revolution consequently sparked an overwhelmingly, if not unmitigatedly, positive change in the United States.

CHAPTER 13

Coming to Terms with the New Age, 1820s–1850s

This chapter covers the effects the "market revolution" had on American urban society, as well as the responses of people to the process. The most fundamental effects were in immigration and the changes it caused in the nation's ethnic makeup, in the growth of cities, social and political troubles, and in changing working conditions that brought labor unrest. Responses to all of these changes were particularly manifested in new types of community groups: labor unions, big-city machines, social reform organizations, utopian settlements, antislavery societies, and the women's rights movement. In this energetic search for continuity, social connection, and social order, Americans tried to come to terms with what was clearly a new age.

Immigration and Ethnicity

Although the market revolution affected all aspects of American life, nowhere was its impact so noticeable as in the cities. It was primarily in cities that the startlingly large number of new immigrants clustered.

Urban America

The market revolution radically altered the American city. Substantial growth stimulated by immigration changed patterns of living and culture. These changes also created the need for social order.

The Labor Movement and Urban Politics

Changes in work led to the erosion of traditional labor organization and politics. Related to individual conditions and immigration, new forms arose.

Social Reform Movements

Evangelical religion stimulated the rise of a broad social reform movement launched largely by the middle class, especially by women. It affected such diverse areas of society as education, prisons, and moral reform. This era also witnessed the emergence of utopianism and new religious sects.

Antislavery and Abolitionism

The antislavery movement gave rise to a strong abolitionist campaign involving whites and blacks. In time, the abolition of slavery became a national political issue.

The Women's Rights Movement

Involvement in social reform movements led women to found organizations to pursue their rights.

Multiple-Choice Questions

1. Which of the following is <u>NOT</u> a reason why immigrants were unwelcome to many Americans?
   (A) They were poor.
   (B) They were Catholic.
   (C) They worked for low wages.
   (D) They filled a need for unskilled labor.
   (E) Americans were unprepared for the immigrants' "foreignness."

2. Until the 1880s, the task of receiving immigrants fell on the
   (A) federal government.
   (B) private charities.
   (C) industrialists.
   (D) religious officials.
   (E) cities.

3. Which one of the following was <u>NOT</u> a belief of the nineteenth-century middle-class reformers?
   (A) They could create the perfect community on earth.
   (B) Human nature was basically good.
   (C) Small-scale sincere responses to social problems could work.
   (D) Religion was often a source for the impulse of reform.
   (E) They were morally certain of what was right.

4. An important common denominator in the public education, temperance, anti-prostitution, and asylum reform movements was
   (A) working class leadership.
   (B) female participation and leadership.
   (C) big city machines.
   (D) leadership by evangelical ministers.
   (E) Southern support.

5. A serious drawback to the reform movement was its
   (A) aggressive morality.
   (B) incremantalism.
   (C) belief in the goodness of human nature.
   (D) engagement in political action.
   (E) social activism.

6. The most successful of the nineteenth-century communitarian movements was
   (A) Oneida.
   (B) Fruitlands.
   (C) New Harmony.
   (D) the Shaker community.
   (E) Mormonism.

7. The American Colonization Society
   (A) focused on sending blacks back to Africa.
   (B) sought the creation of American economic colonies abroad.
   (C) was a group dedicated to helping blacks economically.
   (D) wanted an immediate end to slavery.
   (E) lobbied for rights of free blacks to vote.

8. Similar to evangelical preachers in the nineteenth century, northern abolitionists
   (A) employed a confrontational personal style.
   (B) employed altar calls for the converted.
   (C) treated their opponents with Christian charity.
   (D) opposed emotional responses to the frailties of the human condition.
   (E) used the pulpit as the primary means of publicizing their message.

9. Complicating the efforts of the abolitionists was their
   (A) lack of focus.
   (B) animosity to working-class northerners.
   (C) disagreement on the status of free blacks.
   (D) disagreement on the most effective tactics.
   (E) refusal to denounce slavery on economic terms.

10. The argument of separate spheres was meant to exclude this group from political life:
    (A) African Americans.
    (B) urban poor.
    (C) working class.
    (D) new immigrants.
    (E) women.

Document-Based Question

What concerns and challenges did reformers confront in the antebellum era, and how did they address them?

DOCUMENT 1

Seneca Falls

DOCUMENT 2

THE DRUNKARDS PROGRESS,
FROM THE FIRST GLASS TO THE GRAVE.

DOCUMENT 3

Source: Charles Finney, "What a Revival of Religion Is" (1835)

It is altogether improbable that religion will ever make progress among heathen nations except through the influence of revivals. The attempt is now making to do it by education, and other cautious and gradual improvements. But so long as the laws of mind remain what they are, it cannot be done in this way. There must be excitement sufficient to wake up the dormant moral powers, and roll back the tide of degradation and sin. And precisely so far as our own land approximately to heathenism, it is impossible for God or man to promote religion is such a state of things but by powerful excitements.- This is evident from the fact that this has always been the way in which God has done it. God does not create these excitements, and choose this method to promote religion for nothing, or without reason. Where mankind are so reluctant to obey God, they will not obey until they are excited. For instance, how many there are who know that they ought to be religious, but they are afraid if they become pious they will be laughed at by their companions. Many are wedded to idols, others are procrastinating repentance, until they are settled in life, or until they have secured some favorite worldly interest. Such persons never will give up their false shame, or relinquish their ambitious schemes, till they are so excited that they cannot contain themselves any longer. . . . It is presupposed that the church is sunk down in a backslidden state, and a revival consists in the return of the church from her backsliding, and in the conversion of sinners.

DOCUMENT 4

A Lowell Mill Girl Tells her Story (1836)
Source: Internet Modern History Sourcebook, http://www.fordham.edu/halsall/mod/robinson-lowell.html

The early mill girls were of different ages. Some were not over ten years old; a few were in middle life, but the majority were between the ages of sixteen and twenty-five. The very young girls were called "doffers." They "doffed," or took off, the full bobbins from the spinning frames, and replaced them with empty ones. These mites worked about fifteen minutes every hour and the rest of the time was their own. When the overseer was kind they were allowed to read, knit, or go outside the mill yard to play. They were paid two dollars a week. The working hours of all the girls extended from five o'clock in the morning until seven in the evening, with one half hour each, for breakfast and dinner. Even the doffers were forced to be on duty nearly fourteen hours a day. This was the greatest hardship in the lives of these children. Several years later a ten hour law was passed, but not until long after some of these little doffers were old enough to appear before the legislative committee on the subject, and plead, by their presence, for a reduction of the hours of labor.

DOCUMENT 5

Souce: "Petition of the Catholics of New York" (1840)

Your petitioners have to state further, as grounds of their conscientious objections to those schools, that many of the selections in their elementary reading lessons contain matter prejudicial to the Catholic name and character. The term "POPERY" is repeatedly found in them. This term is known and employed as one of insult and contempt towards the Catholic religion, and it passes into the minds of children with the feeling of which it is the outward expression. Both the historical and religious portions of the reading lessons are selected from Protestant writers, whose prejudices against the Catholic religion render them unworthy of confidence in the mind of your petitioners, at least so far as their own children are concerned. . . .

For these reasons, and others of the same kind, your petitioners cannot, in conscience, and consistently with their sense of duty to God, and to their offspring, intrust the Public

School Society with the office of giving "a right direction to the minds of their children." And yet this Society claims that office, and claims for the discharge of it the Common School Funds, to which your petitioners, in common with other citizens, are contributors. In so far as they are contributors, they are not only deprived to the damage and detriment of their religion, in the minds of their own children, and of the rising generation of the community at large. The contest is between the *guarantied* rights, civil and religious, of the citizen on the one hand, and the pretensions of the Public School Society on the other; and whilst it has been silently going on for years, your petitioners would call the attention of your Honorable Body to its consequences on that class for whom the benefits of public education are most essential-the children of the poor.

DOCUMENT 6

Horace Mann on Education and National Welfare
Source: United States Department of State, International Information Programs,
http://usinfo.state.gov/usa/infousa/facts/democrac/16.htm

Now, surely, nothing but Universal Education can counter-work this tendency to the domination of capital and the servility of labor. If one class possesses all the wealth and the education, while the residue of society is ignorant and poor, it matters not by what name the relation between them may be called; the latter, in fact and in truth, will be the servile dependents and subjects of the former. But if education be equably diffused, it will draw property after it, by the strongest of all attractions; for such a thing never did happen, and never can happen, as that an intelligent and practical body of men should be permanently poor. Property and labor, in different classes, are essentially antagonistic; but property and labor, in the same class, are essentially fraternal. The people of Massachusetts have, in some degree, appreciated the truth, that the unexampled prosperity of the State,—its comfort, its competence, its general intelligence and virtue,—is attributable to the education, more or less perfect, which all its people have received; but are they sensible of a fact equally important?—namely, that it is to this same education that two thirds of the people are indebted for not being, to-day, the vassals of as severe a tyranny, in the form of capital, as the lower classes of Europe are bound to in the form of brute force.

Education, then, beyond all other devices of human origin, is the great equalizer of the conditions of men—the balance-wheel of the social machinery. I do not here mean that it so elevates the moral nature as to make men disdain and abhor the oppression of their fellow-men. This idea pertains to another of its attributes. But I mean that it gives each man the independence and the means, by which he can resist the selfishness of other men. It does better than to disarm the poor of their hostility towards the rich; it prevents being poor. Agrarianism is the revenge of poverty against wealth. The wanton destruction of the property of others,—the burning of hay-ricks and corn-ricks, the demolition of machinery, because it supersedes hand-labor, the sprinkling of vitriol on rich dresses,—is only agrarianism run mad. Education prevents both the revenge and the madness. On the other hand, a fellow-feeling for one's class or caste is the common instinct of hearts not wholly sunk in selfish regards for person, or for family. The spread of education, by enlarging the cultivated class or caste, will open a wider area over which the social feelings will expand; and, if this education should be universal and complete, it would do more than all things else to obliterate factitious distinctions in society.

DOCUMENT 7

Declaration of Sentiments and Resolutions, Woman's Rights Convention,
Seneca Falls, New York (1848)
Source: E. C. Stanton, S. B. Anthony, and Matilda Joslyn Gage, eds., History of Woman Suffrage,
vol. 1
(Rochester, NY: Charles Mann, 1881), pp. 70–72.

We hold these truths to be self-evident: that all men and women are created equal; that they are endowed by their Creator with certain inalienable rights; that among these are life, liberty, and the pursuit of happiness; that to secure these rights governments are instituted, deriving their just powers from the consent of the governed. . .. But when a long train of abuses and usurpations, pursuing invariably the same object evinces a design to reduce them under absolute despotism, it is their duty to throw off such government, and to provide new guards for their future security. Such has been the patient sufferance of the women under this government, and such is now the necessity which constrains them to demand the equal station to which they are entitled.

The history of mankind is a history of repeated injuries and usurpations on the part of man toward woman, having in direct object the establishment of an absolute tyranny over her. To prove this, let facts be submitted to a candid world (...)

Now, in view of this entire disfranchisement of one-half the people of this country, their social and religious degradationÑin view of the unjust laws above mentioned, and because women do feel themselves aggrieved, oppressed, and fraudulently deprived of their most sacred rights, we insist that they have immediate admission to all the rights and privileges which belong to them as citizens of the United States.

DOCUMENT 8

ANSWERS AND EXPLANATIONS

Multiple-Choice Questions

■ **1. (D) is correct.** It would be a mistake to think that immigration was unwelcome to everyone. Industries needed willing workers and western states actively advertised in Europe for settlers. Many of the changes in industry and transportation that accompanied the market revolution would have been impossible without immigrants. In Lowell, Massachusetts, Irish men and women kept the mills operating when the mill operators, facing increasing competition, sought cheaper labor to replace their original labor force of farm women.

■ **2. (E) is correct.** Until the 1880s, the task of receiving immigrants fell completely on cities and states, not the federal government. New York, by far the largest port of entry, did not even establish an official reception center until 1855, when Castle Garden, at the bottom of Manhattan Island (near present-day Battery Park), was so designated.

3. **(C) is correct.** Middle-class people tried to deal with social changes in their communities by joining organizations devoted to reforms. The temperance movement and reforms involving education, prisons and asylums, women's rights, abolitionism, and, above all, the spread of evangelical religion were all concerns of the middle class. The reform message was vastly amplified by inventions such as the steam printing press, which made it possible to publish reform literature in great volume.

4. **(B) is correct.** Women became deeply involved in reform movements through their churches. Nearly every church had a maternal association, where mothers gathered to discuss ways to raise their children as true Christians.

5. **(A) is correct.** One characteristic of the reform movements was their moralistic dogmatism. Reformers were certain they knew what was right and were determined to see their improvements enacted. This attitude was bound to cause controversy: by no means did all Americans share the reformers' beliefs, nor did those for whom it was intended always take kindly to being the targets of the reformers' concern.

6. **(E) is correct.** Mormonism gained rapid distinction for its extraordinary unity under the leadership of its patriarch, Joseph Smith. Close cooperation and hard work made the Mormon community successful, attracting both new followers and the animosity of neighbors, who resented Mormon exclusiveness and economic success.

7. **(A) is correct.** The first attempt to "solve" the problem of slavery was a plan for gradual emancipation of slaves (with compensation to their owners) and their resettlement in Africa. This plan was the work of the American Colonization Society, formed in 1817 by northern religious reformers (Quakers prominent among them) and a number of Southern slave owners, most from the Upper South and the Border States. Northerners were especially happy to send the North's 250,000 black people back to Africa. The American Colonization Society was remarkably ineffective; by 1830, it had managed to send only 1,400 black people to a colony in Liberia, West Africa. Critics pointed out that more slaves were born in a week than the society sent back to Africa in a year.

8. **(A) is correct.** The style of abolitionist writings and speeches was similar to the oratorical style of the religious revivalists. Northern abolitionists believed that a full description of the evils of slavery would force southern slave owners to confront their wrongdoing and lead to a true act of repentance—freeing their slaves. They were confrontational, denunciatory, and personal in their message, much like the evangelical preachers. Southerners, however, regarded abolitionist attacks as libelous and abusive.

9. **(C) is correct.** Although abolitionist groups raised the nation's emotional temperature, they failed to achieve the moral unity they had hoped for, and began to splinter. One perhaps inevitable but nonetheless distressing split was between white and black abolitionists. Frederick Douglas and other free African Americans worked under persistent discrimination, even from antislavery whites. While many white reformers eagerly pressed for civic equality for African Americans, they did not accept the idea of social equality.

10. **(E) is correct.** Women played a vital role in all the social movements of the day. In doing so, they implicitly challenged the popular notion of separate spheres for men and women—the public world for him, home and family for her. The separate spheres argument, although it heaped praise on women for their allegedly superior moral qualities, was meant to exclude them from political life.

Document-Based Question

What concerns and challenges did reformers confront in the antebellum era, and how did they address them?

The antebellum era was a time of great transformation in the United States. There was a significant rise in the number of immigrants coming to America to take advantage of the opportunities offered by the expanding economy, which was transformed by the market revolution and the rise of new industries. This had an effect on the nation's cities, which grew rapidly

(**DOCUMENT 1**). The new cities of this era were characterized by creation of distinct ethnic neighborhoods, racial segregation, increased poverty and poor conditions, and increased class distinctions. Disturbed by what they viewed as significant signs of social ills brought on by such rapid change, American reformers, largely members of the middle and upper class, tackled problems such as the power of the big city machines and civic disorder. Among the many ills reformers saw plaguing society was the damaging effects of alcohol, and the temperance movement to limit alcohol consumption grew rapidly (**DOCUMENT 2**). For many, the drive to limit the consumption of alcohol was tied to what they viewed as the moral decline of American society, and a wave of evangelical religious revivals pulsed through the United States (**DOCUMENT 3**), providing impetus for reformers interested in reshaping American life along stricter lines of moral behavior, which has led many to argue that such reformers were more interested in social control than social reform.

Many reformers were more focused on economic concerns, and viewed the rapid industrialization of the nation as the source of exploitative and unjust conditions for labor. The union movement sought to restore autonomy and status to workers rapidly losing control as traditional patterns of work changed, and workers clashed with owners more frequently (**DOCUMENT 4**). Similarly committed to protecting their own interests, many Americans focused on the reform of specific public institutions to reflect the changing shape of American society. While prisons and asylums drew the attention of many reformers, education was a major source of concern. Alarmed by what they considered Protestant-based public education in the United States, Catholics petitioned the state in New York to reduce their taxes or fund church-sponsored schools (**DOCUMENT 5**), while Horace Mann considered education the source of the economic equality that would erase class distinctions (**DOCUMENT 6**).

In many instances, the roots of these various reform movements can be seen in a desire to fulfill the promise of democracy and equality in the United States. The clearest examples of this can be found in the women's rights movement and antislavery and abolition movements (**DOCUMENTS 7 AND 8**). Both sought to expand the definition of democracy in the United States to include disenfranchised groups through suffrage and the elimination of slavery, but their appeals were often met with derision and violence within the diverse and divided society of antebellum America.

CHAPTER 14

The Territorial Expansion of the United States, 1830s–1850s

This chapter covers the territorial growth of the United States. Supported by the ideology of "manifest destiny," Americans added Oregon, Texas, California, and the Southwest to the nation's territory. Through diplomacy and war, the United States became a continental nation. Settlers repeated the old pattern of initial friendliness to natives and earlier settlers, followed by hostility and domination. Adding new territory also caused intensification of sectional hostility over extending slavery into new territory.

Exploring the West

Economics and the federal government spurred exploration of the West. Companies competing for the fur trade were one source of exploration. After the Louisiana Purchase, the federal government sponsored several expeditions to map the new territory. Expansion followed exploration raising the "Indian problem" again.

The Politics of Expansion

Fueled by the belief in manifest destiny, American expansion followed several paths. Open lands motivated thousands of Americans to follow overland trails to Oregon and California. The Oregon settlement led to a dispute with Great Britain that was resolved diplomatically. In the Southwest, trade led to settlement and forts along the Santa Fe Trail. Americans also settled in Texas, but they eventually rebelled and founded the Republic of Texas, creating a conflict that affected the election of 1844.

The Mexican-American War

Tensions with Mexico, partly fueled by expansionist ideology, led to war. Public opinion was divided on the war, but the United States obtained the present-day Southwest as a result of the war.

California and the Gold Rush

The Russians came first to Spanish California but were followed by the Americans. After the United States annexed California, the discovery of gold spurred immigration by Americans, Chinese, and Mexicans, among others. Mining camps proliferated but most proved temporary settlements.

The Politics of Manifest Destiny

Growing pride in democracy raised American confidence, but the addition of land triggered a growing debate over the extension of slavery.

Multiple-Choice Questions

1. One of the most important factors in the exploration of the West was the
   (A) China trade.
   (B) cattle business.
   (C) search for coal and other minerals.
   (D) search for gold.
   (E) fur trade.

2. The Lewis and Clark expedition was financed by
   (A) the federal government.
   (B) Boston brahmins.
   (C) the personal fortune of Thomas Jefferson.
   (D) subscriptions from land speculators.
   (E) fur traders.

3. The Grand Canyon was first explored by
   (A) Zebulon Pike.
   (B) William Clark.
   (C) Jedediah Smith.
   (D) Major Stephen Long.
   (E) Major John Wesley Powell.

4. The justification for the western removal of the Indians was
   (A) the Indians needed a space where they could live undisturbed by whites.
   (B) to preserve the Indians' way of life.
   (C) the Indians could never be civilized.
   (D) the Indians were misusing the land in the East.
   (E) to give the Indians much-needed arable land.

5. The outcome of Indian removal in the southern part of Indian Territory in the 1830s–1850s was
   (A) almost immediate encroachment by whites on Overland Trails.
   (B) continued fighting among the Indian groups.
   (C) loss of autonomy and tribal identity.
   (D) successful creation of new communities and self-government.
   (E) the total destruction of the Indian tribes.

6. Generally pioneers traveling the Overland Trails in the 1840s and 1850s were
   (A) constantly attacked by Indians.
   (B) likely to experience very little dissension.
   (C) parts of organized westward-moving communities.
   (D) traveling alone for safety and speed.
   (E) bored with routine life-styles.

7. During the Mexican War, northern Whigs began to characterize the war as a/an
   (A) unwinnable conflict.
   (B) racist plot against a weaker nation.
   (C) part of a southern conspiracy to expand slavery.
   (D) Mexican scheme to claim disputed gold fields on the Colorado.
   (E) economic land grab.

8. As commander-in-chief during the war, James K. Polk defined the role of president by
   (A) leaving planning and strategy to the military.
   (B) drawing on his own training to plan military strategy.
   (C) visiting battle sites to keep morale high.
   (D) coordinating both civilian and military goals and needs.
   (E) serving as a battlefield commander and exposing himself to fire.

9. The Mexican-American War began over
   (A) a border dispute.
   (B) a dispute over gold.
   (C) Mexican claims to Louisiana.
   (D) American claims to California.
   (E) an unprovoked Mexican attack on San Antonio.

10. After 1849, California attracted thousands of settlers because of
    (A) cheap land.
    (B) the beautiful climate.
    (C) the discovery of gold.
    (D) the discovery of uranium.
    (E) the discovery of the Comstock Lode.

Document-Based Question

Defend or refute the following statement: The Mexican-American War was an imperialist war.

DOCUMENT 1

The Treaties of Velasco (May 14, 1836)
Source: Texas State Historical Association, Texas History Links, Links to Some Texas History Primary Resource Documents on the Internet, compiled by Roger A. Griffin, Ph.D, Professor of History Emeritus, Austin Community College, Austin, Texas.
http://home.austin.rr.com/rgriffin/texhisdocs.html

ARTICLES OF AGREEMENT AT SAN JACINTO

Whereas, The President Santa Anna, with divers officers of his late army, is a prisoner of war in charge of the army of Texas, and is desirous of terminating the contest now existing between the Government of Texas and that of Mexico, in which desire the Generals above named do fully concur, and Whereas, The President of the Republic of Texas, and the Cabinet, are also willing to stay the further effusion of blood, and to see the two neighboring Republics placed in relations of friendship, on terms of reciprocal advantage;

Therefore, it is agreed by the President Santa Anna, and the Generals Don Vicente Filisola, Don Jose Urea, Don Joaquin Ramires y Sesma, and Don Antonio Gaona...

5th. That the following be, and the same are hereby established and made the lines of demarcation between the two Republics of Mexico and of Texas, to wit: The line shall commence at the estuary or mouth of the Rio Grande, on the western bank thereof, and shall pursue the same bank up the said river, to the point where the river assumes the name of the Rio Bravo del Norte, from which point it shall proceed on the said western bank to the head waters, or source of said river, it being understood that the terms Rio Grande and Rio Bravo del Norte, apply to and designate one and the same stream. From the source of said river, the principal head branch being taken to ascertain that source, a due north line shall be run until it shall intersect the boundary line established and described in the Treaty negotiated by and between the Government of Spain and the Government of the United States of the North; which line was subsequently transferred to, and adopted in the Treaty of limits made between the Government of Mexico and that of the United States; and from this point of intersection the line shall be the same as was made and established in and by the several Treaties above mentioned, to continue to the mouth or outlet of the Sabine river, and from thence to the Gulf of Mexico.

DOCUMENT 2

Source: John L. O'Sullivan, "The Great Nation of Futurity" (1845)

America is destined for better deeds. It is our unparalleled glory that we have no reminiscences of battlefields, but in defense of humanity, of the oppressed of all nations, of the rights of conscience, the rights of personal enfranchisement. Our annals describe no scenes of horrid carnage, where men were led on by hundreds of thousands to slay one another, dupes and victims to emperors, kings, nobles, demons in the human form called heroes. We have had patriots to defend our homes, our liberties, but no aspirants to crowns or thrones; nor have the American people ever suffered themselves to be led on by wicked ambition to depopulate the land, to spread desolation far and wide, that a human being might be placed on a seat of supremacy.

DOCUMENT 3

Source: Thomas Corwin, Against the Mexican War (1847)

What is the territory, Mr. President, which you propose to wrest from Mexico? It is consecrated to the heart of the Mexican by many a well-fought battle with his old Castilian master. His Bunker Hills, and Saratogas, and Yorktowns are there! The Mexican can say, "There I bled for liberty! and shall I surrender that consecrated home of my affections to the Anglo-Saxon invaders? What do they want with it? They have Texas already. They have possessed themselves of the territory between the Nueces and the Rio Grande. What else do they want? To what shall I point my children as memorials of that independence which I bequeath to them, when those battlefields shall have passed from my possession?"

Sir, had one come and demanded Bunker Hill of the people of Massachusetts, had England's lion ever showed himself there, is there a man over thirteen and under ninety who would not have been ready to meet him? Is there a river on this continent that would not have run red with blood? Is there a field but would have been piled high with the unburied bones of slaughtered Americans before these consecrated battlefields of liberty should have been wrested from us? But this same American goes into a sister republic, and says to poor, weak Mexico, "Give up your territory, you are unworthy to possess it; I have got one half already, and all I ask of you is to give up the other!" ....

DOCUMENT 4

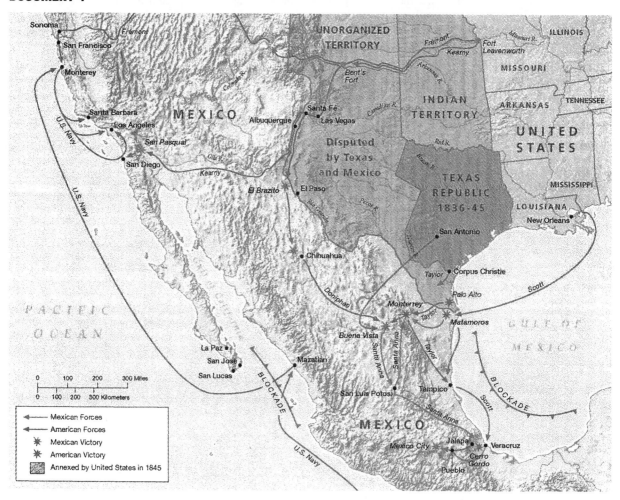

DOCUMENT 5

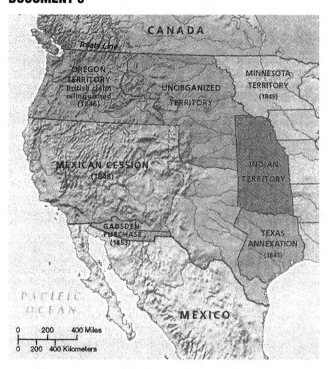

DOCUMENT 6

Source: President Polk Sends a Message to Congress

Mexico has passed the boundary of the United States, has invaded our territory and shed American blood upon American soil. . . . War exists, and, notwithstanding all our efforts to avoid it, exists by the act of Mexico herself.

DOCUMENT 7

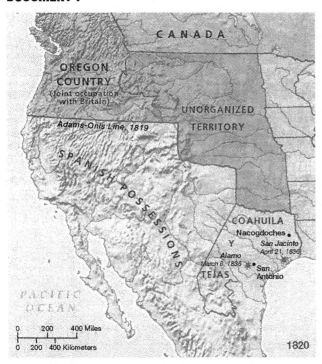

DOCUMENT 8

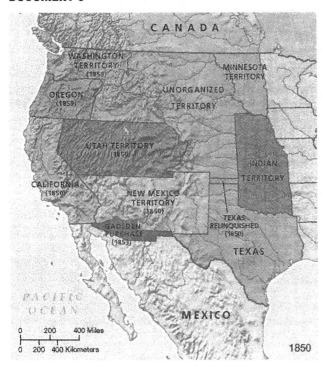

The Territorial Expansion of the United States, 1830s–1850s

Multiple-Choice Questions

■ **1. (E) is correct.** The fur trade, which flourished from the 1670s to the 1840s, was an important spur to exploration on the North American continent. In the 1670s, the British Hudson's Bay Company and its French Canadian rival, Montreal's North West Company, began exploring beyond the Great Lakes in the Canadian West in search of beaver pelts. Not until the 1820s were American companies able to challenge British dominance of the trans-Mississippi fur trade.

■ **2. (A) is correct.** The federal government played a major role in the exploration and development of the West. The exploratory and scientific aspects of the Lewis and Clark expedition in 1804-06 set a precedent for many government-financed quasi-military expeditions.

■ **3. (E) is correct.** The tradition of governmenet-sponsored western exploration continued after the Civil War in the famous geological surveys, the best known of which is the 1869 Grand Canyon exploration by Major John Wesley Powell.

■ **4. (A) is correct.** The justification for this western removal, as Thomas Jefferson had explained early in the century, was the creation of a space where Indian people could live undisturbed by white people while they slowly adjusted to "civilized" ways. But government officals who negotiated the removals failed to predict the tremendous speed at which white people would settle the West.

■ **5. (D) is correct.** The people in the southern part of Indian Territory, in what is now Oklahoma, fared better than other Native Americans. Those members of the southern tribes—the Charokees, Chickasaws, Choctaws, Creeks, and Seminoles—who had survived the trauma of forcible removal from the Southeast in the 1830s, quickly created impressive new communities. The five tribes divided up the territory and established self-governing nations with their own schools and churches. The societies they created were not so different from the American societies from which they had been expelled.

■ **6. (C) is correct.** Few pioneers travled alone, partly because they feared Indian attack (which was rare), but largely because they needed help fording rivers or crossing mountains with heavy wagons. Most Oregon pioneers traveled with their families but usually also joined a larger group, forming a "train."

■ **7. (C) is correct.** As the Mexican-American War dragged on and casualties and costs mounted—13,000 Americans and 50,000 Mexicans died and the United States spent $97 million—opposition increased, especially among northern antislavery Whigs. More and more people came to the opinion that the war was nothing more than a plot by Southerners to expand slavery.

■ **8. (D) is correct.** Although he lacked a military background, Polk assumed the overall planning of the war's strategy. By his personal attention to the coordination of civilian political goals and military requirements, Polk gave a new and expanded definition to the role of president as commander-in-chief during wartime.

■ **9. (A) is correct.** When the Mexican government refused to receive Slidell, sent by President Polk, an angry Polk ordered General Taylor and his forces south to the Rio Grande, into the territory that Mexicans claimed as their soil. In April 1846, a brief skirmish between American and Mexican soliders broke out in the disputed zone. Polk seized the event, sending a war message to Congress: "Mexico has passed the boundary of the United States, has invaded our territory and shed American blood upon American soil…War exists…"

■ **10. (C) is correct.** American annexation at the end of the Mexican-American War changed little for the handful of Amreicans in the California frontier. But then came the Gold Rush of 1849, which changed California permanently. In 1849, as the gold rush began in earnest, San Francisco, the major entry port and supply point, sprang to life. From a settlement of 1,000 in 1848, it grew to a city of 35,000 in 1850.

Document-Based Question

Defend or refute the following statement: The Mexican-American War was started essentially to steal land from Mexico.

The Mexican-American War was driven primarily by a desire for territorial expansion. It was started on false pretenses by a president who had based his campaign on expanding U.S. territory. However, it was not a straightforward "land grab." American expansionism was driven by idealism as well as greed. The Mexican-American War was a product of both.

The roots of the war can be traced back to the American settlement of Mexican Texas. Americans were invited in by the Mexican government, and settled there in droves. They eventually won their independence, and settled that the border between the Republic of Texas and Mexico would be at the Rio Grande River (**DOCUMENT 1**); however, Mexico did not respect the southern boundary set by the treaty, disputing the territory between the Nueces River and the Rio Grande. Texas attempted to be admitted to the United States. However, its annexation was disputed, and it did not gain statehood until 1845, after the election of President James K. Polk.

President Polk's election was widely viewed as a mandate for territorial expansion, and he did not disappoint. In the summer of 1845 he sent an army to defend Texas, and made provisions to take California in the case of war.

The war was not long in coming. Polk sent the Army south, into the disputed territory, without any provocation, though he claimed that the Mexicans had attacked (**DOCUMENT 6**). This claim is crucial to understanding the climate of opinion in the U.S. The American people would not fight a war as an aggressor. Indeed, this idealistic view, that America had only ever fought defensive wars, was an important part of American identity (**DOCUMENT 2**). The idea that America might be a conquering nation was so repugnant to some of Polk's political opponents that some even argued that, should the U.S. win the war, they should not take any Mexican territory (**DOCUMENT 3**).

Despite these anti-expansionist voices, the war continued, and the president did intend to take territory from Mexico. Not a single battle was fought on American soil, and only one was fought in disputed territory (**DOCUMENT 4**). At the end of the war Mexico was forced to cede massive amounts of land to the U.S. (**DOCUMENT 5**). The end to which Polk had started the war had been achieved.

The Mexican-American War was fought for territorial expansion. In 1820 a contemporary American would not recognize the western outline of the United States (**DOCUMENT 7**). By 1850, after the war, it had taken its current shape (**DOCUMENT 8**).

CHAPTER 15

The Coming Crisis, the 1850s

This chapter covers the sectional split between North and South that had been slowly developing since the Missouri Compromise. Thomas Jefferson had called the question of slavery extension "a firebell in the night," and after the Mexican-American War the philosopher Ralph Waldo Emerson expressed the fear that "Mexico will poison us." Their deep concerns were realized as people in the North and South took ever more rigid and determined positions on slavery's extension or elimination. Many Americans in the 1850s, perhaps a majority, felt the issue of slavery had to be permanently settled and expected their political parties to reflect their will. A compromise over territorial gains in 1850 failed to hold and after the Kansas-Nebraska Act of 1854 was passed, a miniature civil war broke out in Kansas. When Lincoln was elected in 1860, many southerners saw him as a purely northern president and several southern states responded by seceding from the union.

America in 1850

By 1850, the United States had experienced tremendous growth and change. An "American Renaissance" of writers developed in the 1850s. But growth and change also raised serious social issues and renewed the debate over slavery. The North and South were divided on slavery creating two opposing sections with very different viewpoints on the future of the United States.

The Compromise of 1850

The issue of the extension of slavery reached a boiling point in 1850. The Compromise of 1850 addressed several major points of tension, but the election of 1852 showed the political party system was weakening while expansionist movements indicated a troubled future.

The Crisis of the National Party System

The Kansas-Nebraska Act triggered a violent confrontation between antislavery and proslavery forces. At the same time, nativism emerged as a growing political force. The political party system underwent major changes as the Whigs disappeared and the Republican Party rose in the North. The election of 1856 was won by the Democrats, but the strong Republican showing indicated future problems.

The Differences Deepen

The Dred Scott decision and the struggle over Kansas constitutions exacerbated the tensions and conflict between North and South. The economic Panic of 1857 further enflamed the dispute. The increasing violence of the slavery issue was shown by John Brown's raid in Virginia.

The South Secedes

The election of 1860 laid bare the differences over ideas of slavery and indicated that few were willing to compromise. Lincoln's election prompted southern states to secede from the Union. As northern leaders grappled with what to do about the secession, the South formed the Confederacy. Lincoln's inauguration indicated he had no desire for war.

Multiple-Choice Questions

1. By 1850, most southern leaders like Calhoun and Toombs
   (A) agreed to confine slavery to the south.
   (B) insisted slavery must be national.
   (C) believed slavery was slowly on its way out.
   (D) emphasized popular sovereignty.
   (E) had organized slave power groups to keep control.

2. The issue of slavery in the territories came to a head when
   (A) California applied for statehood.
   (B) Kansas split on slavery.
   (C) silver was discovered in Nevada.
   (D) Arizona applied for statehood.
   (E) Lewis Cass proposed the principle of popular sovereignty.

3. Solutions proposed for the issue of slavery in the territories included all of the following EXCEPT
   (A) the Wilmot Proviso.
   (B) popular Sovereignty
   (C) the legalization of slavery in all of the Mexican territory.
   (D) the legalization of slavery in California only.
   (E) a stronger fugitive slave law passed.

4. The Kansas-Nebraska Act opened Indian territory to American settlers
   (A) as slave territories.
   (B) under the Wilmot Proviso.
   (C) if they would agree to kill all Indians on sight.
   (D) who were under the age of 50.
   (E) under the principle of popular sovereignty.

5. Stephen Douglas' action in introducing the Kansas-Nebraska Act in 1854 proved to be
   (A) a great political miscalculation.
   (B) his most honorable stand.
   (C) a step closer to the presidency for him.
   (D) a brilliant political move.
   (E) an insignificant political act.

6. The Dred Scott decision held that
   (A) slaves were not citizens and, therefore, could not sue in a court of law.
   (B) slaves had property rights, but only if they were not themselves property.
   (C) slaves were citizens but could not sue in a court of law.
   (D) slaves had no rights before the law.
   (E) the Kansas-Nebraska Act was unconstitutional.

7. The Republicans won the election of 1860 largely because
   (A) their platform had universal appeal.
   (B) of Lincoln's popularity in the South.
   (C) they appealed to the "common man."
   (D) of the personal charm of Abraham Lincoln.
   (E) the Democratic Party split into northern and southern wings.

8. Which one of the following was NOT a plank in the 1860 Republican platform?
   (A) praise for John Brown's raid
   (B) the preservation of the union
   (C) support for a transcontinental railroad
   (D) a higher tariff
   (E) no extension of slavery

9. When Kansas applied for statehood, President James Buchanan
   (A) endorsed the pro-slavery constitution.
   (B) said the issue was a congressional one.
   (C) refused to consider the request at that time.
   (D) accepted the antislavery constitution.
   (E) turned the contested matter over to the Supreme Court for resolution.

10. The only southern state to pass a unanimous vote for secession was
   (A) Texas.
   (B) Virginia.
   (C) Alabama.
   (D) Mississippi.
   (E) South Carolina.

Document-Based Question

The ultimate "cause" of the Civil War has been a matter of intense debate among historians. Evaluate the various factors contributing to the outbreak of war and determine which was the most significant and why.

DOCUMENT 1

Source: William Lloyd Garrison, from The Liberator (1831)

Assenting to the "self-evident truth" maintained in the American Declaration of Independence "that all men are created equal, and endowed by their Creator with certain inalienable rights-among which are life, liberty, and the pursuit of happiness," I shall strenuously contend for the immediate enfranchisement of our slave population. . . . In Park Street Church, on the Fourth of July, 1829, in an address on slavery, I unreflectingly assented to the popular but pernicious doctrine of gradual abolition. I seize this opportunity to make a full and unequivocal recantation, and thus publicly to ask pardon of my God, of my country, and of my brethren the poor slaves, for having uttered a sentiment so full of timidity, injustice, and absurdity. . . .

I am aware that many object to the severity of my language; but is there not cause for severity? I will be as harsh as truth, and as uncompromising as justice. On this subject I do not wish to think, or speak, or write, with moderation. No! No! Tell a man whose house is on fire to give a moderate alarm; tell him to moderately rescue his wife from the hands of the ravisher; tell the mother to gradually extricate her babe from the fire into which it has fallen-but urge me not to use moderation in a cause like the present. I am in earnest-will not equivocate-I will not excuse-I will not retreat in a single inch-and I will be heard.

DOCUMENT 2

Source: Harriet Beecher Stowe, from Uncle Tom's Cabin (1852)

"Well, here's a pious dog, at last, let down among us sinners-a saint, a gentleman, and no less, to talk to us sinners about our sins! Powerful holy crittur, he must be! Here, you rascal, you make believe to be so pious-didn't you never hear, out of yer Bible, 'Servants, obey yer masters'? An't I yer master? Didn't I pay down twelve hundred dollars, cash, for all there is inside yer old cussed black shell? An't yer mine, now, body and soul?" he said, giving Tom a violent kick with his heavy boot; "tell me!"

In the very depth of physical suffering, bowed by brutal oppression, this question shot a gleam of joy and triumph through Tom's soul. He suddenly stretched himself up, and, looking earnestly to heaven, while the tears and blood that flowed down his face mingled, he exclaimed, " No! no! no! my soul an't yours, Mas'r! You haven't bought it-ye can't buy it! It's been bought and paid for by One that is able to keep it. No matter, no matter, you can't harm me!"

"I can't!" said Legree, with a sneer; "we'll see-we'll see! Here Sambo, Quimbo, give this dog such a breakin' in as he won't get over this month!"

DOCUMENT 3

A Dying Statesman Speaks Out Against the Compromise of 1850
Source: The Library of Congress, American Memory: Historical Collections for the National Digital Library
http://lcweb2.loc.gov/cgi-bin/query/r?ammem/mcc:@field(DOCID+@lit(mcc/009))

The result of the whole of these causes combined is that the North has acquired a decided ascendancy over every department of this government, and through it a control over all the powers of the system. A single section, governed by the will of the numerical majority, has now in fact the control of the government and the entire powers of the system. What was once a constitutional federal republic is now converted, in reality, into one as absolute as that of the Autocrat of Russia, and as despotic in its tendency as any absolute government that ever existed.

As, then, the North has the absolute control over the government, it is manifest that on all questions between it and the South, where there is a diversity of interests, the interests of the latter will be sacrificed to the former, however oppressive the effects may be, as the South possesses no means by which it can resist through the action of the government. But if there was no question of vital importance to the South, in reference to which there was a diversity of views between the two sections, this state of things might be endured without the hazard of destruction to the South. There is a question of vital importance to the Southern section, in reference to which the views and feelings of the two sections are as opposite and hostile as they can possibly be.

I refer to the relation between the two races in the Southern section, which constitutes a vital portion of her social organization. Every portion of the North entertains views and feelings more or less hostile to it. Those most opposed and hostile regard it a sin, and consider themselves under most sacred obligation to use every effort to destroy it. Indeed, to the extent that they conceive they have power, they regard themselves as implicated in the sin and responsible for suppressing it by the use of all and every means. Those less opposed and hostile regard it as a crime—an offense against humanity, as they call it— and, although not so fanatical, feel themselves bound to use all efforts to effect the same object; while those who are least opposed and hostile regard it as a blot and a stain on the character of what they call the nation, and feel themselves accordingly bound to give it no countenance or support. On the contrary, the Southern section regards the relation as one which cannot be destroyed without subjecting the two races to the greatest calamity and the section to poverty, desolation, and wretchedness; and accordingly they feel bound by every consideration of interest and safety to defend it.

This hostile feeling on the part of the North toward the social organization of the South long lay dormant, but it only required some cause to act on those who felt most intensely that they were responsible for its continuance to call it into action. The increasing power of this government and of the control of the Northern section over all its departments furnished the cause. It was this which made an impression on the minds of many that there was little or no restraint to prevent the government from doing whatever it might choose to do. This was sufficient of itself to put the most fanatical portion of the North in action for the purpose of destroying the existing relation between the two races in the South.

DOCUMENT 4

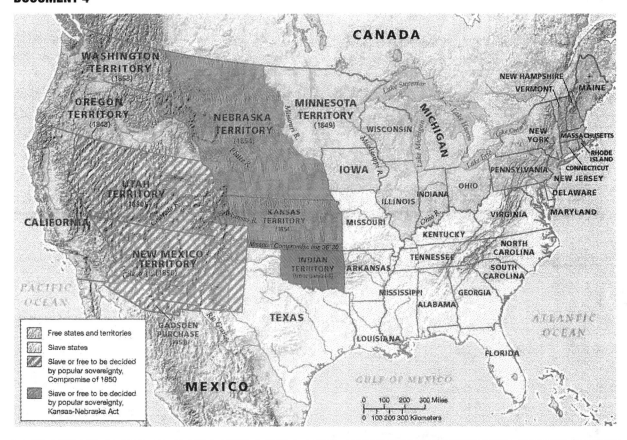

Free states and territories

Slave states

Slave or free to be decided by popular sovereignty, Compromise of 1850

Slave or free to be decided by popular sovereignty, Kansas-Nebraska Act

DOCUMENT 5

BATTLE OF HICKORY POINT, 20 MILES NORTH OF LAWRENCE.

H   JD9512 Recaptured Slave circa 1854
Anthony Burns (1834 - 1862) surrounded by scenes of his capture. He was
arrested in Boston in May 1854 on a charge of theft. Recognised as a
fugitive slave, his return to Virginia was the cause of riots. After he was
bought out of slavery, he later became pastor of a Negro baptist church in
St. Catherine's Canada.
PHOTO: HULTON GETTY / LIAISON AGENCY

DOCUMENT 7

Source: Dred Scott v. Sanford (1857)

The Question is simply this: Can a negro, whose ancestors were imported into this country, and sold as slaves, become a member of the political community formed and brought into existence by the Constitution of the United States, and as such become entitled to all the rights, and privileges, and immunities, guarantied [sic] by that instrument to the citizen? One of which rights is the privilege of suing in a court of the United States in the cases specified in the constitution.

. . . The only matter in issue before the Court, therefore, is, whether the descendants of such slaves, when they shall be emancipated, or who are born of parents who had become free before their birth, are citizens of a State, in the sense which the word citizen is used in the Constitution. . . .

The words "people of the United States" and "citizens" are synonymous terms. . . . They both describe the political body who, according to our republican institutions, form the sovereignty, and who hold the power and conduct the government through their representatives. . . . The question before us is, whether the class of persons described in the plea in abatement compose a portion of this people, and are constituent members of this sovereignty? We think they are not, under the word "citizens" in the Constitution, and can therefore claim none of the rights and privileges which that instrument provides for and secures to citizens of the United States. On the contrary, they were at that time considered as a subordinate and inferior class of beings, who had been subjugated by the dominant race, and whether emancipated or not, yet remained subject to their authority, and had no rights or privileges but such as those who held the power and the government might choose to grant them. . . .

In discussing the question, we must not confound the rights of citizenship which a State may confer within its own limits, and the rights of citizenship as a member of the Union. It does not by any means follow, because he has all the rights and privileges of a citizen of a State, that he must be a citizen of the United States. . . .

In the opinion of the court, the legislation and histories of the times, and the language used in the Declaration of Independence, show, that neither the class of persons who had been imported as slaves, nor their descendants, whether they had become free or not, were then acknowledged as a part of the people, nor intended to be included in the general words used in that memorable instrument. . . .

They had for more than a century before been regarded as beings of an inferior order, and altogether unfit to associate with the white race, either in social or political relations, and so far inferior, that they had no rights which the white man was bound to respect; and that the negro might justly and lawfully be reduced to slavery for his benefit. . . .

. . . there are two clauses in the constitution which point directly and specifically to the negro race as a separate class of persons, and show clearly that they were not regarded as a portion of the people or citizens of the government then formed.

. . . upon full and careful consideration of the subject, the court is of opinion, that, upon the facts stated. . . , Dred

Scott was not a citizen of Missouri within the meaning of the constitution of the United States and not entitled as such to sue in its courts. . . .

DOCUMENT 8

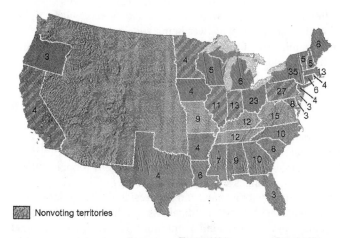

Nonvoting territories

	Electoral Vote (%)	Popular Vote (%)
ABRAHAM LINCOLN (Republican)	180 (59)	1,865,593 (40)
John C. Breckinridge (Southern Democrat)	72 (24)	848,356 (18)
John Bell (Constitutional Union)	39 (13)	592,906 (13)
Stephen A. Douglas (Northern Democrat)	12 (4)	1,382,713 (29)
States that Republicans lost in 1856, won in 1860		

Abraham Lincoln, "A House Divided" (1858)

If we could first know where we are, and whither we are tending, we could better judge what to do and how to do it. We are now far into the fifth year since a policy was initiated with the avowed object, and confident promise, of putting an end to slavery agitation. Under the operation of that policy, that agitation has not only not ceased but has constantly augmented. In my opinion, it will not cease until a crisis shall have been reached and passed. "A house divided against itself cannot stand." I believe this government cannot endure permanently half-slave and half-free. I do not expect the Union to be dissolved-I do not expect the house to fall-but I do expect it will cease to be divided. It will become all one thing or all the other. Either the opponents of slavery will arrest the further spread of it and place it where the public mind shall rest in the belief that it is in the course of ultimate extinction or its advocates will push it forward, till it shall become alike lawful in all the states, old as well as new-North as well as South.

ANSWERS AND EXPLANATIONS

Multiple-Choice Questions

1. **(B) is correct.** Calhoun's and Toombs's position on the territories quickly became southern dogma: anything less than full access to the territories was unconstitutional. On behalf of the South, Calhoun was expressing the belief—and the fear—that his interpretation of the Constitution was the only protection for slave owners, whose right to own slaves (a fundamental right in southern eyes) was being attacked.

2. **(A) is correct.** California's application for statehood set off the debates that became the Compromise of 1850 which brought the issue of slavery in the territories to a head.

3. **(D) is correct.** California applied to the Union as a free state. The Wilmot Proviso proposed outlawing slavery in all the territories. Popular sovereignty and a stronger fugitive slave law were part of the Compromise of 1850. The legalization of slavery in all of the Mexican territory was proposed and rejected.

4. **(E) is correct.** In 1854, Stephen Douglas introduced the Kansas-Nebraska Act, proposing to open those lands that had been the northern part of the Indian Territory to American settlers under the principle of popular sovereignty. He thereby reopened the question of slavery in the territories. Douglas knew he was taking a political risk, but he believed he could satisfy both his expansionist aims and his presidential ambitions.

5. **(A) is correct.** Douglas knew he was taking a political risk, but he believed he could satisfy both his expansionist aims and his presidential ambitions. He was wrong. Instead, he pushed the national party system into crisis, first killing the Whigs and then destroying the Democrats.

6. **(A) is correct.** In *Dred Scott* v. *Sanford*, Chief Justice Roger B. Taney declared the Missouri Compromise unconstitutional. He also asserted that the federal government had no right to interfere with the free movement of property throughout the territories. He dismissed the *Dred Scott* case on the grounds that only citizens could bring suits before federal courts and that black people—slave or free—were not citizens. With this bold judicial intervention into the most heated issue of the day, Taney intended to settle the controversy over the expansion of slavery once and for all. Instead, he inflamed the conflict.

7. **(E) is correct.** The split of the Democratic Party into northern and southern wings that had occurred during President Buchanan's tenure became official at the Democratic nominating conventions in 1860. Northern Democrats nominated Stephen Douglas for president. Southern Democrats nominated Buchanan's Vice-President John C.

Breckinridge of Kentucky. To make matters worse, some southern Whigs joined with border-state nativists to form the Constitutional Union Party, which nominated John Bell of Tennessee. Everyone knew a Republican victory was inevitable.

▓ **8. (A) is correct.** The election of 1860 presented voters with one of the clearest choices in American history. Lincoln stood firmly for slavery's exclusion from the territories. In addition, Republicans offered support for a homestead act (free western lands), for a transcontinental railroad, for other internal improvements, and for a higher tariff. Republicans also condemned John Brown's raid as "the gravest of crimes," repeatedly denied that they favored the social equality of black people, and strenuously affirmed that they sought to preserve the Union.

▓ **9. (A) is correct.** Free-Soil voters boycotted a June 1857 election for representatives to a convention called to write a constitution for Kansas once it reached statehood. As a result, the convention had a proslavery majority that wrote the proslavery Lecompton Constitution and then applied to Congress for admission to the Union under its terms. In the meantime, Free-Soil voters participated in election for the territorial legislature that returned a clear Free-Soil majority. Nevertheless, Buchanan, in the single most disastrous mistake of his administration, endorsed the proslavery constitution, because he feared the loss of the support of southern Democrats. The Leocompton Constitution was eventually defeated in Congress and in a new referendum by the people of Kansas. In 1861, Kansas was admitted as a free state.

▓ **10. (E) is correct.** On December 20, 1860, a state convention in South Carolina, accompanied by all the hoopla and excitement of bands, fireworks displays, and huge rallies, voted unanimously to secede from the Union. In the weeks that followed, conventions in six other southern states (Mississippi, Florida, Alabama, Georgia, Louisiana, and Texas) followed suit, with the support, on average, of 80 percent of their delegates.

Document-Based Question

The ultimate "cause" of the Civil War has been a matter of intense debate among historians. Evaluate the various factors contributing to the outbreak of war and determine which was the most significant and why.

America in the 1850s was a larger, richer and more diverse nation than it had been in 1800. It was also a nation in crisis. Though many Americans believed it was their "manifest destiny" to spread the nation's boundaries from coast to coast, such expansion created problems for the delicate political balance that existed between states with divergent cultures, economic systems, and political goals. The expansion of American territory particularly hinged on the issue of slavery and whether that institution would also spread into the new western territories. Northern opponents of slavery, organized into the antislavery and abolition movements, not only opposed its expansion but called for its outright abolition, creating a powerful movement that exercised influence through the use of moral arguments and impassioned rhetoric (**DOCUMENT 1**). Cultural differences between the North and South also emerged and were evident in the powerful abolitionist literature distributed throughout society, culminating in Harriet Beecher Stowe's stark condemnation of slavery in the hugely successful novel *Uncle Tom's Cabin* (**DOCUMENT 2**).

Of the many attempts to reduce sectional tension by settling issues surrounding the creation of new states, the Compromise of 1850 was made necessary by the hardening of sectional lines and the clear differences between the way northern and southern politicians regarded the relationship between congressional representation and power and the increasing regulatory power of the federal government (**DOCUMENT 3**). But as the 1850s wore on, compromise floundered in the face of increased challenges to the political balance between free and slave states. The Kansas-Nebraska Act hoped to settle the issue by introducing popular sovereignty with regard to the expansion of slavery (**DOCUMENT 4**), but the resulting violence there demonstrated that the issue had become the most divisive the nation had ever seen, as pro-slavery and antislavery advocates clashed in bloody battles in Kansas (**DOCUMENT 5**). This was further proved when northerners fully realized the horrors of slavery with the institution of the Fugitive Slave Act

(**DOCUMENT 6**), which spread antislavery sentiments even more. The movement continued to grow despite the Dred Scott decision, in which the Supreme Court decided that blacks in America were not citizens, which also struck a blow for states' rights (**DOCUMENT 7**). The real division in the nation that had was revealed in the Election of 1860, which centered on the issue of slavery. The new Republican Party captured the presidency (**DOCUMENT 8**). Recognizing that his triumph in the election signaled a break in the Union, as southern states made plans to secede, newly elected President Abraham Lincoln established his commitment to the Union (**DOCUMENT 9**). Now there was no turning back; the crises caused by the various tensions of the 1850s had reached a head, and the North and the South prepared to meet each other in battle.

CHAPTER 16

The Civil War, 1861–1865

This chapter covers the deadliest challenge to community and identity—a civil war. Both sides began the war underestimating its seriousness, scope, and duration. Northern generals such as Grant and Sherman recognized the arrival of a more modern style of warfare and fought accordingly. The entire American community went to war, except ironically the southern planter elite who had the largest stake in the outcome. As American men and women served in the military, helped out in many community support organizations, or fled to the Union lines, their lives changed dramatically. The North's advantage in population and industry finally proved too much for the South to withstand, although victory hung in the balance until nearly the very end of the conflict. Lincoln prepared a generous reconstruction plan that he hoped would rebuild a sense of unity and loyalty. Lee's surrender in April 1865 was marred by the assassination of Lincoln later that same month.

Communities Mobilize for War

The attack on Fort Sumter began the Civil War, leading to mobilization by the Union and the Confederacy. The issue of border state loyalties was decided and the first battle was a harbinger of the long, brutal conflict to come. Both sides entered the war with strengths and weaknesses.

Governments Organize for War

Both Lincoln and Davis prepared their governments for war. In the North, the federal government expanded its powers greatly and engaged in diplomacy to isolate the Confederacy. Jefferson Davis faced difficulties in mobilizing the Confederate government. The Confederate cause was hurt further by economic and diplomatic disappointments.

The Fighting Through 1862

The war was fought on several fronts on land and at sea, including the trans-Mississippi West. Both sides experienced victories and defeats. The Union quickly achieved supremacy of the seas.

The Death of Slavery

The response of African Americans North and South profoundly affected the course of the Civil War. The Emancipation Proclamation led to the enlistment of African Americans into the Union army.

The Front Lines and the Home Front

Deplorable conditions characterized the front lines. Weaponry, medical treatment, and disease all increased casualties, leading to desertions by soldiers on both sides. On the home front, the North experienced political, economic, and social strains while conditions in the South deteriorated.

The Tide Turns

After 1863, the war turned in favor of the North. Military victories with heavy casualties weakened Confederate will and military ability. Lincoln won re-election in 1865 and the war ended the next year; but soon after, Lincoln was assassinated.

Multiple-Choice Questions

1. The most basic similarity between the Union and the Confederacy when the Civil War began was that both sides
   (A) had strong central governments.
   (B) had equal industrial potential.
   (C) had an equal number of states.
   (D) were suitably armed and prepared for war.
   (E) were unprepared for the ordeal that lay ahead.

2. Which of the following was NOT an advantage enjoyed by the South as the Civil War began?
   (A) They were on the defensive, and the North would have to invade.
   (B) They had the most experienced officers.
   (C) the economic power of "King Cotton"
   (D) naval superiority
   (E) the percentage of eligible men in military service

3. Lincoln felt that his primary responsibility as president was to
   (A) free the slaves.
   (B) preserve the Union.
   (C) end all claims to states' rights.
   (D) make the South pay for its defection.
   (E) keep England out of the war.

4. The English did NOT extend diplomatic recognition to the Confederacy because
   (A) English public opinion opposed recognizing a nation based on slavery.
   (B) they were unsure of who was likely to win the war.
   (C) they no longer needed southern cotton.
   (D) they feared war with the Union.
   (E) they did not want to challenge the Monroe Doctrine.

5. The South had problems in financing its war effort because
   (A) state governors refused to impose new taxes.
   (B) the government issued paper money, causing inflation.
   (C) large amounts of borrowing caused inflation.
   (D) none of the above.
   (E) A, B, and C.

6. Lincoln initially resisted announcing a policy to free the slaves for all of the following reasons EXCEPT
   (A) he wanted to encourage pro-Union sentiment.
   (B) a policy to free the slaves would have caused the border states to leave the Union.
   (C) northern public opinion was divided on the slave issue.
   (D) the desire to hold the Republican Party together.
   (E) Lincoln believed that blacks would not make good citizens.

7. The greatest contributors to Lincoln's 1864 re-election victory were
   (A) the women's vote.
   (B) the support of Copperheads.
   (C) the support of Radical Republicans.
   (D) the lack of an alternative.
   (E) the Union soldiers' vote.

8. The use of women in the nursing profession met resistance largely because
   (A) women were too physically weak for such work.
   (B) it was considered an "unseemly" profession for respectable women.
   (C) of the fear they would take diseases home with them.
   (D) women were not used to tending the sick.
   (E) wounded soldiers resented them.

9. Sherman's march to Savannah was designed to
   (A) make it easier for slaves from the Deep South to escape.
   (B) isolate Robert E. Lee's army in Virginia from the rest of the South.
   (C) break southern morale.
   (D) send a message to the French in Mexico and the British on the high seas.
   (E) obtain stored cotton for the industrial mills of the North.

10. Grant's war strategy could be summed up as
    (A) finding as much political as military weakness in your enemy.
    (B) running small, concentrated attacks at predetermined targets.
    (C) the "King of Spades" power of trench warfare.
    (D) massed cavalry and artillery attack.
    (E) find your enemy and keep striking as hard as you can.

Document-Based Question

Describe some of the justifications that Confederates used for secession and for their loyalty to the Confederacy over the Union.

DOCUMENT 1

Source: Jefferson Davis, Address to the Provisional Congress of the Confederate States of America (1861)

The declaration of war made against this Confederacy by Abraham Lincoln, the President of the United States, in his proclamation issued on the 15th day of the present month, rendered it necessary, in my judgment, that you should convene at the earliest practicable moment to devise the measures necessary for the defense of the country. The occasion is indeed an extraordinary one. It justifies me in a brief review of the relations heretofore existing between us and the States which now unite in warfare against us and in a succinct statement of the events which have resulted in this warfare, to the end that mankind may pass intelligent and impartial judgment on its motives and objects. During the war waged against Great Britain by her colonies on this continent a common danger impelled them to a close alliance and to the formation of a Confederation, by the terms of which the colonies, styling themselves States, entered "*severally* into a firm league of friendship with each other for their common defense, the security of their liberties, and their mutual and general welfare, binding themselves to assist each other against all force offered to or attacks made upon them, or any of them, on account of religion, sovereignty, trade, or any other pretense whatever." In order to guard against any misconstruction of their compact, the several States made explicit declaration in a distinct article-that "*each* State *retains its* sovereignty, freedom, and independence, and every power, jurisdiction, and right which is not by this Confederation *expressly delegated* to the United States in Congress assembled." . . .

DOCUMENT 2

The "Cornerstone Speech" (1861)
Source: Henry Cleveland, Alexander H. Stephens, in Public and Private: With Letters and Speeches, Before, During, and Since the War, Philadelphia, 1886, pp. 717–729.
http://www.geocities.com/CollegePark/Quad/6460/doct/861crnrstn.html

Our new government is founded upon exactly the opposite idea; its foundations are laid, its corner-stone rests upon the great truth, that the negro is not equal to the white man; that slavery—subordination to the superior race—is his natural and normal condition. [Applause.] This, our new government, is the first, in the history of the world, based upon this great physical, philosophical, and moral truth. This truth has been slow in the process of its development, like all other truths in the various departments of science. It has been so even amongst us. Many who hear me, perhaps, can recollect well, that this truth was not generally admitted, even within their day. The errors of the past generation still clung to many as late as twenty years ago. Those at the North, who still cling to these errors, with a zeal above knowledge, we justly denominate fanatics. All fanaticism springs from an aberration of the mind—from a defect in reasoning. It is a species of insanity. One of the most striking characteristics of insanity, in many instances, is forming correct conclusions from fancied or erroneous premises; so with the anti-slavery fanatics; their conclusions are right if their premises were. They assume that the negro is equal, and hence conclude that he is entitled to equal privileges and rights with the white man. If their premises were correct, their conclusions would be logical and just—but their premise being wrong, their whole argument fails. I recollect once of having heard a gentleman from one of the northern States, of great power and ability, announce in the House of Representatives, with imposing effect, that we of the South would be compelled, ultimately, to yield upon this subject of slavery, that it was as impossible to war successfully against a principle in politics, as it was in physics or mechanics. That the principle would ultimately prevail. That we, in maintaining slavery as it exists with us, were warring against a principle, a principle founded in nature, the principle of the equality of men. The reply I made to him was, that upon his own grounds, we should, ultimately, succeed, and that he and his associates, in this crusade against our institutions, would ultimately fail. The truth announced, that it was as impossible to war successfully against a principle in politics as it was in physics and mechanics, I admitted; but told him that it was he, and those acting with him, who were warring against a principle. They were attempting to make things equal which the Creator had made unequal.

DOCUMENT 3

Why They Fought (1861)
Source: George Edward Pickett, The Heart of a Soldier, As Revealed in the Intimate Letters of Genl. George E. Pickett
C.S.A.: Electronic Edition.
http://docsouth.unc.edu/pickett/pickett.html#pick33

You know, my little lady, some of those cross-stitched mottoes on the cardboard samplers which used to hang on my nursery wall, such as, "He who provides not for his own household is worse than an infidel" and "Charity begins at home," made a lasting impression upon me; and while I love my neighbor, i.e., my country, I love my household, i.e., my state, more, and I could not be an infidel and lift my sword against my own kith and kin, even though I do believe, my most wise little counselor and confidante, that the measure of American greatness can be achieved only under one flag, and I fear, alas, there can never again reign for either of us the true spirit of national unity whether divided under two flags or united under one…

Now, little one, if you had the very faintest idea how happy a certain captain in the C.S.A. (My, but that "C" looks queer!) would be to look into your beautiful, soul-speaking eyes and hear your wonderfully musical voice, I think you would let him know by wire where he could find you. I shall almost listen for the electricity which says, "I am at —. Come." I know that you will have mercy on your devoted SOLDIER.

Source: Mary Boykin Chesnut, A Confederate Lady's Diary (1861)

I wonder if it be a sin to think slavery a curse to any land. Sumner said not one word of this hated institution which is not true. Men & women are punished when their masters & mistresses are brutes & not when they do wrong-& then we live surrounded by prostitutes. An abandoned woman is sent out of any decent house elsewhere. Who thinks any worse of a Negro or Mulatto woman for being a thing we can't name. God forgive us, but ours is a monstrous system & wrong & iniquity. Perhaps the rest of the world is as bad. This is only what I see: like the patriarchs of old, our men live all in one house with their wives & their concubines, & the Mulattos one sees in every family exactly resemble the white children-& every lady tells you who is the father of all the Mulatto children in everybody's household, but those in her own, she seems to think drop from the clouds or pretends so to think-. Good women we have, but they talk of nastiness tho they never do wrong; they talk day & night of -. My disgust sometimes is boiling over-but they are, I believe, in conduct the purest women God ever made. Thank God for my countrywomen-alas for the men! No worse than men everywhere, but the lower their mistresses, the more degraded they must be.

Source: Charles Harvey Brewster, Three Letters from the Civil War Front (1862)

I don't know but I shall be discharged, as the whole Regiment is almost in a state of mutiny on the Nigger question. Capt Miller the pro slavery Captain of the Shelburne Falls Co undertook with Major Marsh to back him to drive all the Contraband out of camp, he came to me and I had quite a blow up with him. Major Marsh took the Regiment off the camp to drill yesterday while they were gone Capt Miller searched the camp for niggers, but did not find any, this morning they are all here again, this morning placards were found posted around the camp threatening direful things if they persisted in driving them off, which is a most foolish thing, but the men did not come down here to oppress

Niggers and they are not quite brutes yet, as some of their officers are. I have nothing to do with any of the trouble except that I refuse to order off my own servant, in this I am not alone, as Capt Walkly of the Westfield Co has done the same thing, the Officers are divided into two parties on the question, and most bitter and rancorous feelings have been excited which will never be allayed. I do not know how it will all end but I should not be all surprised if they made a fuss about it and should prefer charges against me, Capt Parsons, Lieut Weatherill, the Adjutant, Capt Walkley, Capt Lombard, Lieut Shurtleff, + our one or two others hold the same opinion that I do in the matter. I should hate to have to leave now just as the Regiment is going into active service, but I never will be instrumental in returning a slave to his master in any way shape or manner, I'll die first. Major Marsh well knows that the slaves masters are waiting outside of camp ready to snap them up, and it is inhuman to drive them into their hands, if you could have seen strong men crying like children, at the very thought as I did yesterday you would not blame me for standing out about it nor can one blame the men for showing sympathy for them, for they are from Massachusetts and are entirely unused to such scenes, and cannot recognize this property in human flesh and blood.

DOCUMENT 7

Source: John Dooley, Passages from a Journal (1863)

I tell you, there is no romance in making one of these charges. You might think so from reading 'Charlies O'Malley,' that prodigy of valour, or in reading of any other gallant knight who would as little think of riding over gunners and such like as they would of eating a dozen oysters. But when you rise to your feet as we did today, I tell you the enthusiasm of ardent breasts in many cases ain't there, and instead of burning to avenge the insults of our country, families and altars and firesides, and the thought is most frequently, Oh. if I could just come out of this charge safely how thankful would I be!

ANSWERS AND EXPLANATIONS

Multiple-Choice Questions

■ **1. (E) is correct.** Each nation blamed the other for the breakup of the Union. Each president faced the challenging task of building and maintaining national unity. Each region scorned each other and boasted of their superiority. But the most basic similarity was not apparent: both sides were unprepared for the ordeal that lay ahead.

■ **2. (D) is correct.** The South believed they could win independence as America was able to do in the Revolutionary War because the North would have to invade. Their troops were more experienced than those of the North. The South believed "King Cotton's, economic power would support their effort. Finally, more than a quarter of all the regular army officers chose to side with the South.

■ **3. (B) is correct.** Lincoln actively directed military policy because he realized that a civil war presented problems different than those of a foreign war of conquest. Lincoln wanted above all to persuade the South to rejoin the Union, and his very military order was dictated by the hope of eventual reconciliation—hence his cautiousness, and his acute sense of the role of public opinion.

■ **4. (A) is correct.** Although Southerners had been certain that King Cotton would gain them European support, they were wrong. British public opinion, which had strongly supported the abolition of slavery within the British Empire in the 1830s, would not now countenance the recognition of a new nation based on slavery. British cotton manufacturers found economic alternatives, first using up their backlog of southern cotton and then turning to Egypt and India for new supplies.

5. (E) is correct. Perhaps the greatest southern failure was in the area of finances. At first, the Confederate government tried to raise money from the states, but governors refused new taxes. Heavy borrowing and the printing of great sums of paper money produced runaway inflation. Inflation, in turn, caused incalculable damage to morale and prospects for unity.

6. (E) is correct. Lincoln was acutely aware of divided northern opinions about slavery. His decree after the Union victory at Antietam increased the pressure on the South by directly linking the slave system to the war effort. The final Emancipation Proclamation specifically exempted slaves in the border states so that Lincoln would not lose the support of conservatives. Lincoln's purpose was to meet the abolitionist demand for a war against slavery while not losing the support of conservatives.

7. (E) is correct. After Sherman captured Atlanta jubilation swept through the North. Lincoln won the election with 55 percent of the popular vote. Seventy-eight percent of the soldiers voted for him rather than their former commander General George McClellan.

8. (B) is correct. In addition to supplies, there was also an urgent need for skilled nurses to care for wounded and convalescent soldiers. Nursing within a family context was widely considered to be women's work. Caring for sick family members was a key domestic responsibility of women, and most had considerable experience with it. But taking care of strange men in hospitals was another thing. Under the pressure of wartime necessity, and over the objections of most army doctors—who resented the challenge to their authority from people no different than their daughters or wives—women became army nurses. Hospital nursing, previously considered a job only disreputable women would undertake, now became a suitable vocation for middle-class women.

9. (B) is correct. Sherman's military purpose was to tighten the noose around Robert E. Lee's army in northern Virginia by cutting off Mississippi, Alabama, and Georgia from the rest of the Confederacy. But his second purpose, openly stated, was to make the people of the south horribly sick of war. Accordingly, he told his men to seize, burn, or destroy everything in their path (but, significantly, not to harm civilians).

10. (E) is correct. Grant devised a plan of strangulation and annihilation. While he took on Lee in northern Virginia he sent General Sherman to defeat the Army of Tennessee. Both Grant and Sherman exemplified the new kind of warfare. They aimed to inflict maximum damage on the fabric of southern life, hoping that the South would choose to surrender rather than face total destruction. The decision to broaden the war so that it directly affected civilians was new in American military history, and prefigured the total wars of the twentieth century.

Document-Based Question

Describe some of the justifications that Confederates used for secession and for their loyalty to the Confederacy over the Union.

The Southerners did not perceive themselves as rebels. They viewed secession as legal, and considered themselves the defenders of their homeland against northern aggression. In their eyes, the Civil War was fought in order to defend their homes and their way of life, especially the "peculiar institution" of slavery.

The Confederacy viewed itself as the rightful heir to the legacy of the Founding Fathers of the United States. Those first 13 separate colonies had bound themselves together for their mutual gain, but not in order to give up their individual liberty. The body that oversaw this confederation of states, the federal government, was not to impose its will onto individual states. The Union had overstepped its bounds, and as such the South had both the right and obligation to secede (**DOCUMENT 1**).

Not only had the Union taken liberties with the southern states, but it also defied nature by allowing black people to live as freemen. The Confederate constitution enshrined the enslavement of the black population and presented it as a founding principle of the nation. The Union rejected this principle, and as a consequence the South had to secede (**DOCUMENT 2**).

Though the enslavement of blacks was one of pillars on which southern society rested, not every Southerner thought it good, or just. There were those who saw the violence inherent in the system and denounced it, if only privately (**DOCUMENT 5**). There was also dissention on the question of slavery in the Union ranks. Not every northern soldier opposed slavery, though many did (**DOCUMENT 6**).

Still, even those who opposed slavery had reason to fight for the South. Even some who had served in the Federal Army before secession, and may have sympathized with the Union, came back and enlisted. They could not fight against their friends and family and had more loyalty to their home states than to the federal government (**DOCUMENT 3**). The view that the North was the aggressor in the war was a powerful one. As it was mostly fought on southern soil, the Confederates saw Union soldiers moving through their land, and looting their farms and cities. The Confederate Army was heroic, fighting off the barbarous northern threat (**DOCUMENT 4**).

Ultimately, of course, the war was long and bloody. By the end, though they maintained the justice of their cause, it was very difficult to see any glory in battle (**DOCUMENT 7**). They were able to fight on only because they believed themselves to be right.

CHAPTER 17

Reconstruction, 1863–1877

This chapter treats the Reconstruction Era as a conflict in three dimensions. The first dimension involved who was to conduct it, the executive or the legislative branch. This led to political battles between Johnson and the Radical Republicans. The second dimension was between Radical Republicans and a South still dominated by a planter elite that refused to be reconstructed. The third dimension of conflict was between black and white identified people of all social backgrounds, with the whites trying to diminish any gains of the former slaves by enacting black codes and condoning violence by groups such as the Ku Klux Klan. Eventually, Reconstruction would fail because the Radical Republicans lacked the political power and the will to carry on the struggle, and because the Republican Party became closely identified with northern business interests that cared little for the needs of African Americans, finding it materially profitable to ally themselves with the old planter elite. A disputed election in 1877 ended in a convoluted political compromise that allowed Republican Rutherford Hayes to become president by promising to withdraw federal troops from the South.

The Politics of Reconstruction

The end of the Civil War answered some questions about the nation's future, but raised serious issues about dealing with the South and the 4 million ex-slaves. Disagreement arose between the plans of presidents Lincoln and Johnson versus those of Congress. The Radical Republicans succeeded in implementing their program, including constitutional amendments to guarantee the rights of African Americans.

The Meaning of Freedom

The end of slavery created new opportunities and new challenges for African Americans. The first impulse was to move freely about the country. It soon gave way to attempts to build new communities to accommodate their new status and conditions. Family, churches, and schools served as cornerstones of the new communities, but economic realities of the postwar South severely limited job options. The first attempts to build political power bases also occurred.

Southern Politics and Society

Republicans constituted a minority in the South and faced great challenges in developing the party. Issues also arose over attempts to reconstruct the South and also stimulated a strong conservative Democratic resistance that eventually redeemed state governments from Republican rule. A variety of factors plagued attempts to build a "New South" following northern economic trends.

Reconstructing the North

Following the Civil War, the northern economy followed its path of industrialization and large corporations. The spearhead of development was railroad construction. Economic growth influenced Republicans to ally with businesses, neglecting Radical Republican causes. The depression of 1873 caused great distress and increased tension between labor and capital. Scandals and corruption hurt Republicans in the 1876 election where a stalemate was avoided by a compromise that ended Reconstruction.

and capital. Scandals and corruption hurt Republicans in the 1876 election where a stalemate was avoided by a compromise that ended Reconstruction.

Multiple-Choice Questions

1. Lincoln's Reconstruction program was based on
   (A) punishing the South as much as possible.
   (B) confiscating all southern wealth for the federal government.
   (C) bringing the seceding states back quickly and generously.
   (D) destroying the South's capacity to ever wage war again.
   (E) achieving a fundamental transformation of southern society.

2. Throughout his political career, Andrew Johnson had championed
   (A) African Americans.
   (B) Whig-Republican principles.
   (C) the planter elite.
   (D) Native Americans.
   (E) Yeoman farmers.

3. The "black codes" were
   (A) local constitutions drawn up by freedman to protect themselves.
   (B) federal military enforced rules limiting white violence.
   (C) early attempts state-by-state promoting civil rights.
   (D) the plan to integrate freedmen into society.
   (E) southern laws designed to restrict the freedom of black laborers.

4. In general, freed African Americans in the late 1860s were
   (A) more interested in jobs than politics.
   (B) generally apathetic about political activity.
   (C) highly involved in political activity.
   (D) inching toward the Democratic Party.
   (E) prevented from being too active by dominant Republicans.

5. The Ku Klux Klan Act of 1871
   (A) made it a crime to belong to the Klan.
   (B) set up a police force within the Freedman's Bureau.
   (C) enforced the Civil Rights Act but was almost totally ineffective.
   (D) put an end to the Klan activity.
   (E) made violent infringement of civil rights a federal crime.

6. Which of the following was NOT true of sharecropping in the 1860s?
   (A) It was the dominant form of working the land.
   (B) It stabilized the workforce for planters.
   (C) It offered a way around the shortage of cash and credit that plagued the South.
   (D) Large plantations were broken into family-size farms.
   (E) African Americans welcomed the opportunity that sharecropping presented.

7. Credit Mobilier was an example of
   (A) a large transcontinental railroad system.
   (B) state banking system in the West.
   (C) corruption in railroad promotion.
   (D) the rise of credit extended to southern businesses to get them off their feet.
   (E) government largesse to mining companies.

8. An electoral crisis developed in the Election of 1876 as a result of
   (A) the assassination of the Democratic nominee.
   (B) scandal related to both nominees.
   (C) widespread voter fraud.
   (D) a discrepancy between the popular and electoral votes.
   (E) disputed electoral returns from several states.

9. Which one of the following happened in 1870?
   (A) Suffragists split into moderate and radical groups.
   (B) President Johnson is impeached by the House.
   (C) The "Tweed Ring" is exposed.
   (D) Federal troops are withdrawn from the South.
   (E) The Fifteenth Amendment is ratified but not enforced.

10. At the beginning of Reconstruction, the South was divided into five
    (A) military districts.
    (B) railroad divisions.
    (C) federal government divisions.
    (D) civil rights areas.
    (E) appeals courts districts.

Document-Based Question

Discuss the living conditions of freed blacks in the Reconstruction Era South.

DOCUMENT 1

Source: "Address from the Colored Citizens of Norfolk, Virginia, to the People of the United States" (1865)

We believe our present position is by no means so well understood among the loyal masses of the country, otherwise there would be no delay in granting us the express relief which the nature of the case demands. It must not be forgotten that it is the general assumption, in the South, that the effects of the immortal Emancipation Proclamation of President Lincoln go no further than the emancipation of the Negroes then in slavery, and that it is only constructively even, that that Proclamation can be said, in any legal sense, to have abolished slavery, and even the late constitutional amendment, if duly ratified, can go no further; neither touch, nor can touch, the slave codes of the various southern States, and the laws respecting free people of color consequent therefrom, which, having been passed before the act of secession, are presumed to have lost none of their vitality, but exist, as a convenient engine for our oppression, until repealed by special acts of the State legislature. By these laws, in many of the southern States, it is still a crime for colored men to learn or be taught to read, and their children are doomed to ignorance; there is no provision for insuring the legality of our marriages; we have no right to hold real estate; the public streets and the exercise of our ordinary occupations are forbidden us unless we can produce passes from our employers, or licenses from certain officials; in some States the whole free Negro population is legally liable to exile from the place of its birth, for no crime but that of color; we have no means of legally making or enforcing contracts of any description; we have no right to testify before the courts in any case in which a white man is one of the parties to the suit, we are taxed without representation, and, in short, so far as legal safeguards of our rights are concerned, we are defenceless before our enemies. While this is our position as regards our legal status, before the State laws, we are still more unfortunately situated as regards our late masters. The people of the North, owing to the greater interest excited by war, have heard little or nothing, for the past four years, of the blasphemous and horrible theories formerly propounded for the defence and glorification of human slavery, in the press, the pulpit and legislatures of the southern States; but, though they may have forgotten them, let them be assured that these doctrines have by no means faded from the minds of the people of the South; they cling to these delusions still, and only hug them closer for their recent defeat. Worse than all, they have returned to their homes, with all their old pride and contempt for the Negro transformed into bitter hate for the new-made freeman, who aspires for the suppression of their rebellion.

DOCUMENT 2

Source: Carl Schurz, Report on the Condition of the South (1865)

In which direction will these people be most apt to turn their eyes? Leaving the prejudice of race out of the question, from early youth they have been acquainted with but one system of labor, and with that one system they have been in the habit of identifying all their interests. They know of no way to help themselves but the one they are accustomed to. Another system of labor is presented to them, which, however, owing to circumstances which they do not appreciate, appears at first in an unpromising light. To try it they consider an experiment which they cannot afford to make while their wants are urgent. They have not reasoned calmly enough to convince themselves that the trial must be made. It is, indeed, not wonderful that, under such circumstances, they should study, not how to introduce and develop free labor, but how to avoid its introduction, and how to return as much and as quickly as possible to something like the old order of things. Nor is it wonderful that such studies should find an expression in their attempts at legislation. But the circumstance that this tendency is natural does not render it less dangerous and objectionable. The practical question presents itself: Is the immediate restoration of the late rebel States to absolute self-control so necessary that it must be done even at the risk of endangering one of the great results of the war, and of bringing on in those States insurrection or anarchy, or would it not be better to postpone that restoration until such dangers are passed? If, as long as the change from slavery to free labor is known to the southern people only by its destructive results, these people must be expected to throw obstacles in its way, would it not seem necessary that the movement of social "reconstruction" be kept in the right channel by the hand of the power which originated the change, until that change can have disclosed some of its beneficial effects?

DOCUMENT 3

Source: Clinton B. Fisk, Plain Counsels for Freedmen (1865)

I come to speak to you this evening about work; yes, work, good, honest, hard work. Do not turn away, and say you will not hear me,-that you know all about it, and that it is not a good subject for a lecture.

Listen! The very first verse of the Holy Bible tells us that God is a worker,-that in six days he made all this great world on which we dwell, and the sun and moon and stars.

All the holy angels in heaven are very busy. They go forth to do the will of the Great Being, and find their greatest bliss in action.

Good and great men are all hard workers. And do you know what it is that makes a free state so rich and strong? It is, above all things save God's blessing, patient, honest work.

There is nothing degrading in free labor,-nay, it is most honorable. Why, when God placed Adam and Eve in the garden of Eden, before either of them had ever done any wrong thing, and while they were as pure as the angels, he made gardeners of them. He required them to dress the garden and keep it nice and in good condition.

The blessed Saviour himself worked at the bench, at the carpenter's trade, until he was about thirty years of age.

And yet, some very silly people are above work,-are ashamed to have hard hands,-and do their best to get through the world without honest toil.

But this was not the case with Abraham Lincoln, the man who wrote the Proclamation of Emancipation. He used the hoe, the ax, and the maul, cleared ground, and fenced it with the rails he had split, and was ready to turn his hands to any honest work.

I know that it is quite natural that you should associate work with slavery, and freedom with idleness, because you have seen slaves working all their lives, and free people doing little or nothing. And I should not blame you if you should ask, "What have we gained by freedom, if we are to work, work, work!"

Now, let me explain. A slave works all his life for others. A free man works for himself,- that is, he gets pay for his labor; and if he saves what he earns and manages well, he can get on so well that he may spend the afternoon of his life in his own pleasant home, and never want for any thing. . .

DOCUMENT 4

Source: Mississippi Black Code (1865)

Sec. 6. Be it further enacted, That all contracts for labor made with freedmen, free Negroes, and mulattoes for a longer period than one month shall be in writing and in duplicate, attested and read to said freedman, free Negro, or mulatto, by a beat, city or county officers, or two disinterested white persons of the country in which the labor is to be performed, of which each party shall have one; and said contracts shall be taken and held as entire contracts, and if the laborer shall quit the service of the employer, before expiration of his term of service, without good cause, he shall forfeit his wages for that year, up to the time of quitting.

DOCUMENT 5

The Memphis Riot (1866)

Source: The Freedmen's Bureau Online, Records of the Assistant Commissioner for the State of Tennessee, Bureau of Refugees, Freedmen, and Abandoned Lands, 1865–1869. National Archives Microfilm Publication M999, roll 34 "Reports of Outrages, Riots and Murders, Jan. 15, 1866–Aug. 12, 1868." http://www.freedmensbureau.com/tennessee/outrages/memphisriot.htm

Report of an investigation of the cause, origin, and results of the late riots in the city of Memphis made by Col. Charles F. Johnson, Inspector General States of Ky. and Tennessee and Major T. W. Gilbreth, A. D. C. to Maj. Genl. Howard, Commissioner Bureau R. F. & A. Lands.

The remote cause of the riot as it appears to us is a bitterness of feeling which has always existed between the low whites & blacks, both of whom have long advanced rival claims for superiority, both being as degraded as human beings can possibly be.

In addition to this general feeling of hostility there was an especial hatred among the city police for the Colored Soldiers, who were stationed here for a long time and had recently been discharged from the service of the U.S., which was most cordially reciprocated by the soldiers.

This has frequently resulted in minor affrays not considered worthy of notice by the authorities. These causes combined produced a state of feeling between whites and blacks, which would require only the slightest provocation to bring about an open rupture...

Action of Bvt. Brig. Genl. Ben P. Runkle, Chief Supt., Bureau R.F. and A.L. Sub-District of Memphis

General Runkle was waited upon every hour in the day during the riot, by colored men who begged of him protection for themselves and families, and he, an officer of the Army detailed as Agent of the Freedmen's Bureau was suffered the humiliation of acknowledging his utter inability to protect them in any respect. His personal appearance at the scenes of the riot had no affect on the mob, and he had no troops at his disposal...

The origin and results of the riot may be summed up briefly as follows:

The remote cause was the feeling of bitterness which as always existed between the two classes. The minor affrays which occurred daily, especially between the police and colored persons.

The general tone of certain city papers which in articles that have appeared almost daily, have councilled the low whites to open hostilities with the blacks.

The immediate cause was the collision heretofore spoken of between a few policemen and Negroes on the evening of the 30th of April in which both parties may be equally culpable, followed on the evening of the 1st May by another collision of a more serious nature and subsequently by an indiscriminate attack upon inoffensive colored men and women.

Three Negro churches were burned, also eight (8) school houses, five (5) of which belonged to the United States Government, and about fifty (50) private dwellings, owned, occupied or inhabited by freedmen as homes, and in which they had all their personal property, scanty though it be, yet valuable to them and in many instances containing the hard earnings of months of labor.

DOCUMENT 6

Source: The Fourteenth Amendment (1868)

Sec. 1. All persons born or naturalized in the United States, and subject to the jurisdiction thereof, are citizens of the United States and of the State wherein they reside. No State shall make or enforce any law which shall abridge the privileges or immunities of citizens of the United States; nor shall any State deprive any person of life, liberty, or property, without due process of law; nor deny to any person within its jurisdiction the equal protection of the laws.

Sec. 2. Representatives shall be apportioned among the several States according to their respective numbers, counting the whole number of persons in each State, excluding Indians not taxed. But when the right to vote at any election for the choice of electors for President and Vice President of the United States, Representatives in Congress, the Executive and Judicial officers of a State, or the members of the Legislature thereof, is denied to any of the male inhabitants of such State, being twenty-one years of age, and citizens of the United States, or in any way abridged, except for participation in rebellion, or other crime, the basis of representation therein shall be reduced in the proportion which the number of such male citizens shall bear to the whole number of male citizens twenty-one years of age in such State.

Sec. 3. No person shall be a Senator or Representative in Congress, or elector of President and Vice President, or hold any office, civil or military, under the United States, or under any State, who, having previously taken an oath, as a member of Congress, or as an officer of the United States, or as a member of any State legislature, or as an executive or judicial officer of any State, to support the Constitution of the United States, shall have engaged in insurrection or rebellion against the same, or given aid or comfort to the enemies thereof. But Congress may by a vote of two-thirds of each House, remove such disability.

Sec. 4. The validity of the public debt of the United States, authorized by law, including debts incurred for payment of pensions and bounties for services in suppressing insurrection or rebellion, shall not be questioned. But neither the United States nor any State shall assume or pay any debt or obligation incurred in aid of insurrection or rebellion against the united States, or any claim for the loss or emancipation of any slave; but all such debts, obligations and claims shall be held illegal and void.

Sec. 5. The Congress shall have power to enforce, by appropriate legislation, the provisions of this article.

DOCUMENT 7

Source: James T. Rapier, Testimony Before U.S. Senate Regarding the Agricultural Labor Force in the South (1880)

A. Well, sir, there are several reasons why the colored people desire to emigrate from Alabama; one among them is the poverty of the South. On a large part of it a man cannot make a decent living. Another is their want of school privileges in the State: and there is a majority of the people who believe that they cannot any longer get justice in the courts; and another and the greatest reason is found in the local laws that we have, and which are very oppressive to that class of people in the black belt.

Q. State what some of them are.

A. First, we have only schools about three months in the year, and I suppose I need not say anything more on that head. In reference to the poverty of the soil, 33 to 40 per cent of the lands in Alabama is about all on which a man can make a living.

Q. Do you mean the parts that are subdued?

A. Yes, sir; the arable land. The average is one-third of a bale of cotton to the acre, not making three bales to the hand; and a hundred bushels of corn to the hand, on an average. Then take the price of cotton for the last two years; it has not netted more than $45 to $47.50 to the bale; and I suppose it would not be amiss for me to state something of the plans of working the land in Alabama.

Mr. Vance. It will be very proper.

The Witness. The general plan is that the landlord furnishes the land and the teams and feed for the teams and the implements, for which he draws one half of the crop. I remarked that the three bales of cotton and a hundred bushels of corn is about all that you can make to a hand. We allow in Alabama that much, for that is as much as a man can get out of it, and that is not enough to support his family, including himself and the feed of his family; $95 to $100 is as much as a hand can make, and that is not enough to feed any man in a Christian country. . . .

DOCUMENT 8

Source: A Sharecrop Contract (1882)

To every one applying to rent land upon shares, the following conditions must be read, and agreed to.

To every 30 and 35 acres, I agree to furnish the team, plow, and farming implements, except cotton planters, and I do not agree to furnish a cart to every cropper. The croppers are to have half of the cotton, corn, and fodder (and peas and pumpkins and potatoes if any are planted) if the following conditions are complied with, but-if not-they are to have only two-fifths (2/5). Croppers are to have no part or interest in the cotton seed raised from the crop planted and worked by them. No vine crops of any description, that is, no watermelons, muskmelons, . . . squashes or anything of that kind, except peas and pumpkins, and potatoes, are to be planted in the cotton or corn. All must work under my direction. All plantation work to be done by the croppers. My part of the crop to be housed by them, and the fodder and oats to be hauled and put in the house. All the cotton must be topped about 1st August. If any cropper fails from any cause to save all the fodder from his crop, I am to have enough fodder to make it equal to one-half of the whole if the whole amount of fodder had been saved...

I am to gin & pack all the cotton and charge every cropper an eighteenth of his part, the cropper to furnish his part of the bagging, ties, & twine. The sale of every cropper's part of the cotton to be made by me when and where I choose to sell, and after deducting all they owe me and all sums that I may be responsible for on their accounts, to pay them their half of the net proceeds. Work of every description, particularly the work on fences and ditches, to be done to my satisfaction, and must be done over until I am satisfied that it is done as it should be.

ANSWERS AND EXPLANATIONS

Multiple-Choice Questions

1. **(C) is correct.** Lincoln wanted as soon as possible to get the southern states back in the Union. Lincoln wanted Southerners to get their property back (without slaves) and did not want the South severely punished. Lincoln felt the main part of Reconstruction should be Southerners pledging an allegiance to the United States.

2. **(E) is correct.** Johnson coming from a poor southern background had always championed the yeoman farmers rather than the plantation owners. This led Johnson to be the only Southern politician to side with the Union. This fact made it difficult to understand why Johnson than proceded to punish the South very lightly in his Reconstruction plans.

3. **(E) is correct.** The black codes that were passed by southern state governments included; laws against vagrancy, in which blacks could involuntary be kept on plantations and apprenticeships in which young black males were never paid. The black codes also interfered with the civil rights of blacks; preventing them from owning land, serving on juries or having an interracial marriage.

4. **(C) is correct.** Freed African-Americans became very involved in politics in the late 1960s at many levels. Mass meetings, parades, and petitions demanded civil equality and the right to vote. Statewide conventions in the South concentrated on passing resolutions that united all African Americans. With the First Reconstruction Act of 1867, over 735,000 men registered to vote, under which four-fifths of the eligible voters cast ballots.

5. **(E) is correct.** With the Ku Klux Klan Act of 1871, in addition to federal government intervention under President Grant, the Klan was largely broken and a semblance of law and order was restored. The one place where the federal government had trouble restoring

order was in the western black belt of Alabama, where the Klan still welded considerable power.

6. **(E) is correct.** According to the map concerning sharecropping on page 591, sharecropping is when a person works a piece of land on a plantation in exchange for owning the crop. This became especially prevalent amongst both white and black farmers in the states of Georgia, Alabama, Mississippi, South Carolina, and East Texas during the economic depression of the 1870s.

7. **(C) is correct.** As a way of diverting funds for the building of the Union Pacific Railroad, a group of its stockholders created a dummy business the Credit Mobilier, a construction company. A group of Republican businessmen were given stocks in the company in return for political favors. This was just one of many scandals that rocked the Grant administration.

8. **(D) is correct.** In the election of 1876, there was a heated campaign between Republican Rutherford B. Hayes and Democrat Samuel Tilden. Even though Tilden had more popular and electoral votes than Hayes, he did not have enough electoral votes to officially capture the presidency. The Compromise of 1877 gave Hayes the presidency, while making concessions to the southern states. Dire consequences resulted as the Fourteenth and Fifteenth amendments to the Constitution, in addition to the Civil Rights Act 1866 were effectively nullified.

9. **(E) is correct.** (See Chronology page 598.) In 1870 the fifteenth amendment was ratified into the Constitution. The Amendment stated, "The rights of citizens of the United States should not be denied or abridged on account of race, color or previous condition of servitude." While ratified, it was difficult to enforce down South, where states tried to come up with ways around the amendment such as a poll tax.

10. **(A) is correct.** (See Map page 576.) At the start of Reconstruction the South was divided into five military districts. The districts were made up under the First Reconstruction Act passed over President Johnson's veto. The states would remain under martial law unil they drew up new constitutions that would pledge loyalty to the Union and give universal suffrage to all men.

Document-Based Question

Discuss the living conditions of freed blacks in the Reconstruction Era South.

Though liberated from slavery, the trials of the southern black community were far from over. They were discriminated against, by both private individuals and the state. As they had just been slaves, they had no land of their own and no money to buy it with. These people had a powerful desire to improve their situation, but they received little help from their white neighbors. More often than not, those neighbors went out of their way to hinder the advancement of their former slaves.

In the immediate aftermath of the Civil War, the future was far from certain for recently freed slaves. Though no longer owned by their white neighbors, they had no clear path to success. They were advised to work, and lectured on the value of free labor (**DOCUMENT 3**). Ultimately though, most freed blacks did not end up working for themselves. The majority became sharecroppers on the plantations where they had formerly been slaves. They worked their plots with the owners tools and animals, then gave up the majority of the crop to the owner. If they did not meet their quotas, they were penalized. Though the labor was theirs, they had no control over the sale of crop (**DOCUMENT 8**). With this system of labor in place, some Northerners feared that there would be attempts to reinstate slavery, if not in name then in fact. While the institution no longer existed, there was still a firm belief that blacks were inferior to whites, and consequently belonged in servitude (**DOCUMENT 2**).

Due to this firmly entrenched ideology, blacks remained oppressed in the South (**DOCUMENT 1**). They were legally discriminated against. Many states limited their legal education, did not permit them to vote, and even established labor laws in which whites would have the upper hand (**DOCUMENT 4**). The federal government attempted to prevent this sort of

DOCUMENT 8

Source: A Sharecrop Contract (1882)

To every one applying to rent land upon shares, the following conditions must be read, and agreed to.

To every 30 and 35 acres, I agree to furnish the team, plow, and farming implements, except cotton planters, and I do not agree to furnish a cart to every cropper. The croppers are to have half of the cotton, corn, and fodder (and peas and pumpkins and potatoes if any are planted) if the following conditions are complied with, but-if not-they are to have only two-fifths (2/5). Croppers are to have no part or interest in the cotton seed raised from the crop planted and worked by them. No vine crops of any description, that is, no watermelons, muskmelons, . . . squashes or anything of that kind, except peas and pumpkins, and potatoes, are to be planted in the cotton or corn. All must work under my direction. All plantation work to be done by the croppers. My part of the crop to be housed by them, and the fodder and oats to be hauled and put in the house. All the cotton must be topped about 1st August. If any cropper fails from any cause to save all the fodder from his crop, I am to have enough fodder to make it equal to one-half of the whole if the whole amount of fodder had been saved...

I am to gin & pack all the cotton and charge every cropper an eighteenth of his part, the cropper to furnish his part of the bagging, ties, & twine. The sale of every cropper's part of the cotton to be made by me when and where I choose to sell, and after deducting all they owe me and all sums that I may be responsible for on their accounts, to pay them their half of the net proceeds. Work of every description, particularly the work on fences and ditches, to be done to my satisfaction, and must be done over until I am satisfied that it is done as it should be.

ANSWERS AND EXPLANATIONS

Multiple-Choice Questions

1. (C) is correct. Lincoln wanted as soon as possible to get the southern states back in the Union. Lincoln wanted Southerners to get their property back (without slaves) and did not want the South severely punished. The President also proposed that when the number of any Confederate state's voters who took an oath of allegience reached 10 percent of the number who had ovted in the election of 1860, this group could establish a state government that Lincoln would recognize as legitimate.

2. (E) is correct. Johnson coming from a poor southern background had always championed the yeoman farmers rather than the plantation owners. He was the only Southern politician to side with the Union.

3. (E) is correct. The black codes that were passed by southern state governments included laws against vagrancy, in which blacks could involuntary be kept on plantations and apprenticeships in which young black males were never paid. The black codes also interfered with the civil rights of blacks; preventing them from owning land, serving on juries or having an interracial marriage.

4. (C) is correct. Inclusion, rather than separation, was the objective of early African American political activity. The greatest political activity by African Americans occurred in areas occupied by Union forces during the war. In 1865 and 1866, African Americans throughout the South organized scores of mass meetings, parades, and petitions that demanded civil equality and the right to vote. In the cities, the growing web of churches and fraternal societies helped bolster early efforts at political organization.

With the First Reconstruction Act of 1867, over 735,000 men registered to vote, under which four-fifths of the eligible voters cast ballots.

5. (E) is correct. With the Ku Klux Klan Act of 1871, in addition to federal government intervention under President Grant, the Klan was largely broken and a semblance of law and order was restored.

6. (E) is correct. By the late 1860s, sharecropping had emerged as the dominant form of working the land. Sharecropping represented a compromise between planters and former slaves. Under sharecropping arrangements that were usually very detailed, individual families contracted with landowners to be responsible for a specific plot. Large plantations were thus broken into family-sized farms. Generally, sharecropper families received one-third of the year's crop if the owner furnished implements, seed, and draft animals, or one-half if they provided their own supplies. African Americans preferred sharecropping to gang labor, as it allowed families to set their own hours and tasks and offered freedom from white supervision and control. For planters, the system stabilized the workforce by requiring sharecroppers to remain until the harvest and to employ all family members. It also offered a way around the chronic shortage of cash and credit that plagued the postwar South. Freed people, however, did not aspire to sharecropping.

7. (C) is correct. As a way of diverting funds for the building of the Union Pacific Railroad, a group of its stockholders created a dummy business the Credit Mobilier, a construction company. A group of Republican businessmen were given stocks in the company in return for political favors. This was the worst of many scandals that rocked the Grant administration.

8. (D) is correct. In the election of 1876, there was a heated campaign between Republican Rutherford B. Hayes and Democrat Samuel Tilden. Even though Tilden had more popular and electoral votes than Hayes, he did not have enough electoral votes to officially capture the presidency. The Compromise of 1877 gave Hayes the presidency, while making concessions to the southern states. Concessions to the South effectively nullified the Fourteenth and Fifteenth amendments to the Constitutionand the Civil Rights Act 1866.

9. (E) is correct. In 1870 the fifteenth amendment was ratified into the Constitution. The Amendment stated, "The rights of citizens of the United States should not be denied or abridged on account of race, color or previous condition of servitude." While ratified, it was difficult to enforce down South, where states tried to come up with ways around the amendment such as a poll tax.

10. (A) is correct. (See Map page 576.) At the start of Reconstruction the South was divided into five military districts. The districts were made up under the First Reconstruction Act passed over President Johnson's veto. The states would remain under martial law unil they drew up new constitutions that would pledge loyalty to the Union and give universal suffrage to all men.

Document-Based Question

Discuss the living conditions of freed blacks in the Reconstruction Era South.

Though liberated from slavery, the trials of the southern black community were far from over. They were discriminated against, by both private individuals and the state. As they had just been slaves, they had no land of their own and no money to buy it with. These people had a powerful desire to improve their situation, but they received little help from their white neighbors. More often than not, those neighbors went out of their way to hinder the advancement of their former slaves.

In the immediate aftermath of the Civil War, the future was far from certain for recently freed slaves. Though no longer owned by their white neighbors, they had no clear path to success. They were advised to work, and lectured on the value of free labor (**DOCUMENT 3**). Ultimately though, most freed blacks did not end up working for themselves. The majority became

The Western Landscape

The beauty and grandeur of the western landscape attracted artists and led the United States to set aside huge areas of nature reserves. Legends of the Wild West were fueled by dime novels and shows. Artists and photographers captured western life and Indian culture.

The Transformation of Indian Societies

Government policy attempted to destroy tribal culture and assimilate Indian people into mainstream culture with many negative results. The Ghost Dance represented a last attempt to resist American policies and practices. Throughout the nation, Indian tribes adjusted to their circumstances with mixed results.

Multiple-Choice Questions

1. Sand Creek was the scene of
   (A) an unprovoked massacre of Cheyenne Indians by white civilian "volunteers."
   (B) a bloody battle between the Cheyenne and the Sioux.
   (C) a treaty of friendship between the Cheyenne and the citizens of Colorado.
   (D) an unprovoked massacre of white soldiers by the Sioux.
   (E) an Indian victory over the U.S. 7th Cavalry.

2. The Santa Fe Ring was a group of land spectators, lawyers, and politicians who
   (A) extorted money from the Bureau of Indian Affairs.
   (B) benefited from the Timber Culture Act.
   (C) cheated Mexicanos out of their landholdings.
   (D) conspired to take over New Mexico.
   (E) negotiated the Gadsden Purchase for their railroad route.

3. The Caminetti Act gave the state the power to regulate
   (A) labor.
   (B) indian reservations.
   (C) mines.
   (D) railroads.
   (E) industrial waste.

4. The appearance of groups like Las Gorras Blancas and El Alianzo Hispano-Americano indicated that
   (A) most Mexicanos did not lose status and wages after the Mexican War.
   (B) Anglos were not able to exert influence in the Mexicano community.
   (C) Mexicano and Anglo culture was blending on border areas.
   (D) new literary alliances were being formed in the Mexicano community.
   (E) Mexicanos were challenging the rising Anglo presence.

5. Which one of the following is <u>LEAST</u> descriptive of cowboys in the cattle industry?
   (A) One-fifth to one-third were Indian, Mexican, or African American.
   (B) Most Anglo cowboys came from the North.
   (C) They were seasonal or migrant workers.
   (D) The work was difficult, dangerous and low-paying.
   (E) The camaraderie of cowboys helped them form unions.

6. European immigrants to the Great Plains tended to
   (A) form tight-knit ethnically distinctive communities.
   (B) seek full assimilation into American culture.
   (C) look for secluded areas to form colonies.
   (D) add to the violence and instability of the West.
   (E) settle as individual families isolated on a solitary homestead.

7. The predominant crop of the Great Plains was
   (A) cotton.
   (B) wheat.
   (C) barley.
   (D) rice.
   (E) hay.

8. The FIRST national park in the United States was
   (A) Yosemite.
   (B) Grand Teton.
   (C) Grand Canyon.
   (D) Glacier.
   (E) Yellowstone.

9. The Dawes Act was basically successful in
   (A) establishing Indians as homesteaders.
   (B) undermining tribal sovereignty.
   (C) creating a balance between Anglos and Native Americans.
   (D) reinstating and protecting reservations.
   (E) reaffirming the integrity of Indian cultural institutions.

10. The Timber Culture Act of 1873 was
    (A) favorable to homesteaders.
    (B) successful in restoring forests.
    (C) not very successful but restored some forests.
    (D) enabling to tree diseases.
    (E) helped revive the Great Plains wildlife such as antelope.

Document-Based Question

Many forces contributed to the rapid transformation of the North American West following 1850. Identify, compare, and contrast the various motivations for western settlement and decide which factor was the most decisive in transforming the West.

DOCUMENT 1

DOCUMENT 2

Source: Lydia Allen Rudd, Diary of Westward Travel (1852)

May 14 Just after we started this morning we passed four men dig[g]ing a grave. They were packers. The man that had died was taken sick yesterday noon and died last night. They called it cholera morbus. The corpse lay on the ground a few feet from where they were dig[g]ing. The grave it was a sad sight. . . .

On the bank of the stream waiting to cross, stood a dray with five men harnessed to it bound for California. They must be some of the persevering kind I think. Wanting to go to California more than I do. . . . We passed three more graves this afternoon. . . .

Sept. 5 Traveled eighteen miles today encamped on a slough of powder river poor camp not much grass water nor wood. I am almost dead tonight. I have been sick two or three days with the bowel complaint and am much worse tonight.

Sept. 6 We have not been able to leave this miserable place today. I am not as well as yesterday and no physician to be had. We got a little medicine from a train tonight that has checked the disease some, the first thing that has done me any good.

Sept. 7 . . . I am some better today so much so that they ventured to move me this for the sake of a better camp. Mrs. Girtman is also sick with the same disease. Our cattle are most all of them ailing-there are two more that we expect will die every day. . . .

Oct. 8 started early this morning without any breakfast for the very good reason that we had nothing to eat still three miles from the falls safely landed about eight o'clock tired hungry and with a severe cold from last nights exposure something like civilization here in the shape of three or four houses there is an excuse here for a railroad of a mile and half on which to convey bag[g]age below the falls where they can again take water for the steamboat landing. Harry packed our bag[g]age down the railroad and the rest of us walked the car is drawn across the railroad by a mule and they will car[r]y no persons but sick. We again hired an Indian with his canoe to take us from the falls to the steamboat landing ar[r]ived about sundown a great many emigrants waiting for a chance to leave the steamboat and several flat boats lying ready to start out in the morning encamped on the shore for the night. We have made but eleven miles of travel encamped on the prairie no water for our stock and not much for ourselves.

October 26 . . . we reached Burlington about two o'clock. There is one store one blacksmith shop and three or four dwelling houses. We encamped close by found Mr. Donals in his store an old acquaintance of my husband's. I do not know what we shall yet conclude on doing for the winter. There is no house in town that we can get to winter in. We shall probably stay here tomorrow and by the time know what we are to do for a while at least.

October 27 . . . Our men have been looking around for a house and employment and have been successful for which I feel very thankful. Harry has gone into copartnership with Mr. Donals in the mercantile business and we are to live in the back part of the store for this winter. Henry and Mary are going into Mr. D——house on his farm for the winter one mile from here. Mr. D——will also find him employment if he wants. I expect that we shall not make a claim after all our trouble in getting here on purpose for one. I shall have to be poor and dependent on a man my life time.

DOCUMENT 3

DOCUMENT 4

Source: Horace Greeley, An Overland Journey (1860)

Men and brethen! let us resolve to have a railroad to the Pacific-to have it soon. It will add more to the strength and wealth of our country than would the acquisition of a dozen Cubas. It will prove a bond of union not easily broken, and a new spring to our national industry, prosperity and wealth. It will call new manufactures into existence, and increase the demand for the products of those already existing. It will open new vistas to national and to individual aspiration, and crush out filibusterism by giving a new and wholesome direction to the public mind. My long, fatiguing journey was undertaken in the hope that I might do something toward the early construction of the Pacific Railroad; and I trust that it has not been made wholly in vain.

DOCUMENT 5

Source: Joseph G. McCoy, Historic Sketches of the Cattle Trade of the West and Southwest (1874)

We have in a former paper said that Texan drovers, as a class, were clannish, and easily gulled by promises of high prices for their stock. As an illustration of these statements we cite a certain secret meeting of the drovers held at one of the camps in 1867, whereat they all, after talking the matter over, pledged themselves to hold their cattle for 3 cents per pound gross and to sell none for less. One of the principal arguments used was that their cattle must be worth that price or those Illinoisans would not be expending so much money and labor in preparing facilities for shipping them. To this resolution they adhered persistently, refusing $2.75 per 100 pounds for fully 10,000 head; and afterwards, failing to get their 3 cents on the prairie for their cattle, shipped them to Chicago on their own account and sold them there at $2.25 to $2.50 per 100 pounds; and out of that paid a freight of $150 per car, realizing from $10 to $15 per head less than they had haughtily refused upon the prairie. Some of them refused to accept these prices and packed their cattle upon their own account. Their disappointment and chagrin at their failure to force a buyer to pay 3 cents per pound for their cattle was great and bitter, but their refusal to accept the offer of 23/4 cents per pound was great good fortune to the would-be buyers, for at that price $100,000 would have been lost on 10,000 head of cattle. An attempt was made the following year to form a combination to put up prices; but a burnt child dreads the fire, and the attempted combination failed, and every drover looked out sharply for himself.

DOCUMENT 6

Source: Helen Hunt Jackson, from A Century of Dishonor (1881)

There is not among these three hundred bands of Indians one which has not suffered cruelly at the hands either of the Government or of white settlers. The poorer, the more insignificant, the more helpless the band, the more certain the cruelty and outrage to which they have been subjected. This is especially true of the bands on the Pacific slope. These Indians found themselves of a sudden surrounded by and caught up in the great influx of gold-seeking settlers, as helpless creatures on a shore are caught up in a tidal wave. There was not time for the Government to make treaties; not even time for communities to make laws. The tale of the wrongs, the oppressions, the murders of the Pacific-slope Indians in the last thirty years would be a volume by itself, and is too monstrous to be believed.

It makes little difference, however, where one opens the record of the history of the Indians; every page and every year has its dark stain. The story of one tribe is the story of all, varied only differences of time and place; but neither time nor place makes any difference in the main facts. Colorado is as greedy and unjust in 1880 as was Georgia in 1830, and Ohio in 1795; and the United States Government breaks promises now as deftly as then, and with an added ingenuity from long practice.

One of its strongest supports in so doing is the wide-spread sentiment among the people of dislike to the Indian, of impatience with his presence as a "barrier to civilization" and distrust of it as a possible danger. The old tales of the frontier life, with its horrors of Indian warfare, have gradually, by two or three generations' telling, produced in the average mind something like an hereditary instinct of questioning and unreasoning aversion which it is almost impossible to dislodge or soften. . . .

DOCUMENT 7

Source: Benjamin Harrison, Report on Wounded Knee Massacre and the Decrease in Indian Land Acreage (1891)

Since March 4, 1889, about 23,000,000 acres have been separated from Indian reservations and added to the public domain for the use of those who desired to secure free homes under our beneficent laws. It is difficult to estimate the increase of wealth which will result from the conversion of these waste lands into farms, but it is more difficult to estimate the betterment which will result to the families that have found renewed hope and courage in the ownership of a home and the assurance of a comfortable subsistence under free and healthful conditions. It is also gratifying to be able to feel, as we may, that this work has proceeded upon lines of justice toward the Indian, and that he may now, if he will, secure to himself the good influences of a settled habitation, the fruits of industry, and the security of citizenship.

Multiple-Choice Questions

1. **(A) is correct.** Colorado territorial governor John Evans encouraged white civilians, the Colorado Volunteers, to stage raids through Cheyenne campgrounds. Seeking protection, Chief Black Kettle brought a band of 800 Cheyenne to a U.S. fort and received orders to set up camp at Sand Creek. Several weeks later, the Colorado Volunteers and soldiers attacked. A disorderly group of 700 men, many of them drunk, slaughtered 105 Cheyenne women and children and 28 men.

2. **(C) is correct.** Although the Treaty of Guadalupe Hidalgo stated that all Hispanics were formally guaranteed citizenship and the "free enjoyment of their liberty and property," local "Anglos" (as the Mexicans called white Americans) often violated these provisions and, through fraud or coercion, took control of the land. The Santa Fe Ring stole millions of acres from the public domain and grabbed over 80 percent of the Mexicano landholdings in New Mexico alone.

3. **(C) is correct.** In 1893, Congress finally passed the Caminetti Act, giving the state the power to regulate the mines. (The act also created the Sacramento River Commission, which began to replace free-flowing rivers with canals and dams.) Underground mining continued unregulated, using up whole forests for timbers and filling the air with dangerous, sulfurous smoke.

4. **(E) is correct.** As late as the 1880s, Las Gorras Blancas, a band of agrarian rebels in New Mexico, were destroying railroad ties and farm machines and posting demands for justice on fences of the new Anglo farms and ranches. In 1890, Las Gorras turned from social banditry to political organization. Along similar lines, *El Aliazno Hispano-Americano* was formed "to protect and fight for the rights of Spanish Americans" through political action.

5. **(B) is correct.** Cowboys were usually paid in one lump sum at the end of the drive. Scurvy was a widespread ailment and the cowboys worked without protection from rain or hail, and severe dust storms could cause temporary blindness. Aided by the legendary camaraderie fostered in the otherwise desolate conditions of the long drive, cowboys, along with miners, were among the first western workers to organize against employers. Like other parts of the West, the cattle range was ethnically diverse. Between one-fifth and one-third of all workers were Indian, Mexican, or African American.

6. **(A) is correct.** Having traveled the huge distance with kin or members of their Old World villages, immigrants tended to form tight-knit communities on the Great Plains. Many married within their own group. Like many Mexicanos in the Southwest, several immigrant groups retained their languages into the twentieth century, usually by sponsoring parochial school systems and publishing their own newspapers.

7. **(B) is correct.** Fields of wheat dominated the local environs.

8. **(E) is correct.** In 1864, Congress passed the Yosemite Act, which placed the spectacular cliffs and giant sequoias under the management of the state of California. In 1872, Congress named Yellowstone the first national park. Yosemite and Sequoia in California, Crater Lake in Oregon, Mount Rainier in Washington, and Glacier in Montana all became national parks between 1890 and 1910.

9. **(B) is correct.** The Dawes Severalty Act, passed by Congress in 1887, established federal policy for decades to come. The act allowed the president to distribute land, not to tribes, but to individuals legally "severed" from their tribes. Those individuals who accepted the land allotment of 160 acres and agreed to allow the government to sell unallotted tribal lands could petition to become citizens of the United States. The Dawes Act successfully undermined tribal sovereignty but offered little compensation. Indian religions and sacred ceremonies were banned, the telling of legends and myths forbidden, and shaman and medicine men imprisoned or exiled for continuing traditional practices.

■ **10. (C) is correct.** In 1873, Congress passed the Timber Culture Act, which allotted homesteaders an additional 160 acres of land in return for planting and cultivating 40 acres of trees. Because residence was not required, and because tree planting could not be assessed for at least 13 years, speculators filed for several claims at once, then turned around and sold the land without having planted a single tree. Although some forests were restored, neither the weather nor the soil improved.

Document-Based Question

Many forces contributed to the rapid transformation of the North American West following 1850. Identify, compare and contrast the various motivations for western settlement and decide which factor was the most decisive in transforming the West.

From 1850 to 1900, the North American West underwent a series of changes that completely transformed that area from a rural, unsettled and vast landscape into a settled region bustling with commercial and industrial energy **(DOCUMENT 1)**. It also became a land dominated by Americans of European ancestry, as the expansion of the United States, aided by military strength, defeated the traditional Native American population of the region. Various motivations for western settlement fostered these changes. While many traveled west with the hope that they could share in the fabulous gold and silver claims of some successful pioneers, many had more modest dreams, hoping to purchase or claim land for themselves and their families and thereby gain a measure of economic independence **(DOCUMENT 2)**. Yet others yearned for more independence from the power of state and federal governments over their beliefs and values **(DOCUMENT 3)**. At the root of these motives, some believe, is a specific desire for a more individualized experience of freedom, helping to establish the West's image as a home for rugged individualists.

However, many larger forces expanded westward in order to take advantage of the resources of the area. Industry viewed the wealth of natural resources as a valuable boon to trade, and soon the expansion of the railroad into the West was viewed as a necessary step in the ongoing development of the American economy **(DOCUMENT 4)**. Similarly, new and old Westerners alike participated in the transformation of the West as they developed regionally specific industries and markets **(DOCUMENT 5)**. However, western settlers and expansionists believed that the Native Americans were an impediment to the achievement of their goals. In addition, many Americans viewed the native tribes as examples of "uncivilized" peoples who would prevent the achievement of a greater United States **(DOCUMENT 7)**. The ongoing conflict between the United States and the native peoples of the land quickly became a losing battle for the Native Americans, as the United States marshaled its forces to defeat them in the name of national wealth and power **(DOCUMENT 6)**.

CHAPTER 19

The Incorporation of America, 1865–1900

This chapter covers the industrialization of America from 1865 to 1900. This transformation was based on railroad expansion, which in turn encouraged other industries as well as the development of large-scale corporations. Labor unions organized on a national level for the first time to counter the size and power of the employers, but with only mixed success. America also continued to urbanize, with rapid unplanned growth of the cities that, among other things, produced residential patterns reflecting social class divisions. The South tried to participate in the growth under the motto of the "New South," but the results generally reinforced old social and economic patterns. The "Gospel of Wealth," conceived by industrial giant Andrew Carnegie, and similar ideas reinforced differences between the rising middle class and the factory workers, but leisure-time activities such as sports added to national unity and a distinctive American identity.

The Rise of Industry, The Triumph of Business

Advances in technology, mechanization, and an expanded market for goods contributed to new strategies of business organization. The trend was toward large corporations and a philosophy of wealth rationalized the methods used by business leaders to secure their wealth.

Labor in the Age of Big Business

Economic development profoundly affected the conditions of employment and work. While the number of jobs expanded, discrimination limited the opportunities of certain groups. Seeking improvement, workers formed unions that provided a variety of services and representation, with mixed results.

The New South

The movement to promote industrialization and the exploitation of resources of the South achieved limited success. Labor opportunities largely followed racial lines and were not affected by European immigration. The Piedmont was most affected by the New South movement; its industry was organized around mill towns.

The Industrial City

Industrialization fueled the growth of cities that were populated by migrants from rural areas and immigrants. Architectural and transportation advances influenced urban development. Rapid, expansive growth caused environmental and health problems that were ameliorated by medical discoveries and public-health campaigns.

The Rise of Consumer Society

Between approximately 1875 and 1900, the standard of living rose, though unevenly. The newly rich industrialists formed a new class based on wealth and conspicuous consumption. At the same time, new middle and working classes emerged that also developed their own values and cultures.

Cultures in Conflict, Culture in Common

The growth of cities and industries led to the expansion of the education system, the development of urban parks, and the increased appeal of popular entertainment and spectator sports. Different values and behavior created tensions among classes, but changes were made to accommodate the diversity of the population.

Multiple-Choice Questions

1. By 1900, the United States was _____ in the world in terms of productivity.
   (A) first
   (B) third
   (C) fourth
   (D) tenth
   (E) twelfth

2. Horizontal combinations like the Standard Oil trust
   (A) helped to raise workers' wages.
   (B) served to limit production.
   (C) promoted free-market capitalism.
   (D) allowed for unlimited competition.
   (E) secured control over output and prices.

3. The "Gospel of Wealth"
   (A) justified the ruthless behaviors of entrepreneurs like Rockefeller.
   (B) held that "greed is good."
   (C) held that God always helps the poor.
   (D) held that God provides wealth and that individual initiative counts for little.
   (E) advocated a strong welfare system.

4. The Chinese Exclusion Act involved all of the following EXCEPT
   (A) prohibited Chinese children from attending public schools.
   (B) suspended Chinese immigration.
   (C) limited the civil rights of resident Chinese.
   (D) forbade Chinese naturalization.
   (E) it did all of these things.

5. The Haymarket Square incident in 1886
   (A) helped fill the ranks of the Knights of Labor and the AFL.
   (B) succeeded in obtaining more support for the eight-hour day.

   (C) weakened the existing wage system.
   (D) weakened labor unions particularly the Knights of Labor.
   (E) helped create the IWW.

6. By 1890, approximately what fraction of the population lived in cities?
   (A) one-third
   (B) one-half
   (C) three-fifths
   (D) two-thirds
   (E) three-fourths

7. The proponents of a "New South" envisioned the South as
   (A) a vast agrarian area supplying needed cash crops.
   (B) an area of sturdy yeoman farmers.
   (C) the primary supplier of raw materials to northern industry.
   (D) an area that promoted industrial development and welcomed northern investors.
   (E) a bucolic mix of agriculture and industry moving towards self-sufficiency.

8. African-American workers in the New South
   (A) were strictly segregated.
   (B) made the same wages as their white counterparts.
   (C) were guaranteed equal opportunity by law.
   (D) benefited as new opportunities opened for unskilled labor.
   (E) were attracted to the skilled trades.

9. All of the following were considered lower-class pastimes in the Gilded Age EXCEPT
   (A) bicycling.
   (B) public parks.
   (C) baseball.
   (D) ragtime music.
   (E) vaudeville.

10. More common ground could be found between members of the middle and working class with
    (A) urban park systems.
    (B) public high school education.
    (C) speakeasies.
    (D) religious events.
    (E) ragtime and baseball.

Document-Based Question

Analyze the effect that the rise of industry had on the distribution of wealth in the United States.

DOCUMENT 1

Source: Progress and Poverty (1879)

The poverty which in the midst of abundance pinches and embrutes men, and all the manifold evils which flow from it, spring from a denial of justice. In permitting the monopolization of the opportunities which nature freely offers to all, we have ignored the fundamental law of justice—for, so far as we can see, when we view things upon a large scale, justice seems to be the supreme law of the universe. But by sweeping away this injustice and asserting the rights of all men to natural opportunities, we shall conform ourselves to the law—we shall remove the great cause of unnatural inequality in the distribution of wealth and power; we shall abolish poverty; tame the ruthless passions of greed; dry up the springs of vice and misery; light in dark places the lamp of knowledge; give new vigor to invention and a fresh impulse to discovery; substitute political strength for political weakness; and make tyranny and anarchy impossible.

DOCUMENT 2

Source: Charles Loring Brace, "The Life of the Street Rats" (1872)

Seventeen years ago, my attention had been called to the extraordinarily degraded condition of the children in a district lying on the west side of the city, between Seventeenth and Nineteenth Streets, and the Seventh and Tenth Avenues. A certain block, called "Misery Row," in Tenth Avenue, was the main seed-bed of crime and poverty in the quarter, and was also invariably a "fever-nest." Here the poor obtained wretched rooms at a comparatively low rent; these they sub-let, and thus, in little, crowded, close tenements, were herded men, women and children of all ages. The parents were invariably given to hard drinking, and the children were sent out to beg or to steal. Besides them, other children, who were orphans, or who had run away from drunkards' homes, or had been working on the canal-boats that discharged on the docks near by, drifted into the quarter, as if attracted by the atmosphere of crime and laziness that prevailed in the neighborhood. These slept around the breweries of the ward, or on the hay-barges, or in the old sheds of Eighteenth and Nineteenth Streets. They were mere children, and kept life together by all sorts of street-jobs-helping the brewery laborers, blackening boots, sweeping sidewalks, "smashing baggages" (as they called it), and the like. Herding together, they soon began to form an unconscious society for vagrancy and idleness. Finding that work brought but poor pay, they tried shorter roads to getting money by petty [sic] thefts, in which they were very adroit. Even if they earned a considerable sum by a lucky day's job, they quickly spent it in gambling, or for some folly.

DOCUMENT 3

Source: Address by George Engel, Condemned Haymarket Anarchist (1886)

Of what does my crime consist?

That I have labored to bring about a system of society by which it is impossible for one to hoard millions, through the improvements in machinery, while the great masses sink to degradation and misery. As water and air are free to all, so should the inventions of scientific men be applied for the benefit of all. The statute laws we have are in opposition to the laws of nature, in that they rob the great masses of their rights "to life, liberty, and the pursuit of happiness."

I am too much a man of feeling not to battle against the societary conditions of today. Every considerate person must combat a system which makes it possible for the individual to rake and hoard millions in a few years, while, on the other side, thousands become tramps and beggars.

Is it to be wondered at that under such circumstances men arise, who strive and struggle to create other conditions, where the humane humanity shall take precedence of all other considerations. This is the aim of Socialism, and to this I joyfully subscribe.

DOCUMENT 4

Source: Edward Bellamy, from Looking Backward (1888)

"As no such thing as the labor question is known nowadays," replied Dr. Leete, "and there is no way in which it could arise, I suppose we may claim to have solved it. . . . The solution came as the result of a process of industrial evolution which could not have terminated otherwise. All that society had to do was to recognize and cooperate with that evolution, when its tendency had become unmistakable." . . .

"Meanwhile, without being in the smallest degree checked by the clamor against it, the absorption of business by ever larger monopolies continued. In the United States there was not, after the beginning of the last quarter of the century, any opportunity whatever for individual enterprise in any important field of industry, unless backed by great capital. During the last decade of the century, such small businesses as still remained were fast-failing survivals of a past epoch. . . . The railroads had gone on combining till a few great syndicates controlled every rail in the land. In manufactories, every important staple was controlled by a syndicate. These syndicates, pools, trusts, or whatever their name, fixed prices and crushed all competition except when combinations as vast as themselves arose. Then a struggle, resulting in still greater consolidation, ensued.

" . . . The movement toward the conduct of business by larger and larger aggregations of capital, the tendency toward monopolies, which had been so desperately and vainly resisted, was recognized at last, in its true significance, as a process which only needed to complete its logical evolution to open a golden future to humanity.

"Early in the last century the evolution was completed by the final consolidation of the entire capital of the nation. The industry and commerce of the country, ceasing to be conducted by a set of irresponsible corporations and syndicates of private persons at their caprice and for their profit, were intrusted to a single syndicate representing the people, to be conducted in the common interest for the common profit. The nation, that is to say, organized as the one great business corporation in which all other corporations were absorbed. . . ."

DOCUMENT 5

Scientific Management (1919)
Source: Frederick Winslow Taylor, The Principles of Scientific Management (New York: Harper, 1919), pp. 9–16.

The principal object of management should be to secure the maximum prosperity for the employer, coupled with the maximum prosperity for each employé.

The words "maximum prosperity" are used, in their broad sense, to mean not only large dividends for the company or owner, but the development of every branch of the business to its highest state of excellence, so that the prosperity may be permanent.

In the same way maximum prosperity for each employé means not only higher wages than are usually received by men of his class, but, of more importance still, it also means the development of each man to his state of maximum efficiency, so that he may be able to do, generally speaking, the highest grade of work for which his natural abilities fit him, and it further means giving him, when possible, this class of work to do.

It would seem to be so self-evident that maximum prosperity for the employer, coupled with maximum prosperity for the employé, ought to be the two leading objects of management, that even to state this fact should be unnecessary. And yet there is no question that, throughout the industrial world, a large part of the organization of employers, as well as employés, is for war rather than peace, and that perhaps the majority on either side do not believe that it is possible so to arrange their mutual relations that their interests become identical.

DOCUMENT 6

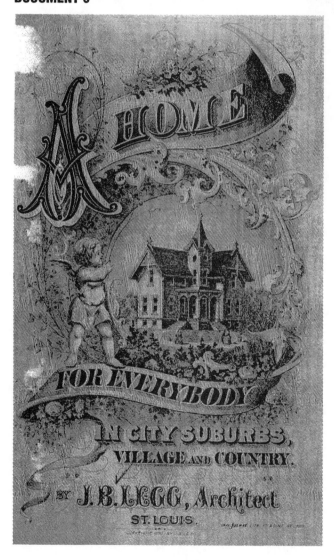

ANSWERS AND EXPLANATIONS

Multiple-Choice Questions

■ **1. (A) is correct.** Industry grew at a pace that was not only unprecedented but previously unimaginable. In 1865, the annual production of goods was estimated at $2 billion; by 1900, it stood at $13 billion, transforming the United States from fourth to first in the world in terms of productivity. By the early twentieth century, American industry manufactured one-third of the world's goods.

■ **2. (E) is correct.** *Horizontal combination* entailed gaining control of the market for a single product. Standard Oil Company, founded by John D. Rockefeller in 1870, operated out of Cleveland in a highly competitive but lucrative field. Rockefeller first secured preferential rates from railroads eager to ensure a steady supply of oil. He then convinced or coerced local oil operators to sell their stock to him. The Standard Oil Trust, established in 1882, controlled more than ninety percent of the nation's oil-refining industry.

■ **3. (A) is correct.** Ninety percent of the nation's business leaders were Protestant and the majority attended church services regularly. They attributed their personal achievements to hard work and perseverance and made these the principal tenets of a new faith that imbued the pursuit of wealth with old-time religious zeal. One version of this "gospel of wealth" justified the ruthless behavior of the so-called "robber barons" who accumulated unprecedented wealth and power through shady deals and conspiracies.

■ **4. (A) is correct.** Congress responded to anti-Chinese sentiments by passing the Chinese Exclusion Act in 1882. The Act suspended Chinese immigration for ten years, limited the civil rights of resident Chinese, and forbade their naturalization.

■ **5. (D) is correct.** Following a series of confrontations between strikers and authorities, a protest against police violence at Chicago's Haymarket Square seemed to be ending quietly until someone threw a bomb that killed one policeman and left seven others fatally wounded. Police responded by firing wildly into the crowd, killing an equal number. A group of anarchists were arrested and sentenced to death after a sensational trial, although no evidence linked the accused to the bombing. The Knights of Labor were crushed.

Employers' associations successfully pooled funds to rid their factories of troublesome agitators, and announced that companies would no longer bargain with unions.

6. (A) is correct. The population of cities grew at double the rate of the nation's population as a whole. In 1860, only sixteen cities had more than 50,000 residents. By 1890, one-third of Americans were city dwellers. Eleven cities claimed more than 250,000 people.

7. (D) is correct. A vocal and powerful new group of Southerners headed by Henry Woodfin Grady, editor of the *Atlanta Constitution*, insisted that the region enjoyed a great potential in its abundant natural resources of coal, iron, turpentine, tobacco, and lumber. Grady and his peers envisioned a "New South" where modern textile mills operated efficiently and profitably, close to the sources of raw goods, the expansive fields of cotton, and plentiful and cheap supply of labor, unrestricted by unions or by legal limitations on the employment of children. Arguing against those planters who aspired to rejuvenate the agricultural economy based on the cultivation of a few staple crops, this group forcefully promoted industrial development and welcomed northern investors.

8. (A) is correct. For the most part, African Americans were limited to unskilled, low-paying jobs. In the textile mills and cigarette factories, which employed both black and white workers, the workforce was rigidly segregated. African Americans were assigned mainly to janitorial jobs and rarely worked alongside the white workers who tended the machines.

9. (A) is correct. Bicycles cost $100 and were considered a symbol of middle-class prosperity.

10. (E) is correct. Toward the end of the century, the younger members of the urban middle class had begun to find common ground in lower-class pastimes, especially ragtime music. Middle-class urban dwellers began to seek out ragtime bands, and congregated in nightclubs and even on the rooftops of posh hotels to listen and dance and even to drink. Baseball also bridged middle- and lower-class interests. As attendance continued to grow, the enthusiasm for baseball straddled major social divisions, bringing together Americans of many backgrounds, if only on a limited basis.

Document-Based Question

Analyze the effect that the rise of industry had on the distribution of wealth in the United States in the late 19th century.

In the latter part of the 19th century a revolution took place in the organization of business. Due to the the invention of large-scale, labor-saving machinery, companies were able to operate on a larger scale than they ever had before. One of the results of this new form of business organization was an increased polarization of wealth, and a high level of social stratification.

The new business model was typified by John Rockefeller's Standard Oil. By a combination of vertigal integration and horizontal combination, which he achieved by underselling his competitors until they had to sell out to him, he was able to control ninety percent of the country's oil production. He was the archetype of the "robber baron," the monopolist who was viewed by the public as having a stranglehold on both government and other businesses **(DOCUMENT 9)**.

Working in his refineries, as well as in other large factories, was a lower class. These people lived in abject poverty. Their homes were crowded tenements. Many of them were driven to crime, as work did not pay well. Children were often orphaned thought industrial accidents. **(DOCUMENT 2)**. Many of these poor were immigrants, who had come to the United States looking for a better life. Instead, they were looked down on by natives and forced to work for low wages **(DOCUMENT 7)**.

Aside from the rich and the poor, there was a new and growing middle class, filling the new middle-management jobs created by vertical integration. They were moving out to larger homes in newly created suburbs **(DOCUMENT 6)**. They also had increased leisure time, and used it in a number of ways, among which was playing in parks in their new neighborhoods **(DOCUMENT 8)**, as well as watching sports and visiting amusement parks like Coney Island.

The contrast between rich and poor was noticed, and deemed a problem that needed to be solved (**DOCUMENT 1**). There were different approaches to the issue. Many of the working poor turned to unionism, in an attempt to force higher wages from their employers. It was in this era that the AFL and the Knights of Labor were founded. Some resorted to the more extreme solution of joining socialist organizations (**DOCUMENT 3**). To some of them, the increased monopolization and social stratification was only an intermediate stage. Eventually, the entire means of production would be a giant monopoly held in the hand of the people, for their own benefit (**DOCUMENT 4**). Finally, there were those who believed that the stratification was simply a result of mismanagement. A firm organized in the proper, scientific way would maximize profits both for the employer and his employees, allowing everybody to do well (**DOCUMENT 5**).

The new system of business organization at the end of the 19th century created a situation where the gap between rich and poor was constantly growing. This situation was ripe for reform, something which the progressives would attempt to address at the beginning of the 20th century.

CHAPTER 20

Commonwealth and Empire, 1870–1900

This chapter covers the conflicts between the Populist movements and those groups that held most of the nation's wealth and power. Mass political movements of farmers and workers were organized. These movements were also actively supported and shaped by women who were struggling to gain their own civil and voting rights. There was a moment of democratic promise when Americans might have established a commonwealth based on agreement of the people for the common good. Instead, a national governing class and a growing bureaucratic state emerged. While debating their domestic future, most Americans seemed united in pursuing an empire. Anti-imperialists could do little more than criticize from the sidelines as the United States acquired numerous territories and took an interventionist stance toward others.

Toward a National Governing Class

In the last three decades of the nineteenth century, the expansion and growth of the economy caused a similar trend in all levels of government. The modern apparatus of departments, cabinets, and agencies rose in the federal government. Legislatures controlled political power and patronage flourished as machine politics became prevalent. In response, reformers promoted civil service and improving public services.

Farmers and Workers Organize Their Communities

Facing hard times and a loss of status and power, farmers and workers formed organizations both to provide services and to protest against conditions. In both cases, the railroads were a major target. The strike of 1877 was a peak of labor unrest. Women played important roles in farm and labor movements. They also founded other organizations. The Populist movement united farmers and workers in a short-lived reform and third-party movement.

The Crisis of the 1890s

A long, severe depression caused high unemployment and hardship. Strikes, often violent, broke out across the nation. At the same time, religious leaders developed the social gospel doctrine to promote social reform that aided the poor. The economic crisis of the 1890s weakened the two-party system. The Populists mounted a third-party threat but were co-opted by the Democrats. The Republicans won the 1896 election.

The Age of Segregation

During this period, nativism and racism arose. The institution of Jim Crow laws led to violence against African Americans and, in the South, reform dissipated into racism.

"Imperialism of Righteousness"

Many Americans believed the economic problems of the 1890s showed the need for the United States to expand. In part, there were ideas that the American civilization and the white race were superior to other cultures and peoples. Religious evangelism was one aspect of overseas expansion, but many in government and business desired an overseas empire. The United States acquired overseas territories through war and annexation.

The Spanish-American War

Support for the Cuban independence movement and yellow journalism helped precipitate the Spanish-American War. The short conflict established the United States as an imperialist nation, but expansion aroused strong opposition from many Americans.

Multiple-Choice Questions

1. The Interstate Commerce Commission was established in 1887 to
   (A) regulate the trade unions.
   (B) control interstate criminal activity.
   (C) break up the monopolistic trusts.
   (D) promote multinational corporations.
   (E) regulate the railroads.

2. In general, the presidents of the last quarter of the nineteenth century
   (A) willingly yielded power to Congress and the states.
   (B) yielded to the courts.
   (C) used their office to enrich themselves.
   (D) increased the power of the presidency and controlled Congress.
   (E) were very charismatic individuals.

3. Passage of the Pendleton Act in 1883 indicated
   (A) the success of a bipartisan effort to lower the tariff.
   (B) Congress's desire to control big business.
   (C) both parties recognized a need to professionalize government service.
   (D) the desire of voters to curb the power of political parties.
   (E) congressional concern over the chaos in the railroad industry.

4. The largest women's organization in the world in the late nineteenth century was
   (A) the patrons of Husbandry.
   (B) the National Women's Alliance.
   (C) the Woman's League for Equal Rights.
   (D) the National Organization for Women.
   (E) the Woman's Christian Temperance Union.

5. The Social Gospel movement was largely guided by
   (A) Catholic priests.
   (B) Baptist ministers.
   (C) women.
   (D) Unitarians.
   (E) party bosses.

6. In *Plessy* v. *Ferguson* and *Cumming* v. *Richmond County Board of Education*, the Supreme Court upheld legislation that
   (A) required the integration of public schools.
   (B) denied illegal immigrants the right to attend public schools.
   (C) formally segregated facilities including schools.
   (D) effectively put off the question of segregation.
   (E) allowed poll taxes and literacy requirements for voting.

7. Alfred Thayer Mahan helped define American policy in the 1880s with his work about the influence of which of the following on history?
   (A) imperialism
   (B) Christianity
   (C) sea power
   (D) discovery
   (E) disease

8. Hawaii was annexed
   (A) to protect American missionaries from cannibalism.
   (B) for imperialistic reasons.
   (C) for the coffee.
   (D) to rid the island of the oppressive regime of King Kalakaua.
   (E) to bring land reform to the Hawaiian peasants.

9. In the Platt Amendment on Cuba, the United States
   (A) declared Cuba independent from Spain.
   (B) utilized the Monroe Doctrine against Hawaii.
   (C) denied any intent of annexing the island.
   (D) allied with Cuban rebels against the Spanish imperialists.
   (E) called for the right to intervene to protect its interests in Cuba.

10. The acquisition of the Philippines by the United States
   (A) assured Philippine independence.
   (B) ended the Philippine independence movement.
   (C) gave control of the government to Emilio Aguinaldo.
   (D) resulted in a four-year war of conquest by the Americans.
   (E) started a period of great reform in the Philippines.

Document-Based Question

How were racial and ethnic differences employed to define social and political institutions from 1870 to 1900, and what effect did this have on the exercise of power by different groups of Americans?

DOCUMENT 1

Anglo-Saxon Culture Under Siege (1885)
Source: Josiah Strong, Our Country (New York: Taylor and Baker for the American Home Missionary Society, 1885), pp. 40–46.

2. We can only glance at the political aspects of immigration. As we have already seen, it is immigration whichhas fed fat the liquor power; and there is a liquor vote. Immigration furnishes most of the victims of Mormonism; and there is a Mormon vote. Immigration is the strength of the Catholic church; and there is a Catholic vote. Immigration is the mother and nurse of American socialism; and there is to be a socialist vote. Immigration tends strongly to the cities, and gives to them their political complexion. And there is no more serious menace to our civilization than our rabble-ruled cities. These several perils, all of which are enhanced by immigration, will be considered in succeeding chapters.

Many American citizens are not Americanized. It is as unfortunate as it is natural, that foreigners in this country should cherish their own language and peculiar customs, and carry their nationality, as a distinct factor, into our politics. Immigration has created the "German vote" and the "Irish vote," for which politicians bid, and which have already been decisive of state elections, and might easily determine national. A mass of men but little acquainted with our institutions, who will act in concert and who are controlled largely by their appetites and prejudices, constitute a very paradise for demagogues.

We have seen that immigration is detrimental to popular morals. It has a like influence upon popular intelligence, for the percentage of illiteracy among the foreign-born population is thirty-eight per cent greater than among the nativeborn whites. Thus immigration complicates our moral and political problems by swelling our dangerous classes. And as immigration is to increase much more rapidly than the population, we may infer that the dangerous classes are to increase more rapidly than hitherto.4 It goes without saying, that there is a dead-line of ignorance and vice in every republic, and when it is touched by the average citizen, free institutions perish; for intelligence and virtue are as essential to the life of a republic as are brain and heart to the life of a man.

DOCUMENT 2

Source: The Secret Oath of the American Protective Association (1893)

I do most solemnly promise and swear that I will always, to the utmost of my ability, labor, plead, and wage a continuous warfare against ignorance and fanaticism; that I will use my utmost power to strike the shackles and chains of blind obedience to the Roman Catholic Church from the hampered and bound consciences of a priest-ridden and church-oppressed people; that I will never allow anyone, a member of the Roman Catholic Church, to become a member of this order, I knowing him to be such; that I will use my influence to promote the interest of all Protestants everywhere in the world that I may be; that I will not employ a Roman Catholic in any capacity, if I can procure the services of a Protestant.

I furthermore promise and swear that I will not aid in building or maintaining, by my resources, any Roman Catholic church or institution of their sect or creed whatsoever, but will do all in my power to retard and break down the power of the Pope, in this country or any other; that I will not enter into any controversy with a Roman Catholic upon the subject of this order, nor will I enter into any agreement with a Roman Catholic to strike or create a disturbance whereby the Catholic employees may undermine and substitute their Protestant co-workers; that in all grievances I will seek only Protestants, and counsel with them to the exclusion of all Roman Catholics, and will not make known to them anything of any nature matured at such conferences.

I furthermore promise and swear that I will not countenance the nomination, in any caucus or convention, of a Roman Catholic for any office in the gift of the American people, and that I will not vote for, or counsel others to vote for, any Roman Catholic, but will vote only for a Protestant, so far as may lie in my power (should there be two Roman Catholics in opposite tickets, I will erase the name on the ticket I vote); that I will at all times endeavor to place the political positions of this government in the hands of Protestants, to the entire exclusion of the Roman Catholic Church, of the members thereof, and the mandate of the Pope.

To all of which I do most solemnly promise and swear, so help me God.

Amen.

DOCUMENT 3

Source: Booker T. Washington, Atlanta Exposition Address (1895)

To those of the white race who look to the incoming of those of foreign birth and strange tongue and habits for the prosperity of the South, were I permitted I would repeat what I say to my own race, "Cast down your bucket where you are." Cast it down among the eight millions of Negroes whose habits you know, whose fidelity and love you have tested in days when to have proved treacherous meant the ruin of your firesides. Cast down your bucket among these people who have, without strikes and labour wars, tilled your fields, cleared your forests, built your railroads and cities, and brought forth treasures from the bowels of the earth. . . . Casting down your bucket among my people . . . you will find that they will buy your surplus land, make blossom the waste places in your fields, and run your factories. While doing this, you can be sure in the future, as in the past, that you and your families will be surrounded by the most patient, faithful, lawabiding, and unresentful people that the world has seen. . . . In all things that are purely social we can be as separate as the fingers, yet one as the hand in all things essential to mutual progress. . . .

DOCUMENT 4

Source: From Plessy v. Ferguson (1896)

This case turns upon the constitutionality of an act of the general assembly of the state of Louisiana, passed in 1890, providing for separate railway carriages for the white and colored races. . . .

The constitutionality of this act is attacked upon the ground that it conflicts both with the 13th Amendment of the Constitution, abolishing slavery, and the 14th Amendment, which prohibits certain restrictive legislation on the part of the states.

1. That it does not conflict with the 13th Amendment, which abolished slavery and involuntary servitude, except as a punishment for crime, is too clear for argument. . . .

Indeed, we do not understand that the 13th Amendment is strenuously relied upon by the plaintiff. . . .

The object of the [14th] amendment was undoubtedly to enforce the absolute equality of the two races before the law, but in the nature of things it could not have been intended to abolish distinctions based upon color, or to enforce social, as distinguished from political, equality, or a commingling of the two races upon terms unsatisfactory to either. Laws permitting, and even requiring their separation in places where they are liable to be brought into contact do not necessarily imply the inferiority of either race to the other, and have been generally, if not universally, recognized as within the competency of the state legislatures in the exercise of their police power. . . .

We consider the underlying fallacy of the plaintiff's argument to consist in the assumption that the enforced separation of the two races stamps the colored race with a badge of inferiority. If this be so, it is not by reason of anything found in the act, but solely because the colored race chooses to put that construction upon it. . . .

The argument also assumes that social prejudice may be overcome by legislation, and that equal rights cannot be secured to the Negro except by an enforced commingling of the two races. We cannot accept this proposition. If the two races are to meet on terms of social equality, it must be the result of natural affinities, a mutual appreciation of each other's merits and a voluntary consent of individuals. . . . Legislation is powerless to eradicate racial instincts or abolish distinctions based upon physical differences and the attempt to do so can only result in accentuating the difficulties of the present situation. If the civil and political right of both races be equal, one cannot be inferior to the other civilly or politically. If one race be inferior to the other socially, the Constitution of the United States cannot put them upon the same plane.

DOCUMENT 5

Source: W. E. B. Du Bois, from "Of Mr. Booker T. Washington and Others" (1903)

The question then comes: Is it possible, and probable, that nine millions of men can make effective progress in economic lines if they are deprived of political rights, made a servile caste, and allowed only the most meagre chance for developing their exceptional men? If history and reason give any distinct answer to these questions, it is an emphatic No. . . .

. . . while it is a great truth to say that the Negro must strive and strive mightily to help himself, it is equally true that unless his striving be not simply seconded, but rather aroused and encouraged, by the initiative of the richer and wiser environing group, he cannot hope for great success.

. . . So far as Mr. Washington preaches Thrift, Patience, and Industrial Training for the masses, we must hold up his hands and strive with him, rejoicing in his honors and glorying in the strength of this Joshua called of God and of man to lead the headless host. But so far as Mr. Washington apologizes for injustice, North or South, does not rightly value the privilege and duty of voting, belittles the emasculating effects of caste distinctions, and opposes the higher training and ambition of our brighter minds,-so far as he, the South, or the Nation, does this, we must unceasingly and firmly oppose them.

DOCUMENT 6

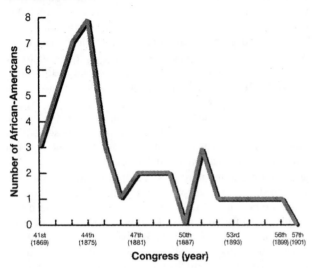

DOCUMENT 7

Lee Chew, Life of a Chinese Immigrant (1903)
Source: From The Independent, 54 (2818), February 19, 1903, 417–423.

When I first opened a laundry it was in company with a partner, who had been in the business for some years. We went to a town about 500 miles inland, where a railroad was building. We got a board shanty and worked for the men employed by the railroads....

We were three years with the railroad, and then went to the mines, where we made plenty of money in gold dust, but had a hard time, for many of the miners were wild men who carried revolvers and after drinking would come into our place to shoot and steal shirts, for which we had to pay. One of these men hit his head hard against a flat iron and all the miners came and broke our laundry, chasing us out of town. They were going to hang us. We lost all our property and $365 in money, which a member of the mob must have found.

Luckily most of our money was in the hands of Chinese bankers in San Francisco. I drew $500 and went East to Chicago, where I had a laundry for three years, during which I increased my capital to $2,500. After that I was four years in Detroit. I went home to China in 1897, but returned in 1898, and began a laundry business in Buffalo.

The ordinary laundry shop is generally divided into three rooms. In front is the room where the customers are received, behind that a bedroom and in the back the work shop, which is also the dining room and kitchen. The stove and cooking utensils are the same as those of the Americans....

I have found out, during my residence in this country, that much of the Chinese prejudice against Americans is unfounded, and I no longer put faith in the wild tales that were told about them in our village, tho some of the Chinese, who have been here twenty years and who are learned men, still believe that there is no marriage in this country, that the land is infested with demons and that all the people are given over to general wickedness.

I know better. Americans are not all bad, nor are they wicked wizards. Still, they have their faults, and their treatment of us is outrageous....

The reason why so many Chinese go into the laundry business in this country is because it requires little capital and is one of the few opportunities that are open....

There is no reason for the prejudice against the Chinese. The cheap labor cry was always a falsehood. Their labor was never cheap, and is not cheap now. It has always commanded the highest market price. But the trouble is that the Chinese are such excellent and faithful workers that bosses will have no others when they can get them. If you look at men working on the street you will find an overseer for every four or five of them. That watching is not necessary for Chinese. They work as well when left to themselves as they do when some one is looking at them....

DOCUMENT 8

Source: Albert Beveridge, "The March of the Flag" (1898)

Hawaii is ours, Puerto Rico is to be ours; at the prayer of her people Cuba finally will be ours; in the islands of the East, even to the gates of Asia, coaling stations are to be ours at the very least; the flag of a liberal government is to float over the Philippines, and may it be the banner that Taylor unfurled in Texas and Fr mont carried to the coast.

The Opposition tells us that we ought not to govern a people without their consent. I answer, The rule of liberty that all just government derives its authority from the consent of the governed, applies only to those who are capable of self-government. We govern the Indians without their consent, we govern our territories without their consent, we govern our children without their consent. How do they know that our government would be without their consent?

Would not the people of the Philippines prefer the just, human, civilizing government of this Republic to the savage, bloody rule of pillage and extortion from which we have rescued them?

And, regardless of this formula of words made only for enlightened, self-governing people, do we owe no duty to the world? Shall we turn these peoples back to the reeking hands from which we have taken them? Shall we abandon them, with Germany, England, Japan, hungering for them? Shall we save them from those nations, to give them a self-rule of tragedy? . . . Then, like men and not like children, let us on to our tasks, our mission, and our destiny.

ANSWERS AND EXPLANATIONS

Multiple-Choice Questions

1. **(E) is correct.** The nation's first independent regulatory agency took charge of the nation's most import industry. The Interstate Commerce Commission (ICC) was created in 1887 to bring order to the growing patchwork of state laws concerning railroads.

2. **(A) is correct.** Presidents of the last quarter century—Hayes, Garfield, Arthur, Cleveland and Harrison—lacked luster. They willingly yielded power to Congress and the state legislatures. Both presidendtial popular vote and congressional races were tight in the late 1800s.

3. **(C) is correct.** In January 1883, a bipartisan congressional majority passed the Pendleton Civil Service Reform Act. This measure allowed the president to create, with Senate approval, a three-person commission to draw up a set of guidelines for executive and legislateive appointments. The commission established a system of standards for various federal jobs and instituted "open, competitive examinations for testing the fitness of applications for public serve." Although patronage did not disappear entirely, many departments of the federal government took on a professional character.

4. **(E) is correct.** Frances E. Willard was the most famous woman of the nineteenth century. From 1878 until her death in 1897, Willliard presided over the Woman's Christian Temperance Union (WCTU), at the time the largest organization of women in the world.

5. **(C) is correct.** Women guided the social gospel movement in their communities. The WCTU trained hundreds and thousands of Protestant women in social uplift. By the mid-1880s, in nearly every city, groups of white women affiliated with various evangelical Protestant sects were raising funds.

6. **(C) is correct.** In *Plessy* v. *Ferguson*, the Supreme Court upheld a Louisiana state law formally sergregating railroad passenger cars on the basis of the "separate but equal" doctrine, and thereby established a precedent for segregation, North as well as South. In *Cumming* v. *Richmond County Board of Education*, the Supreme Court allowed separate schools for blacks and whites, even where facilities for African American children did not exist.

7. **(C) is correct.** Congress established the Naval War College in Newport, Rhode Island, in 1884, to train the officer corps. One of its first presidents, Captain Alfred Thayer Mahan, prescribed an imperialist strategy based on command of the seas. Mahan insisted that international strength rested not only on open markets, but on the control of colonies through its sea power. He advocated the annexation of bases in the Caribbean and the Pacific to enhance the navy's ability to threaten or wage warfare.

8. **(B) is correct.** Hawai'i was viewed as a stepping stone to the vast Asian markets. In 1887, a new treaty allowed the United States to build a naval base at Pearl Harbor on the island of Oahu. Imperialism guided the American interest in acquiring Hawai'i.

9. **(E) is correct.** Under the Platt Amendment, sponsored by Republican Senator Orville H. Platt of Connecticut in 1901, Cuba was required to provide land for American bases to devote national revenues to pay back debts to the United States; to sign no treaty that would be detrimental to American interests; and to acknowledge the right of the United States to intervene at any time to protect its interest in Cuba.

10. **(D) is correct.** The acquisition of the Philippines by the United States resulted in a four-year war of conquest by the Americans. The Filipino rebels at first welcomed American troops and fought with them against Spain. But when the Spanish-American War ended and they perceived that American troops were not preparing to leave, the rebels, led by Emilio Aguinaldo, turned against their former allies and attacked the American base operations in Manila in February 1899. Predicting a brief skirmish, American commanders seriously undersestimated the population's capacity to endure great suffering for the sake of independence. The resulting conflict took the form of modern guerrilla warfare, with brutalities on both sides. On some of the Philippine islands, intermittent fighting lasted until 1935.

Document-Based Question

How were racial and ethnic differences employed to define social and political institutions from 1870 to 1900, and what effect did this have on the exercise of power by different groups of Americans?

Following the Civil War, American political and social institutions underwent dramatic changes. Rapid industrial and urban growth, the emergence of new forms of agricultural production, westward expansion, immigration, and America's increased role in world affairs caused a variety of responses. One of those responses was an increased nativism, evident in the various attempts made by those considered "old-stock Americans" to question the value of developments such as immigration (**DOCUMENT 1**). Many even formed "protective associations" designed to limit the influence of those they viewed as damaging to the American way of life (**DOCUMENT 2**). These groups relied on prejudicial descriptions of and assumptions about different immigrant and ethnic groups to foster unified attempts to disenfranchise and disempower those they feared and disliked.

Long accustomed to also being the target of such attempts, some African Americans sought to accommodate themselves to this development in the interest of survival and to point out the strengths they could bring to society and industry (**DOCUMENT 3**). Despite such muted pleas for recognition, however, the increased restrictions on African Americans were codified in the Supreme Court case *Plessy* v. *Ferguson*, which stripped African Americans of their claims to civic equality through the institution of a "separate but equal" doctrine (**DOCUMENT 4**). This led many African Americans to question accommodation as a means toward equality, and a new attempt to achieve equality emerged that was more radical, demanding immediate recognition and equality and tying the achievement of equality to voting rights (**DOCUMENT 5**). Unfortunately, such rights were not achieved at that time, and the legal and political status of African Americans continued to decline (**DOCUMENT 6**).

Yet African Americans were not alone in their struggle for equality. Asian immigrants were often targets of legal restrictions and violence, and their lives were often framed within economic competition (**DOCUMENT 7**). Competition, ethnic and racial prejudice, and suspicion similarly informed the foreign policy of the United States as it entered the world stage. As the United States expanded its hegemony over different parts of the world, it often defined other nations as less civilized and capable, and therefore justifying the idea that it was the destiny of the United States to spread its institutions (**DOCUMENT 8**). As the United States established itself as a dominant power, the power structure at home reflected the same racial and ethnic ordering of society.

CHAPTER 21

Urban America and the Progressive Era, 1900–1917

This chapter covers the accelerated urbanization of America in the first years of the twentieth century, and the social problems that resulted from rapid unplanned growth of the cities. Both political bosses and reformers tried to respond to the reality of an industrialized and urbanized America. Social Darwinism was challenged by the progressives, who had a new, though sometimes inconsistent, vision of the American community. Progressives viewed the government as an ally in achieving realistic and pragmatic reforms. The climate for reform was created by several new or transformed professions, including social workers, social scientists at universities, and investigative journalists. Both major political parties came to embrace progressive views. Presidents Roosevelt, Taft, and Wilson based their programs on these new ideas. Although much was accomplished, the progressive movement lacked unity and failed to adequately address issues of class, race, or sex. Legislation was not always enforced or had unintended negative consequences. In the long run, politics was affected by the demands for social justice and attempts were made to confront the problems of rapid industrialization and urbanization.

The Currents of Progressivism

Progressives launched a comprehensive reform campaign. Women acted as spearheads of reforms that touched all levels of government and focused on problems in cities. Reformers used the press to pursue their programs and intellectuals actively participated in reform efforts.

Social Control and Its Limits

Fears of moral decline led some reformers to seek social control of immigrants, workers, and African Americans. Their efforts met with mixed results.

Working-class Communities and Protest

Immigrants from Europe, North America, and Asia flooded into the United States creating crowded urban communities in large cities. Deplorable working conditions in the garment trades led to unions and strikes, but it took a tragic fire for the New York state government to institute legal reform. In many cases, immigrants populated company towns but these too experienced violent labor conflicts. During this period, two national unions emerged. In addition, a group of bohemian intellectuals became involved in radical causes.

Women's Movements and Black Awakening

Women and African Americans actively pursued reform agenda. Women's organizations took up numerous causes and sought to cross class lines. A major issue was birth control. African Americans responded to legal segregation in two distinct ways: accommodation and activism.

National Progressivism

The progressive movement reached the national level after Theodore Roosevelt became president. Roosevelt championed government regulation to achieve reform and became involved in areas such as business and conservation of the natural environment. His successor, William Howard Taft, was more restrained in his reform efforts. The election of 1912 became a referendum on reform agenda. Wilson won the election and began implementing much of his program.

Multiple-Choice Questions

1. In general, progressives were
   - (A) optimistic about citizens improving socio-economic conditions.
   - (B) pessimistic about the ability of people to reform.
   - (C) revolutionaries who wanted to organize cells for soldiers.
   - (D) applying the ideas of Social Darwinism as reforms.
   - (E) anti-political, preferring to emphasize improving individual character.

2. What was the major reason progressive women like Jane Addams turned to settlement work?
   - (A) They were dissatisfied with the choices that society offered to women.
   - (B) They thought that women are more compassionate than men.
   - (C) Settlement work commanded higher salaries.
   - (D) Settlement work required less professional training.
   - (E) Society offered no other employment opportunities.

3. Party machines were powerful because they were
   - (A) crusaders against vice.
   - (B) champions of immigration restrictions.
   - (C) supported by the military.
   - (D) in control of most state legislatures.
   - (E) organized and delivered needed services.

4. Southern progressives agreed to the disfranchisement and segregation of African Americans because
   - (A) progressives did not want to lose political control to Democrats.
   - (B) they felt they couldn't win on the issue.
   - (C) progressives wanted protection from the Ku Klux Klan.
   - (D) disenfranchisement would allow poor whites to be upwardly mobile.
   - (E) progressives shared the same racist views as others in southern society.

5. The Woman's Christian Temperance Union's efforts at prohibition and other social reforms allowed women to
   - (A) fuse public concerns with moral guardianship.
   - (B) seek control without the vote.
   - (C) remove unwanted elements in society.
   - (D) collect contributions for political parties.
   - (E) keep wives and mothers in the home.

6. Both prohibition and ending prostitution were efforts by the progressive reformers to control
   - (A) state politicians who obstructed progressive reform.
   - (B) the migrating agricultural workers.
   - (C) city bosses and city machines.
   - (D) the growing middle class.
   - (E) the new, predominantly Catholic and Jewish, immigrants.

7. Progressive reformers believed the primary purpose of public education was to
   - (A) assimilate new immigrants.
   - (B) create an aristocracy of the able.
   - (C) prepare immigrant children for college.
   - (D) teach immigrant children a trade.
   - (E) allow the poor and the rich to mingle in a democratic manner.

8. As a result of the Triangle Shirtwaist Company fire, the following positive action was taken:
   - (A) improvement of safety conditions and limiting working hours for women.
   - (B) women were allowed to unionize.
   - (C) women received large annual bonuses.

(D) women were allowed to remain home with their families.

(E) women received health care and paid vacations.

9. The American Federation of Labor organized
   (A) immigrant labor.
   (B) all labor.
   (C) unskilled labor.
   (D) chinese labor.
   (E) skilled labor.

10. President Theodore Roosevelt's support for the Hepburn Act and the Pure Food and Drug Act reflected his beliefs in
    (A) an economy based on a small competitive business.
    (B) keeping government out of big business.
    (C) the ability of big business to reform itself.
    (D) free enterprise.
    (E) regulating big business.

Document-Based Question

What themes united different groups of progressive reformers and how were those themes evident in the reform activities and philosophies of these groups?

DOCUMENT 1

Source: Lincoln Steffens, from The Shame of the Cities (1904)

The machine controls the whole process of voting, and practices fraud at every stage. The assessor's list is the voting list, and the assessor is the machine's man. . . . The assessor pads the list with the names of dead dogs, children, and non-existent persons. One newspaper printed the picture of a dog, another that of a little four-year-old negro boy, down on such a list. A ring orator in a speech resenting sneers at his ward as "low down" reminded his hearers that that was the ward of Independence Hall, and naming over signers of the Declaration of Independence, he closed his highest flight of eloquence with the statement that "these men, the fathers of American liberty, voted down here once. And," he added, with a catching grin, "they vote here yet." Rudolph Blankenburg, a persistent fighter for the right and the use of the right to vote (and, by the way, an immigrant), sent out just before one election a registered letter to each voter on the rolls of a certain selected division. Sixty-three per cent were returned marked "not at," "removed," "deceased," etc. From one four-story house where forty-four voters were addressed, eighteen letters came back undelivered; from another of forty-eight voters, came back forty-one letters; from another sixty-one out of sixty-two; from another, forty-four out of forty-seven. Six houses in one division were assessed at one hundred and seventy-two voters, more than the votes cast in the previous election in any one of two hundred entire divisions.

DOCUMENT 2

Source: Walker Percy, "Birmingham under the Commission Plan" (1911)

Commission government in Birmingham has been an unqualified business success. With the appointment of our commissioners there dawned a new day in our civic progress. We are realizing the fruition of long cherished hopes. The same sort of fidelity, honesty, energy, loyalty and intelligence is being displayed by these public employees that we have been accustomed to expect from private employees. A dollar of city money in Birmingham can buy as much in labor, service, and material as a dollar of individual money. When the commissioners entered upon their duties, Birmingham's floating debt under aldermanic government had been piling up with alarming rapidity. A favored bank had selfishly dominated the city's finances, and the other banking institutions of the city had felt that it was useless for them to consider, or endeavor to aid in, the city's financial problems. Practically all of the Birmingham bankers were enthusiastic believers in commission government, and have rallied in loyal support of the new administration. . . .

DOCUMENT 3

Source: Platform Adopted by the National Negro Committee (1909)

We denounce the ever-growing oppression of our 10,000,000 colored fellow citizens as the greatest menace that threatens the country. Often plundered of their just share of the public funds, robbed of nearly all part in the government, segregated by common carriers, some murdered with impunity, and all treated with open contempt by officials, they are held in some States in practical slavery to the white community. The systematic persecution of law-abiding citizens and their disfranchisement on account of their race alone is a crime that will ultimately drag down to an infamous end any nation that allows it to be practiced, and it bears most heavily on those poor white farmers and laborers whose economic position is most similar to that of the persecuted race.

The nearest hope lies in the immediate and patiently continued enlightenment of the people who have been inveigled into a campaign of oppression. The spoils of persecution should not go to enrich any class or classes of the population. Indeed persecution of organized workers, peonage, enslavement of prisoners, and even disfranchisement already threaten large bodies of whites in many Southern States.

We agree fully with the prevailing opinion that the transformation of the unskilled colored laborers in industry and agriculture into skilled workers is of vital importance to that race and to the nation, but we demand for the Negroes, as for all others, a free and complete education, whether by city, State or nation, a grammar school and industrial training for all and technical, professional, and academic education for the most gifted.

But the public schools assigned to the Negro of whatever kind or grade will never receive a fair and equal treatment until he is given equal treatment in the Legislature and before the law. Nor will the practically educated Negro, no matter how valuable to the community he may prove, be given a fair return for his labor or encouraged to put forth his best efforts or given the chance to develop that efficiency that comes only outside the school until he is respected in his legal rights as a man and a citizen.

We regard with grave concern the attempt manifest South and North to deny black men the right to work and to enforce this demand by violence and bloodshed. Such a question is too fundamental and clear even to be submitted to arbitration. The late strike in Georgia is not simply a demand that Negroes be displaced, but that proven and efficient men be made to surrender their long-followed means of livelihood to white competitors.

As first and immediate steps toward remedying these national wrongs, so full of peril for the whites as well as the blacks of all sections, we demand of Congress and the Executive:

(1) That the Constitution be strictly enforced and the civil rights guaranteed under the Fourteenth Amendment be secured impartially to all.

(2) That there be equal educational opportunities for all and in all the States, and that public school expenditure be the same for the Negro and white child.

(3) That in accordance with the Fifteenth Amendment the right of the Negro to the ballot on the same terms as other citizens be recognized in every part of the country.

DOCUMENT 4

Source: Helen M. Todd, "Getting Out the Vote" (1911)

We opened our plea for women by showing our audience that the mother and wife could not long protect herself and her children unless she had a vote. That the milk the city mother gave her baby; the school her children were educated in; the purity of the water they drank; the prices she paid for meat and clothes; the very wages her husband received; the sanitary and moral condition of the streets her children passed through were all matters of politics. When once we had clearly established the fact that women wanted to vote to protect their homes we had won a large part of our audience. . .

No words can better express the soul of the woman's movement, lying back of the practical cry of "Votes for Women," better than this sentence which had captured the attention of both Mother Jones and the hired girl, "Bread for all, and Roses too." Not at once; but woman is the mothering element in the world and her vote will go toward helping forward the time when life's Bread, which is home, shelter and security, and the Roses of life, music, education, nature and books, shall be the heritage of every child that is born in the country, in the government of which she has a voice.

There will be no prisons, no scaffolds, no children in factories, no girls driven on the street to earn their bread, in the day when there shall be "Bread for all, and Roses too."

To help to make such a civilization possible is the meaning of "Votes for Women." It was the power of this idea which sent the women of Illinois "down State" on their automobile campaign.

DOCUMENT 5

DOCUMENT 6

Source: Louis Brandeis, Other People's Money and How the Bankers Use It (1913)

The fact that industrial monopolies arrest development is more serious even than the direct burden imposed through extortionate prices. But the most harm-bearing incident of the trusts is their promotion of financial concentration. Industrial trusts feed the money trust. Practically every trust created has destroyed the financial independence of some communities and of many properties; for it has centered the financing of a large part of whole lines of business in New York, and this usually with one of a few banking houses. This is well illustrated by the Steel Trust, which is a trust of trusts; that is, the Steel Trust combines in one huge holding com-pany the trusts previously formed in the different branches of the steel business. Thus the Tube Trust combined 17 tube mills, located in 16 different cities, scattered over 5 states and owned by 13 different companies. The wire trust combined 19 mills; the sheet steel trust 26; the bridge and structural trust 27; and the tin plate trust 36; all scattered similarly over many states. Finally these and other companies were formed into the United States Steel Corporation, combining 228 companies in all, located in 127 cities and towns, scattered over 18 states. Before the combinations were effected, nearly every one of these companies was owned largely by those who managed it, and had been financed, to a large extent, in the place, or in the state, in which it was located.

DOCUMENT 7

Source: Eugene V. Debs, "The Outlook for Socialism in the United States" (1900)

As a rule, large capitalists are Republicans and small capitalists are Democrats, but workingmen must remember that they are all capitalists, and that the many small ones, like the fewer large ones, are all politically supporting their class interests, and this is always and everywhere the capitalist class.

Whether the means of production-that is to say, the land, mines, factories, machinery, etc.-are owned by a few large Republican capitalists, who organize a trust, or whether they be owned by a lot of small Democratic capitalists, who are opposed to the trust, is all the same to the working class. Let the capitalists, large and small, fight this out among themselves.

The working class must get rid of the whole brood of masters and exploiters, and put themselves in possession and control of the means of production, that they may have steady employment without consulting a capitalist employer, large or small, and that they may get the wealth their labor produces, all of it, and enjoy with their families the fruits of their industry in comfortable and happy homes, abundant and wholesome food, proper clothing and all other things necessary to "life, liberty and the pursuit of happiness." It is therefore a question not of "reform," the mask of fraud, but of revolution. The capitalist system must be overthrown, class rule abolished and wage slavery supplanted by cooperative industry.

DOCUMENT 8

DOCUMENT 9

Source: Jane Addams, Twenty Years at Hull House (1910)

The Settlement . . . is an experimental effort to aid the solution of the social and industrial problems which are engendered by the modern conditions of life in a great city. It insists that these problems are not confined to any one portion of a city. It is an attempt to relieve, at the same time, the overaccumulation at one end of society and the destitution at the other, but it assumes that this overaccumulation and destitution is most sorely felt in the things that pertain to social and educational advantages… It should demand from its residents a scientific patience in the accumulation of facts and the steady holding of their sympathies as one of the best instruments for that accumulation. It must be grounded in a philosophy whose foundation is on the solidarity of the human race, a philosophy which will not waver when the race happens to be represented by a drunken woman or an idiot boy. Its residents must be emptied of all conceit of opinion and all self-assertion, and ready to arouse and interpret the public opinion of their neighborhood. They must be content to live quietly side by side with their neighbors, until they grow into a sense of relationship and mutual interests. Their neighbors are held apart by differences of race and language which the residents can more easily overcome. They are bound to see the needs of their neighborhood as a whole, to furnish data for legislation, and to use their influence to secure it. In short, residents are pledged to devote themselves to the duties of good citizenship and to the arousing of the social energies which too largely lie dormant in every neighborhood given over to industrialism. They are bound to regard the entire life of their city as organic, to make an effort to unify it, and to protest against its over-differentiation

ANSWERS AND EXPLANATIONS

Multiple-Choice Questions

■ **1. (A) is correct.** Progressives were optimistic about the ability of citizens improving socio-economic conditions within government. They shared a fundamental ethos, or belief, that America need a new social consciousness to cope with the problems brought on by the enormous rush of economic and social change in the post-Civil War decades.

■ **2. (A) is correct.** Jane Addams founded one of the first settlement houses, Hull House, in Chicago in 1889, after years of struggling to find work and a social identity equal to her talents. Many educated women were dissatisfied with the life choices conventionally available to them: early marriage or traditional female professions of teaching, nursing, and library work.

■ **3. (E) is correct.** By the turn of the century, Democratic Party machines, usually dominated by first- and second-generation Irish, controlled the political life of most large American cities. The keys to machine strength were disciplined organization and the delivery of essential services to both immigrant communities and business elites. The successful machine politician viewed his work as a business, and he accumulated his capital by serving people who needed assistance.

■ **4. (E) is correct.** In the South, the populist tradition of the 1880s and the 1890s had been based in part on a biracial politics of protest. But Southern progressivism was for white people only. Indeed, Southern progressives believed that the disfranchisement of black voters and the creation of a legally segregated public sphere were necessary preconditions for political and social reform.

■ **5. (A) is correct.** During the last two decades of the nineteenth century, the Woman's Christian Temperance Union had grown into a powerful mass organization. The WCTU appealed especially to women angered by men who used alcohol and then abused their wives and children. It directed most of its work toward ending the production, sale, and consumption of alcohol. But local WCTU chapters put their energy into non-temperance activities as well, including homeless shelters, Sunday schools, prision reform, child nurseries, and woman suffrage. The WCTU thus provided women with a political forum in which they could fuse their traditional moral posture as guaradians of the home with broader public concerns.

▨ **6. (E) is correct.** Between 1908 and 1914, exposés of the "white slave traffic" became a national sensation. Dozens of books, articles, and motion pictures alleged an international conspiracy to seduce and sell girls into prostitution. Most of these materials exaggerated the practices they attacked. They also made foreigners, especially Jews and southern Europeans, scapegoats for the sexual anxieties of native-born whites.

▨ **7. (A) is correct.** Progressive educators look to the public school primarily as an agent of "Americanization." Elwood Cubberley, a leading educational reformer, expressed the view that schools could be the vehicle by which immigrant children could break free of the parochial ethnic neighborhood.

▨ **8. (A) is correct.** In the bitter aftermath of the fire, women progressives joined with Tammany Hall leaders Al Smith, Robert Wagner, and Big Tim Sullivan to create a New York State Factory Investigation Commission. Under Perkins's vigorous leadership, the commission conducted an unprecedented round of public hearings and on-site inspections, leading to a series of state laws that dramatically improved the safety conditions and limited the hours for working women and children.

▨ **9. (E) is correct.** Following the depression of the 1890s, the American Federation of Labor emerged as the strongest and most stable organization of workers. Samuel Gompers's strategy of recruiting skilled labor into unions organized by craft had paid off.

▨ **10. (E) is correct.** President Theodore Roosevelt's support for the Hepburn Act and the Pure Food and Drug Act reflected his beliefs in regulating big business. The acts expanded the regulatory power of the federal government. The battles surrounding these reforms demonstrate how progressive measures often attracted supporters with competing motives. In both cases, supporters hailed the new laws as providing consumer protection against adulterated or fraudulently labeled food and drugs.

Document-Based Question

What themes united different groups of progressive reformers and how were those themes evident in the reform activities and philosophies of these groups?

The Progressive movement was not one single unified reform attempt but was instead a series of divergent local and national reform activities that shared common themes. Progressives responded to the problems caused by increased urbanization, concerns over expanding and often corrupt government practices, the rapid growth of American business and industry, and the resultant changes these developments had on American society. Bolstered by an optimistic faith in the idea of progress, progressives employed a number of different tactics in a variety of areas to bring positive improvements that would help America better handle its new conditions. Some reformers focused on the need to improve and alter the structure of urban government, which had long been a subject of muckraking exposes that unearthed the inherent corruption of the older city machine politics (**DOCUMENT 1**). Experimenting with new forms of governmental structure was one way of attacking this problem (**DOCUMENT 2**). Many viewed the drive to create "good government" as a way to expand democracy in the United States. On a national level, the direct election of senators was achieved through the passage of a constitutional amendment, but for many Americans, this was not enough to fulfill the promises of American democracy. African Americans, increasingly limited in political and economic power by the institution of legal segregation in the late nineteenth century, united to demand more political and civic equality (**DOCUMENT 3**). Similarly, women continued their suffrage campaign, often stressing the improvements to society that could be made through women's greater political participation (**DOCUMENT 4**).

Related to the campaigns for good government was the attempt of reformers to address the increased power of big business and industry. President Theodore Roosevelt, responding to public concerns over the rapid consolidation of American business, which many believed would threaten competition, initiated a series of attacks on large corporations, earning a reputation as a "trustbuster" (**DOCUMENT 5**). Lawyer and future Supreme Court justice Louis Brandeis similarly criticized the trend toward consolidation (**DOCUMENT 6**). Labor often rejected the validity of corporate and business power altogether, as demonstrated by the program of the growing Socialist movement in the United States, which fought for worker control over industry as a way ameliorating inequality in American society (**DOCUMENT 7**). Many sympathized with the plight of the workers, and labor organizations and worker strikes were viewed by many as the answer to the problems created by industrialization and corporate development (**DOCUMENT 8**). Still others worked to address the poor urban conditions in which most workers, many of whom were immigrants, lived and struggled to assimilate into American society. Though there is a debate about whether such workers were actually trying to exercise social control over the new urban masses, such urban social reforms were often broad-based attempts to address many of the Progressive Era concerns, including corrupt government, labor justice, and poor urban conditions (**DOCUMENT 9**).

CHAPTER 22

World War I, 1914–1920

This chapter begins with the activist foreign policy of progressive presidents Roosevelt, Taft, and Wilson. America became more interventionist in the Western Hemisphere, but when war broke out in Europe in 1914, most Americans did not see any national interest at stake. However, eventually the United States joined the Allies when Germany broke its pledges to restrict the use of the submarine. Americans mobilized rapidly, accepting unprecedented governmental control. A drive to mobilize Americans' minds led to domestic hostility toward ethnic groups and "reds," and serious violations of civil rights that went largely unpunished. The war also affected women and African Americans. Wilson took his "Fourteen Points" to the Peace Conference in Paris with the goal of establishing a new international order, but opponents in Europe and at home, along with Wilson's own uncompromising attitude ultimately defeated him. U.S. victory in World War I did not prevent the country from becoming a reluctant, even "isolationist" world power. In the 1920 election, Americans overwhelmingly chose Republican Warren Harding's "normalcy" and sought to put the turbulence of the progressive and war years behind them.

Becoming a World Power

Theodore Roosevelt's aggressive foreign policy made the United States a world power. He used force and diplomacy to pursue his goals. William Howard Taft continued the U.S. role as police power stressing economic means, though he too used military force. Woodrow Wilson tried to blend morality and realism in foreign policy but experienced difficulties in dealing with the Mexican Revolution.

The Great War

When World War I erupted, the United States adopted a policy of neutrality that proved impossible to maintain. Despite strong opposition, Wilson launched a preparedness program in 1916. German actions in 1917 led Wilson to declare war on that nation and its allies.

American Mobilization

The United States was unprepared for war and the government was uncertain about the public's willingness to fight. The Committee on Public Information mobilized popular support for the war and opposition faded. The greatest challenge was raising, training, and deploying military forces. African Americans experienced racism from American military figures but received much better treatment from the French. By 1918, American forces joined the fighting in France. Eight months later, the war ended, thanks in part to American involvement.

Over Here

In one sense, the progressive movement reached its ultimate in the government's regulation of American society during World War I. Industry, fuel, and food were all regulated by government committees. War bond drives financed much of the war costs. The stress on efficiency influenced postwar business development. Labor also faced regulations but won many rights. The radical labor movement, however, was decimated.

Another major aspect was the entry of women in the workplace and their wartime service helped secure passage of women suffrage. Moral reformers achieved their goal of prohibition. Another area receiving attention was public health.

Repression and Reaction

As the government tried to unify public opinion behind the war, it cracked down on dissenters and radicals, especially in the wake of the Russian Revolution. Tensions also arose over the African American migration to northern cities. The war's end ushered in a brief period of militant labor activities that largely failed.

An Uneasy Peace

Wilson went to the Versailles conference with a comprehensive plan for peace but was unable to implement much of his program. The treaty dealt harshly with Germany. Wilson also faced resistance at home and Congress did not approve the treaty. The Russian Revolution produced a Red Scare in the United States. Seeking less turmoil and a break from two decades of change, the American people elected Harding as president.

Multiple-Choice Questions

1. The Roosevelt Corollary was issued because
   (A) Roosevelt wanted to prevent armed European intervention in South America.
   (B) Roosevelt was afraid of losing face in Europe.
   (C) Roosevelt wanted to prevent the Japanese from colonizing Nicaragua.
   (D) Roosevelt wanted to assure European creditors access to Latin markets.
   (E) Roosevelt wanted an open door policy toward China.

2. William Howard Taft's Central American policy depended on
   (A) good will toward all nations.
   (B) the carrot and the stick.
   (C) dollars and guns.
   (D) big stick diplomacy.
   (E) giving foreigners access to U.S. land.

3. Wilson's efforts to manage the Mexican Revolution and protect U.S. interests in Mexico resulted in
   (A) a legacy of suspicion and mistrust between the two nations.
   (B) cooperation between the nations that culminated in NAFTA.
   (C) an era of good feelings between the nations.
   (D) a war between Mexico and the United States.
   (E) Pancho Villa's resignation from the Mexican Parliament.

4. The greatest barrier to true U.S. neutrality was
   (A) economic ties to the allies.
   (B) a huge pacifist movement in the United States.
   (C) U.S. citizens' undivided support for England.
   (D) a total commitment to the Central Powers.
   (E) a desire by American arms manufactures to sell to all sides.

5. Which of the following is NOT true of the Committee on Public Information?
   (A) Chairman George Creel took it from government news coordination to promoting the war effort.
   (B) The committee created massive writings, films, and advertising for the war.
   (C) Film stars were recruited to sell war bonds.
   (D) It wanted to mold Americans into a "white hot mass."
   (E) Creel's materials played up the "Old World" ties of Americans.

6. Feminist Carrie Chapman Catt supported women working in the war service because she believed ultimately this would give women
   (A) suffrage.
   (B) social respect.
   (C) employment.
   (D) the right to hold office.
   (E) increases in wages after the war.

7. Which of the following was NOT one of the Fourteen Points of President Wilson?
   (A) reduced armaments
   (B) open covenants
   (C) controlled trade
   (D) mediation for colonial claims
   (E) the setting of postwar boundaries

8. Which of the following was a governmental tool, used during WWI, to destroy radical labor unions like IWW?
   (A) the Espionage Act.
   (B) the National Labor Relation Control Act.
   (C) encouraging radical union leaders to join more respectable unions.
   (D) drafting radical labor leaders into the military.
   (E) increasing wages for all labor and thereby removing the need for unions.

9. In the ratification debate on the Versailles Treaty, Senator Lodge and his supporters focused on
   (A) congressional authority to declare war if the United States was in the League of Nations.
   (B) opposing entry into the war in the first place.
   (C) mechanisms for the preservation of civil rights in Europe.
   (D) isolationism as the best position for American security in the postwar world.
   (E) fighting all versions of the treaty.

10. WWI inflamed hatred against all of the following groups EXCEPT
    (A) the American Federation of Labor.
    (B) Socialists.
    (C) dissenters.
    (D) African Americans.
    (E) Radicals.

Document-Based Question

There are both internationalist and Isolationist streams in the history of American thought. Discuss the role that this continuing debate played in the period surrounding World War I.

DOCUMENT 1

DOCUMENT 2

THE WORLD'S CONSTABLE

DOCUMENT 3

Source: Woodrow Wilson, The Fourteen Points (1918)

We entered this war because violations of right had occurred which touched us to the quick and made the life of our own people impossible unless they were corrected and the world secure once for all against their recurrence.

What we demand in this war, therefore, is nothing peculiar to ourselves. It is that the world be made fit and safe to live in; and particularly that it be made safe for every peace-loving nation which, like our own, wishes to live its own life, determine its own institutions, be assured of justice and fair dealing by the other peoples of the world as against force and selfish aggressions...

14. A general association of nations must be formed under specific covenants for the purpose of affording mutual guarantees of political independence and territorial integrity to great and small states alike.

DOCUMENT 4

Source: Boy Scouts of America from, "Boy Scouts Support the War Effort" (1917)

This patriotic service will be rendered under the slogan: "EVERY SCOUT TO BOOST AMERICA" AS A GOVERNMENT DISPATCH BEARER. The World War is for liberty and democracy.

America has long been recognized as the leader among nations standing for liberty and democracy. American entered the war as a sacred duty to uphold the principles of liberty and democracy.

As a democracy, our country faces great danger-not so much from submarines, battleships and armies, because, thanks to our allies, our enemies have apparently little chance of reaching our shores.

Our danger is from within. Our enemies have representatives everywhere; they tell lies; they mispresent the truth; they deceive our own people; they are a real menace to our country.

DOCUMENT 5

The Great War
Source: Francis Whiting Halsey, The Literary Digest History of the World War vol. IV (New York 1920), pp. 26–32.

Observers felt that the President, while reading his address, did not know how thoroughly the whole country not only sympathized with him in the great crisis, but voiced its sincere determination to support him, until he had heard the cheers that greeted a later passage as he delivered it slowly, almost haltingly at times, but with deep emphasis, as follows:

"With a profound sense of the solemn and even tragical character of the step I am taking, and of the grave responsibilities which it involves, but in unhesitating obedience to what I deem my constitutional duty, I advise that the Congress declare the recent course of the Imperial German Government to be in fact nothing less than war against the Government and People of the United States; that it formally accept the status of belligerent which has thus been thrust upon it; and that it take immediate steps not only to put the country in a more thorough state of defense, but also to exert all its power and employ all its resources to bring the Government of the German Empire to terms and end the war."

DOCUMENT 6

Source: Warren G. Harding, Campaign Speech at Boston (1920)

This republic has its ample tasks. If we put an end to false economics which lure humanity to utter chaos, ours will be the commanding example of world leadership today. If we can prove a representative popular government under which a citizenship seeks what it may do for the government rather than what the government may do for individuals, we shall do more to make democracy safe for the world than all armed conflict ever recorded. The world needs to be reminded that all human ills are not curable by legislation, and that quantity of statutory enactment and excess of government offer no substitute for quality of citizenship. . . .

My best judgment of America's needs is to steady down, to get squarely on our feet, to make sure of the right path. Let's get out of the fevered delirium of war, with the hallucination that all the money in the world is to be made in the madness of war and the wildness of its aftermath. Let us stop to consider that tranquility at home is more precious than peace abroad, and that both our good fortune and our eminence are dependent on the normal forward stride of all the American people

DOCUMENT 7

Source: American Troops in the Trenches (1918)

July 21.—What a week this has been in the world's history! A week ago, while the French were celebrating Bastille Day, the Germans, strong in hope because of two preceding drives, were making ready for another great effort. On the 15th they launched an attack from Château-Thierry to north of Châlons on a 100-kilometer front. They crossed the Marne and moved a short distance toward their objectives. Then, out of a clear sky, July 18, came Foch's blow from Soissons to Château-Thierry. On Thursday and Friday French and Americans fought ahead, and then today they hit Ludendorff a body blow south of the Marne. The week started with a formidable German offensive. The week ends with a great allied offensive.

Americans, French, English—all the Allies—now face the fury of the German high command, with its great military machine. That machine is big and powerful, but it is not the machine it used to be. The morale of the German Army is weakening from day to day. The size of the German Army is growing surely less day by day.

The morale of the allied armies is getting better every day, and because of America the size of the allied armies is growing day by day. The defeat of Germany is but a matter of time. How much time no one can say. America should rejoice, but America should not be overconfident. But for what France has to be thankful for America has a just right to be thankful for, too.

ANSWERS AND EXPLANATIONS

Multiple-Choice Questions

1. **(A) is correct.** To prevent armed intervention by the Europeans over the Panama Canal affair, Roosevelt proclaimed what became known as the Roosevelt Corollary to the Monroe Doctrine. "Chronic wrongdoing, or an impotence which results in a general loosening of the ties of civilized society," the statement read, justified "the exercise of an international police power" anywhere in the hemisphere. Roosevelt used the corollary to justify U.S. intervention in the region, beginning with the Dominican Republic in 1905.

2. **(C) is correct.** Roosevelt's successor, William Howard Taft, believed he could replace the militarism of the big stick with the more subtle and effective weapon of business investment. Taft and his secretary of state, corporate lawyer Philander C. Knox, followed a strategy (called "dollar diplomacy" by critics) in which they assumed that political influence would follow increased U.S. trade and investment. But dollar diplomacy ended up requiring military support. The Taft administration sent the navy and the marines to intervene in political disputes in Honduras and Nicaragua, propping up factions pledged to protect American business interests.

3. **(A) is correct.** Wilson's attempt to guide the course of Mexico's revolution and protect U.S. interests left a bitter legacy of suspicion and distrust in Mexico. It also suggested the limits of a foreign policy tied to a moral vision rooted in the idea of American exceptionalism.

4. **(A) is correct.** President Wilson issued a formal proclamation of neutrality and urged citizens to be "impartial in thought as well as in action." In practice, powerful cultural, political, and economic factors made the impartiality advocated by Wilson impossible. The U.S. population included many ethnic groups with close emotional ties to the Old World. About one-third of Americans were either foreign-born or had one or both parents who were immigrants. Strong support for the Allies and the Central Powers could be found amongst Americans.

5. **(E) is correct.** Just a week after signing the war declaration, Wilson created the Committee on Public Information (CPI) to organize public opinion. It was dominated by its civilian chairman, the journalist and reformer George Creel. Creel quickly transformed the CPI from its original function as coordinator of government news into a sophisticated and aggressive agency for promoting the war. CPI committees produced more than 100 million pieces of literature—pamphlets, articles, books—that explained the causes and meaning of the war. It also called upon movie stars to help sell war bonds at huge rallies. The CPI also urged ethnic Americans to abandon their Old World ties.

6. **(A) is correct.** Most of the leading lights of The Women's Peace Party, Florence Kelley, Lillian D. Wald, and Carrie Chapman Catt, threw themselves into volunteer war work. Catt, leader of the huge National American Woman Suffrage Association (NAWSA) believed that supporting the war might help women win the right to vote.

7. **(C) is correct.** The Fourteen Points, as a blueprint for peace, contained three main elements. First, Wilson offered a series of specific proposals for setting postwar boundaries in Europe and creating new countries out of the collapsed Austro-Hungarian and Ottoman empires. The key idea here was the right of all peoples to "national self-determination." Second, Wilson listed general principles for governing international conduct, including freedom of the seas, free trade, open covenants instead of secret treaties, reduced armaments, and meditation for competing colonial claims. Third, and most important, Wilson called for a League of Nations to help implement these principles and resolve future disputes.

■ **8. (A) is correct.** The Espionage Act contained vague prohibitions against obstructing the nation's war effort. Under its authority, Justice Department agents swooped down on IWW offices, arresting more than 300 people and confiscating files. The mass trials and convictions that followed broke the back of America's radical labor movement and marked the beginning of a powerful wave of political repression.

■ **9. (A) is correct.** The influential opponents of the Treaty of Versailles were led by Republican Henry Cabot Lodge of Massachusetts, a powerful majority leader of the Senate. They had strong reservations about the League of Nations, especially the provisions for collective security in the event of a member nation being attacked. Lodge argued that the provision impinged on congressional authority to declare war and placed unacceptable constraints on the nation's ability to pursue an independent foreign policy.

■ **10. (A) is correct.** As the demand for labor intensified, the federal government was forced to recognize that labor, like any other resource or commodity, would have to be more carefully tended to than in peacetime. For the war's duration, working people generally enjoyed higher wages and a better standard of living. Trade unions, especially those affiliated with the American Federation of Labor (AFL), experienced a sharp rise in membership. In effect, the government took in labor as a junior partner in the mobilization of the economy.

Document-Based Question

There are both internationalist and isolationist streams in the history of American thought.
Discuss the role that this continuing debate played in the period surrounding World War I.

The United States has always had an ambiguous relationship with the rest of the world. Though Washington warned against entangling foreign alliances in his farewell address, there have always been those who saw benefits in working with foreign governments. At the beginning of the twentieth century internationalist thinking was on the upswing, culminating with the American participation in World War I, but afterward war weariness pushed the country back into an isolationist perspective.

Theodore Roosevelt's presidency was one that stressed internationalism. Aside from his imperial adventures in the Philippines and Cuba, Roosevelt also won the Nobel Peace Prize for helping to end the Russo-Japanese war. However, his efforts were not viewed by every American as appropriate. He was mocked by some as "the world's constable," a busybody interfering where he had no business (**DOCUMENT 2**).

Woodrow Wilson continued Roosevelt's internationalist policies. He interfered frequently in South American politics, attempting to sow liberty there, in his view. He was also mocked (**DOCUMENT 1**), though others approved of his efforts, When the war in Europe started, he kept the United States neutral. In fact, he ran for a second term with the slogan, "I Kept America Out of the War." However, he was looking for a way to get involved, and he soon had one. Germany's policy of unrestricted submarine warfare was considered sufficient excuse to declare war. When Wilson did so, he had the whole nation behind him (**DOCUMENT 5**).

The entire country threw itself into the war effort. Men signed up for the newly instituted draft in droves (though the fact that they needed to be drafted may be a sign that they were less enthusiastic than they liked to pretend). Women were co-opted into the workforce. Even children did what they could (**DOCUMENT 4**). The soldiers in the trenches were confident of success (**DOCUMENT 7**). The spirit of international cooperation was high.

At the end of the war, Wilson continued his internationist policies. At the Versaille conferences he pushed an agenda that promoted national determination for the citizens of the now defunct German and Ottoman empires. He also wanted to create an international body to adjudicate disputes between countries, a League of Nations (**DOCUMENT 3**). However, at this point America's isolationist streak asserted itself. The Senate refused to ratify a treaty that subjected America's foreign policy to foreign approval. They would not join the League. At the end of the war, Americans wanted to turn inward. They were tired of getting involved in Europes troubles. Instead, they wanted to heal their wounds and deal with American issues (**DOCUMENT 6**).

The beginning of the twentieth century was a period of strong internationalist tendencies in the United States. However, the trauma of the First World War caused Americans to rethink these policies and return to a more traditional isolationist perspective.

CHAPTER 23

The Twenties, 1920–1929

This chapter covers the many changes in American life in the 1920s. After the war, Presidents Harding, Coolidge, and Hoover continued to encourage a foreign policy that would enhance American capitalism. A second Industrial Revolution of sorts took place, based on greatly expanded use of electrical power, a flood of consumer goods, easy credit, and new scientific management methods. The "Auto Age" produced profound changes in American life and housing patterns. Some areas such as agriculture, railroads, coal mining, and textile manufacturing did not share in the postwar prosperity. A new mass culture defined by radio, movies, music, newspapers, and advertising encouraged a kind of national community. Some groups such as the Ku Klux Klan resisted modernity, but met with mixed results. The postponement of democratic promise continued to stir reaction in women's groups, in Mexican Americans and most especially the "New Negro." Intellectuals tried to put into writing the alienation and doubts connected with headlong pursuit of material prosperity.

Postwar Prosperity and its Price

The twenties ushered in the second Industrial Revolution that stimulated a boom in several industries. At the same time, the modern corporation changed how business was organized and worked. Prosperity fostered the corporate idea of welfare capitalism while unions declined. The epitome of the new age was the automobile that influenced where people lived, their daily life, and their leisure activities, among many other things. Despite the appearance of prosperity, several sectors of the economy experienced significant declines.

The New Mass Culture

New media transformed American culture in the 1920s. Popular entertainment, sports, journalism, and advertising encouraged the culture of consumption and the idea of celebrity. The media promoted a new morality that celebrated sensuality and personal pleasure.

Resistance to Modernity

Not all Americans embraced modern changes. Especially outside big cities, resistance to modern trends and longing for the past was evident in several movements, including prohibition, immigration, the Ku Klux Klan, and religious fundamentalism.

The State, the Economy, and Business

The Republican presidents promoted a business-government partnership that stressed business profits. Despite abuses and scandals, the nation experienced general prosperity. The issue of war reparations also arose but was settled by an "American plan." During the early twenties, naval disarmament treaties were signed. United States foreign policy aimed to promote business expansion overseas.

Promises Postponed

Prosperity did not lead to advances in status and rights for several groups. Though winning the right to vote, women faced strong barriers to achieving other political, social, and economic gains but did make some progress. Mexican immigration increased and while immigrants faced racism they built strong communities. African Americans also emerged from the war with mixed feelings. They developed a strong movement based on race pride and consciousness that led to a rich cultural flowering. Intellectuals were another group who felt alienated. They developed a strong literary tradition. The opposing forces evident in the 1920s came to a head in the 1928 election that was won by Herbert Hoover.

Multiple-Choice Questions

1. Suburban living during the 1920s was possible because of
   (A) land grants to construction companies.
   (B) the urban housing debacle.
   (C) government grant money for mortgages.
   (D) subsidized housing.
   (E) the growth of the automobile industry and mass transit.

2. Large employers implemented welfare capitalism in an effort to
   (A) undermine unions.
   (B) meet government standards.
   (C) strengthen unions.
   (D) fulfill their strong social conscience.
   (E) keep workers employed.

3. In 1913 it took thirteen hours to produce one automobile. By 1925, Henry Ford's new plants were producing one
   (A) every ten seconds.
   (B) every ninety minutes.
   (C) in one hour.
   (D) every two hours.
   (E) every three hours.

4. One reason why the coal industry declined was
   (A) oil and natural gas became the dominant energy sources.
   (B) a dramatic shortage.
   (C) coal was too dirty.
   (D) coal owners switched to other energy sources.
   (E) the natural sources of coal disappeared.

5. The movie industry in the 1920s entered a new phase with the studio system which meant
   (A) depending on Wall Street investors for financing.
   (B) exaggerating the star-celebrity cult.
   (C) controlling production, distribution, and exhibition.
   (D) only three studios could produce movies.
   (E) increasing the advertising element of moviemaking.

6. Which of the following contributed to a more open treatment of sexuality in the 1920s?
   (A) Sigmund Freud stressed puritanical behavior.
   (B) the third "Great Awakening."
   (C) Victorian parents allowed more permissiveness.
   (D) the government educated the public on the dangers of puritanical behavior.
   (E) more education about birth control

7. A call for immigration restrictions resulted from
   (A) a form of racism directed at immigrants from eastern and southern Europe.
   (B) a dislike of northern and western Europeans.
   (C) a dislike of Asians and Hispanic peoples.
   (D) a feeling that the U.S. population had reached its maximum capacity.
   (E) a feeling that new immigrants would use up too much of the existing farm land.

8. This president lamented that the job was too much for him and his friends were a worse problem than his enemies:
   (A) Calvin Coolidge.
   (B) Herbert Hoover.
   (C) Warren G. Harding.
   (D) Woodrow Wilson.
   (E) Theodore Roosevelt

9. The "associative state" that President Hoover proposed relied on
   (A) an aggressive overseas expansion of business as well as exports.
   (B) union, government, and business cooperation.
   (C) the pacific tendencies of Americans and Europeans.
   (D) voluntary collaboration between business, consumers, farmers, and workers.
   (E) volunteers who performed a variety of civic responsibilities.

10. The National American Woman Suffrage Association and the National Woman's Party argued over the following:
   (A) which group gave more protection to immigrants.
   (B) methods for achieving full suffrage.
   (C) which group should become involved in the next presidential election.
   (D) which group had a greater social conscience.
   (E) labor laws to protect women.

Document-Based Question

The 1920s are often viewed as the era that signaled the onset of "modernity" in American culture. In what ways can American culture in the 1920s be seen as a battleground of conflicting responses and reactions to modernity?

DOCUMENT 1

The Sahara of the Bozart (1920)
Source: H.L. Mencken, Prejudices 2nd Series, (New York: A. A. Knopf, 1920), pp. 136–154.

Consider, for example, the present estate and dignity of Virginia—in the great days indubitably the premier American state, the mother of Presidents and statesmen, the home of the first American university worthy of the name, the arbiter elegantiarum of the western world. Well, observe Virginia to-day. It is years since a first-rate man, save only Cabell, has come out of it; it is years since an idea has come out of it. The old aristocracy went down the red gullet of war; the poor white trash are now in the saddle. Politics in Virginia are cheap, ignorant, parochial, idiotic; there is scarcely a man in office above the rank of a professional job-seeker; the political doctrine that prevails is made up of hand-me-downs from the bumpkinry of the Middle West—Bryanism, Prohibition, vice crusading, all that sort of filthy claptrap; the administration of the law is turned over to professors of Puritanism and espionage; a Washington or a Jefferson, dumped there by some act of God, would be denounced as a scoundrel and jailed overnight. Elegance, esprit, culture? Virginia has no art, no literature, no philosophy, no mind or aspiration of her own. Her education has sunk to the Baptist seminary level; not a single contribution to human knowledge has come out of her colleges in twenty-five years; she spends less than half upon her common schools, per capita, than any northern state spends. In brief, an intellectual Gobi or Lapland. Urbanity, politesse, chivalry? Go to! It was in Virginia that they invented the device of searching for contraband whisky in women's underwear.

. . . There remains, at the top, a ghost of the old aristocracy, a bit wistful and infinitely charming. But it has lost all its old leadership to fabulous monsters from the lower depths; it is submerged in an industrial plutocracy that is ignorant and ignominious. The mind of the state, as it is revealed to the nation, is pathetically naïve and inconsequential.

It no longer reacts with energy and elasticity to great problems. It has fallen to the bombastic trivialities of the camp-meeting and the chautauqua.

DOCUMENT 2

DOCUMENT 3

Source: Advertisements (1925, 1927)

Advertisement for Berkey & Gay Furniture Company (1925)

Do they know Your son at MALUCIO's?

There's a hole in the door at Malucio's. Ring the bell and a pair of eyes will look coldly out at you. If you are known you will get in. Malucio has to be careful.

There have been riotous nights at Malucio's. Tragic nights, too. But somehow the fat little man has managed to avoid the law.

Almost every town has its Malucio's. Some, brightly disguised as cabarets-others, mere back street filling stations for pocket flasks.

But every Malucio will tell you the same thing. His best customers are not the ne'er-do-wells of other years. They are the young people-frequently, the best young people of the town.

Malucio has put one over on the American home. Ultimately he will be driven out. Until then THE HOME MUST BID MORE INTELLIGENTLY FOR MALUCIO'S BUSINESS.

There are many reasons why it is profitable and wise to furnish the home attractively, but one of these, and not the least, is-Malucio's.

The younger generation is sensitive to beauty, princely proud, and will not entertain in homes of which it is secretly ashamed.

But make your rooms attractive, appeal to the vaulting pride of youth, and you may worry that much less about Malucio's-and the other modern frivolities that his name symbolizes.

A guest room smartly and tastefully furnished-a refined and attractive dining room-will more than hold their own against the tinsel cheapness of Malucio's.

Nor is good furniture any longer a luxury for the favored few. THE PRESCOTT suite shown above, for instance, is a moderately priced pattern, conforming in every detail to the finest Berkey & Gay standards.

In style, in the selection of rare and beautiful woods, and in the rich texture of the finish and hand decorating, it reveals the skill of craftsmen long expert in the art of quality furniture making.

The PRESCOTT is typical of values now on display at the store of your local Berkey & Gay dealer. Depend on his showing you furniture in which you may take deep pride-beautiful, well built, luxuriously finished, and moderately priced.

There is a Berkey & Gay pattern suited to every home-an infinite variety of styles at prices ranging all the way from $350 to $6,000.

DOCUMENT 4

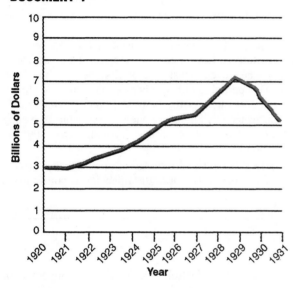

DOCUMENT 5

Family Planning (1926)
Source: Margaret Sanger, Happiness in Marriage (1926) pp. 191–203.

We must recognize that the whole position of womanhood has changed today. Not so many years ago it was assumed to be a just and natural state of affairs that marriage was considered as nothing but a preliminary to motherhood. A girl passed from the guardianship of her father or nearest male relative to that of her husband. She had no will, no wishes of her own. Hers not to question why, but merely to fulfill duties imposed upon her by the man into whose care she was given.

Today women are on the whole much more individual. They possess as strong likes and dislikes as men. They live more and more on the plane of social equality with men. They are better companions. We should be glad that there is more enjoyable companionship and real friendship between men and women.

This very fact, it is true, complicates the marriage relation, and at the same time enables it. Marriage no longer means the slavish subservience of the woman to the will of the man. It means, instead, the union of two strong and highly individualized natures. Their first problem is to find out just what the terms of this partnership are to be. Understanding full and complete cannot come all at once, in one revealing flash. It takes time to arrive at a full and sympathetic understanding of each other, and mutually to arrange lives to increase this understanding. Out of the mutual adjustments, harmony must grow and discords gradually disappear.

These results cannot be obtained if the problem of parenthood is thrust upon the young husband and wife before they are spiritually and economically prepared to meet it. For naturally the coming of the first baby means that all other problems must be thrust aside. That baby is a great fact, a reality that must be met. Preparations must be made for its coming. The layette must be prepared. The doctor must be consulted. The health of the wife may need consideration. The young mother will probably prefer to go to the hospital. All of these preparations are small compared to the régime after the coming of the infant.

In the wife who has lived through a happy marriage, for whom the bonds of passionate love have been fully cemented, maternal desire is intensified and matured. Motherhood becomes for such a woman not a penalty or a punishment, but the road by which she travels onward toward completely rounded self-development. Motherhood thus helps her toward the unfolding and realization of her higher nature.

Her children are not mere accidents, the outcome of chance. When motherhood is a mere accident, as so often it is in the early years of careless or reckless marriages, a constant fear of pregnancy may poison the days and nights of the young mother. Her marriage is thus converted into a tragedy. Motherhood becomes for her a horror instead of a joyfully fulfilled function.

Millions of marriages have been blighted, not because of any lack of love between the young husband and wife, but because children have come too soon. Often these brides become mothers before they have reached even physical maturity, before they have completed the period of adolescence. This period in our race is as a rule complete around the age of twenty-three. Motherhood is possible after the first menstruation. But what is physically possible is very often from every other point of view inadvisable. A young woman should be fully matured from every point of view—physically, mentally and psychically before maternity is thrust upon her.

Those who advise early maternity neglect the spiritual foundation upon which marriage must inevitably be built. This takes time. They also ignore the financial responsibility a family brings.

DOCUMENT 6

The New Woman

In this excerpt, an anonymous female student from Detroit revealed the growing power of the movies and celebrity culture on her and her friends.

Goodness knows, you learn plenty about love from the movies. That's their long run; you learn more from actual experience, though! You do see how the golddigger systematically gets the poor fish in tow. . . . You meet the flapper, the good girl, 'n' all the feminine types and their little tricks of the trade. We pick up their snappy comebacks which are most handy . . .

In this excerpt, Mary Garden explains her reasons for "bobbing," and what it symbolizes for her.

Bobbed hair is a state of mind and not merely a new manner of dressing my head. It typifies growth, alertness, up-todateness, and is part of the expression of the élan vital! [spirit] . . . I consider getting rid of our long hair one of the many little shackles that women have cast aside in their passage to freedom. Whatever helps their emancipation, however small it may seem, is well worth while.

Multiple-Choice Questions

▨ **1. (E) is correct.** The middle and upper classes moved to the suburbs in the 1920s thanks to improvements in transportation and mass transit. Due to mass production, the automobile became affordable to the average American, letting people explore outside their own community.

▨ **2. (A) is correct.** Welfare capitalism was a response to coporate leaders' fear of the power of unions. In welfare capitalism, corporations offered employees stock plans, health insurance, and attempted to make better working conditions. Still, unions continued because industries still faced the problems of low wages, long hours, and unhealthy working conditions.

▨ **3. (A) is correct.** With the continous assembly line, Henry Ford's company drastically reduced the worker hours it took to make a single automobile. Everything on the factory floor was in constant movement. Due to this, Ford shrewdly increased wages and lowered working hours which increased efficiency and morale within his factories.

▨ **4. (A) is correct.** Due to the increase in natural gas and oil, demand for coal decreased. This combined with new mining technology and losing strikes depleted the coal workforce, seriously damaging the economies in Appalachia and the southern Midwest.

▨ **5. (C) is correct.** Each studio in addition to controlling all aspects of the movie industry, controlled thousands of movie theaters across the country. The industry moved from silent movies to "talkies," which carried subject matters such as musicals, gangster films, and screwball comedies.

▨ **6. (E) is correct.** Sex education began to appear in the 1920s, with Margaret Sanger becoming the nation's leading advocate on birth control. In her journal, *Birth Control Review,* Sanger argued that contraceptives should be made freely available to all women.

▨ **7. (A) is correct.** Between 1891 and 1920 a new wave of 10.5 million immigrants arrived from northern and eastern Europe. These "new immigrants" were mostly Catholic and Jewish. They were darker skinned and looked more exotic and foreign, therefore people wondered if they would conform to the nation's political and cultural values.

▨ **8. (C) is correct.** Even though he looked the part of President, Harding was exposed for his shallowness, intellectual weakness, and favoritism towards his friends, known as the "Ohio Gang." After his death in office from a heart attack in 1923, widespread corruption in his administration was discovered. Harding is considered by most historians to be one of the weaker chief executives in our nation's history.

▨ **9. (D) is correct.** President Hoover believed in old-fashioned individualism, in which he not only wanted a favorable business climate, but one in which the government actively supported the business community. The "associative state" became the main occupation of the Department of Commerce during the Hoover administration.

▨ **10. (E) is correct.** The National American Woman's Suffrage Association argued for not just suffrage, but equal rights in the workplace and protections in the law for women and children. The National Woman's Party on the other hand, downplayed the issue of suffrage, while arguing that protective legislation for women enforced stereotyping even more, preventing women from competing with men in the workplace.

ANSWERS AND EXPLANATIONS

Multiple-Choice Questions

1. (E) is correct. The middle and upper classes moved to the suburbs in the 1920s thanks to improvements in transportation and mass transit. Due to mass production, the automobile became affordable to the average American, letting people explore outside their own community.

2. (A) is correct. Welfare capitalism was a response to coporate leaders' fear of the power of unions. In welfare capitalism, corporations offered employees stock plans, health insurance, and attempted to make better working conditions. Still, unions continued because industries still faced the problems of low wages, long hours, and unhealthy working conditions.

3. (B) is correct. With the continous assembly line, Henry Ford's company drastically reduced the worker hours it took to make a single automobile. Everything on the factory floor was in constant movement. Due to this, Ford shrewdly increased wages and lowered working hours which increased efficiency and morale within his factories.

4. (A) is correct. Due to the increase in natural gas and oil, demand for coal decreased. This combined with new mining technology and losing strikes depleted the coal workforce, seriously damaging the economies in Appalachia and the southern Midwest.

5. (C) is correct. Each studio in addition to controlling all aspects of the movie industry, controlled thousands of movie theaters across the country. The industry moved from silent movies to "talkies," which carried subject matters such as musicals, gangster films, and screwball comedies.

6. (E) is correct. Sex education began to appear in the 1920s, with Margaret Sanger becoming the nation's leading advocate on birth control. In her journal, *Birth Control Review,* Sanger argued that contraceptives should be made freely available to all women.

7. (A) is correct. Between 1891 and 1920 a new wave of 10.5 million immigrants arrived from northern and eastern Europe. These "new immigrants" were mostly Catholic and Jewish. They were darker skinned and looked more exotic and foreign, therefore people wondered if they would conform to the nation's political and cultural values.

8. (C) is correct. Even though he looked the part of President, Harding was exposed for his shallowness, intellectual weakness, and favoritism towards his friends, known as the "Ohio Gang." After his death in office from a heart attack in 1923, widespread corruption in his administration was discovered.

9. (D) is correct. President Hoover believed in old-fashioned individualism, in which he not only wanted a favorable business climate, but one in which the government actively supported the business community. The "associative state" became the main occupation of the Department of Commerce during the Hoover administration.

10. (E) is correct. The National American Woman's Suffrage Association argued for not just suffrage, but equal rights in the workplace and protections in the law for women and children. The National Woman's Party on the other hand, downplayed the issue of suffrage, while arguing that protective legislation for women enforced stereotyping even more, preventing women from competing with men in the workplace.

CHAPTER 24

The Great Depression and the New Deal, 1929–1940

This chapter covers the cumulative effects of underlying weaknesses in the American economy and the stock market crash that led to the Great Depression. Many unemployed workers blamed themselves rather than the system, but they increasingly began to look to the government for some relief. President Hoover remained committed to budget balancing and a relatively limited response to the crisis, but frightened and angry voters elected an avowed Democratic reformer, Franklin Delano Roosevelt. His original "New Deal" of 1933 was mostly a cooperative business–government venture, but the "Second New Deal" that followed made a more dramatic shift toward direct government intervention in the economy and direct aid to the unemployed. Neither was as radical as some critics accused Roosevelt of being. Other critics said he was not radical enough. Roosevelt's own ability to inspire, the activism of his wife, Eleanor, and the action-oriented programs of the two New Deals helped restore American confidence, even though none of these issues ended the depression. FDR's impatience with the Supreme Court and his attempt to pack it in 1938 cost him considerable political influence. Deep poverty was not really touched by the programs and minorities did not make major gains, but they did form a coalition of voters that supported the Democratic Party, despite Roosevelt's sometimes uncertain fortunes.

Hard Times

The stock market crash triggered the Great Depression, though underlying economic weaknesses caused the downturn. The sharp decline led to mass unemployment that caused great stress and strains on American society and families. Hoover's attempts to deal with the depression proved ineffective and led to a protest by veterans. The election of 1932 pit Hoover against the reform-minded Franklin Delano Roosevelt, who won a landslide victory.

FDR and the First New Deal

Upon becoming president, Franklin D. Roosevelt sought to bolster confidence both through his words and his actions. In the first hundred days of his term, Roosevelt pushed through several reform programs, addressing various economic and societal problems.

Left Turn and the Second New Deal

Faced with critics on the right and left, Roosevelt responded with the Second New Deal that addressed several remaining issues. Labor responded to the depression by developing the CIO and increasing union membership in large-scale mass production industries. The 1936 election was referendum on the New Deal as Roosevelt won by a stunning landslide.

The New Deal in the South and the West

The New Deal in the South and West touched on environmental concerns and the Indians. Programs aimed at addressing problems that arose from poor weather conditions, the state of the land, and water resources, in part to improve agriculture and conserve the environment. Programs also aimed at reversing government policies on Indians.

Depression-Era Culture

American culture was profoundly affected by the depression. Government sponsorship revived the arts and also stimulated the documenting of the state of the nation and its people. The movies and radio experienced golden ages as they sought to entertain the American people. The power of radio was demonstrated by its influence on the popularity of big-band swing music.

The Limits of Reform

Frustrated with their decisions, Roosevelt tried to change the number of Supreme Court judges, experiencing failure. The New Deal provided women with a temporary increase in women's political influence. Hardest hit by the depression, minorities received some help from the New Deal, but their experience was mixed. By the late 1930s, the New Deal had not ended the depression, as the 1937 recession showed.

Multiple-Choice Questions

1. Which of the following allowed investors to buy stock easily in the 1920s?
   (A) the destruction of the gold standard
   (B) keeping the nation on the gold standard
   (C) buying on margin
   (D) buying stock through the mail
   (E) providing employee stock options

2. Hoover's most important institutional response to the depression was
   (A) the War Finance Corporation.
   (B) the Civilian Conservation Corporation.
   (C) the National Labor Relations Act.
   (D) the Federal Relief Act.
   (E) the Reconstruction Finance Corporation.

3. All of the following were New Deal reform measures implemented in the first 100 days EXCEPT
   (A) the Emergency Banking Act.
   (B) the Civilian Conservation Corps.
   (C) the Federal Emergency Relief Administration.
   (D) the National Labor Relations Act.
   (E) the Agricultural Adjustment Administration.

4. One of the anti-Roosevelt groups, the American Liberty League
   (A) funded Father Charles Coughlin's Wall Street attacks.
   (B) was made up of Republicans and conservative Democrats.
   (C) proposed a more radical solution to the depression.
   (D) demanded more socialistic programs from the New Deal.
   (E) proposed the "old age revolving pension plan."

5. Why did FDR's advisers promote turning left and concentrating on social reform during the second 100 days of the New Deal?
   (A) pressure from Sinclair, Townsend, and Long
   (B) leftward pressure from the public
   (C) pressure from Coughlin, the Liberty League, and Republicans
   (D) pressure from traditional Democrats
   (E) pressure from labor unions

6. The CIO differed from the AFL in that
   (A) the union organized African Americans, women, and unskilled labor.
   (B) it distinguished between various gradations of labor.
   (C) the union organized only skilled labor.
   (D) the union organized only craft labor.
   (E) the union organized only women in the garment industry.

7. Besides providing the cheapest electricity in the United States, the Grand Coulee Dam also
   (A) became a significant tourist attraction.
   (B) destroyed the initiative of local farmers.
   (C) brought African American farmers to the region.

(D) produced wealth for Mexican American workers.

(E) brought new manufacturing to the region.

8. Which one of the following was NOT one of the ways that Eleanor Roosevelt saw her job as First Lady?
(A) a ceremonial position
(B) an influence with her husband on behalf of her causes
(C) a base for independent action
(D) a guardian of human values within the administration.
(E) a buffer between depression victims and government bureaucracy

9. President Roosevelt's attempts to restructure the Supreme Court in 1937
(A) passed overwhelmingly in Congress.
(B) resulted in an overturning of all his New Deal programs.

(C) cost him in political power in Congress, including his own party.
(D) shifted the balance of power to the court.
(E) delighted conservatives but appalled his liberal supporters.

10. California repatriated Mexicans and Mexican Americans because
(A) of pressure from unemployed whites who wanted the work held by Mexicans.
(B) Mexican Americans were willing to go anywhere for work.
(C) Mexico experienced labor shortages.
(D) Mexican Americans found better opportunities in other states.
(E) American Indians demanded these scarce jobs.

Document-Based Question

The crisis of the Great Depression was met with many different political responses. Identify and explain the various political approaches advanced to end the depression. What did they share in common with traditional American political ideologies and how did they differ from those ideologies?

DOCUMENT 1

Source: Herbert Hoover, Speech at New York City (1932)

We have heard a great deal in this campaign about reactionaries, conservatives, progressives, liberals and radicals. I think I belong to every group. I have not yet heard an attempt by any one of the orators who mouth these phrases to define the principles upon which they base these classifications. There is one thing I can say without any question of doubt-that is, that the spirit of liberalism is to create free men; it is not the regimentation of men under government. It is not the extension of bureaucracy. I have said in this city before now that you cannot extend the mastery of government over the daily life of a people without somewhere making it master of people's souls and thoughts. Expansion of government in business means that the government in order to protect itself from the political consequences of its errors or even its successes is driven irresistibly without peace to greater and greater control of the nation's press and platform. Free speech does not live many hours after free industry and free commerce die. It is a false liberalism that interprets itself into government operation of business. Every step in that direction poisons the very roots of liberalism. It poisons political equality, free speech, free press and equality of opportunity. It is the road not to liberty, but to less liberty. True liberalism is found not in striving to spread bureaucracy, but in striving to set bounds to it. It is found in an endeavor to extend cooperation between free men. True liberalism seeks all legitimate freedom first in the confident belief that without such freedom the pursuit of other blessings is in vain. Liberalism is a force truly of the spirit proceeding from the deep realization that economic freedom cannot be sacrificed if political freedom is to be preserved.

Source: Franklin Delano Roosevelt, Speech at San Francisco (1932)

As I see it, the task of Government in its relation to business is to assist the development of an economic declaration of rights, an economic constitutional order. This is the common task of statesman and business man. It is the minimum requirement of a more permanently safe order of things. . . .

The Declaration of Independence discusses the problem of Government in terms of a contract. Government is a relation of give and take, a contract, perforce, if we would follow the thinking out of which it grew. Under such a contract rulers were accorded power, and the people consented to that power on consideration that they be accorded certain rights. The task of statesmanship has always been the re-definition of these rights in terms of a changing and growing social order. New conditions impose new requirements upon Government and those who conduct Government. . . .

I feel that we are coming to a view through the drift of our legislation and our public thinking in the past quarter century that private economic power is, to enlarge an old phrase, a public trust as well. I hold that continued enjoyment of that power by any individual or group must depend upon the fulfillment of that trust. The men who have reached the summit of American business life know this best; happily, many of these urge the binding quality of this greater social contract.

The terms of that contract are as old as the Republic, and as new as the new economic order.

(...)

This implication is, briefly, that the responsible heads of finance and industry instead of acting each for himself, must work together to achieve the common end. They must, where necessary, sacrifice this or that private advantage; and in reciprocal self-denial must seek a general advantage. It is here that formal Government-political Government, if you choose-comes in. Whenever in the pursuit of this objective the lone wolf, the unethical competitor, the reckless promoter, the Ishmael or Insull whose hand is against every man's, declines to join in achieving an end recognized as being for the public welfare, and threatens to drag the industry back to a state of anarchy, the Government may properly be asked to apply restraint. Likewise, should the group ever use its collective power contrary to the public welfare, the Government must be swift to enter and protect the public interest.

DOCUMENT 3

DOCUMENT 4

Share the Wealth

Source: Huey Long, *Every Man A King* (New Orleans, National Book Co., 1933), pp. 290–298.

But, oh, Mr. President, if we could simply let the people enjoy the wealth and the accumulations and the contrivances that we have. If, with the invention of every machine, we could secure the education of every man; if with increased production of every kind there could be less toil, more hours of pleasure and recreation; if there could be a happy and contented people enjoying what the Almighty has made it possible to provide; if there could be people clothed with the materials that we have to clothe them with today, and no place to put them; if the people could be fed with the food that we have to feed them with, and no place to put it; if the people could be sheltered in the homes we have today, that the Federal Land Bank has taken away from them because they cannot pay the interest on the mortgages—if that could be done, if we could distribute this surplus wealth, while leaving these rich people all the luxuries they can possibly use, what a different world this would be.

We can do this. If we do not, we will leave these masters of finance and fame and fortune like the man in the book of old, who said to himself, so the Bible tells us:

"I will pull down my barns, and build greater; and there will I bestow all my fruits and my goods.

"And I will say to my soul: Soul, thou hast much goods laid up for many years; take thine ease, eat, drink and be merry.

"But God said unto him: Thou fool, this night thy soul shalt be required of thee."

While the tax bills were pending before the United States Senate in 1932, I proposed a resolution which provided that the tax bills should be so revamped that no one man should be allowed to have an income of more than one million dollars a year; that no one person should inherit in a lifetime more than five million dollars without working for it. The effect of that resolution was that when a man made one million dollars in a year, the government of the United States would receive the balance; and when a rich man died, he could not leave one child more than five million dollars, and the balance would go to the government of the United States.

This would have meant that much of the taxes would have been paid by the so-called upper classes, and that instead of the funds of the government being sucked from the bottom and exploited by the classes at the top, the classes at the top would have paid the taxes to be filtered out to the masses at the bottom, through the various general works and compensations supported by the government.

DOCUMENT 5

Source: Father Charles E. Coughlin, "A Third Party" (1936)

Thus, with the advent of our scientific era, with its far-flung fields, its spacious factories, its humming motors, its thundering locomotives, its highly trained mechanics, it is inconceivable how such a thing as a so-called depression should blight the lives of an entire nation when there was a plenitude of everything surrounding us, only to be withheld from us because the so-called leaders of high finance persisted in clinging to an outworn theory of privately issued money, the medium through which wealth is distributed.

I challenged this private control and creation of money because it was alien to our Constitution, which says "Congress shall have the right to coin and regulate the value of money." I challenged this system of permitting a small group of private citizens to create money and credit out of nothing, to issue it into circulation through loans and to demand that borrowers repay them with money which represented real goods, real labor and real service. I advocated that it be replaced by the American system-namely, that the creation and control of money and credit are the rights of the people through their democratic government. . . .

ANSWERS AND EXPLANATIONS

Multiple-Choice Questions

1. (C) is correct. Only about 4 million Americans owned any stocks at all, out of a total population of 120 million. Many of these stock buyers had been lured into the market through easy-credit, margin accounts. Margin accounts allowed investors to purchase stocks by making a small down payment (as low as 10 percent), borrowing the rest from a broker, and using the shares as collateral, or security, on the loan. "Buying on the margin" brought new customers to the stock market. Investment trusts, similar to today's mutual funds, attracted many new investors with promises of high returns based on their managers' expert knowledge of the market.

2. (E) is correct. The Hoover administration's most important institutional response to the depression was the Reconstruction Finance Corporation (RFC), established in 1932 and based on the War Finance Corporation of the World War I years. The RFC was designed to make government credit available to ailing banks, railroads, insurance companies, and other businesses, thereby stimulating economic activity. The key assumption here was that the credit problem was one of supply (for businesses) rather than demand (from consumers). But given the public's low purchasing power, most businesses were not interested in obtaining loans for expansion.

3. (D) is correct. From March to June 1933—"the Hundred Days"—FDR pushed through Congress an extraordinary number of acts designed to combat various aspects of the depression. The Civilian Corporation Corps (CCC), established in March as an unemployment relief effort, provided work for jobless young men in protecting and conserving the nation's national resources. The Agricultural Adjustment Act (AAA) was set up to provide immediate relief to the nation's farmers. The Emergency Banking Relief Act enlarged federal authority over private banks, allowing for government loans to private banks. The Federal Emergency Relief Administration directed federal money for relief, funneling it through state and local governments.

4. (B) is correct. Criticism of the New Deal came from the right and the left. On the right, pro-Republican newspapers and the American Liberty League, a group of conservative businessmen organized in 1934, denounced Roosevelt and his advisers. They held the administration responsible for what they considered an attack on property rights, the growing welfare state, and the decline of personal liberty. Dominated by wealthy executives of DuPont and General Motors, the league attracted support from a group of conservative Democrats as well.

5. (A) is correct. The popularity of leaders such as Sinclair, Townsend, and Long suggested Roosevelt might be losing electoral support among workers, farmers, the elderly, and the unemployed. In early 1935, Roosevelt and his closets advisers responded by turning left and concentrating on a new program of social reform. They had three major goals: strengthening the national commitment to creating jobs; providing security against old age, unemployment, and illness; and improving housing conditions and cleaning slums.

6. (A) is correct. At the 1935 AFL convention, a group of more militant union officials led by John L. Lewis and Sidney Hillman formed the Committee for Industrial Organization (CIO). Their goal was to organize mass-production workers by industry rather than by craft. They emphasized the need for opening the new unions to all, regardless of a worker's level of skill. And they differed from nearly all old-line AFL unions by calling for the inclusion of black and women workers. In 1938, CIO unions, now boasting nearly 4 million members, withdrew from the AFL and reorganized themselves as the Congress of Industrial Organizations.

7. (E) is correct. The largest power and irrigation project of all was the Ground Coulee Dam, northwest of Spokane, Washington. Completed in 1941, it was designed to convert the power of the Columbia River into cheap electricity, and to irrigate previously uncultivated land, thereby stimulating the economic development of the Pacific Northwest. In the longer run, Grand Coulee provided the cheapest electricity in the United States, and helped attract new manufacturing to a region previously dependent on the export of raw materials, such as lumber and metals.

8. (A) is correct. Eleanor Roosevelt actively used her prominence as First Lady to fight for the liberal causes she believed in. She revolutionized the role of the political life by taking a position involving no institutional duties and turning it into a base for independent action. Privately, she enjoyed great influence with her husband, and her support for a cause could give it instant credibility. She saw herself as the guardian of "human values" within the administration, a buffer between depression victims and government bureaucracy.

9. (C) is correct. Roosevelt's court-packing scheme met determined opposition from a coalition of conservatives and outraged New Dealers in the Congress. The Court fight badly weakened Roosevelt's relations with Congress. Many more conservative Democrats now felt free to oppose further New Deal measures.

10. (A) is correct. Southwestern communities, responding to racial hostility from unemployed whites and looking for ways to reduce their welfare burden, campaigned to deport Mexicans and Mexican Americans. Employers, private charities, and the Immigration and Naturalization Service joined in this effort. Authorities made little effort to distinguish citizens from aliens: most of the children they deported had been born in the United States and were citizens. Overall, nearly one-half million left the United States during the decade.

Document-Based Question

The crisis of the Great Depression was met with many different political responses. Identify and explain the various political approaches advanced to end the depression. What did they share in common with traditional American political ideologies and how did they differ from those ideologies?

The Great Depression struck fear and desolation in the hearts and minds of Americans, who looked to the government as a source of relief and reform as never before in American history. But there was no consensus on the best way to solve the crisis, and a variety of political responses and plans were offered as options to Americans. For many Americans, the leading presidential candidates of 1932, the worst year of the depression, provided a stark contrast in differing viewpoints on the very role of government and its relationship to business. President Herbert Hoover stood firm on the principles of traditional liberalism, which limited the regulatory power of the state and espoused a laissez-faire approach to the economy even in the midst of its collapse (**DOCUMENT 1**). Challenger Franklin Delano Roosevelt, while campaigning in San Francisco in 1932, told the audience at the Commonwealth Club that responsible government was activist government, providing guidance to an ailing economy as part of the government's traditional contract to secure the welfare of its citizens (**DOCUMENT 2**). Roosevelt's election to the presidency signaled that many Americans now believed with the president that the federal government must exercise some control over the economy and even initiate economic programs of its own. Roosevelt's New Deal began to do this through the creation of such programs as the Resettlement Administration, Public Works Administration, Tennessee Valley Authority, and Civilian Conservation Corps (**DOCUMENT 3**). But the problems of the Great Depression continued, witnessed by high rates of unemployment and homelessness, and Americans soon began to seek out other possible political alternatives. Senator Huey Long, the flamboyant machine boss of Louisiana, proposed radical reform of the property and tax structure of the United States, and "Share Our Wealth" clubs sprang up across the country in support of Long's plan (**DOCUMENT 4**). Former Roosevelt supporter the Reverend Charles Coughlin, the famous "Radio Priest" similarly supported radical changes to the nation's economic system, proposing the circulation of more money (**DOCUMENT 5**). For many others, the abstractions of political platforms did not address their immediate concerns. Workers continued to employ their own strategies by going on strike, but despite support from the federal government for worker's rights in the Wagner Act, such activities were often met with violent reprisals from owners (**DOCUMENT 6**).

CHAPTER 25

World War II, 1941–1945

This chapter covers American involvement in World War II and its effects on the United States. At the height of the depression, America tried to legislate isolation from any future foreign conflicts by enacting a series of Neutrality Acts, but as wars broke out first in Asia and Africa and then in Europe, the United States gradually amended these laws or President Roosevelt managed to find ways to moderate their effects. Even before Pearl Harbor, the United States was involved in a naval conflict with Germany in the North Atlantic. U.S. policy sought to deal with Hitler's Germany as the most serious enemy, but the Japanese attack on Pearl Harbor partly changed that. The United States and its allies were on the defensive until mid-1942, when the North African counter-offensive, the Battle of Stalingrad in Soviet Russia, and the Coral Sea-Midway victories in the Pacific marked the turning of the tide. The war became a battle of production, with the United States possessing enormous advantages. While the United States fought the war for democracy, some constituencies still had to fight for democracy at home. The home front's involvement in the war changed the lives of many women and African Americans, who became essential to the wartime economy. Japanese Americans, mostly from the West Coast, experienced a humiliating and unjust detention even as many of their sons served with distinction in Europe. The United States became the world's greatest single power and stood at the center of global politics. Roosevelt and his successor, Harry Truman, worked with a range of politicians and experts to develop a new foreign policy to face these changing conditions.

The Coming of World War II

War broke out first in Asia in the early 1930s and later spread to Africa and Europe. Japan, Italy, and Germany were the aggressors. Following public opinion, the U.S. government pursued neutrality, but after the conflict expanded to include Russia, France, and Great Britain, Roosevelt launched a preparedness campaign. The Japanese attack on Pearl Harbor brought the United States into the Second World War.

Arsenal of Democracy

The government comprehensively mobilized the nation for war. Propaganda fueled public support and the New Deal focus quickly switched to a win-the-war effort based on reorienting the economy to military production. The economic conversion ended the depression. Increased production fueled profits and job opportunities, especially for minorities and women. Growing labor unrest before the United States entered the conflict ceased and unions began admitting African Americans.

The Home Front

The war drastically altered life in the United States. Families faced new strains and pressures. Japanese Americans suffered the worst discrimination, but African Americans seeking a victory at war and for their rights also experienced mixed results, as did Mexican Americans. Popular culture promoted the "good war" to Americans of all ages.

Men and Women in Uniform

The military was unprepared for combat when war broke out. The draft organized the male population for military service. The process of building the military transformed the officer corps and facilitated the forging of bonds among military personnel while "Americanizing" immigrant groups. Women joined the military and played important roles. Despite racism, the same was true of minorities. Great emphasis was placed on building a medical corps to handle casualties. A major problem was the deplorable conditions American POWs lived under, especially those captured by the Japanese.

The World at War

The war was fought on several fronts. Until 1942, the Allies were on the defensive. A variety of successes changed the tide of the conflict. In Europe, the war was fought in the air and on the ground, with the Soviets bearing most of the ground war burden. English and American forces approached Europe from two directions, first through North Africa and Italy and then across France. During this period, air strikes on Germany also occurred. The war in the Pacific involved naval battles and island-hopping invasions. When the war ended in Europe, all resources were trained on Japan. Air strikes took a heavy toll on the Japanese.

The Last Stages of War

By 1945, the war was coming to a close. Americans learned about the extent of the Holocaust, though not until the concentration camps were liberated was the full horror known. At the Yalta Conference, Roosevelt, Stalin, and Churchill negotiated terms to end the war and plan for the peace. Roosevelt's death thrust Harry Truman into the presidency. One of his first decisions was to drop the atomic bomb on Japan, ending World War II.

Multiple-Choice Questions

1. The shadows of war in Europe in the 1930s did NOT include which if the following events?
   (A) Italy's invasion of Ethiopia
   (B) German occupation of the Rhineland
   (C) German seizure of Czechoslovakia
   (D) German invasion of the Soviet Union
   (E) Kristallnacht

2. All of the following promoted isolationism EXCEPT
   (A) Franklin Roosevelt.
   (B) Charles A. Lindbergh.
   (C) American First Committee.
   (D) college students.
   (E) Socialist Norman Thomas.

3. Why did President Roosevelt encourage the passage of the Lend-Lease Act?
   (A) He was trying to promote a one-world government.
   (B) He wanted to help the American economy.
   (C) He wanted to provide aid to Britain in its struggle against Germany.
   (D) He wanted to aid Italy in its struggle against Germany.
   (E) He wanted to get Congress involved in the European crisis.

4. During the war the U.S. budget grew how many times larger than the whole New Deal?
   (A) two
   (B) four
   (C) three
   (D) ten
   (E) twelve

5. Basically, the United States won World War II by
   (A) military power.
   (B) strategy.
   (C) outproducing its enemies.
   (D) espionage.
   (E) superior soldiers.

6. Women in the military worked in
   (A) mechanical repairs.
   (B) secretarial positions.
   (C) combat missions.
   (D) kitchen duties.
   (E) nursing and administration.

7. The majority of African American soldiers served in which capacity during World War II?
   (A) in construction and stevedore work
   (B) on the front lines
   (C) on naval vessels in the Pacific
   (D) in European foxholes
   (E) training other soldiers for combat

8. All of the following were participants at Yalta EXCEPT
   (A) Franklin Roosevelt.
   (B) Winston Churchill.
   (C) Joseph Stalin.
   (D) Charles de Gaulle.
   (E) all were participants.

9. The struggle for which island in 1945 was more bloody for the United States than Normandy?
   (A) Tarawa
   (B) Guam
   (C) Okinawa
   (D) Guadalcanal
   (E) Midway

10. By the time the Allies met at Yalta, Roosevelt realized that neither the Soviets nor the British would accept
    (A) spheres of influence.
    (B) the Atlantic Charter.
    (C) conditional surrender.
    (D) not opening a second front.
    (E) American domination of the postwar world.

Document-Based Question

World War 2 was known as the Good War. In what ways is that an accurate description and in ways does it fall short?

DOCUMENT 1

Source: Charles Lindbergh, Radio Address (1941)

In time of war, truth is always replaced by propaganda. I do not believe we should be too quick to criticize the actions of a belligerent nation. There is always the question whether we, ourselves, would do better under similar circumstances. But we in this country have a right to think of the welfare of America first, just as the people in England thought first of their own country when they encouraged the smaller nations of Europe to fight against hopeless odds. When England asks us to enter this war, she is considering her own future and that of her Empire. In making our reply, I believe we should consider the future of the United States and that of the Western Hemisphere.

It is not only our right, but it is our obligation as American citizens, to look at this war objectively and to weigh our chances for success if we should enter it. I have attempted to do this, especially from the standpoint of aviation; and I have been forced to the conclusion that we cannot win this war for England, regardless of how much assistance we extend.

DOCUMENT 2

Source: Franklin Delano Roosevelt, Annual Message to Congress (1941)

Just as our national policy in internal affairs has been based upon a decent respect for the rights and the dignity of all our fellow men within our gates, so our national policy in foreign affairs has been based on a decent respect for the rights and dignity of all nations, large and small. And the justice of morality must and will win in the end.

Our national policy is this:

First, by an impressive expression of the public will and without regard to partisanship, we are committed to all inclusive national defense.

Second, by an impressive expression of the public will and without regard to partisanship, we are committed to full support of all those resolute peoples, everywhere, who are resisting aggression and are thereby keeping war away from our hemisphere. By this support, we express our determination that the democratic cause shall prevail, and we strengthen the defense and security of our own nation.

Third, by an impressive expression of the public will and without regard to partisanship, we are committed to the proposition that principles of morality and considerations for our own security will never permit us to acquiesce in a peace dictated by aggressors and sponsored by appeasers. We know that enduring peace cannot be bought at the cost of other people's freedom. . . .

DOCUMENT 3

Japanese Relocation Order February 19, 1942
Source: Henry Steele Commanger, Documents of American History (New York: Appleton-Century-Crofts, 1949), pp. 464–465; Japanese Relocation Order; Federal Register, vol. VII, No. 38.

EXECUTIVE ORDER

Authorizing the Secretary of War to Prescribe Military Areas

Whereas the successful prosecution of the war requires every possible protection against espionage and against sabotage to national-defense materials, national-defense premises, and national-defense utilities. . . .

Now, therefore, by virtue of the authority vested in me as President of the United States, and Commander in Chief of the Army and Navy, I hereby authorize and direct the Secretary of War, and the Military Commanders whom he may from time to time designate, whenever he or any designated Commander deems such action necessary or desirable, to prescribe military areas in such places and of such extent as he or the appropriate Military Commander may determine, from which any or all persons may be excluded, and with respect to which, the right of any person to enter, remain in, or leave shall be subject to whatever restrictions the Secretary of War or the appropriate Military Commander may impose in his discretion. The Secretary of War is hereby authorized to provide for residents of any such area who are excluded therefrom, such transportation, food, shelter, and other accommodations as may be necessary, in the judgment of the Secretary of War or the said Military Commander, and until other arrangements are made, to accomplish the purpose of this order. The designation of military areas in any region or locality shall supersede designations of prohibited and restricted areas by the Attorney General under the Proclamations of December 7 and 8, 1941, and shall supersede the responsibility and authority of the Attorney General under the said Proclamations in respect of such prohibited and restricted areas.

I hereby further authorize and direct the Secretary of War and the said Military Commanders to take such other steps as he or the appropriate Military Commander may deem advisable to enforce compliance with the restrictions applicable to each Military area hereinabove authorized to be designated, including the use of Federal troops and other Federal Agencies, with authority to accept assistance of state and local agencies.

I hereby further authorize and direct all Executive Departments, independent establishments and other Federal Agencies, to assist the Secretary of War or the said Military Commanders in carrying out this Executive Order, including the furnishing of medical aid, hospitalization, food, clothing, transportation, use of land, shelter, and other supplies, equipment, utilities, facilities, and services. . . .

FRANKLIN D. ROOSEVELT

DOCUMENT 4

Source: Sterling A. Brown, "Out of Their Mouths" (1942)

White liberal: "This Negro soldier was sitting on a seat opposite to a white man. The bus was not crowded, and he wasn't sitting in front of any white. But the driver came back and told him to move. He refused. The driver shouted, 'I'm gonna move you.' The Negro took his coat off and said, 'Well I'm fixing to go off and fight for democracy. I might as well start right now.' And I want to tell you that bus driver backed down. It did me good to see it."

DOCUMENT 5

Source: Langston Hughes, Bequmont to Detroit 1943

Looky here, America
What you done done—
Let things drift
Until the riots come

Yet you say we're fighting
For democracy.
Then why don't democracy
Include me?

I ask you this question
Cause I want to know
How long I got to fight
BOTH HITLER—AND JIM CROW.

ANSWERS AND EXPLANATIONS

Multiple-Choice Questions

1. (D) is correct. The shadows of war did not include German invasion of the Soviet Union. In 1935, Italy invaded Ethiopia and formally claimed the impoverished African kingdom as a colony. In 1936, Hitler sent 35,000 troops to occupy the Rhieland, a region demilitarized by the Versailles treaty. On the night of November 9, 1938, Nazi storm troopers rounded up Jews, beating them mercilessly and murdering an untold number. They smashed windows in Jewish shops, hospitals, and orphanages and burned synagogues to the ground. This attack came to be known as *Kristallnacht*.

2. (A) is correct. Franklin Roosevelt did not promote isolationism. College students, seeing themselves as future cannon fodder, began to demonstrate against the war. In 1938, Socialist Norman Thomas gathered leading liberals and trade unionists into the Keep American Out of War Congress. In 1940, the arch-conservative Committee to Defend America First was formed to oppose U.S. intervention. Additionally, the American First Committee quickly gained attention because its members included well-known personalities such as Charles A. Lindbergh.

3. (C) is correct. President Roosevelt encouraged the passage of the Lend-Lease Act to give aid to Britain in its struggle against Germany. The Lend-Lease Act made Great Britain the first beneficiary of massive aid in which the United States made arrangements for the transfer of war supplies, including food, machinery, and services to nations whose defense was considered vital to the defense of the United States.

4. (D) is correct. During World War II the federal budget grew to 10 times the previous level, as established in the New Deal. War bought a huge expansion of the federal government and under government pressure, industry shifted to defense production.

5. (C) is correct. The decisive factor for victory, even more than military prowess and superior strategy, would be, many observers agreed, the ability of the United States to outproduce it enemies. The country enjoyed many advantages to meet this challenge: a large industrial base, abundant natural resources, and a civilian population large enough to permit it to increase both its labor force and its armed forces.

6. (B) is correct. The vast majority of women in the military remained far from battlefronts. Many women were stationed within the United States, where they served in administration, communications, clerical, or health-care facilities.

7. (A) is correct. The Selective Service Act, in response to the demands of African American leaders, specified that "there shall be no discrimination against any person on account of race or color." The draft brought hundreds of thousands of young black men into the Army, and African Americans enlisted at a rate of 60 percent, about their proportion of the general population. The majority served in the Signal Engineer, Quartermaster Corps, mainly in construction or stevedore work. Only toward the end of the war, when the shortage of infantry neared a crisis, were African Americans permitted to rise to combat status.

8. (D) is correct. Charles de Gaulle was not a participant at the Yalta Conference. In early February 1945, Roosevelt held his last meeting with Churchill and Stalin at Yalta, a Crimean resort on the Black Sea.

9. (C) is correct. The stuggle for the island of Okinawa, 350 miles southwest of the home islands of Japan and the site of vital airbases, proved even bloodier than the Normandy invasion. The invasion of the island, which began on Easter Sunday, April 1, 1945, was the largest amphibious operation mounted by Americans in the Pacific war.

10. (B) is correct. In preparing for the end of the war, Alllied leaders began to reassess their goals. The Atlantic Charter, drawn up before the United States had entered the war, stated noble objectives for the world after the defeat of facism. Now, four years later, Roosevelt—ill and exhausted—realized that neither Great Britain nor the Soviet Union intended to abide by any code or conduct that compromised its national security or conflicted with its economic interests in other nations or in colonial territories.

Document-Based Question

World War II was known as the Good War. In what ways is that an accurate description and in ways does it fall short?

World War II was known as the Good War. In some ways this is an accurate description. The fight against fascism was a noble fight. In other ways, however, wartime America was not such a good place. Racial prejudice still existed, directed against both African Americans and Japanese Americans, who were sent to detainment camps. The country had ideals of freedom that it was fighting for, but the United States had yet to fully live up to them.

The Second World War was presented as a fight against fascism, and for liberty and democracy. This is the sort of battle that America had always claimed as its own. However, in leading up to the war, it was not clear that the United States would get involved. There were prominent Americans arguing that the European war was not America's business (**DOCUMENT 1**). President Roosevelt disputed this view, claiming that the fight for democracy is always America's business (**DOCUMENT 2**). However, he was not able to bring the United States fully into the war until after the bombing of Pearl Harbor. The devastation that Japan wreaked on the American naval base was enough of a cause to bring the entire country around (**DOCUMENT 6**).

The war continued to be presented as a fight for democracy, and there is no question that the enemy was evil. One only needs to see pictures of the horrors that were visited on the Jews of Europe by the Nazis (**DOCUMENT 7**) to realize that the fight was a good one.

However, the battle for liberty at home had still not been won. Once the war with Japan had begun, prejudice against Japanese Americans reared its ugly head. This led to President Roosevelt's Executive Order relocating the Japanese American population of the West Coast into internment camps (**DOCUMENT 3**), in violation of their civil liberties. Prejudice against African

Americans also continued. Though permitted to join the armed services, they were still discriminated against in many ways. Jim Crow laws in the South segregated the black population from the white population (**DOCUMENT 4**). America still had a ways to go.

Despite this discrimination, many African Americans still viewed the war as a good one. Langston Hughes wrote a poem in which he compared the battle against Jim Crow to the battle against Hitler (**DOCUMENT 5**). He is pointing out the irony of a country that would confront the evil of German racism without confronting its own homegrown racism. At the same time, he maintains that the battle against Hitler is a good one.

World War II was known as the Good War, and in many ways it was. However, it also had some ugly aspects for America, ways in which it does not live up to its vaunted title.

CHAPTER 26

The Cold War, 1945–1952

This chapter covers the beginning of the cold war under Harry Truman's presidency, and how it affected both foreign and domestic policies. Peace after World War II was marred by a powerful rivalry between the United States and Soviet Russia. Truman and his advisors introduced the basic cold war doctrine of "containment" in the Truman Doctrine, the Marshall Plan, and the North Atlantic Treaty Organization (NATO). With the victory of the Communist People's Liberation Army in China (1949) and the outbreak of the Korean War (1950), the cold war was extended to the Asian mainland as well. The cold war prompted the United States to rebuild its World War II enemies of Germany and Japan as counterweights to the Soviets. At home, Americans wanted to return to normal by bringing the troops home, resuming spending for consumer goods, and reestablishing family life, but many changing social patterns brought anxieties. A second "Red Scare" was caused by heated cold war rhetoric of a bipartisan foreign policy and Truman's government loyalty oath program, but Senator Joseph McCarthy's tactics in the first half of the 1950s symbolized the era. Defense spending increased and the American economy became dependent on it to maintain growth and avoid renewed depression. Truman tried to extend elements of the New Deal in his "Fair Deal," but this effort met with minimal success.

Global Insecurities at War's End

The end of World War II did not end global insecurities. The United States emerged as the world's greatest power but the future remained uncertain. The alliance with the Soviet Union showed strains, but hope remained for collective security under the United Nations.

The Policy of Containment

The growing split between the Soviet Union and the United States led President Truman to develop a policy of containment to block communist expansion. A cornerstone of Truman's doctrine was providing financial aid to nations fighting communism, and economic aid to rebuild Europe. A crisis over Berlin led to the creation of NATO, a political alliance, to block Soviet expansion in Europe.

Cold War Liberalism

Truman was unable to enlarge the New Deal, but he did maintain a strong federal government. Truman faced strong opposition in Congress and his popularity dropped. Still, Truman won reelection in 1948 and proclaimed his "Fair Deal," though foreign affairs soon occupied most of his attention.

The Cold War at Home

Often under the call for national security, the fear of communism spread throughout the nation in the late 1940s and early 1950s. The government, aided by the media, led the anticommunist crusade that profoundly affected many individuals and the American public. The Red Scare fostered loyalty programs for federal government employees, congressional investigations into Hollywood that led to blacklists, and much publicized spy trials of government officials and scientists. The peak was reached when Senator Joseph McCarthy launched his anticommunist campaign. His failure diffused the fears of many Americans.

Cold War Culture

The growing cold war abroad and the Red Scare at home created anxiety and fear among many Americans, as well as fears of a declining economy. These emotions found expression in popular culture, especially movies. Strengthened by prosperity, family life supplied security and stability for many Americans. The increasing rates of childbirth and consumer spending led many women to work, though staying home was promoted by numerous sources. Defense spending most affected the West, especially California, where older and newer communities arose as part of the growing military-industrial partnership. At the same time, patriotism surged and was evident in the "Zeal for Democracy" campaign and the stress on the American way of life, though some protested against the uneven application of democracy.

Stalemate for the Democrats

Events in Asia in the late 1940s and early 1950s heightened cold war tensions. The communist victory in China and the Korean War led to a steep decline to Truman's popularity. Running as a peace candidate, Dwight D. Eisenhower won the 1952 presidential election.

Multiple-Choice Questions

1. Economists recommended the U.S. should _____ at the end of WWII.
   (A) search for new markets
   (B) build up the military
   (C) become more self-sufficient
   (D) balance the budget
   (E) collect higher taxes

2. The Truman Doctrine committed the United States to
   (A) intervening to prevent further communist takeover attempts.
   (B) reinstating the Monroe Doctrine.
   (C) sending combat troops to the Middle East.
   (D) supporting United Nations efforts to stabilize countries.
   (E) reducing the U.S. military presence abroad.

3. The Marshall Plan for European nations reflected the Truman administration's fear of
   (A) a Soviet invasion of Western Europe.
   (B) atomic testing in Eastern Europe.
   (C) military confrontation between the two Germanys.
   (D) political consequences of economic chaos.
   (E) chinese intervention in Europe.

4. In response to NATO allying with a rearmed West Germany, the Soviet Union organized the
   (A) Warsaw Pact.
   (B) Eastern European Treaty Organization.
   (C) Berlin Wall.
   (D) Solidarity Pact.
   (E) SEATO Pact.

5. Why did the United States decide to build up the Japanese economy?
   (A) Japan would serve in the anti-communist bloc.
   (B) Japan's anger at Germany would be an asset.
   (C) Japanese consumers would purchase American goods.
   (D) This would allow American consumers to buy cheap Japanese goods.

6. Truman used the threat of communism to provide
(A) defense spending.
(B) martial law.
(C) democracy.
(D) new Deal programs.
(E) the Fair Deal program.

7. In his "Lincoln Day" speech in 1950, Senator Joseph R. McCarthy claimed that
(A) there were 200 communists working in the State Department.
(B) Truman was a closet communist.
(C) the army was ignoring the communist threat.
(D) a military takeover of the United States by the communists was imminent.
(E) Whittaker Chambers, Alger Hiss, and the Rosenberg had sold secrets to the Soviets.

8. Which one of the following was NOT a result of U.S. involvement in the Korean War?
(A) The principle of containment was extended.
(B) The U.S. and the People's Republic of China became unwavering enemies.
(C) There was a heightened commitment to Southeast Asia.
(D) Containment had been extended beyond Europe.
(E) The containment principle was repudiated as a viable policy.

9. All of the following caused anxiety during the 1950s EXCEPT
(A) the suburbs as prime nuclear targets.
(B) Cold War rhetoric.
(C) nuclear proliferation.
(D) economic woes.
(E) the belief that the executive branch had become too powerful.

10. In his 1952 presidential campaign, Republican candidate Eisenhower projected an image of a/an
(A) aggressive anticommunist who would get total victory in Korea.
(B) moderate but firm candidate who could achieve honorable peace in Korea.
(C) liberal who would pull America out of Korea.
(D) reformer who could fulfill the dreams of the New Deal.
(E) conservative determined to undo remaining elements of the New Deal.

Document-Based Question

Defend or refute the following statement: The Marshall Plan was motivated by Cold War considerations.

DOCUMENT 1

Source: George F. Kennan, "Long Telegram" (1946)

We have here a political force committed fanatically to the belief that with US there can be no permanent modus vivendi, that it is desirable and necessary that the internal harmony of our society be disrupted, our traditional way of life be destroyed, the international authority of our state be broken, if Soviet power is to be secure. This political force has complete power of disposition over energies of one of world's greatest peoples and resources of world's richest national territory, and is borne along by deep and powerful currents of Russian nationalism. In addition, it has an elaborate and far flung apparatus for exertion of its influence in other countries, and apparatus of amazing flexibility and versatility, managed by people whose experience and skill in underground methods are presumably without parallel in history. Finally, it is seemingly inaccessible to considerations of reality in its basic reactions. For it, the vast fund of objective fact about human society is not, as with us, the measure against which outlook is constantly being tested and re-formed, but a grab bag from which individual items are selected arbitrarily and tendentiously to bolster an outlook already preconceived. This is admittedly not a pleasant picture. Problem of how to cope with this force in [is] undoubtedly greatest task our diplomacy has ever faced and probably greatest it will ever have to face. It should be point of departure from which our political general staff work at present juncture should proceed. It should be approached with same thoroughness and care as solution of major strategic problem in war, and if necessary, with no smaller outlay in planning effort. I cannot attempt to suggest all answers here. But I would like to record my conviction that problem is within our power to solve-and that without recourse to any general military conflict.

DOCUMENT 2

Source: Kenneth MacFarland, "The Unfinished Work" (1946)

One who traveled about over the country a year ago this month, talking with taxi drivers, bell hops, policemen, business employees, and others who reflect the thinking of the man-on-the-street, found the conversation all to be along the same lines. The war was over, the boys would be coming home now, rationing would end. Truman was doing better than expected, we must resolutely work together to build one world in which war would be outlawed and the principles of the Atlantic Charter would hold sway. The keynote a year ago was one of joyous relief that the bloodiest conflict in all history had ended in complete victory over the enemy, and a feeling of faith that we had at last learned our lesson sufficiently well to outlaw war. There was confidence that an effective United Nations organization would be developed.

But today, one year after, that buoyant faith has turned to cynicism. Hope in the United Nations is largely gone. The average American has already resigned himself to a future in which there will be at least two worlds instead of one. Having given up his hope for a better world, the average man has ceased to realize how terribly important it is that we keep striving, and he has settled down to bickering over a myriad of minor issues here on the domestic scene. . . .

There is a strange fear and insecurity in America today. The people fear that in winning the war we introduced a new power into the world which may in turn engulf us.

DOCUMENT 3

Source: George Marshall, The Marshall Plan (1947)

Aside from the demoralizing effect on the world at large and the possibilities of disturbances arising as a result of the desperation of the people concerned, the consequences of the economy of the United States should be apparent to all. It is logical that the United States should do whatever it is able to do to assist in the return of normal economic health in the world, without which there can be no political stability and no assured peace. Our policy is directed not against any country or doctrine but against hunger, poverty, desperation, and chaos. Its purpose should be the revival of a working economy in the world so as to permit the emergence of political and social conditions in which free institutions can exist.

DOCUMENT 4

Containment (1947)
Source: "X." "The Sources of Soviet Conduct," Foreign Affairs vol. 25 no. 4 (July 1947), pp. 566–582.

This means that we are going to continue for a long time to find the Russians difficult to deal with. It does not mean that they should be considered as embarked upon a do-or-die program to overthrow our society by a given date. The theory of the inevitability of the eventual fall of capitalism has the fortunate connotation that there is no hurry about it. The forces of progress can take their time in preparing the final coup de grâce. Meanwhile, what is vital is that the "Socialist fatherland"—that oasis of power which has been already won for Socialism in the person of the Soviet Union—should be cherished and defended by all good Communists at home and abroad, its fortunes promoted, its enemies badgered and confounded. The promotion of premature, "adventuristic" revolutionary projects abroad which might embarrass Soviet power in any way would be an inexcusable, even a counter-revolutionary act. The cause of Socialism is the support and promotion of Soviet power, as defined in Moscow...

These considerations make Soviet diplomacy at once easier and more difficult to deal with than the diplomacy of individual aggressive leaders like Napoleon and Hitler. On the one hand it is more sensitive to contrary force, more ready to yield on individual sectors of the diplomatic front when that force is felt to be too strong, and thus more rational in the logic and rhetoric of power. On the other hand it cannot be easily defeated or discouraged by a single victory on the part of its opponents. And the patient persistence by which it is animated means that it can be effectively countered not by sporadic acts which represent the momentary whims of democratic opinion but only by intelligent long-range policies on the part of Russia's adversaries—policies no less steady in their purpose, and no less variegated and resourceful in their applications, than those of the Soviet Union itself.

In these circumstances it is clear that the main element of any United States policy toward the Soviet Union must be that of a long-term, patient but firm and vigilant containment of Russian expansive tendencies. It is important to note, however, that such a policy has nothing to do with outward histrionics: with threats or blustering or superfluous gestures of outward "toughness." While the Kremlin is basically flexible in its reaction to political realities, it is by no means unamenable to considerations of prestige. Like almost any other government, it can be placed by tactless and threatening gestures in a position where it cannot afford to yield even though this might be dictated by its sense of realism. The Russian leaders are keen judges of human psychology, and as such they are highly conscious that loss of temper and of self-control is never a source of strength in political affairs. They are quick to exploit such evidences of weakness. For these reasons, it is a sine qua non of successful dealing with Russia that the foreign government in question should remain at all times cool and collected and that its demands on Russian policy should be put forward in such a manner as to leave the way open for a compliance not too detrimental to Russian prestige.

DOCUMENT 5

Source: Harry S Truman, The Truman Doctrine (1947)

At the present moment in world history nearly every nation must choose between alternative ways of life. The choice is too often not a free one.

One way of life is based upon the will of the majority, and is distinguished by free institutions, representative government, free elections, guaranties of individual liberty, freedom of speech and religion, and freedom from political oppression.

The second way of life is based upon the will of a minority forcibly imposed upon the majority. It relies upon terror and oppression, a controlled press and radio, fixed elections, and the suppression of personal freedoms.

I believe that it must be the policy of the United States to support free peoples who are resisting attempted subjugation by armed minorities or by outside pressures.

I believe that we must assist free peoples to work out their own destinies in their own way.

I believe that our help should be primarily through economic and financial aid, which is essential to economic stability and orderly political processes.

The world is not static, and the status quo is not sacred. But we cannot allow changes in the status quo in violation of the Charter of the United Nations by such methods as coercion, or by such subterfuges as political infiltration. In helping free and independent nations to maintain their freedom, the United States will be giving effect to the principles of the Charter of the United Nations. . . .

The seeds of totalitarian regimes are nurtured by misery and want. They spread and grow in the evil soil of poverty and strife. They reach their full growth when the hope of a people for a better life has died. We must keep that hope alive.

The free peoples of the world look to us for support in maintaining their freedoms.

If we falter in our leadership, we may endanger the peace of the world-and we shall surely endanger the welfare of our own Nation.

DOCUMENT 6

Source: National Security Council Memorandum Number 68 (1950)

In the light of present and prospective Soviet atomic capabilities, the action which can be taken under present programs and plans, however, becomes dangerously inadequate, in both timing and scope, to accomplish the rapid progress toward the attainment of the United States political, economic, and military objectives which is now imperative.

A continuation of present trends would result in a serious decline in the strength of the free world relative to the Soviet Union and its satellites. This unfavorable trend arises from the inadequacy of current programs and plans rather than from any error in our objectives and aims. These trends lead in the direction of isolation, not by deliberate decision but by lack of the necessary basis for a vigorous initiative in the conflict with the Soviet Union.

Our position as the center of power in the free world places a heavy responsibility upon the United States for leadership. We must organize and enlist the energies and resources of the free world in a positive program for peace which will frustrate the Kremlin design for world domination by creating a situation in the free world to which the Kremlin will be compelled to adjust. Without such a cooperative effort, led by the United States, we will have to make gradual withdrawals under pressure until we discover one day that we have sacrificed positions of vital interest.

It is imperative that this trend be reversed by a much more rapid and concerted build-up of the actual strength of both the United States and the other nations of the free world. The analysis shows that this will be costly and will involve significant domestic financial and economic adjustments.

The execution of such a build-up, however, requires that the United States have an affirmative program beyond the solely defensive one of countering the threat posed by the Soviet Union. This program must light the path to peace and order among nations in a system based on freedom and justice, as contemplated in the Charter of the United Nations. Further, it must envisage the political and economic measures with which and the military shield behind which the free world can work to frustrate the Kremlin design by the strategy of the cold war; for every consideration of devotion to our fundamental values and to our national security demands that we achieve our objectives by the strategy of the cold war, building up our military strength in order that it may not have to be used. The only sure victory lies in the frustration of the Kremlin design by the steady development of the moral and material strength of the free world and its projection into the Soviet world in such a way as to bring about an internal change in the Soviet system. Such a positive program-harmonious with our fundamental national purpose and our objectives-is necessary if we are to regain and retain the initiative and to win and hold the necessary popular support and cooperation in the United States and the rest of the free world.

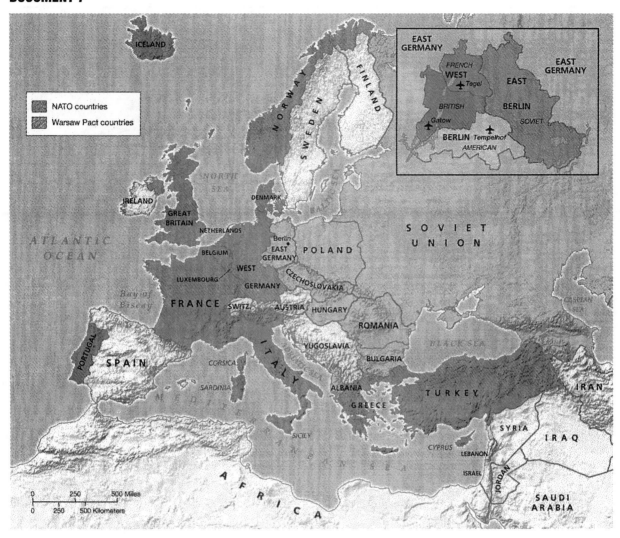

ANSWERS AND EXPLANATIONS

Multiple-Choice Questions

■ **1. (A) is correct.** Just to maintain the current level of growth, the United States needed an estimated $14 billion in exports—an unprecedented amount. U.S. business and government leaders became determined to integrate Western Europe and Asia into a liberal international economy open to American trade and investment. During the final stages of the war, President Roosevelt's advisers laid plans to establish U.S. primacy in the postwar global economy.

■ **2. (A) is correct.** The 1947 Truman Doctrine pledged the United States to the containment of communism in Europe and elsewhere. The doctrine was the foundation of Truman's foreign policy. It impelled the United States to support any nation whose stability was threatened by communism or the Soviet Union.

DOCUMENT 7

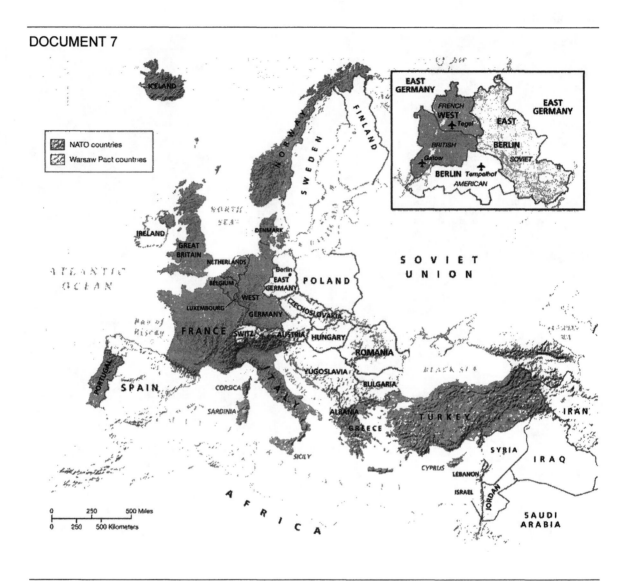

ANSWERS AND EXPLANATIONS

Multiple-Choice Questions

1. (A) is correct. Just to maintain the current level of growth, the United States needed an estimated $14 billion in exports—an unprecedented amount. Many business leaders even looked to the Soviet Union as a potential trading partner. U.S. business and government leaders became determined to integrate Western Europe and Asia into a liberal international economy open to American trade and investment. During the final stages of the war, President Roosevelt's advisers laid plans to establish U.S. primacy in the postwar global economy.

2. (A) is correct. The 1947 Truman Doctrine pledged the United States to the containment of communism in Europe and elsewhere. The doctrine was the foundation of

A year before the plan was offered, it had become abundantly clear to even U.S. civilians that the world was being split in two (**DOCUMENT 2**). U.S. policy makers were certain that the USSR had no desire for coexistence. There would be no sharing the world with the communists (**DOCUMENT 1**). It was necessary to form a strategy to deal with them.

The strategy became known as containment. As the Soviets were willing to be patient in their battle with the United States, America would also have to be willing to be deliberate. The plan would be to prevent the USSR from expanding, while waiting for its inevitable collapse (**DOCUMENT 4**). One of the ways in which this plan was to be executed was to give aid to "free peoples," so that they would be able to keep off "the communist yoke" (**DOCUMENT 5**). Though Marshall claimed that the goal of the plan was to alleviate suffering in Europe (**DOCUMENT 3**), it was part of this larger scheme of containment. By giving aid to European countries the United States was attempting to prevent them from falling to communism.

By 1950, the United States had changed course in its strategy for fighting communism in the world. A decision had been made to be more aggressive in combating communist interests (**DOCUMENT 6**). However, the Marshall Plan belongs to an earlier time, and was firmly a part of early containment strategy.

CHAPTER 27

America at Midcentury, 1952–1963

This chapter covers American society at midcentury from the premier performance of Elvis Presley in 1954 to the assassination of John F. Kennedy in 1963. This era enjoyed the prosperity of post-World War II through the growth of suburban life and the emergence of youth culture. Americans reflected a fierce desire for consumer goods and "the good life." Deeply held popular belief in a continuously expanding economy and a steady increase in the standard of living helped shape social life and politics throughout the postwar era. Overall, the nation's public culture presented a powerful consensus based on the idea that the American dream was available to all who worked for it.

American Society at Midcentury

The election of Dwight D. Eisenhower changed the tone of government as he sought a more conservative, corporate commonwealth. During his presidency, the federal government built on the growing prosperity to subsidize programs that helped Americans pursue higher education and buy homes, especially in new suburbs. The suburban boom strengthened domestic ideals but also provoked criticism for creating a dull, conformist lifestyle, among other things. During the 1950s, labor unions reached a peak of membership and power. In part due to federal laws, higher education expanded greatly. At the same time, dramatic improvements in medical care made it possible for Americans to live longer, healthier lives.

Youth Culture

After World War II, increasing attention was directed at American youth. The rising birthrates in the late 1930s onward made young people a potent market. Teenagers gained a special status. They developed their own culture, especially rock 'n' roll music that drew heavily on black music and made black performers popular among white youth. Tensions arose over the status of teenagers and was partly reflected in an increase in juvenile delinquency.

Mass Culture and Its Discontents

The rise of television contributed to the development of a mass culture that reflected many of the conformists tendencies of the postwar era. Criticism of mass culture came from the right and the left. The Beats offered strong dissent of conformity both in their writing and their lifestyles.

The Cold War Continued

The waging of the Cold War changed when Eisenhower became president. He focused on using massive retaliation to resolve disputes. Summit meetings between Eisenhower and Khruschev lessened tensions. Eisenhower's policy also employed covert action in several nations as Eisenhower feared a domino effect of communism. When his term ended, Eisenhower left office warning against the growing military-industrial complex.

John F. Kennedy and the New Frontier

The election of John F. Kennedy changed the direction of the nation. His New Frontier represented a return to liberal, activist politics but faced opposition from Congress. Still, Kennedy successfully implemented several social programs and energized the space program. In foreign policy, Kennedy followed the cold war policies. He tried to ease tensions with the Soviets but confronted several crises. His assassination sent the nation into shock.

Multiple-Choice Questions

1. In the book *The Affluent Society*, John Kenneth Galbraith argued that Americans should spend more on social services and less on
   (A) stocks and bonds.
   (B) space exploration
   (C) military spending.
   (D) education.
   (E) consumer goods.

2. Eisenhower achieved all of the following EXCEPT
   (A) major reductions in defense spending.
   (B) accepted New Deal legacy of greater federal social responsibility.
   (C) appointed businessmen to his Cabinet.
   (D) deregulated the environment.
   (E) created the Department of Health, Education, and Welfare.

3. The following was a NEGATIVE effect of the Federal Housing Administration (FHA):
   (A) it took the initiative out of buying a home.
   (B) FHA issued long-term mortgage loans.
   (C) FHA subsidized the housing industry.
   (D) FHA required less than 10 percent down payment on loans.
   (E) FHA policies inscribed racial and income segregation into public policy.

4. Betty Friedan's work *The Feminine Mystique*
   (A) celebrated suburban life and the nuclear family.
   (B) articulated the frustrations of suburban women.
   (C) urged women to be more accepting of their role as wives and mothers.
   (D) chronicled the hazards of working women.
   (E) stressed the power of positive thinking to middle-class women.

5. The American Medical Association (AMA) blocked
   (A) federal involvement in health care.
   (B) health research.
   (C) increases in prices for drugs and medical treatment.
   (D) medical insurance policies.
   (E) research for "wonder drugs."

6. Many southerners seemed to fear rock 'n' roll music because
   (A) white females might become attracted to black performers.
   (B) it promoted a dubious morality.
   (C) it might bring more northerners into the region.
   (D) it would destroy parental authority.
   (E) it would surpass country music.

7. Television did all of the following EXCEPT
   (A) created overnight fads.
   (B) reshaped leisure time.
   (C) created a sophisticated, urbane culture.
   (D) reshaped political life.
   (E) reshaped consumption.

8. Eisenhower's foreign policy depended on nuclear armaments and
   (A) covert activity.
   (B) a significant increase in the number of American soldiers.
   (C) expanding the space program.
   (D) forcing the Soviets out of Eastern Europe.
   (E) massive increases in military spending.

9. In Guatemala, the CIA worked to promote the benefit of
   (A) United Fruit Company.
   (B) the Rockefeller Corporation.
   (C) General Motors Company.
   (D) General Electric Company.
   (E) Kaiser Aluminum.

10. Under President Kennedy, advisory functions and details of running the Executive Branch
   (A) became micromanaged by the president.
   (B) shifted from the cabinet to the White House staff.
   (C) were ignored and weakened the presidency.
   (D) fell under cabinet offices.
   (E) were covered by civil-service employees.

Document-Based Question

The 1950s are often presented as an era of consensus, when people chose to conform rather than rock the boat. Is this characterization accurate?

DOCUMENT 1

DOCUMENT 2

DOCUMENT 3

Numbers in Millions (% of total population)

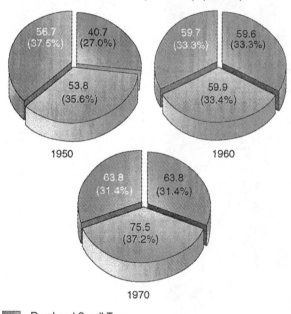

Rural and Small Towns

Suburbs

Central Cities

DOCUMENT 6

The Feminine Mystique (1963)
Source: Betty Friedan, The Feminine Mystique, (New York: Norton, 1963), pp. 15–32.

The suburban housewife—she was the dream image of the young American women and the envy, it was said, of women all over the world. The American housewife—freed by science and labor-saving appliances from the drudgery, the dangers of childbirth and the illnesses of her grandmother. She was healthy, beautiful, educated, concerned only about her husband, her children, her home. She had found true feminine fulfillment. As a housewife and mother, she was respected as a full and equal partner to man in his world. She was free to choose automobiles, clothes, appliances, supermarkets; she had everything that women ever dreamed of.

In the fifteen years after World War II, this mystique of feminine fulfillment became the cherished and self-perpetuating core of contemporary American culture. Millions of women lived their lives in the image of those pretty pictures of the American suburban housewife, kissing their husbands goodbye in front of the picture window, depositing their stationwagonsful of children at school, and smiling as they ran the new electric waxer over the spotless kitchen floor. They baked their own bread, sewed their own and their children's clothes, kept their new washing machines and dryers running all day. They changed the sheets on the beds twice a week instead of once, took the rug-hooking class in adult education, and pitied their poor frustrated mothers, who had dreamed of having a career. Their only dream was to be perfect wives and mothers; their highest ambition to have five children and a beautiful house, their only fight to get and keep their husbands. They had no thought for the unfeminine problems of the world outside the home; they wanted the men to make the major decisions. They gloried in their role as women, and wrote proudly on the census blank: "Occupation: housewife."

DOCUMENT 7

Source: Alan Ginsberg, Howl (1955)

I saw the best minds of my generation destroyed
by madness, starving hysterical naked,
dragging themselves through the negro streets at dawn
looking for an angry fix,
angelheaded hipsters burning for the ancient heavenly connection
to the starry dynamo in the machinery of night

DOCUMENT 8

Source: Brown v. Board of Education (1954)

Mr. Chief Justice Warren delivered the opinion of the Court
In the first cases in this Court construing the Fourteenth Amendment, decided shortly after its adoption, the Court interpreted it as proscribing all state-imposed discriminations against the Negro race. The doctrine of "separate but equal" did not make its appearance in this Court until 1896 in the case of Plessy v. Ferguson, supra, involving not education but transportation. American courts have since labored with the doctrine for over half a century. In this Court, there have been six cases involving the "separate but equal" doctrine in the field of public education. . . . In none of these cases was it necessary to examine the doctrine to grant relief to the Negro plaintiff. And in Sweatt v. Painter . . . the Court expressly reserved decision on the question of whether Plessy v. Ferguson should be held inapplicable to public education...

We come then to the question presented: Does segregation of children in public schools solely on the basis of race, even though the physical facilities and other "tangible" factors may be equal, deprive the children of the minority group of equal education opportunities? We believe that it does...

We conclude that in the field of public education the doctrine of "separate but equal" has no place. Separate educational facilities are inherently unequal. Therefore, we hold that the plaintiffs and others similarly situated for whom the actions have been brought are, by reason of the segregation complained of, deprived of the equal protection of the laws guaranteed by the Fourteenth Amendment. This disposition makes unnecessary any discussion whether such segregation also violates the Due Process Clause of the Fourteenth Amendment.

ANSWERS AND EXPLANATIONS

Multiple-Choice Questions

1. (E) is correct. With the title of his influential work, *The Affluent Society*, economist John Kenneth Galbraith gave a label to postwar America. Galbraith observed that American capitalism had worked "quite brilliantly" in the years since World War II. But Americans, he argued, needed to spend less on personal consumption and devote more public funds to schools, medical care, cultural activities, and social services.

2. (A) is correct. Eisenhower did not achieve major reductions in defense spending. Eisenhower wanted to run government in a businesslike manner while letting the states and corporate interests guide domestic policy and the economy. He appointed nine businessmen to his first cabinet. At the same time, Eisenhower accepted the New Deal legacy of greater federal responsibility for social welfare. Eisenhower deregulated the environment with the Submerged Lands Act in 1953, which transferred $40 billion worth of disputed offshore oil lands from the federal government to the Gulf states. Ike also created the Department of Health, Education and Welfare, appointing Oveta Culp Hobby as its secretary, making her the second woman to hold a cabinet post.

3. (E) is correct. The Federal Housing Administration and its policies had long-range drawbacks. FHA went overwhelming to new residential developments, usually on the fringes of urban areas, hastening the decline of older, inner-city neighborhoods. A bias toward suburban middle-class communities manifested itself in several ways, such as the requirement for an "unbiased professional estimate" rating the property, the prospective borrower, and the neighborhood. In practice, these estimates resulted in blatant discrimination against communities that were racially mixed. The FHA's Undwriting Manual bluntly warned: "If a neighborhood is to retain stability, it is necessary that properties shall continue to be occupied by the same social and racial classes."

4. (B) is correct. Betty Friedan's *The Feminine Mystique* articulated the frustrations of suburban women and helped to launch a revived feminist movement.

5. (A) is correct. The American Medical Association (AMA) lobbied hard against efforts to expand government responsibility for the public's health. President Harry Truman had advanced a plan for national health insurance, to be run along the lines of Social Security. President Dwight Eisenhower had proposed a program that would offer government assistance to private health insurance companies. The AMA denounced both proposals as "socialized medicine."

6. (A) is correct. Many adults held rock 'n' roll responsible for the apparent decline in parental control over teens. Much of the opposition to rock 'n' roll, particularly in the South, played on long-standing racist fears that white females might become attracted to black music and black performers.

7. (C) is correct. Television did not create a sophisticated, urbane culture. Television reshaped consumption and transformed the advertising industry, creating slick thirty-second commercials. Television also demonstrated a unique ability to create overnight fads and crazes across the nation. It allowed performers, such as Elvis Presley, to catapult from a regional success to international stardom. Television also reshaped leisure time and political life, as was evident in the 1960 presidential election.

■ **8. (A) is correct.** Eisenhower developed new strategies for containment and for the support of the United States power abroad, including a greater reliance on nuclear weapons and the aggressive use of the Central Intelligence Agency (CIA) for covert action.

■ **9. (A) is correct.** The most publicized CIA intervention of the Eisenhower years took place in Guatemala, where a fragile democracy had taken root in 1944. A challenge to the long-standing dominance of the American-based United Fruit Company by Guatemalan President Jácobo Arbenz Guzmán resulted in CIA and military intervention.

■ **10. (B) is correct.** Overall, Kennedy's most long-lasting achievement as president may have been his strengthening of the executive branch itself. He insisted on direct presidential control of details that Eisenhower had left to advisers and appointees. Moreover, under Kennedy the White House staff assumed many of the decision-making and advisory functions previously held by cabinet members.

Document-Based Question

The 1950s are often presented as an era of consensus, when people chose to conform rather than rock the boat. Is this characterization accurate?

The clichéd presentation of the 1950s as an era of conformity and consensus has more than an element of truth to it. However, at the same time that this conservative mass culture was being produced, there was also a strong undercurrent of tension and rebellion.

There is no doubt that the mass culture of the 1950s was one that encouraged conformity. In the aftermath of the Second World War, veterans were granted a number of benefits, including low-interest mortgages. Many of them used these loans in order to purchase houses in the newly built suburbs. These suburbs consisted of thousands of nearly identical houses, on small plots, built in neat rows (**DOCUMENT 1**). By the 1950s suburbs housed over thirty five percent of the country's population (**DOCUMENT 5**). Many of the residents of these suburbs commuted to work in cities on newly built rail lines. Cars full of neatly dressed men, in nearly identical suits and hats, all reading newspapers, would travel together every morning and every evening (**DOCUMENT 2**).

Popular culture was also conformist in many ways. The urban ethnic comedies of the early years of television had given way to television comedies about suburban, Protestant whites. Even those television programs which did not quite fit the mold, such as the popular program *I Love Lucy*, were presented as being watched by an "ideal" family, which fits the stereotypical mode (**DOCUMENT 3**). Even the stereotypical picture of a suburban marriage was often accurate, though frequently to the detriment of the wife's mental health (**DOCUMENT 6**).

Though all of these images are accurate, there were other trends during the 1950s which do not fit this mold, such as the growth of youth culture. Young people had emerged as their own demographic. They had their own tastes, which were different from their parents'. An example of this is the spread of rock 'n' roll music. This sexually charged form of popular dance music spread though the teenage demographic (**DOCUMENT 4**). Another, similar, counterexample is the beat movement. A group of young dissatisfied poets in New York, centered around Jack Kerouac and Alan Ginsberg, the beats did not conform to the image of the consensus. They wrote about an entire generation that felt detached from the broader culture (**DOCUMENT 7**). Finally, the civil rights movement also made quite a bit of headway in this period. Segregation in schools was deemed unconstitutional (**DOCUMENT 8**).

A culture of conformity certainly existed in the 1950s, but it was counter-balanced by another, nonconforming culture.

CHAPTER 28

The Civil Rights Movement, 1945–1966

This chapter covers the mass movements for civil rights beginning in the black community and then extending to the Mexican American, Puerto Rican, Asian, and American Indian communities as well. This era, often called the "Second Reconstruction," saw advances against segregation through federal court decisions and more direct demonstrations as black leaders forced the larger community to face segregation issues. The Civil Rights Act of 1964 and the Voting Rights Act of 1965 reinforced political equality, but economic and social equality did not automatically follow. The persistence of poverty, entrenched racism, and racially segregated "ghetto" slums brought about a split within the formerly united black community over what goals the movement should subsequently pursue. The civil rights movement overall created new pride and expectation as well as anger and a more militant "Black Power" movement.

Origins of the Movement

The migration of African Americans to northern cities led to increased economic and political opportunities. Voting power and legal action by the NAACP led to increased civil rights. In the South, segregation prevailed. After World War II, the NAACP's legal strategy culminated in the victory in *Brown* v. *Board of Education* that ended segregation in the schools. A crisis in Little Rock, Arkansas, forced President Eisenhower to use National Guard troops to integrate the schools there.

No Easy Road to Freedom, 1957–1962

African Americans used several nonviolent strategies to obtain civil rights, including boycotts, sit-ins, and freedom rides. A number of organizations emerged to pursue civil rights. Their campaigns often proved successful but met with strong resistance in the South.

The Movement at High Tide, 1963–1965

Between 1963 and 1965, civil rights activities reached new heights and registered important victories. The campaign in Birmingham, Alabama, met strong, violent resistance but resulted in several gains. The March on Washington attracted 250,000 people and, after the assassination of John Kennedy, led to passage of the Civil Rights Act. Direct action continued with the Mississippi Freedom Summer, which suffered tragic violence. A different movement was founded by Malcolm X, who stressed militancy and black consciousness. In 1964, the Selma protests helped secure passage of the Voting Rights Act.

Civil Rights Beyond Black and White

The African American civil rights movement stimulated similar efforts by Mexican Americans, Puerto Ricans, Indian peoples, and Asian Americans. Each group pursued goals connected to their specific situation using a variety of strategies.

Multiple-Choice Questions

1. Rosa Parks was arrested in Montgomery, Alabama, because she refused to
   (A) pay her fare up front and re-enter the bus from the back.
   (B) ride on a blacks-only bus.
   (C) yield her seat to a white passenger.
   (D) get up from a segregated lunch counter.
   (E) sit in the back of the bus.

2. This African American Nobel Prize winner refused a government appointment because he did not want to subject his family to humiliating segregation laws in Washington, D.C.
   (A) Ralph Abernathy
   (B) James Farmer
   (C) Ralph Bunche
   (D) W.E.B. Du Bois.
   (E) Martin Luther King, Jr.

3. In regard to civil rights, the most important department of the Kennedy administration was
   (A) the Agriculture Department.
   (B) the Interior Department.
   (C) the State Department.
   (D) the Health, Education, and Welfare Department.
   (E) the Justice Department.

4. Why did civil rights leaders promote the March on Washington?
   (A) to demonstrate on behalf of integrated busing
   (B) to pressure Kennedy into offering a civil rights bill
   (C) to pressure southern Republicans into supporting the civil rights bill
   (D) to pressure southern police brutality
   (E) to pressure Congress into passing JFK's civil rights bill

5. The Voting Rights Act provided for
   (A) federal supervision of registration in certain southern states and counties.
   (B) a poll tax to pay for civil rights education.
   (C) the registration of all white southern voters.
   (D) a declaration of party affiliation.
   (E) a literacy requirement for voting.

6. Mississippi Freedom Summer was successful in
   (A) reaching the coalition ideal of the beloved community.
   (B) registering black voters with minimal violence.
   (C) using white volunteers to minimize violence against their cause.
   (D) focusing attention on racism.
   (E) ending voting abuses in Mississippi.

7. The National Congress of American Indians took a cue from the civil rights movement and
   (A) mixed peaceful and violent protest.
   (B) used the courts to gain rights.
   (C) assimilated into the mainstream culture.
   (D) separated from mainstream Americans.
   (E) declared that only Indians could declare termination.

8. The great migration from 1945 to 1964 signified by East Harlem was largely driven by
   (A) African Americans.
   (B) Puerto Ricans.
   (C) Native Americans.
   (D) Mexicans.
   (E) Germans.

9. With the change in the Immigration and Nationality Act of 1965, which group was not the largest Asian American group in 1985, as it had been in 1960?
   (A) Chinese
   (B) Vietnamese
   (C) Korean
   (D) Cambodians
   (E) Japanese

10. Jackie Robinson became the first African American in major league baseball in
    (A) 1941.
    (B) 1946.
    (C) 1947.
    (D) 1952.
    (E) 1954.

Document-Based Question

The civil rights movement has been called America's Second Reconstruction because it fulfilled many of the promises made to African Americans in the aftermath of the Civil War. A long time in coming, the civil rights movement was characterized by both "top-down" administrative changes in the structure and practice of American government as well as the committed actions of a grassroots activist movement. How did these two forces work together to effect change, and did one influence the outcome more than the other?

DOCUMENT 1

Source: *Brown* v. *Board of Education* (1954)

We come then to the question presented: Does segregation of children in public schools solely on the basis of race, even though the physical facilities and other "tangible" factors may be equal, deprive the children of the minority group of equal education opportunities? We believe that it does.

In *Sweatt* v. *Painter* . . . in finding that a segregated law school for Negroes could not provide them equal education opportunities, the Court relied in large part on "those qualities which are incapable of objective measurement but which make for greatness in a law school." In *McLaurin* v. *Oklahoma State Regents* . . . the Court, in requiring that a Negro admitted to a white graduate school be treated like all other students, again resorted to intangible considerations: ". . . his ability to study, to engage in discussions and exchange views with other students, and in general, to learn his profession." Such considerations apply with added force to children in grade and high schools. To separate them from others of similar age and qualifications solely because of their race generates a feeling of inferiority as to their status in the community that may affect their hearts and minds in a way unlikely ever to be undone. The effect of this separation on their educational opportunities was well stated by a finding in the Kansas case by a court which nevertheless felt compelled to rule against the Negro plaintiffs:

Segregation of white and colored children in public schools has a detrimental effect upon the colored children. The impact is greater when it has the sanction of the law; for the policy of separating the races is usually interpreted as denoting the inferiority of the Negro group. A sense of inferiority affects the motivation of a child to learn. Segregation with the sanction of law, therefore, has a tendency to retard the education and mental development of negro children and to deprive them of some of the benefits they would receive in a racial[ly] integrated school system.

Whatever may have been the extent of psychological knowledge at the time of *Plessy* v. *Ferguson*, this finding is amply supported by modern authority. Any language in *Plessy* v. *Ferguson* contrary to this finding is rejected.

We conclude that in the field of public education the doctrine of "separate but equal" has no place. Separate educational facilities are inherently unequal. Therefore, we hold that the plaintiffs and others similarly situated for whom the actions have been brought are, by reason of the segregation complained of, deprived of the equal protection of the laws guaranteed by the Fourteenth Amendment. This disposition makes unnecessary any discussion whether such segregation also violates the Due Process Clause of the Fourteenth Amendment.

DOCUMENT 2

DOCUMENT 3

Source: Charles Sherrod, Student Nonviolent Coordinating Committee Memorandum (1961)

The night of the first Mass Meeting came! The church was packed before eight o'clock. People were everywhere, in the aisles, sitting and standing in the choir stands, hanging over the railing of the balcony upstairs, sitting in trees outside near windows, and about twenty or thirty ministers sat on the pulpit in chairs and on the floor side by side. There was no bickering. Soon a young doctor of the community took charge of the gathering, leading in the freedom songs which have grown out of the student movement during the last two years. Petitions were laid before Almighty God by one of the ministers and a challenge was directed to the assembly by the young doctor. Then arose a tall, silver-haired, outspoken veteran of the struggle. He spoke [in a] slow and determined [manner]. He referred to attempts last year to unify the community in protest against literary abuse of black men in the local paper and filled in with vivid detail the developments to the date of the Mass Meeting. Appearing also on the program was the indefatigable, only, local Negro lawyer, C. B. King. He stood flatfooted and thundered with his explosively deep voice, striking at both the inaction of the church and its hypocrisy. He also condemned local leadership in other areas for procrastination. At times he sounded like the prophet of doom but before he had finished, in his highly polished speech, he declared that our only hope was unity. This had been the real reason for the Mass Meeting-to weld the community into one bond of reason and emotion. The force to do this was generated by accounts of the released who individually described the physical situation and mental state of each, in jail.

When the last speaker among the students, Bertha Gober, had finished, there was nothing left to say. Tears filled the eyes of hard, grown men who had known personally and seen with their own eyes merciless atrocities committed by small men without conscience. As

Bertha, with her small frame and baby voice told of spending Thanksgiving in jail along with other physical inconveniences, there was not a dry eye to be found. And when we rose to sing "We Shall Overcome," nobody could imagine what kept the top of the church on four corners. It was as if everyone had been lifted up on high and had been granted voices to sing with the celestial chorus in another time and in another place.

DOCUMENT 4

DOCUMENT 5

Source: The Civil Rights Act of 1964

TITLE II

Injunctive Relief Against Discrimination in Places of Public Accommodation

Sec. 201. (a) All persons shall be entitled to the full and equal enjoyment of the goods, services, facilities, privileges, advantages, and accommodations of any place of public accommodation, as defined in this section, without discrimination or segregation on the ground of race, color, religion, or national origin.

(b) Each of the following establishments which serves the public is a place of public accommodation within the meaning of this title if its operations affect commerce, or if discrimination or segregation by it is supported by State action:

(1) any inn, motel, or other establishment which provides lodging to transient guests, other than an establishment located within a building which contains not more than five rooms for rent or hire and which is actually occupied by the proprietor of such establishment as his residence;

(2) any restaurant, cafeteria, lunch room, lunch counter, soda fountain, or other activity principally engaged in selling food for consumption on the premises. . . .

(3) any motion picture house, theater, concert hall, sports arena, stadium, or other place of exhibition or entertainment.

. . .

(d) Discrimination or segregation by an establishment is supported by State action within the meaning of this title if such discrimination or segregation (1) is carried on under color of any law, statute, ordinance, or regulation; or (2) is carried on under color of any custom or usage required or enforced by officials of the State or political subdivision thereof. . . .

Sec. 202. All persons shall be entitled to be free, at any establishment or place, from discrimination or segregation of any kind on the ground of race, color, religion, or national origin, if such discrimination or segregation is or purports to be required by any law, statute, ordinance, regulation, rule, or order of a State or any agency or political subdivision thereof. . . .

Sec. 206. (a) Whenever the Attorney General has reasonable cause to believe that any person or group of persons is engaged in a pattern of practice of resistance to the full enjoyment of any of the rights secured by this title, the Attorney General may bring a civil action in the appropriate district court of the United States by filing with it a complaint . . . requesting such preventive relief, including an application for a permanent or temporary injunction, restraining order or other order against the person or persons responsible for such pattern or practice, as he deems necessary to insure the full enjoyment of the rights herein described.

DOCUMENT 6

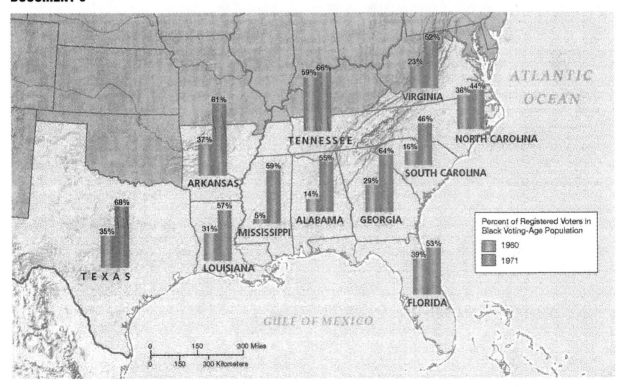

Multiple-Choice Questions

1. (C) is correct. When Rosa Parks refused to give up her seat to a white person in Montgomery, Alabama, in 1955, she gavalnized 30,000 members of the black community into a bus boycott. While Martin Luther King, Jr. is credited with being the undisputed leader of the civil rights movement, it was Parks who started the movement.

2. (C) is correct. Bunche won the Nobel Peace Prize in 1950 for arranging an Arab-Israeli truce in 1948. Bunche, if he took the position in Washington D.C., would have been the undersecretary of state.

3. (E) is correct. The Justice Department in fact had a Civil Rights division, which was established in 1957. This part of the Justice Department gave the attorney general the right to seek court injunctions to protect the rights of people to vote. President Kennedy's brother, Robert, as attorney general, was extremely active in fighting segregation.

4. (E) is correct. Kennedy's proposed civil rights bill included: ensure voting rights, outlaw segregation in public facilities, and bolster the federal government to deny funds for discriminatory programs. Leaders from every civil rights organization in the country put aside their differences and marched on Washington D.C.

5. (A) is correct. The Voting Rights Act of 1965 also outlawed literacy tests and other discriminatory practices in voting registration. The Voting Rights Act dramatically increased black voter registration in the Deep South.

6. (D) is correct. The Mississippi Freedom Summer joined black and white civil rights activists together in attempts to increase voter registration and fight discrimination. This movement attempted to fight racism in the state that was the most segregated in the union. Despite shootings, arrests, beatings, and bombings of black churches, the Freedom movement raised awareness to the nation about the racism in Mississippi.

7. (B) is correct. The Native Americans used the court system to protect sovereign rights. The most important court decision that came out of this was the *United States* v. *Wheeler* decision of 1978, which reasserted the principle of "unique and limited sovereignty" to the Native Americans.

8. (B) is correct. The *el barrio* of East Harlem was created in large part due to the direct air service between Puerto Rico and New York City. By 1970, Puerto Ricans made up 10 percent of New York City's overall population.

9. (E) is correct. The Immigration and Nationality Act of 1965 made it easier for people all over Asia to come to the United States, when before it was mainly just the Japanese. This act made it so 11 million Asians had immigrated to the United States before the end of the century. By 1985, Chinese and Filipinos became the largest group of immigrants coming from Asia.

10. (C) is correct. In 1947, Jackie Robinson broke the color barrier in major league baseball. Playing for the Brooklyn Dodgers, Robinson, despite enduring racist taunts from fans and players alike, opened the major leagues for African American players after him.

Document-Based Question

The civil rights movement has been called America's Second Reconstruction because it fulfilled many of the promises made to African Americans in the aftermath of the Civil War. A long time in coming, the civil rights movement was characterized by both "top-down" administrative changes in the structure and practice of American government as well as the committed actions of a grassroots activist movement. How did these two forces work together to effect change, and did one influence the outcome more than the other?

African Americans struggled to achieve full political and legal equality following the abolition of slavery, only to see their hopes dashed by the institution of legal segregation in many parts of the country, especially the South, and *de facto* segregation caused by economic equality and unofficial discriminatory policies in the North. Well into the twentieth century, African Americans were forced into second-class citizenship, relegated to menial and low-paying jobs, and without recourse when their civil rights were violated by both law and custom. However, African Americans were galvanized by the broad social and economic changes generated by World War II and a series of significant events, including the desegregation of the armed forces following the war, propelled many to further challenge institutionalized racism in the United States. At the same time, the federal government was expanding its role and took on the divisive issue, no longer shirking its responsibility to upholding the guarantees of the Constitution. Both the institutional reform of the federal government and the grassroots activities of activists formed the civil rights movement of the 1950s and 1960s, often working together, sometimes at odds with one another.

The first sign that change would come from the government occurred in the landmark Supreme Court decision *Brown* v. *Board of Education of Topeka, Kansas*, in which the "separate but equal" precedent established by *Plessy* v. *Ferguson* in 1896 was overturned with regard to public education (**DOCUMENT 1**). Attempts to desegregate other forms of segregation followed, as African Americans challenged public accommodations all over the South, as demonstrated in the successful Montgomery Bus Boycott led by the Reverend Dr. Martin Luther King, Jr. The success of such popular protests provided an example of effective non-violent protest to African Americans, and students soon became committed to fighting segregation, holding demonstrations such as the Greensboro, North Carolina, lunch counter sit-in (**DOCUMENT 2**). As students throughout the nation became committed to the movement, they formed the Student Non-Violent Coordinating Committee. Dedicated to the principles of non-violence, SNCC spread throughout the South as students entered even the poorest and most frightened communities, educating African Americans about their rights and organizing them into a powerful force for change (**DOCUMENT 3**). Often risking their lives, these young men and women worked the front lines of social change (**DOCUMENT 4**). Such activity was not ignored by the federal government, which recognized the dramatic moral force of the civil rights movement as well as its legitimate claims regarding the rights of all citizens. A result of political compromise following the assassination of John F. Kennedy, the Civil Rights Act of 1964 that President Lyndon Johnson signed followed up on the *Brown* decision by destroying the legal basis of segregation in areas outside of education (**DOCUMENT 5**). Perhaps the most far-reaching change in the political structure, though, was created by the Voting Rights Act of 1965, which provided federal support for African American voting rights and succeeded in securing such rights for African Americans throughout the South (**DOCUMENT 6**). By the end of the 1960s, African Americans had made great strides in their ongoing struggle for equality.

CHAPTER 29

War Abroad, War at Home, 1965–1974

This chapter covers the Vietnam conflict, the longest and least successful war in American history. The period of greatest involvement was from 1965 to 1974, and because of the aggressive military policies of the administration, it became known as "Johnson's war" and then "Nixon's war." The war and actions against it diverted the domestic agendas of President Johnson and student reform groups. Ironically, President Nixon proved not to be as conservative as expected in some social reform areas. He was also able to make a major foreign policy opening to Communist China and subsequently to Soviet Russia. The civil rights movement spurred demands from other groups, including college students, gays, women, Latinos, Asian Americans, and Indians. The Vietnam War and the agendas of the various groups dominated both the 1968 and 1972 presidential elections. The year 1968 was also a key turning point on the battlefield, with the dramatic North Vietnamese "Tet" offensive. While the Americans finally won all the battles, live television footage and interviews with demoralized soldiers shocked the nation because of the gap it illustrated between rosy predictions of impending victory and actual facts. Martin Luther King, Jr. and Robert F. Kennedy were assassinated in rapid succession during the 1968 presidential campaign. The 1968 Democratic Convention in Chicago was engulfed in great street demonstrations and violence, much of which was also televised. The national mood was dismal and the events of the Nixon administration and Watergate did nothing to rebuild a national political or social consensus.

Vietnam: America's Longest War

Inheriting U. S. involvement in Vietnam, Lyndon Johnson expanded the American role to full-fledged war after the Tonkin Gulf resolution. The U.S. strategy of attrition failed due to North Vietnam's resolve. The media eventually accused Johnson of creating a credibility gap between official reports on the war and its reality. Criticism soon spread to Congress, and its continuation affected domestic policy.

A Generation in Conflict

The sixties generation was the largest and best-educated generation in American history. A minority of this generation began protesting the Vietnam War and other social ills. Many had taken part in civil rights demonstrations and they started protesting on college campuses, soon mobilizing large numbers of young people and others to take part in mass demonstrations. Conversely, large numbers of young men served as teenage soldiers in Vietnam, experiencing frustration and alienation amid the horror of combat in tropical swamps and rain forests.

Wars on Poverty

In 1964, Lyndon Johnson proclaimed his Great Society program that was designed to wage war on poverty. Programs were developed to improve opportunities in education and employment, empower communities, and increase social welfare. Part of the problem was the continuing decline of the cities. The deteriorating conditions helped precipitate a number of urban uprisings by African Americans.

1968

One of the most turbulent and influential years in American history was 1968. The Vietnam War experienced its most destructive fighting. Two major leaders were assassinated. The Democratic convention in Chicago was accompanied by a full-scale riot. Lastly, student radical and antiwar protests erupted throughout Europe and in Japan.

The Politics of Identity

In the late 1960s, numerous movements either intensified their efforts or emerged. Some African Americans embraced Black Power. The women's and gay liberation movements became powerful voices for their respective rights, while Chicano nationalism and Red Power identified the Mexican-American and Indian peoples movements. Asian Americans also became actively involved in rights movements.

The Nixon Presidency

The conservative backlash to the liberal and radical movements of the 1960s helped Richard Nixon win the 1968 election. Nixon also campaigned on winning peace with honor, but his escalation of the conflict into Cambodia triggered a massive, national antiwar protest. At the same time, Nixon worked to normalize relations with China. Domestically, he supported both liberal and conservative programs.

Watergate

The Nixon White House engaged in covert actions overseas and dirty tricks at home. His illegal actions during the 1972 presidential campaign eventually erupted into the Watergate scandal that led to convictions of several Nixon appointees and the resignation of the president.

Multiple-Choice Questions

1. Why did President Johnson <u>NOT</u> want his administration to lose in Vietnam?
   (A) It would hurt him in the upcoming election.
   (B) Johnson was a military-minded president.
   (C) He was afraid Vietnam was becoming imperialist.
   (D) Johnson understood the political price Eisenhower paid over losing China.
   (E) The Democratic Party wanted a war to help the economy.

2. The SDS called on the government for
   (A) immediate withdrawal of U.S. troops from Vietnam.
   (B) gradual withdrawal followed by limited bombing.
   (C) the impeachment of Johnson.
   (D) increased military funding.
   (E) a peace march on Washington.

3. Which of the following is <u>LEAST</u> likely to be one of the communities of Harrington's *Other America*?
   (A) the Appalachian Mountain area
   (B) a counterculture commune
   (C) the Deep South
   (D) an inner city
   (E) all these communities were affected

4. All of the following were problems for urban centers <u>EXCEPT</u>
   (A) increase in pollution.
   (B) employment opportunities declined.
   (C) housing shortages for the poor.
   (D) income for white Americans declined dramatically.
   (E) low wages for the poor.

5. This 1968 presidential candidate was so popular on campuses that his campaign was called the "Children's Crusade."
   (A) Robert Kennedy
   (B) Hubert Humphrey
   (C) Eugene J. McCarthy
   (D) Richard Nixon
   (E) George C. Wallace

6. Most of the activism of young women in the women's liberation movement was in
   (A) flamboyant radical activities.
   (B) consciousness-raising groups.
   (C) marching.
   (D) antiwar protests.
   (E) writing.

7. The following was a consequence of Martin Luther King's assassination:
   (A) a desire for whites and blacks to work together.
   (B) Johnson attended the funeral.
   (C) banks issued loans to rebuild inner-city neighborhoods.
   (D) southern congressmen understood their black constituents.
   (E) blacks developed deep feelings of mistrust for whites.

8. In 1970, hoping to deliver a knockout blow to the North Vietnamese, President Nixon
   (A) launched the Vietnamese Plan.
   (B) ordered the bombing and invasion of Cambodia.
   (C) ordered the bombing of Thailand.
   (D) announced a cease-fire in Laos and Cambodia.
   (E) began Operation Rolling Thunder.

9. The most dramatic foreign policy move of the Nixon presidency involved
   (A) negotiating an Arab-Israeli peace accord.
   (B) reopening diplomatic relations with Cuba.
   (C) his visit to the People's Republic of China.
   (D) his visit to the Soviet Union.
   (E) signing a comprehensive nuclear test ban treaty with the Soviets.

10. What was the most enduring component of Black Power?
   (A) more cross-racial understanding
   (B) a militant leadership
   (C) cultural nationalism
   (D) self-help programs
   (E) scholarship money for black youths

Document-Based Question

The dominant mood of consensus in the postwar years gave way in the 1960s, as different groups in American society advanced new interpretations of American ideals such as liberty and equality. What did these groups advocate, and how did they contribute to the dramatic political dialogues of the era?

DOCUMENT 1

Source: Students for a Democratic Society, The Port Huron Statement (1962)

We are the people of this generation, bred in at least modest comfort, housed now in the universities, looking uncomfortably to the world we inherit.

When we were kids the United States was the wealthiest and strongest country in the world; the only one with the atom bomb, the least scarred by modern war, an initiator of the United Nations that we thought would distribute Western influence throughout the world. Freedom and equality for each individual, government of, by, and for the people-these American values we found good, principles by which we could live as men. Many of us began maturing in complacency.

As we grew, however, our comfort was penetrated by events too troubling to dismiss. First, the permeating and victimizing fact of human degradation, symbolized by the Southern struggle against racial bigotry, compelled most of us from silence to activism. Second, the enclosing fact of the Cold War, symbolized by the presence of the Bomb, brought awareness that we ourselves, and our friends, and millions of abstract "others" we knew more directly because of our common peril, might die at any time. We might deliberately ignore, or avoid or fail to feel all other human problems, but not these two, for these were too immediate and crushing in their impact, too challenging in the demand that we as individuals take the responsibility for encounter and resolution.

DOCUMENT 2

Source: Betty Friedan, The Feminine Mystique (1963)

I began to see in a strange new light the American return to early marriage and the large families that are causing the population explosion; the recent movement to natural childbirth and breastfeeding; suburban conformity, and the new neuroses, character pathologies and sexual problems being reported by the doctors. I began to see new dimensions to old problems that have long been taken for granted among women: menstrual difficulties, sexual frigidity, promiscuity, pregnancy fears, childbirth depression, the high incidence of emotional breakdown and suicide among women in their twenties and thirties, the menopause crises, the so-called passivity and immaturity of American men, the discrepancy between women's tested intellectual abilities in childhood and their adult achievement, the changing incidence of adult sexual orgasm in American women, and persistent problems in psychotherapy and in women's education.

If I am right, the problem that has no name stirring in the minds of so many American women today is not a matter of loss of femininity or too much education, or the demands of domesticity. It is far more important than anyone recognizes. It is the key to these other new and old problems which have been torturing women and their husbands and children, and puzzling their doctors and educators for years. It may well be the key to our future as a nation and a culture. We can no longer ignore that voice within women that says: "I want something more than my husband and children and my home."

DOCUMENT 3

Source: National Organization for Women, Statement of Purpose (1966)

Discrimination in employment on the basis of sex is now prohibited by federal law, in Title VII of the Civil Rights Act of 1964. . . . Until now, too few women's organizations and official spokesmen have been willing to speak out against these dangers facing women. Too many women have been restrained by the fear of being called "feminist."

There is no civil rights movement to speak for women, as there has been for Negroes and other victims of discrimination. The National Organization for Women must therefore begin to speak.

WE BELIEVE that the power of American law, and the protection guaranteed by the U.S. Constitution to the civil rights of all individuals, must be effectively applied and enforced to isolate and remove patterns of sex discrimination, to ensure equality of opportunity in employment and education, and equality of civil and political rights and responsibilities on behalf of women, as well as for Negroes and other deprived groups.

WE REALIZE that women's problems are linked to many broader questions of social justice; their solution will require concerted action by many groups. . . .

WE DO NOT ACCEPT the token appointment of a few women to high-level positions in government and industry as a substitute for a serious continuing effort to recruit and advance women according to their individual abilities. To this end, we urge American government and industry to mobilize the same resources of ingenuity and command with which they have solved problems of far greater difficulty than those now impeding the progress of women.

WE BELIEVE that this nation has a capacity at least as great as other nations, to innovate new social institutions which will enable women to enjoy true equality of opportunity and responsibility in society, without conflict with their responsibilities as mothers and homemakers. . . .

. . . WE REJECT the assumption that these problems are the unique responsibility of each individual woman, rather than a basic social dilemma which society must solve. . . .

DOCUMENT 4

Source: Stokely Carmichael and Charles Hamilton, from Black Power (1967)

Next we deal with the term "integration." According to its advocates, social justice will be accomplished by "integrating the Negro into the mainstream institutions of the society from which he has been traditionally excluded." This concept is based on the assumption that there is nothing of value in the black community and that little of value could be created among black people. The thing to do is to siphon off the "acceptable" black people into the surrounding middle-class white community.

The goals of integrationists are middle-class goals, articulated primarily by a small group of Negroes with middle-class aspirations or status. . . .

Secondly, while color blindness may be a sound goal ultimately, we must realize that race is an overwhelming fact of life in this historical period. There is no black man in the country who can live "simply as a man." His blackness is an ever-present fact of this racist society, whether he recognizes it or not. It is unlikely that this or the next generation will witness the time when race will no longer be relevant in the conduct of public affairs and in public policy decision-making. . . .

"Integration" as a goal today speaks to the problem of blackness not only in an unrealistic way but also in a despicable way. It is based on complete acceptance of the fact that in order to have a decent house or education, black people must move into a white neighborhood or send their children to a white school. This reinforces, among both black and white, the idea that "white" is automatically superior and "black" is by definition inferior. For this reason, "integration" is a subterfuge for the maintenance of white supremacy.

DOCUMENT 5

DOCUMENT 6

Source: The Gay Liberation Front, Come Out (1970)

Bernard: I see the Gay Liberation Movement as a process which will help liberate gay people by making them fully part of the whole liberation movement. The movement for change in the system that will eventually annihilate any form of oppression. Before GLF I was active in these movements, but anonymously-nobody was conscious of the fact that I was homosexual. I think the only way we can gain respect for ourselves and any of the help that we need from everyone else in overcoming our oppression is by showing that we participate even though they don't understand why we participate. I think even among a lot of our own people we have to fight for the right to participate as homosexuals.

Bob: I've always been active as a homosexual. Openly, but never publicly. In the past six or seven months I have suddenly found myself living the life of a public homosexual. I find resentment in many parts of the movement. When I find it, I confront it. This is very healthy for me; and it's very healthy for the movement. We cant hold the movement up as being any better or any worse than the rest of us. Gay Liberation to me is seeing 35 or 40 homosexuals marching as homosexuals in a vigil to free political prisoners. We have been political prisoners, and we will be political prisoners. Homosexuals are beginning to see themselves as an oppressed minority. I don't think homosexuality is a magic tie that binds us all but in a sense there is something. It's being proud of ourselves. And I think that's what liberation will help us find-a pride that we can just stand up and be proud of ourselves as human beings.

Bernard: I want to bring up the past in one way. When I was among young people, we had no way of expressing this. I never felt sick, although the attitude then was that we were a sickness. I could only fight this when I talked to individuals. We had no public way of fighting it. And it's exciting to be able to do it now, and the fight must be a very conscious fight.

DOCUMENT 7

Multiple-Choice Questions

1. (A) is correct. Facing a presidential election in November 1964, Johnson knew that a major military setback would cripple his election campaign. When Johnson faced the 1968 election campaign, the turmoil in Vietnam led him to announce that he would not seek the Democratic Party's nomination.

2. (A) is correct. Campus organizations such as SDS encouraged college students to take a militant stand against the war, calling for an immediate and unconditional withdrawal of U.S. troops from Vietnam.

3. (B) is correct. Michael Harrington's *The Other America* (1962) argued that one-fifth of the nation—as many as 40 to 50 million people—suffered from bad housing, malnutrition, poor medical care, and other deprivations of poverty. Harrington documented the miseries of the rejects of society who simply did not exist for affluent suburbanites or the mass media. These arguments motivated President Johnson to expand the antipoverty program that he had inherited from the Kennedy administration and declare a "war on poverty."

4. (D) is correct. The federal government encouraged "redlining," which left people in poor neighborhoods without access to building loans. In these areas, the supply of adequate housing declined sharply. Urban employment opportunities declined along with the urban housing stock. Black unemployment, however, was nearly twice that of white unemployment. Pollution became an increasingly pervasive urban problem. Despite deteriorating conditions, millions of Americans continued to move into the cities. Many had fled rural poverty only to find themselves earning minimum wages at best and living in miserable, racially segregated neighborhoods.

5. (C) is correct. Eugene McCarthy felt that the Vietnam War was a mirror of injustice at home. He garnered support from liberal Democrats and white suburbanites. On college campuses, his popularity with antiwar students was so great that his campaign became known as the "Children's Crusade."

6. (B) is correct. The majority involved in the women's liberation movement were less flamboyant women who were simply trying to rise above the limitations imposed on them because of their gender. Most of their activism took place outside of the limelight in consciousness-raising (CR) groups. CR groups brought women together to discuss the relationship between public events and private lives, particularly between politics and sexuality.

7. (E) is correct. After the death of Dr. King, riots broke out in more than 100 cities. By week's end, nearly 27,000 African Americans had been jailed. The physical scars of these riots remained for years, as banks redlined black neighborhoods and refused funds for rebuilding. The psychic scar survived even longer. With King's death, his vision of humanity as a "Beloved Community" faded.

8. (B) is correct. On April 30, 1970, Nixon made one of the most controversial decisions of his presidency. Without seeking congressional approval, he ordered U.S. troops to invade the tiny nation of Cambodia. Nixon had hoped in this way to end North Vietnamese infiltration into the South, but he had also decided to live up to what he privately called his "wild man" or "mad bomber" reputation. The enemy would be unable to anticipate the location or severity of the next U.S. strike, Nixon reasoned, and would thus feel compelled to negotiate.

9. (C) is correct. In 1972, Richard and Pat Nixon flew to Beijing. It was a momentous and surprising event, one that marked a new era in East-West diplomacy. The president's move successfully increased diplomatic pressure on the Soviet Union but simultaneously weakened the Nationalist Chinese government in Taiwan, which now slipped into virtual diplomatic obscurity.

ANSWERS AND EXPLANATIONS

Multiple-Choice Questions

1. (A) is correct. Facing a presidential election in November 1964, Johnson knew that a major military setback would cripple his election campaign. But he was equally determined to avoid the fate of President Truman, who had bogged down politically after "losing" China to communism and producing a stalemate in Korea. When Johnson faced the 1968 election campaign, the turmoil in Vietnam led him to announce that he would not seek the Democratic Party's nomination.

2. (A) is correct. Campus organizations such as SDS encouraged college students to take a militant stand against the war, calling for an immediate and unconditional withdrawal of U.S. troops from Vietnam.

3. (B) is correct. Michael Harrington's *The Other America* (1962) argued that one-fifth of the nation—as many as 40 to 50 million people—suffered from bad housing, malnutrition, poor medical care, and other deprivations of poverty. Harrington documented the miseries of the rejects of society who simply did not exist for affluent suburbanites or the mass media. These arguments motivated President Johnson to expand the antipoverty program that he had inherited from the Kennedy administration and declare a "war on poverty."

4. (D) is correct. The federal government encouraged "redlining," which left people in poor neighborhoods without access to building loans. In these areas, the supply of adequate housing declined sharply. Urban employment opportunities declined along with the urban housing stock. Black unemployment, however, was nearly twice that of white unemployment. Pollution became an increasingly pervasive urban problem. Despite deteriorating conditions, millions of Americans continued to move into the cities. Many had fled rural poverty only to find themselves earning minimum wages at best and living in miserable, racially segregated neighborhoods.

5. (C) is correct. Eugene McCarthy felt that the Vietnam War was a mirror of injustice at home. He garnered support from liberal Democrats and white suburbanites. On college campuses, his popularity with antiwar students was so great that his campaign became known as the "children's crusade."

6. (B) is correct. The majority involved in the women's liberation movement were less flamboyant women who were simply trying to rise above the limitations imposed on them because of their gender. Most of their activism took place outside of the limelight in consciousness-raising (CR) groups. CR groups brought women together to discuss the relationship between public events and private lives, particularly between politics and sexuality.

7. (E) is correct. After the death of Dr. King, riots broke out in more than 100 cities. By week's end, nearly 27,000 African Americans had been jailed. The physical scars of these riots remained for years, as banks redlined black neighborhoods and refused funds for rebuilding. The psychic scar survived even longer. With King's death, his vision of humanity as a "Beloved Community" faded.

8. (B) is correct. On April 30, 1970, Nixon made one of the most controversial decisions of his presidency. Without seeking congressional approval, he ordered U.S. troops to invade the tiny nation of Cambodia. Nixon had hoped in this way to end North Vietnamese infiltration into the South, but he had also decided to live up to what he privately called his "wild man" or "mad bomber" reputation. The enemy would be unable to anticipate the location or severity of the next U.S. strike, Nixon reasoned, and would thus feel compelled to negotiate.

9. (C) is correct. In 1972, Richard and Pat Nixon flew to Beijing. It was a momentous and surprising event, one that marked a new era in East-West diplomacy. The president's

CHAPTER 30

The Conservative Ascendancy, 1974–1991

This chapter covers the Ford, Carter, and Reagan administrations and their attempts to respond to changing conditions. Americans finally became painfully aware of the high price of cold war military defenses, and in the aftermath of Watergate had little confidence in the federal government's ability to act effectively or honestly. Grassroots political activity increased but did not expand nationally. Foreign policy under Ford and Carter experienced highs and lows. A new conservatism, driven by a revived religious right, was energetic and contributed to the election of Ronald Reagan. Reagan energized the nation but his domestic efforts and foreign policies had mixed results. A major achievement was better relations with the Soviet Union.

The Overextended Society

In the 1970s, American society was in transition. The economy was shaken by a variety of domestic and international forces. The hard times hit the working class the hardest. Two very different regions were evident. The Sunbelt appeared prosperous but was subject to boom-and-bust cycles, while the Snowbelt showed signs of severe decline. The policies of presidents Ford and Carter failed to improve economic conditions. Political mobilization in the 1970s focused on communities. Minorities gained political power and political office but reforms were difficult due to fiscal problems. A mix of federal government, community organizations, and philanthropic foundations sponsored initiatives to rebuild the cities. In addition, environmental crises shocked communities and the nation, stimulating the environmental movement. Retirees and urban problems fueled growth in small towns, but some residents protested against new subdivisions.

The New Conservatism

The expansion of government and the drive to promote so-called traditional values led to the creation of the New Right. Evangelical Christianity played a strong role in this movement, which opposed liberal issues. Another political trend of the 1970s was disengagement from politics in favor of personal growth and self-indulgence. Popular culture reflected these new trends.

Adjusting to a New World

After the Vietnam War, U.S. foreign policy was reassessed. Economics and other considerations led to a thaw in the cold war. President Jimmy Carter's defense of human rights introduced morality into American foreign policy and helped negotiate a major Middle East agreement between Israel and Egypt. He also set the stage for Panama to gain ownership and control of the Panama Canal, but backed repressive dictators in Central America in certain cases. A major problem for Carter was handling unexpected developments in Central America, Africa, and Central Asia. His biggest challenge was the Iran hostage crisis. As his first term ended, Carter announced that the nation was experiencing a crisis of confidence that hurt his popularity. Ronald Reagan easily won the 1980 election.

Reagan Revolution

Ronald Reagan attempted to reshape the American political and social scene along conservative lines. His ability to communicate with the American people made him extremely popular. In domestic affairs, he stressed supply-side economics but his reductions were countered by massive defense spending. Reagan supported business interests over labor, favoring deregulation of business. The economic recovery helped Reagan win a landslide victory in 1984. Reagan's economic policies had mixed results as the nation moved from a brief recession to a recovery to a fiscal crisis, due to the rising national debt. The stock scandal of the late 1980s also affected the economy.

Best of Times, Worst of Times

Entrepreneurship and moneymaking dominated the 1980s, but the celebration of wealth was not shared by all. Affluent Americans tended to do well, but a two-tiered society was developing. The gap between the rich and poor widened and the opportunities to climb to middle-class status diminished. Minorities and women were hit particularly hard by the economic gap. Other issues also affected the nation: drug use became more widespread, AIDS was a new disease that achieved epidemic proportions, and homelessness became a chronic problem.

Reagan's Foreign Policy

Reagan wanted to restore America's world leadership. His strong anticommunism dominated his foreign policy. In Central America, the Reagan administration engaged in covert activities to stem communist influence. Changes occurred with the opening up of Soviet society to discussion and change. Gorbachev headed negotiations to end the arms race and Reagan responded positively. But the Iran-Contra scandal tarnished the Reagan administration, leading to several resignations and convictions for illegal acts.

Multiple-Choice Questions

1. In the 1970s, a combination of skyrocketing prices, rising unemployment, and low economic growth was termed
   (A) inflation.
   (B) recession.
   (C) downturn.
   (D) stagflation.
   (E) depression.

2. The oil crisis of 1973 caused
   (A) an economic downturn.
   (B) panic in the streets.
   (C) a drop in oil prices.
   (D) a drop in production.
   (E) an alliance with the Soviet Union.

3. By 1980, two out of the three most populous states were in the Sunbelt; they were
   (A) Florida and California.
   (B) Arizona and Texas.
   (C) Florida and Texas.
   (D) Arkansas and Florida.
   (E) Texas and California.

4. Why were Americans becoming more concerned with the environment in the 1970s?
   (A) It was more visible.
   (B) Increasing rates of cancer were revealed.
   (C) The issue received constant publicity in the media.
   (D) The lumbering and mining interests stressed environmental issues.
   (E) Environmental quality was part of the Democratic platform.

5. Proposition 13 in California symbolized
   (A) an environmental backlash.
   (B) exurbia protest.
   (C) a taxpayer revolt.
   (D) support for capital punishment.
   (E) an affirmative-action coalition.

6. An advocate of supply-side economics would support
   (A) stimulating the economy through government spending.
   (B) emphasizing individual saving.
   (C) lowering taxes but continuing public spending.
   (D) keynesian economics.
   (E) giving investors greater incentives.

7. Why did the federal debt mushroom under Reagan?
   (A) Government spending increased overall in a dramatic fashion in the 1980s.
   (B) His forced spending increases and rejected tax plan caused a slowdown.
   (C) A rise in unemployment forced more welfare spending.
   (D) Expenditures on the space program tripled due to SDI.
   (E) U.S. companies exported more than they imported.

8. Which of the following was NOT a policy of Soviet leader Gorbachev?
   (A) perestroika
   (B) Strategic Defense Initiative
   (C) glasnost
   (D) zero option
   (E) restructuring

9. Gorbachev believed that the way to improve the Soviet economy was to
   (A) halt the arms race.
   (B) cut capital gain taxes.
   (C) get more consumer items in the country.
   (D) print more money.
   (E) establish a form of modified capitalism.

10. The "New Right" united traditional pro-business conservatives with a new constituency of
    (A) Christians who supported traditional moral values.
    (B) poor rural whites.
    (C) paramilitary groups of white supremacists.
    (D) conservative union members.
    (E) anticommunist groups.

Document-Based Question

Though not considered as divisive an era as the 1960s, the 1970s and 1980s witnessed new divisions in American society. How did these differences reveal the conflicting values of Americans at this time?

DOCUMENT 1

Source: Roe v. Wade (1973)

The principal thrust of appellant's attack on the Texas statutes is that they improperly invade a right, said to be possessed by the pregnant women, to choose to terminate her pregnancy. Appellant would discover this right in the concept of personal "liberty" embodied in the Fourteenth Amendment's Due Process Clause; or in personal, marital, familial, and sexual privacy said to be protected by the Bill of Rights or its penumbras, see Griswold v. Connecticut, 381 U.S. 479 (1965); Eisenstadt v. Baird, 405 U.S. 438 (1972); id., at 460 (White, J., concurring); or among those rights reserved to the people by the Ninth Amendment, Griswold v. Connecticut, 381 U. S., at 486 (Goldberg, J., concurring) . . . .

The Constitution does not explicitly mention any right of privacy. In a line of decisions, however, going back perhaps as far as Union Pacific R. Co. v. Botsford, 141 U.S. 250, 251 (1891), the Court has recognized that a right of personal privacy, or a guarantee of certain areas or zones of privacy, does exist under the Constitution. . . .

This right of privacy, whether it be founded in the Fourteenth Amendment's concept of personal liberty and restrictions upon state action, as we feel it is, or, as the District Court determined, in the Ninth Amendment's reservation of rights to the people, is broad enough to encompass a women's decision whether or not to terminate her pregnancy. The detriment that the state would impose upon the pregnant woman by denying this choice altogether is apparent. Specific and direct harm medically diagnosable even in early pregnancy may be involved. Maternity, or additional offspring, may force upon the woman a distressful life and future. Psychological harm may be imminent. Mental and physical health may be taxed by child care. There is also the distress, for all concerned, associated with the unwanted child, and there is the problem of bringing a child into a family already unable, psychologically and otherwise, to care for it. In other cases, as in this one, the additional difficulties and continuing stigma of unwed motherhood may be involved. All these are factors the woman and her responsible physician necessarily will consider in consultation.

The Constitution does not define "person" in so many words. Section 1 of the Fourteenth Amendment contains three references to "person." The first, in defining "citizens," speaks of "persons born or naturalized in the United States." The word also appears both in the Due Process Clause and in the Equal Protection Clause. "Person" is used in other places in the Constitution. . . . in nearly all these instances, the use of the word is such that it has application only postnatally. None indicates, with any assurance, that it has any possible pre-natal application.

Texas urges that, apart from the Fourteenth Amendment, life begins at conception and is present throughout pregnancy, and that, therefore, the state has a compelling interest in protecting that life from and after conception. We need not resolve the difficult question of when life begins. When those trained in the respective disciplines of medicine, philosophy, and theology are unable to arrive at any consensus, the judiciary, at this point in the development of man's knowledge, is not in a position to speculate as to the answer. . . .

In areas other than criminal abortion the law has been reluctant to endorse any theory that life, as we recognize it, begins before live birth or to accord legal rights to the unborn except in narrowly defined situations and except when the rights are contingent upon live birth. . . .

In short, the unborn have never been recognized in the law as persons in the whole sense. . . .

DOCUMENT 2

Asked of those who said they had heard of or read about the Equal Rights Amendment: Do you favor or oppose this amendment?

Favor	58%
Oppose	24%
No opinion	18%

By Sex

Male

Favor	63%
Oppose	22%
No opinion	15%

Female

Favor	54%
Oppose	25%
No opinion	21%

Interviewing Date 3/7–10/1975, Survey #925-K

DOCUMENT 3

Source: Ronald Reagan, First Inaugural Address (1981)

In this present crisis, government is not the solution to our problem.

From time to time, we have been tempted to believe that society has become too complex to be managed by self-rule, that government by an elite group is superior over government for, by, and of the people. But if no one among us is capable of governing himself, then who among us has the capacity to govern someone else? All of us together, in and out of government, must bear the burden. The solutions we seek must be equitable, with no one group singled out to pay a higher price.

We hear much of special interest groups. Our concern must be for a special interest group that has been too long neglected. It knows no sectional boundaries or ethnic and racial divisions, and it crosses political party lines. It is made up of men and women who raise our food, patrol our streets, man our mines and our factories, teach our children, keep our homes, and heal us when we are sick-professionals, industrialists, shopkeepers, clerks, cabbies, and truckdrivers. They are, in short, "We the people," this breed called Americans.

Well, this administration's objective will be a healthy, vigorous, growing economy that provides equal opportunity for all Americans, with no barriers born of bigotry or discrimination. Putting America back to work means putting all Americans back to work. Ending inflation means freeing all Americans from the terror of runaway living costs. All must share in the productive work of this "new beginning" and all must share in the bounty of a revived economy. With the idealism and fair play which are the core of our system and our strength, we can have a strong and prosperous America at peace with itself and the world.

So, as we begin, let us take inventory. We are a nation that has a government-not the other way around. And this makes us special among the nations of the Earth. Our Government has no power except that granted it by the people. It is time to check and reverse the growth of government which shows signs of having grown beyond the consent of the governed.

It is my intention to curb the size and influence of the Federal establishment and to demand recognition of the distinction between the powers granted to the Federal Government and those reserved to the States or to the people. All of us need to be reminded that the Federal Government did not create the States; the States created the Federal Government.

DOCUMENT 4

DOCUMENT 5

Source: Patricia Morrisroe, "The New Class" (1985)

Six floors above the Handlers, Linda and Mark Reiner also had to redo their apartment completely. "It was considered the worst disaster in the building," Linda says. "The walls, which were painted magenta, royal blue, and orange, were falling down. But we really wanted to live here. We recognized how the West Side was growing, and we wanted to be a part of that."

Two years ago, they moved from a house in Hewlett Harbor, where Mark Reiner had a medical practice. "It was a risk giving up everything," he says, "but Hewlett Harbor was very sterile and uniform."

"That's why we didn't want the East Side," adds Linda, who until recently was a practicing psychologist. "Now I sell real estate," she says. "I became addicted to it while we were looking for this apartment." The au pair brings their two-year-old son into the living room to say good night. "You wouldn't believe the children's playground in the park," Linda says. "You can barely get a place for your kid in the sandbox."

"Everybody wants to come here," says Mark. "There's nothing more exciting than living in a neighborhood in transition. It's sad, because a lot of people who live here can't afford to shop in the stores. But they're being pushed out of Manhattan, not just the West Side."

"The West Side makes you feel the difference between the haves and the have-nots," says Linda, who is dressed in a silk Chanel shirt, black pants, and pumps. "Right in our building, there's a real schism between the pre-conversion and post-conversion people. A new breed is taking over, and there's a lot of hostility. People are separated by age and economic class. The senior citizens got insider prices so low that there's a lot of resentment on all sides. At a recent meeting, one elderly person shouted, 'Well, I'm not rich like you.' But what can you do?"

"Basically, we're very optimistic," Mark says. "We feel good about the changes. The neighborhood is going to continue to improve."

Linda nods. "Definitely," she says. "For the West Side, there's no turning back."

ANSWERS AND EXPLANATIONS

Multiple-Choice Questions

■ **1. (D) is correct.** In the 1970s, Americans faced an unfamiliar combination of skyrocketing prices, rising unemployment, and low economic growth. Economists termed this novel condition "stagflation." The annual rate of economic growth slowed by almost one-quarter from its robust 3.2 percent average of the 1950s. By 1975, the unemployment rate had reached nearly 9 percent, its highest level since the Great Depression, and it remained close to 7 percent for most of the rest of the decade. Inflation, meanwhile, reached double-digits.

■ **2. (A) is correct.** The United States, which used about 70 percent of all oil produced in the world, had found the domestic supply sufficient until the mid-1950s. But rising demand had outstripped national reserves, and by 1973 the nation was importing one-third of its crude oil, mainly from the Middle East. With the cost of gasoline, oil, and electricity up, many other prices also rose, from apartment rents and telephone bills to restaurant checks. Whatever the causes, the oil crisis played a major role in the economic downturn.

▓ **3. (E) is correct.** The South witnessed a dramatic turnaround in demographic and economic trends. While manufacturing and highly subsidized agribusiness flourished, southern cities reversed the century-long trend of out-migration among African Americans. Aided by air conditioning, water diversions, public improvements, and large-scale development, California became the nation's most populous state; Texas moved to third, behind New York.

▓ **4. (B) is correct.** Early in the 1970s, the discovery of high rates of cancer and birth defects in Love Canal, near Buffalo, New York, had offered compelling evidence of a growing danger to many American communities. Here toxic wastes had oozed into basements and backyards, and residents organized a vigorous publicity campaign to draw attention to the grim situation.

▓ **5. (C) is correct.** Sizable numbers of taxpayers resented the tax hikes required to fund government programs that benefited minorities, provided expanded social services for the poor, or protected the environment at the expense of economic development. In 1978, California voters staged a "taxpayers' revolt," approving Proposition 13, which cut property taxes and government revenues for social programs and education.

▓ **6. (D) is correct.** Supply-side economics emphasized productivity and sought plans to raise it. It also abhorred big government, calling for simultaneous tax cuts and reductions in public spending. This combination would give private entrepreneurs and investors greater incentives to start businesses, take risks, invest capital, and thereby create new wealth and jobs. Whatever revenues were lost in lower tax rates would be offset by revenue from economic growth. At the same time, spending cuts would keep the federal deficit under control and thereby keep interest rates down.

▓ **7. (A) is correct.** Although President Reagan had promised to balance the federal budget, his policies had the opposite effect. A major contributor to the national debt was the multi-billion dollar defense budget. The national debt tripled, growing from $914 billion in 1980 to over $2.7 trillion in 1989.

▓ **8. (B) is correct.** In 1983 President Reagan introduced an unsettling new element into superpower relations when he presented his Strategic Defense Initiative (SDI) the plan for a space-based ballistic-missile defense system that journalists dubbed "Star Wars." Gorbachev's radical new program of economic and political reform included *glasnost* (openness) and *perestroika* (restructuring).

▓ **9. (A) is correct.** Over 10 percent of the Soviet GNO went to defense spending, while the majority of its citizens still struggled to find even the most basic consumer items in shops. Gorbachev thus took the lead to end the arms race with the Untied States.

▓ **10. (A) is correct.** By the end of the 1970s, evangelical Christians had become the backbone of the New Right and chief fund-raisers for key organizations such as the National Conservative Political Action Committee and, most especially, the Moral Majority. They united behind major conservative and political leaders not merely to promote an ideology but to target specific issues that they believed further undermined what they termed "traditional family values."

Document-Based Question

Though not considered as divisive an era as the 1960s, the 1970s and 1980s witnessed new divisions in American society. How did these differences reveal the conflicting values of Americans at this time?

The social and political challenges of the 1960s ushered in an era of profound social change, in which new developments expanded legal interpretations of individual liberty and led to increased choices for many Americans (**DOCUMENT 1**). Though most Americans embraced such changes (**DOCUMENT 2**), many believed that the ideals of feminist and civil rights activists had forsaken more traditional values. This ushered in a conservative social movement that asserted an opposing social agenda from the one forged by the liberation movements of the 1960s. This movement built upon the conservative political resurgence that began with the candidacy of Barry Goldwater in the 1964 presidential election, and soon fiscal conservatives began to assert their own program for change, which included a retreat from the liberal state to a more *laissez-faire* government, in order to combat the declining economy of the United States. Arguing that government had become too big and regulatory, constricting the free-enterprise system and preventing growth, conservatives helped propel former movie actor Ronald Reagan to the White House in 1980. Reagan firmly supported the limitation of government, especially with regard to the economy (**DOCUMENT 3**). Though deregulation and tax cuts created a brief surge in economic activity (**DOCUMENT 4**), many Americans, especially those at the bottom of the economic structure, witnessed a decline in their economic status. For those who benefited from the new economic policies, life was now defined by status and consumption (**DOCUMENT 5**). In the midst of all the new divisions in American society, though, certain issues crossed class lines, and Americans were forced to respond to new threats including a renewed Cold War, increased tension in the Middle East, and the spread of a devastating new virus that first emerged in American's gay communities but soon touched every strata of American society (**DOCUMENT 6**).

CHAPTER 31

Toward a Transnational America, since 1988

This chapter covers the development of a transnational America. A major shift for the country was the end of the cold war. In 1992, Democrats under Clinton recaptured the presidency by becoming more centrist themselves, but they were continually challenged by a resurgent New Right. Economic competition with Europe and Pacific Rim nations replaced cold war ideological struggles, but military problems would still remain in various areas, particularly the Middle East. Presidents Bush and Clinton would look for collective responses to international crises through the U.N. and other international organizations. Greater reliance on lower-wage service workers and the reduced need for the "military-industrial complex" continued to reinforce the growing inequities among Americans. American communities struggled to respond to a more global, service-oriented, "high-tech" economy. George W. Bush won a hotly disputed election in 2000. His administration took a conservative stance on the environment but the focus changed dramatically with the war on terrorism after the horrific terrorist attack on the World Trade Center and the Pentagon.

"A Kinder, Gentler Nation"

The collapse of communism did not bring an era of peace. Conflicts broke out in the Middle East and the Balkans that involved the United States militarily. The aftermath of the Gulf War was worsening tensions in the Middle East. U.S. success in the Persian Gulf War marked the high point of the Bush presidency. However, despite his popularity, divisive economic issues proved to be his downfall. Reflect and Respond What caused the Gulf War and were the goals of the war attained? See textbook section The Persian Gulf War.

The Clinton Presidency

Human rights emerged as a central theme of Bill Clinton's foreign policy, especially following demonstrations in the People's Republic of China, but modified his stance after becoming president. Presiding over one of the strongest and longest economic booms in American history also proved to boost Clinton's popularity throughout his two terms in office.

Changing American Communities

The recession and budget deficits of the late 1980s helped Bill Clinton win the 1992 election. Clinton broke the gridlock between Democrats and Republicans to pass legislation on welfare reform and trade. The economy boomed, with growth occurring through the changes in the economy epitomized by Silicon Valley. Developments in media and information technology helped create an electronic culture. Another trend was a large increase in immigration, especially from Latin America and Asia, which led to the development of new communities and cultural expressions.

A New Age of Anxiety

The economic prosperity did not touch every American. Significant numbers of African Americans and Latinos lived in poverty and were subject to greater police scrutiny and imprisonment. Tensions rose between various groups, raising the issue of race. At the same time, terrorist attacks grew more violent and frequent, with tragic consequences. Amid this turbulence, a debate emerged between conservatives and liberals over multiculturalism, abortion, gay rights, and evolution. In government, the election of young conservative Republicans who gained control of Congress in 1994 created conflict with the Clinton administration. Clinton won reelection but soon was embroiled in scandals concerning sex allegations and eventually in impeachment proceedings.

The New Millennium

George W. Bush won the hotly disputed election of 2000. He showed a conservative bent by pushing through a tax cut and his environmental policies. The globalization movement focused on the economy but the power of multinational corporations in the United States, Europe, and Japan prompted criticisms.

Multiple-Choice Questions

1. George H. W. Bush supported all of the following EXCEPT
   (A) the Americans with Disabilities Act.
   (B) tripling the budget for the war on drugs.
   (C) the invasion of Panama to capture General Noriega.
   (D) the family-leave bill.
   (E) the funding of new prisons.

2. The United States' response to Iraq's invasion of Kuwait was to
   (A) organize immediately an alliance to force Iraq out.
   (B) declare war on Iraq in January 1991.
   (C) swiftly bomb the Iraqi's out of Kuwait.
   (D) recognize Iraq as a bulwark against Iran.
   (E) demonize Saddam Hussein in November to justify an attack.

3. The Persian Gulf War
   (A) was fought almost exclusively by traditional means.
   (B) brought greater freedom to minorities in Iraq.
   (C) led to the capture of Saddam Hussein.
   (D) produced extensive ecological damage.
   (E) had a surprisingly few civilian deaths.

4. In the 1992 campaign, Clinton adopted all of the following positions EXCEPT
   (A) be tough on crime.
   (B) reduce the bureaucracy.
   (C) privatize Social Security.
   (D) cut taxes for the middle class.
   (E) reforming welfare.

5. All of the following are true of Silicon Valley EXCEPT
   (A) its early firms began by relying on military contracts.
   (B) it had no real competition anywhere.
   (C) it benefited from having a cheap, nonunion labor pool.
   (D) its growth exploded with the consumer electronics revolution.
   (E) it boosted the greatest concentration of new wealth in the United States.

6. The census of 2000 showed that
   (A) Latin Americans were the fastest growing ethnic group.
   (B) immigrants avoided older northern cities altogether.
   (C) New York had the highest percentage of foreign born.

(D) Hispanics had replaced African Americans as the largest minority group in the nation.
(E) the Immigration Act of 1965 had favored highly skilled Asians.

7. The Immigration Act of 1965
   (A) restated the national origins quotas.
   (B) kept out Asians.
   (C) set limits for Latin Americans.
   (D) offered amnesty to undocumented workers.
   (E) favored immigration from the Western Hemisphere.

8. Which of the following is NOT true of the Kyoto Protocol?
   (A) It outlined targets and timetables for the reduction of greenhouse gases.
   (B) President George W. Bush signed it.
   (C) Richer, industrialized countries were to take the lead. Mexico.
   (D) 178 countries signed it.
   (E) Russia supported it.

9. The boom of the 1990s
   (A) left a higher percentage of people in poverty than ever.
   (B) allowed women to earn much more compared to men.
   (C) did little to close the gap between the best and poorest paid.
   (D) promoted a real improvement in race relations.
   (E) closed the gap between the best and poorest paid citizens with the increase in minimum wage.

10. After the removal of the Taliban Regime in Afghanistan in 2001, Osama bin Laden most likely
    (A) was killed at Tora Bora.
    (B) escaped into the unruly tribal areas of Pakistan.
    (C) was hidden by the Pakistani government.
    (D) moved to Iran.
    (E) died to kidney failure due to a lack of medical care.

Document-Based Question

Discuss the legacy of the Clinton presidency in foreign and domestic policy.

DOCUMENT 1

DOCUMENT 2

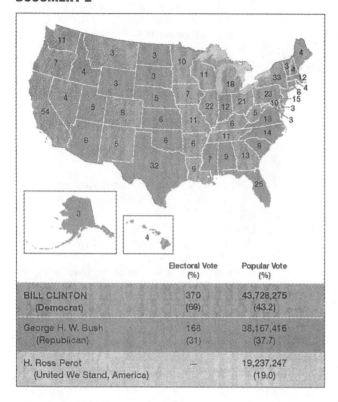

	Electoral Vote (%)	Popular Vote (%)
BILL CLINTON (Democrat)	370 (69)	43,728,275 (43.2)
George H. W. Bush (Republican)	168 (31)	38,167,416 (37.7)
H. Ross Perot (United We Stand, America)	—	19,237,247 (19.0)

DOCUMENT 3

DOCUMENT 4

DOCUMENT 5

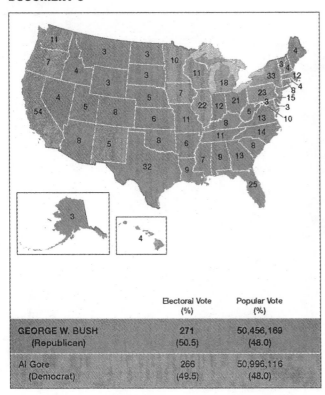

	Electoral Vote (%)	Popular Vote (%)
GEORGE W. BUSH (Republican)	271 (50.5)	50,456,169 (48.0)
Al Gore (Democrat)	266 (49.5)	50,996,116 (48.0)

Multiple-Choice Questions

1. (D) is correct. President George H.W. Bush did not support the family-leave bill, but he did continue President Reagan's war on drugs. He appointed William Bennet as the new "drug czar" and tripled funding for more police and the construction of more prisons. In December 1989, President Bush sent U.S. troops to Panama on a mission to capture General Manuel Noriega, an international drug dealer who at one time had been on the CIA payroll. As a self-proclaimed "compassionate" Republican, President Bush gave his support to the Americans With Disabilities Act.

2. (E) is correct. The United States responded swiftly to the news of the invasion. In early November, President Bush announced a change in policy to what he called "an offensive military option." Administration officials now demonized Saddam Hussein as another Adolf Hitler.

3. (D) is correct. The ecological damage in the Gulf region was extensive and long-lasting. Oil fires burned out of control.

4. (C) is correct. The Democratic Leadership Council set itself to rebuild the party "by redefining and reclaiming the political center." Clinton carried this mission to the White House, presenting an agenda that included balancing the federal budget, reforming welfare, reducing crime, promoting economic growth, and ensuring a strong national defense. Reducing the size of the federal government and promoting free markets worldwide became hallmarks of his administration. President Clinton did not attempt or promise to privatize Social Security.

5. (B) is correct. Silicon Valley did have competition. Silicon Valley was part of a global enterprise. Its firms were closely linked to the microelectronic industry of the greater Pacific Rim. The end of the cold war and the accompanying decline in military spending in the United States forced high-tech firms in California into greater competition on the world market and especially against similar companies in Japan, Korea, China, and Malaysia.

6. (E) is correct. The Immigration Act of 1965, passed almost unnoticed in the context of the egalitarian political climate created by the civil rights movement. The act abolished the discriminatory national origins quotas that had been in place since the 1920s. It also limited immigration from the Western Hemisphere for the first time, while giving preferences to people from the nations of the Eastern Hemisphere who had specialized job skills and training.

7. (C) is correct. The Immigration Act of 1965 set limits on Western Hemisphere immigration and the tempted many thousands of people from Latin America to enter the United States illegally. By the mid-1980s, growing concern over "illegal aliens" had become a hotly debated political issue, particularly in the Southwest.

8. (D) is correct. The map displays the number of foreign-born residents of New York City. In 200, there were 2 million foreign-born residents of New York City, or 36 percent of its population, with the largest number of residents coming from the Dominican Republic.

9. (C) is correct. The 2000 census also revealed sharp divisions among Americans. Although the poverty rate had dropped to 11.3 percent of the population, near the lowest level ever recorded, more than 31 million people still lived in poverty. Moreover, the new economy had done little to close the gap between the highest and lowest income earners.

10. (B) is correct. Intensive bombing routed the last remnants of Taliban and Al Qaeda forces from the mountain cave complex of Tora Bora. But bin Laden and much of the Al Qaeda leadership escaped into the tribal areas of Pakistan to the south and east. Despite a massive manhunt and the aid of Pakistan's government, American forces proved unable to capture bin Laden as of mid-2006.

ANSWERS AND EXPLANATIONS

Multiple-Choice Questions

1. (D) is correct. President George H.W. Bush did not support the family-leave bill, but he did continue President Reagan's war on drugs. He appointed William Bennet as the new "drug czar" and tripled funding for more police and the construction of more prisons. In December 1989, President Bush sent U.S. troops to Panama on a mission to capture General Manuel Noriega, an international drug dealer who at one time had been on the CIA payroll. As a self-proclaimed "compassionate" Republican, President Bush gave his support to the Americans With Disabilities Act.

2. (E) is correct. The United States responded swiftly to the news of the invasion. In early November, President Bush announced a change in policy to what he called "an offensive military option." Administration officials now demonized Saddam Hussein as another Adolf Hitler.

3. (D) is correct. The ecological damage in the Gulf region was extensive and long-lasting. Oil fires burned out of control. Human rights groups reported an appalling death toll among civilians.

4. (C) is correct. The Democratic Leadership Council set itself to rebuild the party "by redefining and reclaiming the political center." Clinton carried this mission to the White House, presenting an agenda that included balancing the federal budget, reforming welfare, reducing crime, promoting economic growth, and ensuring a strong national defense. Reducing the size of the federal government and promoting free markets worldwide became hallmarks of his administration. President Clinton did not attempt or promise to privatize Social Security.

5. (B) is correct. Silicon Valley did have competition. Silicon Valley was part of a global enterprise. Its firms were closely linked to the microelectronic industry of the greater Pacific Rim. The end of the cold war and the accompanying decline in military spending in the United States forced high-tech firms in California into greater competition on the world market and especially against similar companies in Japan, Korea, China, and Malaysia.

6. (E) is correct. The Immigration Act of 1965, passed almost unnoticed in the context of the egalitarian political climate created by the civil rights movement. The act abolished the discriminatory national origins quotas that had been in place since the 1920s. It also limited immigration from the Western Hemisphere for the first time, while giving preferences to people from the nations of the Eastern Hemisphere who had specialized job skills and training.

7. (C) is correct. The Immigration Act of 1965 set limits on Western Hemisphere immigration and tempted many thousands of people from Latin America to enter the United States illegally. By the mid-1980s, growing concern over "illegal aliens" had become a hotly debated political issue, particularly in the Southwest.

8. (B) is correct. Shortly after taking office, President George W. Bush announced his opposition to the terms of the Kyoto Protocol, leaving 178 other countries to agree to mandatory reductions in greenhouse gases without the participation of the United States. The Kyoto Protocol outlined targets and timetables for the reduction of greenhouse gases and required the richer, industrialized countries to take the lead, specifying an average 5.2 percent reduction from 1990s levels by 2012.

9. (C) is correct. The 2000 census revealed sharp divisions among Americans. Although the poverty rate had dropped to 11.3 percent of the population, near the lowest level ever recorded, more than 31 million people still lived in poverty. Moreover, the new economy had done little to close the gap between the highest and lowest income earners.

10. (B) is correct. Intensive bombing routed the last remnants of Taliban and Al Qaeda forces from the mountain cave complex of Tora Bora. But bin Laden and much of the Al Qaeda leadership escaped into the tribal areas of Pakistan to the south and east. Despite a massive manhunt and the aid of Pakistan's government, American forces proved unable to capture bin Laden, as of the end of 2006.

Document-Based Question

Discuss the legacy of the Clinton presidency in foreign and domestic policy.

In 1992 William Jefferson Clinton ended 12 years of Republican control of the Executive branch. A member of the Democratic Leadership Council, a group of centrist Democrats, the former Arkansas governor presided over one of the largest economic booms in American history. He was also able to pass a substantial amount of his legislative agenda. However, a scandal-plagued second term left him unable to deal with the growing threat of international terror, leaving a mixed legacy to his successor.

Running in 1992 against two older, more conservative opponents, (**DOCUMENT 1**) President Clinton was able to co-opt a substantial amount of the conservative agenda, while also maintaining loyalty to his liberal Democratic base. This strategy of triangulation led him to a decisive victory (**DOCUMENT 2**). Despite the fact that for most of his Presidency he was fighting a Republican Congress (**DOCUMENT 7**), he had many legislative successes. They include the North American Free Trade Agreement, the Welfare Reform Act, and the signing of 1993's Family and Medical leave act. At the end of his first term, substantial anti-immigration legislation was proposed, but never passed (**DOCUMENT 6**). His one major legislative failure was his inability to succeed with his wife's healthcare reform program.

The country had unparalleled economic success during the Clinton Presidency. The spread of computer technology and the internet created an information revolution. It became possible for a woman sitting in a public library in New York to quickly contact somebody anywhere in the world (**DOCUMENT 3**).

Though the economy continued to be strong, Clinton's second term was not as successful as his first. Plagued by scandals, both personal and financial, Clinton became only the third president to be successfully impeached, though he was acquitted by the Senate.

Another problem, which had plagued him during his first term, also reasserted itself. In 1993 Islamic terrorists associated with Osama Bin Laden had attempted unsuccessfully to bomb the World Trade Center in New York. In 1998, Islamic terrorists bombed US embassies in Africa (**DOCUMENT 4**), and at the very end of his term, in October 2000, they killed 17 American sailors aboard the USS Cole. This problem was not systematically addressed by the Clinton Administration.

Though he left office with the economy still booming, President Clinton's record was unable to secure the office for his vice-president. Though Al Gore won the popular vote, by the smallest margin since 1960, he was unable to win the electoral vote, or even to win his home state (**DOCUMENT 5**). Overall, the Clinton legacy is a mixed one.

8. In contrast to the Chesapeake, New England communities
   (A) had better relationships with the Indians.
   (B) imported indentured servants who later became freemen.
   (C) were mainly family groups.
   (D) developed self-government.
   (E) were Anglican in religion.

9. In the task system governing slave labor on the low country plantations, slaves
   (A) who finished their tasks were free to use their remaining time for their own pursuits.
   (B) were forced to work in large groups.
   (C) had no time to take care of their personal needs.
   (D) were primarily used to grow tobacco and cotton.
   (E) were required to work indoors after finishing their outdoor tasks.

10. The Navigation Acts passed between 1660 and 1696
    (A) opened trade within the British Empire to any nation.
    (B) encouraged colonial manufacturing.
    (C) consolidated English colonies into one centralized trading unit.
    (D) defined the role colonies would play within the future British Empire.
    (E) forbade customs collectors from going into warehouses to look for smuggled goods.

11. Roger Williams is to *The Bloudy Tenet of Persecution* as _____ is to *Letter on Tolerance*.
    (A) Cotton Mather
    (B) Thomas Whitfield
    (C) John Williams
    (D) Benjamin Franklin
    (E) John Locke

12. The British colonial group most comfortable with religious and ethnic pluralism was the
    (A) Puritans.
    (B) Anglicans.
    (C) Huguenots.
    (D) Quakers.
    (E) Catholics.

13. As a result of various experiences in the French and Indian War, many American colonists
    (A) became more sympathetic to Indians.
    (B) desired a strong empire to protect them.
    (C) began to feel distinct from the British.
    (D) sought new alliances with the French.
    (E) experienced a weakening of intercolonial identity.

14. The primary purpose of the Sugar Act was to
    (A) raise revenue to defray expenses of the Seven Years' War.
    (B) assert economic control.
    (C) punish the colonists for their poor performance during the Seven Years' War.
    (D) regulate trade within the empire.
    (E) eliminate colonial trade with other nations.

15. The local militias that fought in the Revolutionary War
    (A) were raised by instituting a draft.
    (B) provided the military expertise that ultimately defeated the British.
    (C) were well-trained fighting forces.
    (D) exhibited surprising military discipline.
    (E) suffered appalling rates of desertion.

16. The French committed themselves to recognize American independence
    (A) on the insistence of Jefferson, the head of the American diplomatic delegation in Paris.
    (B) after Saratoga and fears of British conciliation.
    (C) when Jefferson threatened to invade France.
    (D) after the British launched an attack on a French supply ship entering the Boston harbor.
    (E) to support the principles of anti-colonialism and opposition to monarchism.

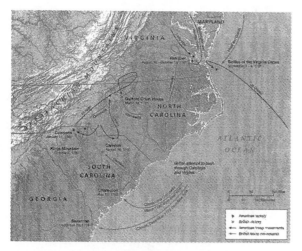

17. The map of fighting in the South from 1778 to 1781 shows that
    (A) the British had difficulty in the Lower South along the coast.
    (B) the British lost battles mostly in the interior.
    (C) the British won everywhere and retreated needlessly.
    (D) the British fought their way to Virginia through eastern Carolina.
    (E) the Americans controlled the coast.

18. The Articles of Confederation were not actually ratified until
    (A) 1789.
    (B) 1781.
    (C) 1782.
    (D) 1783.
    (E) 1785.

19. "One of the compromises at the Convention was over the slave population and was settled by the 'three-fifths rule'." This meant that
    (A) three-fifths of a state's voters had to be white.
    (B) up to three-fifths of slaves were eligible to vote.
    (C) a slave's vote counted three-fifths of a white person's vote.
    (D) five slaves equaled three freemen in population's representation.
    (E) three-fifths of the state had to vote on slave issues.

20. In his first "Report on the Public Credit," Alexander Hamilton proposed
    (A) the establishment of a centralized Bank of the United States.
    (B) high protective tariffs.
    (C) creating an income tax to pay the war debt.
    (D) funding the domestic debt and sharing the profits with its original holders.
    (E) that the federal government assumes remaining state Revolutionary War debts.

21. Which one of the following gives the correct sequence of these events?
    (A) Mint Act, First Bank of the United States, First Census
    (B) XYZ, Citizen Genet, French Revolution begins
    (C) Sedition Act, Indian Intercourse Act, Judiciary Act
    (D) Whiskey Rebellion, First Bank of the United States, Fries Rebellion
    (E) Annapolis Convention, Constitutional Convention, Bill of Rights

22. The period between 1800 and 1850 in the United States was characterized by
    (A) a decline in the overall population.
    (B) a dramatic expansion of population to the West.
    (C) declining westward expansion due to fear of Indian attacks.
    (D) the tremendous growth of Atlantic seaboard cities.
    (E) a decrease in the birthrate across the nation as a whole.

23. The Land Act of 1820
    (A) granted squatters preemptive rights.
    (B) granted land to War of 1812 veterans.
    (C) promoted corporate agriculture.
    (D) outlawed speculator purchases.
    (E) lowered the minimum purchase.

24. Which one of the following was NOT true of Jefferson's political philosophy?
    (A) America's room to grow ensured a Republican form of government.
    (B) Yeoman rural communities were essential for a republic.
    (C) America's resources would overcome Malthusian predictions.
    (D) Manufacturing and industrialization would enrich America.
    (E) Rural contact with the cycles of nature was essential for a republic to grow.

25. Which one of the following is <u>NOT</u> a negative effect that King Cotton had on the economy of the South?
   (A) Most acreage was devoted to growing cotton.
   (B) Attention was drawn away from the development of southern cities.
   (C) Slavery was more firmly entrenched.
   (D) Most mercantile services were in northern hands.
   (E) Industrial growth lagged behind the North.

26. Ironically, both enslaved and free black people could be in these occupations in the South while denied them in the North.
   (A) professions like medicine and law
   (B) skilled trades like carpentry and smithing
   (C) butlers and valets
   (D) farming and fishing
   (E) domestic service

27. While slavery and slave owners dominated the South and its economic system, this number of southerners did <u>NOT</u> own slaves.
   (A) one-half
   (B) three-fifths
   (C) two-thirds
   (D) three-quarters
   (E) four-fifths

28. The Second American Party System was based on
   (A) economic privation.
   (B) elite families.
   (C) favorable Supreme Court decisions.
   (D) favoritism.
   (E) mass participation.

29. Daniel Webster, John C. Calhoun, and Henry Clay were examples of
   (A) leading sectional politicians.
   (B) anti-slavery zealots.
   (C) crafty deal makers.
   (D) men from the West who had the "common touch."
   (E) candidates with family money to finance new mass campaigning.

30. In New England, these two conditions for rapid industrialization could be found.
   (A) canals and railroads
   (B) swift rivers and wealthy investors
   (C) investors and railroads
   (D) education population and shipping
   (E) commercial farms and mining

31. Which one of the following has the <u>LEAST</u> in common with the other four?
   (A) central workshops
   (B) per-piece wages
   (C) putting-out system
   (D) artisan tradition
   (E) merchant capitalists

32. The agenda for reform in the 1820s and 1830s was set by the
   (A) new emerging middle class.
   (B) impoverished lower class.
   (C) wealthy elite.
   (D) political machine.
   (E) New England reformers.

33. All of the following factors worked against the union movement <u>EXCEPT</u>
   (A) their own exclusiveness.
   (B) the legal system.
   (C) the perception that they were dangerous to the public order.
   (D) big city machines.
   (E) employers.

34. By 1848, the United States had gained all of the following territories <u>EXCEPT</u>
   (A) California.
   (B) Texas.
   (C) the Oregon Territory.
   (D) Georgia.
   (E) Alaska.

35. The map of territory added (1845–1853) shows that
    (A) the Mexican Cession of 1848 included much of present-day Texas.
    (B) Texas as annexed in 1845 is basically the same as present-day Texas.
    (C) the Mexican Cession extended north from Mexico to Canada.
    (D) the Gadsden Purchase was nearly half as large as the Mexican Cession.
    (E) Indian Territory is approximately as large as the Mexican Cession.

36. Americans justified their restless expansion in all of the following ways EXCEPT
    (A) Americans had a God-given right to bring the benefits of American democracy to others.
    (B) the nation's prosperity depended on expansion.
    (C) it was the Americans' duty to Christianize the Indians.
    (D) Canada and Mexico should belong to the United States.
    (E) pride in the size and power of America.

37. John Brown's raid shocked the South because
    (A) it aroused the South's great fear of a slave rebellion.
    (B) they did not realize that whites cared this much about slavery.
    (C) it was so successful.
    (D) Brown was tried and hanged; he was recovering from wounds suffered in the raid.
    (E) so many people died in vain.

38. The Republican victory in 1860
    (A) was won by a landslide.
    (B) was the immediate cause for the first southern states to secede.
    (C) was the party's last for 12 years.
    (D) was acclaimed by North and South alike.
    (E) proved the validity of the Electoral College.

39. Union victories at Forts Henry and Donelson, Shiloh and Vicksburg successfully achieved this Union War goal:
    (A) cut off the Confederate states west of the Mississippi.
    (B) improved morale.
    (C) obtained stored up cotton from southern docks.
    (D) seized the resource-rich Lower South.
    (E) isolated South Carolina.

40. Initially the Union's strategy was to
    (A) invade the South.
    (B) overwhelm the South with its better-trained army.
    (C) fight a limited war by strangling the South with a blockade.
    (D) select certain targets and attack with small guerilla forces.
    (E) lure the South into invading the North.

41. In 1860, the South held 25 percent of the nation's wealth. By 1870, it controlled this percent:
    (A) 2
    (B) 8
    (C) 12
    (D) 15
    (E) 30

42. In order to build a new political coalition of northern Democrats, southern Unionists and conservative Republicans, President Johnson used THIS term rather than "reconstruction":
    (A) renewal
    (B) restoration
    (C) realignment
    (D) reconciliation
    (E) Republican construction

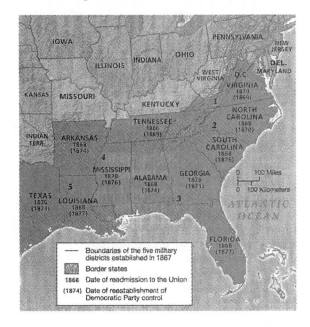

43. The map on the Reconstruction of the South (1866–1877) shows that all of the former Confederate states were readmitted to the Union by
   (A) 1868.
   (B) 1872.
   (C) 1874.
   (D) 1877.
   (E) 1870.

44. One result of the Reconstruction era for women was the
   (A) establishment of an independent suffrage movement.
   (B) temporary retrenchment of the suffrage movement.
   (C) weakening of ideas about reforms for women.
   (D) vote for freed blacks made it easier to argue for women suffrage.
   (E) fragmentation of state governments divided radicals.

45. The Dawes Act was to most Indian tribes as THIS act was to the Five Civilized Tribes:
   (A) Edmunds Act
   (B) Acheson Act
   (C) Morrill Act
   (D) Hatch Act
   (E) Curtis Act

46. More than any other industry or commercial enterprise, this group fostered western expansion.
   (A) missionaries
   (B) land speculators
   (C) miners
   (D) fur traders
   (E) farmers

47. Some Mormons engaged in the controversial practice of
   (A) bigamy.
   (B) miscegenation.
   (C) polygamy.
   (D) communal property.
   (E) monogamy.

48. The most significant development shaping the American economy after the Civil War was the
   (A) invention of the cotton gin.
   (B) growth of the arms industry.
   (C) growth of the meat packing industry.

   (D) decline in the railroads.
   (E) emergence and consolidation of large-scale corporations.

49. The largest proportion of persons who filled jobs in industry in the second half of the nineteenth century came from
   (A) the American family farm.
   (B) the South.
   (C) Europe and Asia.
   (D) Latin America.
   (E) Scandinavia.

50. The map of Strikes by State as of 1880 shows that the states with the most strikes were
   (A) Massachusetts, New Jersey, and Virginia.
   (B) New York, Pennsylvania, and Ohio.
   (C) Illinois, Missouri, and Michigan.
   (D) Minnesota, Wisconsin, and Iowa.
   (E) Kentucky, Indiana, and Delaware.

51. The Social Gospel movement was a/an
   (A) attempt to apply Christian ideals to social ills.
   (B) way to justify high society using Christian principles.
   (C) means to unite various populist groups.
   (D) Union movement based on Catholic traditions.
   (E) outgrowth of the WCTU.

52. William Jennings Bryan's "Cross of Gold" speech advocated
   (A) the free silver issue.
   (B) progressive income taxes.
   (C) a gold standard.
   (D) a national bank.
   (E) gold for the working man.

53. Progressive reformers believed in all of the following EXCEPT
    (A) rugged individualism.
    (B) opposition to urban growth and unfettered capitalism.
    (C) common bonds to make society more affluent.
    (D) they were optimistic about the future.
    (E) the active use of government.

54. Progressive critics of machine politics exaggerated the power of these machines; in reality, their power was limited by
    (A) state legislatures.
    (B) Supreme Court rulings.
    (C) immigrants.
    (D) religious organizations.
    (E) Congress.

55. Many businessmen supported Prohibition because
    (A) farmers would be more supportive of industrialists.
    (B) a happy family life made a happy worker.
    (C) closing saloons would increase the productivity of the worker.
    (D) unruly immigrants would return to their homeland.
    (E) consumers would have more money to spend on consumer goods.

56. The progressive diplomacy of Presidents Roosevelt, Taft, and Wilson
    (A) stressed a moral God-given role for the United States.
    (B) stressed the civil rights of the people in all nations.
    (C) followed the principle of national self-determination.
    (D) favored commercial expansion and avoided military involvement.
    (E) aimed to keep intrusive American businesses out of other countries.

57. The Zimmerman note was a coded message proposing an alliance between Germany and
    (A) Canada.
    (B) Mexico.
    (C) France.
    (D) Russia.
    (E) Italy.

58. The most important and long-lasting economic legacy of WWI was
    (A) the breakup of corporations.
    (B) a nationalized industrial base.
    (C) implementation of a government-corporate partnership.
    (D) the reduction of government.
    (E) an increase in family owned businesses.

59. Why did the American economy change from producer-durable goods to a consumer-durable goods economy?
    (A) mass production
    (B) inflation
    (C) labor shortages
    (D) high wages
    (E) lack of raw materials

60. Hoover had a strong commitment to the principle of
    (A) a chicken in every pot.
    (B) "rugged individualism."
    (C) government assistance to individuals.
    (D) executive intervention in Supreme Court decisions.
    (E) government assistance to unions.

61. The following was the most powerful sign of a deepening depression in the early 1930s:
    (A) rising unemployment
    (B) inflation
    (C) closed offices
    (D) government welfare
    (E) soup kitchens

62. The major significance of the Social Security Act of 1935 was
    (A) it established the principle of national responsibility for citizens.
    (B) it reestablished state control of the dole.
    (C) it provided unemployment benefits to everyone.
    (D) it provided retirement funds to all citizens.
    (E) it allowed for future formation of unions.

63. All of the following are members of the New Deal voting coalition EXCEPT
    (A) chamber of commerce members.
    (B) white southern Democrats.
    (C) big city political machines.
    (D) industrial workers.
    (E) Depression hit farmers.

64. In the Atlantic Charter, the undersigned pledged
    (A) self-determination.
    (B) a European currency and a unified
        economy.
    (C) future colonial rights.
    (D) economic support for the Soviet Union.
    (E) freedom of the seas.

65. The War Powers Act empowered Roosevelt to
    do all of the following EXCEPT
    (A) seize property owned by American citizens.
    (B) create new agencies.
    (C) reorganize the federal government.
    (D) censor all news.
    (E) seize property owned by foreigners.

66. The following was Stalin's response to the
    unification of Western Germany:
    (A) Stalin sought to stop it in the Untied
        Nations.
    (B) Stalin declared a blockade on Poland.
    (C) Stalin threatened to use nuclear weapons
        against the U.S.
    (D) The Soviets built the Berlin Wall.
    (E) Stalin stopped all traffic to West Berlin.

67. These two trends encouraged a change in the
    middle-class family:
    (A) higher wages and more college-educated
        parents
    (B) the baby boom and high rates of consumer
        spending
    (C) birth control and returning veterans
    (D) younger marriages and fewer children
    (E) inflation and higher military spending

68. The GI Bill of Rights
    (A) provided educational grants to veterans.
    (B) is an affirmative action program for
        veterans.
    (C) gave veterans a substantial reenlistment
        bonus.
    (D) guaranteed future employment for returning
        veterans.
    (E) gave bonuses only to Korean War veterans.

69. The Soviet launching of *Sputnik* prompted the
    (A) Nuclear Proliferation Act.
    (B) Federal Highway Act.
    (C) National Defense Education Act.
    (D) GI Bill of Rights.
    (E) Submerged Lands Act.

70. Why did Truman issue an executive order
    barring segregation in the armed forces?
    (A) to attract African American voters for the
        1948 election
    (B) He could then draft fewer white youth into
        the military.
    (C) because he was deeply committed to civil
        rights
    (D) Truman was trying to undercut Strom
        Thurmond's independent candidacy.
    (E) Officers in the military were requesting
        integration.

71. In the late 1940s, the Supreme Court ruled in
    Mendez v. *Westminster* that
    (A) language was not a barrier to citizenship.
    (B) the separate but equal doctrine applied to
        Mexican Americans.
    (C) Mexican Americans could not be excluded
        from jury lists.
    (D) the use of literacy tests for voters was
        illegal.
    (E) segregation of Mexican Americans was
        unconstitutional.

72. U.S. government Indian policy from 1954 to
    1962 was dominated by House Concurrent
    Resolution 108 which stressed
    (A) termination of tribes as a legal entity.
    (B) retention of tribal designations in
        determining tribal status.
    (C) limited sovereignty.
    (D) relocating Indians to reservations.
    (E) the concept of ethnic Indians as opposed to
        tribal identity.

73. Which one of the following was NOT a success
    of groups like SDS?
    (A) College students realized their political
        power.
    (B) They encouraged the poor to take action.
    (C) They popularized a new style of activist
        politics.
    (D) They allied with liberal Democrats.
    (E) They popularized the idea of "participatory
        democracy."

74. The following is true of the sixties generation:
    (A) They were out only to "feel good."
    (B) They agreed with their parents.
    (C) They were highly educated.
    (D) They were conservative.
    (E) They were apathetic about politics.

75. During the 1970s, organized labor experienced its only real growth among
    (A) public employees.
    (B) truckers.
    (C) restaurant employees.
    (D) quality circle companies.
    (E) agribusiness.

76. President Carter's deregulation of the nation's banks resulted in
    (A) bank failures.
    (B) fewer loans and less economic stimulation.
    (C) increased bank profits.
    (D) deregulation of other industries.
    (E) an end to inflation.

Asked of those who said they had heard of or read about the Equal Rights Amendment: Do you favor or oppose this amendment?

Favor	58%
Oppose	24%
No opinion	18%

By Sex

Male

Favor	63%
Oppose	22%
No opinion	15%

Female

Favor	54%
Oppose	25%
No opinion	21%

Interviewing Date 3/7–10/1975, Survey #925-K

77. The table of the Gallup Poll on the Equal Rights Amendment, 1975 shows all of the following EXCEPT
    (A) 63 percent of men favored it.
    (B) 54 percent of women favored it.
    (C) 21 percent of women had no opinion.
    (D) 25 percent of men had no opinion.
    (E) 25 percent of women opposed it.

78. Before becoming president, George H. W. Bush had held all of the following positions EXCEPT
    (A) director of the FBI.
    (B) ambassador to the United Nations.
    (C) envoy to China.
    (D) Vice President of the United States.
    (E) leader in the Texas oil industry.

79. The Gramm-Rudman Act
    (A) forced Bush to obtain a war resolution from Congress.
    (B) mandated automatic spending cuts to balance the budget.
    (C) regulated the savings and loan industry.
    (D) provided the nation a tax cut to fight the recession.
    (E) established the Federal Reserve and FDIC.

80. Under George W. Bush, the United States economy
    (A) entered a new period of rapid growth.
    (B) strengthened the dollar against other currencies.
    (C) made U.S. investments more attractive to foreigners.
    (D) slowed while budget deficits rose.
    (E) found that interest rates rose dramatically as the economy grew stronger.

Document-Based Question

Some argue that the United States is the product of an ongoing debate about the nature of liberty and equality, resulting in the continued expansion of democracy. Considering the changes the United States experienced from the Revolutionary War to the Civil War, do you agree or disagree with this assessment?

USE THE FOLLOWING DOCUMENTS AND YOUR KNOWLEDGE OF THE PERIOD TO CONSTRUCT YOUR ESSAY.

DOCUMENT 1

James Madison Defends the Constitution (1788)
Source: Jonathan Elliot, ed., The Debates in the Several State Conventions on the Adoption of the Federal Constitution. 2nd ed., 5 vols. (Philadelphia: J. B. Lippincott Company, 1907).

By the new system, a majority of the states cannot introduce amendments; nor are all the states required for that purpose; three fourths of them must concur in alterations; in this there is a departure from the federal idea. The members to the national House of Representatives are to be chosen by the people at large, in proportion to the numbers in the respective districts. When we come to the Senate, its members are elected by the states in their equal and political capacity. But had the government been completely consolidated, the Senate would have been chosen by the people in their individual capacity, in the same manner as the members of the other house. Thus it is of a complicated nature; and this complication, I trust, will be found to exclude the evils of absolute consolidation, as well as of a mere confederacy. If Virginia was separated from all the states, her power and authority would extend to all cases: in like manner, were all powers vested in the general government, it would be a consolidated government; but the powers of the federal government are enumerated; it can only operate in certain cases; it has legislative powers on defined and limited objects, beyond which it cannot extend its jurisdiction.

DOCUMENT 2

Source: Divergent Reactions to Shays's Rebellion
THOMAS JEFFERSON TO JAMES MADISON

Paris, January 30th, 1787
Dear Sir,
My last to you was of the 16th of December; since which, I have received yours of November 25 and December 4, which afforded me, as your letters always do, a treat on matters public, individual, and economical. I am impatient to learn your sentiments on the late troubles in the Eastern states. So far as I have yet seen, they do not appear to threaten serious consequences. Those states have suffered by the stoppage of the channels of their commerce, which have not yet found other issues. This must render money scarce and make the people uneasy. This uneasiness has produced acts absolutely unjustifiable; but I hope they will provoke no severities from their governments. A consciousness of those in power that their administration of the public affairs has been honest may, perhaps, produce too great a degree of indignation; and those characters, wherein fear predominates over hope, may apprehend too much from these instances of irregularity. They may conclude too hastily that nature has formed man insusceptible of any other government than that of force, a conclusion not founded in truth or experience.
Societies exist under three forms, sufficiently distinguishable: (1) without government, as among our Indians; (2) under governments, wherein the will of everyone has a just influence, as is the case in England, in a slight degree, and in our states, in a great one; (3) under governments of force, as is the case in all other monarchies, and in most of the other republics.
To have an idea of the curse of existence under these last, they must be seen. It is a government of wolves over sheep. It is a problem, not clear in my mind, that the first condition is not the best. But I believe it to be inconsistent with any great degree of population. The second state has a great deal of good in it. The mass of mankind under that enjoys a precious degree of liberty and happiness. It has its evils, too, the principal of which is the turbulence to which it is subject. But weigh this against the oppressions of monarchy, and it becomes nothing. Malo periculosam libertatem quam quietam servitutem. Even this evil is productive of good. It prevents the degeneracy of government and nourishes a general attention to the public affairs.

I hold it that a little rebellion now and then is a good thing, and as necessary in the political world as storms in the physical. Unsuccessful rebellions, indeed, generally establish the encroachments on the rights of the people which have produced them. An observation of this truth should render honest republican governors so mild in their punishment of rebellions as not to discourage them too much. It is a medicine necessary for the sound health of government. . . .

Yours affectionately,

Th. Jefferson

DOCUMENT 3

Source: The "Distracting Question" in Philadelphia (1787)

Mr. GHORUM. supported the propriety of establishing numbers as the rule. He said that in Massts. estimates hadbeen taken in the different towns, and that persons had been curious enough to compare these estimates with the respective numbers of people; and it had been found even including Boston, that the most exact proportion prevailed between numbers & property. He was aware that there might be some weight in what had fallen from his colleague, as to the umbrage which might be taken by the people of the Eastern States. But he recollected that when the proposition of Congs. for changing the 8th. art: of Confedn. was before the Legislature of Massts. the only difficulty then was to satisfy them that the negroes ought not to have been counted equally with whites instead of being counted in the ratio of three fifths only.

Mr. WILSON did not well see on what principle the admission of blacks in the proportion of three fifths could be explained. Are they admitted as Citizens? then why are they not admitted on an equality with White Citizens? are they admitted as property? then why is not other property admitted into the computation? These were difficulties however which he thought must be overruled by the necessity of compromise. He had some apprehensions also from the tendency of the blending of the blacks with the whites, to give disgust to the people of Pena. as had been intimated by his Colleague [Mr. Govr. Morris]. But he differed from him in thinking numbers of inhabts. so incorrect a measure of wealth. He had seen the Western settlemts. of Pa. and on a comparison of them with the City of Philada. could discover little other difference, than that property was more unequally divided among individuals here than there. Taking the same number in the aggregate in the two situations he believed there would be little difference in their wealth and ability to contribute to the public wants.

DOCUMENT 4

Source: The Alien and Sedition Acts (1798)

SEC. 2. And be it further enacted, That if any person shall write, print, utter or publish, or shall cause or procure to be written, printed, uttered or published, or shall knowingly and willingly assist or aid in writing, printing, uttering or publishing any false, scandalous and malicious writing or writings against the government of the United States, or the President of the United States, with intent to defame the said government, or either house of the said Congress, or the said President, or to bring them, or either of them, into contempt or disrepute; or to excite against them, or either or any of them, the hatred of the good people of the United States, or to stir up sedition within the United States, or to excite any unlawful combinations therein, for opposing (or resisting any law of the United States,) or any act of the President of the United States, done in pursuance of any such law, or of the powers in him vested by the Constitution of the United States, or to resist, oppose, or defeat any such law or act, or to aid, encourage or abet any hostile designs of any foreign nation against the United States, their people or government, then such person, being thereof convicted before any court of the United States having jurisdiction thereof, shall be punished by a fine not exceeding two thousand dollars, and by imprisonment not exceeding two years.

DOCUMENT 5

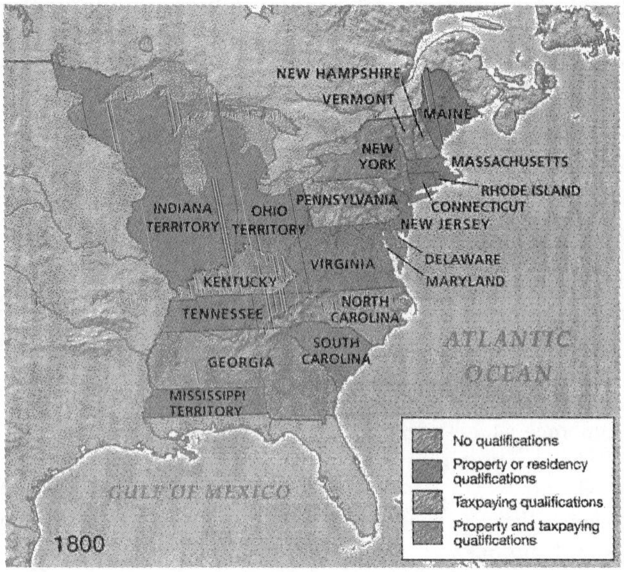
NEW HAMPSHIRE
VERMONT
MAINE
NEW YORK
MASSACHUSETTS
RHODE ISLAND
CONNECTICUT
PENNSYLVANIA
NEW JERSEY
INDIANA TERRITORY
OHIO TERRITORY
DELAWARE
VIRGINIA
MARYLAND
KENTUCKY
NORTH CAROLINA
TENNESSEE
SOUTH CAROLINA
GEORGIA
ATLANTIC OCEAN
MISSISSIPPI TERRITORY
GULF OF MEXICO
1800
No qualifications
Property or residency qualifications
Taxpaying qualifications
Property and taxpaying qualifications

DOCUMENT 6

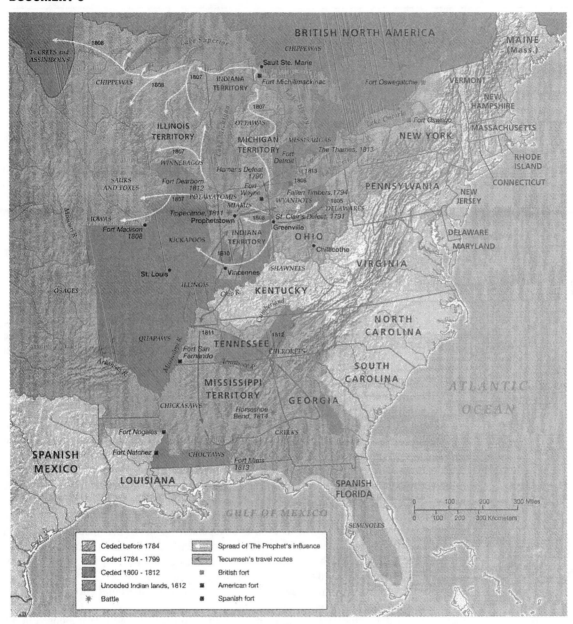

Legend:
- Ceded before 1784
- Ceded 1784 - 1799
- Ceded 1800 - 1812
- Unceded Indian lands, 1812
- ✳ Battle
- Spread of The Prophet's influence
- Tecumseh's travel routes
- British fort
- American fort
- Spanish fort

DOCUMENT 7

Source: A Black Abolitionist Speaks Out (1829)

Are we MEN! !—I ask you, my brethren, are we MEN? Did our Creator make us to be slaves to dust and ashes like ourselves? Are they not dying worms as well as we? Have they not to make their appearance before the tribunal of Heaven, to answer for the deeds done in the body, as well as we? Have we any other Master but Jesus Christ alone? Is he not their Master as well as ours?—What right then, have we to obey and call any other Master, but Himself? How we could be so submissive to a gang of men, whom we cannot tell whether they are as good as ourselves or not, I never could conceive. However, this is shut up with the Lord, and we cannot precisely tell—but I declare, we judge men by their works.

The whites have always been an unjust, jealous, unmerciful, avaricious and blood-thirsty set of beings, always seeking after power and authority. . . .

DOCUMENT 8

Declaration of Sentiments and Resolutions, Woman's Rights Convention, Seneca Falls, New York (1848)
Source: E. C. Stanton, S. B. Anthony, and Matilda Joslyn Gage, eds., History of Woman Suffrage, vol. 1 (Rochester, NY: Charles Mann, 1881), pp. 70–72.

We hold these truths to be self-evident: that all men and women are created equal; that they are endowed by their Creator with certain inalienable rights; that among these are life, liberty, and the pursuit of happiness; that to secure these rights governments are instituted, deriving their just powers from the consent of the governed. . . . But when a long train of abuses and usurpations, pursuing invariably the same object evinces a design to reduce them under absolute despotism, it is their duty to throw off such government, and to provide new guards for their future security. Such has been the patient sufferance of the women under this government, and such is now the necessity which constrains them to demand the equal station to which they are entitled.

DOCUMENT 9

Source: Dred Scott v. Sanford (1857)

The Question is simply this: Can a negro, whose ancestors were imported into this country, and sold as slaves, become a member of the political community formed and brought into existence by the Constitution of the United States, and as such become entitled to all the rights, and privileges, and immunities, guarantied [sic] by that instrument to the citizen? One of which rights is the privilege of suing in a court of the United States in the cases specified in the constitution.

. . . . The question before us is, whether the class of persons described in the plea in abatement compose a portion of this people, and are constituent members of this sovereignty? We think they are not, under the word "citizens" in the Constitution, and can therefore claim none of the rights and privileges which that instrument provides for and secures to citizens of the United States. ..In discussing the question, we must not confound the rights of citizenship which a State may confer within its own limits, and the rights of citizenship as a member of the Union. It does not by any means follow, because he has all the rights and privileges of a citizen of a State, that he must be a citizen of the United States. . . . In the opinion of the court, the legislation and histories of the times, and the language used in the Declaration of Independence, show, that neither the class of persons who had been imported as slaves, nor their descendants, whether they had become free or not, were then acknowledged as a part of the people, nor intended to be included in the general words used in that memorable instrument. . . . They had for more than a century before been regarded as beings of an inferior order, and altogether unfit to associate with the white race, either in social or political relations, and so far inferior, that they had no rights which the white man was bound to respect; and that the negro might justly and lawfully be reduced to slavery for his benefit. . . .

. . . there are two clauses in the constitution which point directly and specifically to the negro race as a separate class of persons, and show clearly that they were not regarded as a portion of the people or citizens of the government then formed. . . . upon full and careful consideration of the subject, the court is of opinion, that, upon the facts stated. . . , Dred Scott was not a citizen of Missouri within the meaning of the constitution of the United States and not entitled as such to sue in its courts. . . .

Multiple-Choice Questions

1. (E) is correct. Farming created the material basis for much greater social complexity. Greater population density prompted the development of significantly more elaborate systems of kinship, and families began grouping themselves into clans.

2. (E) is correct. Archaeological finds suggest the growing complexity of early Indian communities. The systematic butchering of animals required a sophisticated division of labor among dozens of men and women and the cooperation of a number of communities.

3. (B) is correct. Although the Spanish had superior arms, that was not the principal cause of their success. Most importantly, Cortés brilliantly exploited the resentment of the many peoples who lived under Aztec domination, forging Spanish-Indian alliances that became a model for the subsequent European colonization of the Americas.

4. (B) is correct. In the sixteenth century, the Spanish first invaded the Caribbean and used it to stage their successive wars of conquest in North and South America. The French penetrated much further inland than any European power, other than the Spanish.

5. (D) is correct. The Indians were not simply the victims of European traders. Cutthroat competition among traders provided them with the opportunity to hold out for what they considered good prices. But the fur trade was essentially an unequal exchange with furs selling in Europe for 10 or 20 times what Indians received for them.

6. (E) is correct. The Jamestown colonists included adventurers, gentleman, and "ne'er-do-wells." They had come to find gold and a passage to the Indies, and failing at both they spent their time gaming and drinking. They survived only because of Powhatan's material assistance. But as more colonists arrived from England, and demands for food escalated, Powhatan had second thoughts. During the winter of 1609–1610, more than four hundred colonists starved and a number resorted to cannibalism. Only sixty remained alive by the spring.

7. (A) is correct. Most indentured servants were young, unskilled males, who served for two to seven years; but some were skilled craftsmen, unmarried women, or even parentless children. The majority were convicts of vagabonds.

8. (C) is correct. The group that founded the first English colony in New England was mostly families but included a substantial number of single men hired by investors.

9. (A) is correct. Colonial records reveal that some Africans acquired farms, servants, and slaves of their own. They must have hired themselves out during their free time to earn enough to gain freedom for themselves.

10. (D) is correct. The Acts created the legal and institutional infrastructure of the British colonial system. The acts defined the colonies as both suppliers of raw materials and as markets for English manufactured goods. Merchants from other nations were expressly forbidden to trade in the colonies, and commodities from the colonies had to be shipped in vessels built in England or the British colonies themselves.

11. (E) is correct. John Locke argued in his *Letter on Tolerance* (1688) that church and state were voluntary societies and could only work through persuasion. That a religion was sanctioned by the state was no evidence of its truth, because different nations had different official religions.

12. (D) is correct. The Quakers who founded Pennsylvania were generally comfortable with religious and ethnic pluralism. Many of the founders of the Society of Friends had been imprisoned for their beliefs in pre-Restoration England and they were determined to prevent a repetition of this injustice in their province.

13. (C) is correct. The conclusion of the Seven Years' War left most colonists proud of their place in the British Empire. But during the war, many had begun to note important contrasts between themselves and the mother country. The soldiers of the British army shocked Americans with their profane, lewd, and violent behavior. But the colonists were equally shocked by the swift and terrible punishment that aristocratic officers used to keep these soldiers in line. The Seven Years' War also strengthened a sense of identity among the colonies.

14. (A) is correct. The cost of maintaining 10,000 troops in North America added to the enormous debt Britain had run up during the war and created a desperate need for additional revenues. In 1764, Chancellor of the Exchequer George Grenville decided to obtain the needed revenue from America, pushing through Parliament a measure known as the Sugar Act which placed a duty on sugar imported into the colonies.

15. (E) is correct. Serving short terms of enlistment, often with officers of their own choosing, militiamen resisted discipline. Indeed, in the face of battle, militia companies demonstrated appalling rates of desertion.

16. (B) is correct. The victory at Saratoga, as well as fears of British conciliation with the revolutionaries, had persuaded French Foreign Minister Vergennes to tie France to the United States. In mid-December 1777, he informed Benjamin Franklin that the king's council had decided to recognize American independence.

17. (B) is correct. Losses in the interior of the Lower South led Cornwallis to retreat to Yorktown where he would eventually be forced to surrender.

18. (B) is correct. In 1781, Virginia, the state with the most extensive western claims promised to cede its lands. Maryland then agreed to ratification, and in March, the Articles of Confederation took effect.

19. (D) is correct. To boost their power, southerners wanted slaves included in the population census for the purpose of determining proportional representation, but wanted them excluded when it came to apportioning taxes. Northerners agreed to count five slaves as the equivalent of three freemen.

20. (E) is correct. In 1790, Treasury Secretary Hamilton submitted a "Report on the Public Credit," recommending that the federal government assume the obligations accumulated by the states during the 15 years and redeem the national debt—owed to both domestic and foreign lenders—by agreeing to a new issue of interest-bearing bonds.

21. (E) is correct. The 1786 Annapolis Convention proposed modifying the Articles of Confederation. Next, the Constitutional Convention drafted the Constitution and the Bill of Rights was the first ten amendments to the Constitution.

22. (B) is correct. Growth by migration was greatest in the trans-Appalachian West, a region that was already home to approximately 100,000 Indians. From 1800 to 1850, in an extraordinary burst of territorial expansion, Americans surged westward all the way to the Pacific.

23. (E) is correct. Congress passed the most liberal land law in American history in 1820. Congress set the price of land at $1.25 an acre, the minimum purchase at eighty acres (in contrast to the 640-acre minimum in 1785) and a down payment of $100 in cash.

24. (D) is correct. Jefferson envisioned a nation of small family farms clustered together in rural communities—an agrarian republic. He believed that only a nation of roughly equal yeoman farmers, each secure in his own possessions and not dependent on someone else for his livelihood, would exhibit the concern for the community good that was essential in a republic.

25. (A) is correct. Cotton was far from being the only crop farmed by southerners; the South actually devoted more acreage to corn than to cotton in 1860, but its vast profitability affected all aspects of society.

26. (B) is correct. Most free black people lived in the countryside of the Upper South where they worked as tenant farmers or farm laborers. Although they were discriminated against in employment and in social life, there were opportunities for skilled black craftsmen in trades such as blacksmithing and carpentry.

27. (C) is correct. Although two-thirds of all southerners did not own slaves, slave owners dominated the social and political life of the region.

28. (E) is correct. The political struggles of the Jackson era, coupled with the dramatic social changes caused by expansion and economic growth, created the basic pattern of American politics: two major parties, each with at least some appeal among voters of all social classes and in all sections of the country.

29. (A) is correct. John C. Calhoun wholehearted identified with southern interests, first and foremost among which was the expansion and preservation of slavery. Northerner Daniel Webster was the outstanding orator of the age and the main spokesman for the new northern interests, supporting a high protective tariff, a national bank, and a strong federal government. Henry Clay, spokesman of the West was always eager to forge political compromises. Clay worked to incorporate western desires for cheap and good transportation into national politics.

30. (B) is correct. The rivers of New England were quickly dotted with mills wherever waterpower could be tapped. Wealthy merchants like Samuel Slater and Francis Cabot Lowell used their financial power to establish these mills.

31. (D) is correct. The immense increase in productivity made possible by the principles of division of labor and specialization, described by the other four terms, destroyed artisan production and the apprenticeship system.

32. (A) is correct. Much of America was swept by the fervor of moralistic reform and it was the new middle-class that set the agenda for reform. Reform efforts arose from the recognition that the traditional methods of small-scale local relief were no longer adequate.

33. (D) is correct. Through machine politics, workers, although they lacked the political or organizational strength to challenge the harmful effects of the market revolution, could use their numbers to ameliorate some of its effects at the local level. The machines themselves offered personal ties and loyalties—community feelings—to recent arrivals in big cities and help in hard times to workers who cast their votes directly.

34. (E) is correct. Georgia was on of the Thirteen Colonies. The Treaty of Guadalupe Hidalgo ceded California to the Untied States. Texas joined the Union in 1845 and an 1846 treaty with Britain established the boundaries of Oregon Territory.

35. (A) is correct. The Mexican Cession established the present-day boundary of Texas, the Rio Grande River, and included much of its present-day land area.

36. (D) is correct. Arguments for expansion included a God-given right to bring the benefits of democracy to other, more backward peoples; pride in what America had achieved, missionary zeal, and racist attitudes toward other peoples. Finally, some argued that America needed to expand trade with Asia to maintain its prosperity, reaching the Pacific was an important step towards this goal.

37. (A) is correct. Brown's raid shocked the South because it aroused the greatest fear, that of a slave rebellion. Southerners believed that northern abolitionists were provoking slave revolts; a suspicion apparently confirmed when documents captured at Harpers Ferry revealed that Brown had the financial support of half a dozen members of the northern elite. Even more shocking to southerners than the raid itself, was the extent of northern mourning for Brown's death.

38. (B) is correct. The results of the election shocked southerners. They were humiliated and frightened by the prospect of becoming a permanent minority in a political system dominated by a party pledged to the elimination of slavery. In southern eyes, the Republican triumph meant that they would become unequal partners in the federal enterprise, their way of life (the slave system) existing on borrowed time.

39. (A) is correct. After Grant's victory at Vicksburg on July 4, 1863 the Union controlled the entire Mississippi River and could cut off the western part of the Confederacy from the east.

40. (C) is correct. The initial northern strategy, dubbed by critics as the Anaconda Plan envisaged slowly squeezing the South with a blockade at sea and on the Mississippi River. It was proposed by the general-in-chief Winfield Scott because it avoided invasion and conquest in the hope that a strained South would recognize the inevitability of defeat and thus surrender.

41. (B) is correct. It would take the South's economy a generation to overcome the severe blows dealt by the Civil War. In 1860, the South held roughly 25 percent of the nation's wealth; a decade later it controlled only 12 percent.

42. (B) is correct. Andrew Johnson used the term "restoration" rather than "reconstruction." A lifelong Democrat with ambitions to be elected president on his own in 1868, Johnson hoped to build a new political coalition composed of northern Democrats, conservative Republicans, and southern Unionists.

43. (E) is correct. In 1870 the last five former Confederate states, Texas, Virginia, Georgia, and Mississippi were re-admitted to the Union.

44. (A) is correct. Women did not win the vote during the period of Reconstruction, but they did establish an independent suffrage movement that eventually drew millions of women into political life.

45. (E) is correct. In 1898, Congress passed the Curtis Act, which formally ended Indian communal land ownership and thereby legally dissolved Indian Territory. Similar to the Dawes Act, this directed most Indian nations to dismantle their governments, abandon their estates, and join the ranks of other homesteaders.

46. (C) is correct. The discovery of gold in California in 1848 roused fortune seekers from across the United States, Europe, and as far away as Chile and China. More than any other industry, the mining corporations laid the basis for a new economy as well as an interim government and established many of the region's first white settlements.

47. (C) is correct. Joseph Smith, the founder of the Church of Jesus Christ of Latter-Day Saints, was murdered after he announced that an angel had told him that it is "the will of Heaven that a man have more than one wife." The Mormons migrated in 1846–1847 to the Great Salt Lake Basin to form an independent theocratic state and to affirm the sanctity of plural marriage, or polygamy.

48. (E) is correct. At the time of the Civil War, the typical American business firm was a small enterprise, owned and managed by a single family, and producing goods for a local or regional market. By 1900, businesses depending on large-scale investments had organized as corporations and grown to unforeseen size.

49. (C) is correct. The new system of production required a vast number of people. Lured by the promise of a paying job in industry, many young men and women fled the family farm for the factory. By far, the largest proportion came from Europe or Asia.

50. (B) is correct. New York, Pennsylvania and Ohio all experienced between 90 and 304 strikes per state in 1880.

51. (A) is correct. Ministers called for civil service reform and the end of child labor. Supporting labor's rights to organize and, if necessary, to strike, they petitioned government officials to regulate corporations and place a limit on profits. Ministers felt that the Church should take an active part in the fight against social injustice.

52. (A) is correct. The upshot of Bryan's speech was that the government should expand the money supply by purchasing and coining all the silver offered to it.

53. (A) is correct. Progressives advocated ending political corruption, bringing more businesslike methods to governing, and offering a more compassionate legislative response to the excesses of industrialism. They were optimistic, angry over the excesses of industrial capitalism and urban growth, and believed citizens needed to intervene actively, both politically and morally, to improve social conditions.

54. (A) is correct. In order to satisfy their constituencies, machine politicians often allied themselves with progressive reformers in state legislatures.

55. (C) is correct. Businessmen saw a link between closing a community's saloons and increasing the productivity of its workers.

56. (A) is correct. The "progressive diplomacy" of Roosevelt, Taft, and Wilson, reflected a view of world affairs that stressed moralism, order, and a special, even God-given role for the United States. Commercial expansion was backed by a growing military presence in the Caribbean, Asia, and Mexico.

57. (B) is correct. The Zimmerman note was intercepted by U.S. officials and proposed an alliance between Germany and Mexico if the Untied States entered the war. It suggested Mexico take up arms against the U.S. and reclaim the lost territory in New Mexico, Texas, and Arizona.

58. (C) is correct. The most important and long-lasting economic legacy of the war was the organizational shift towards corporatism in American business. The wartime need for efficient management, manufacturing, and distribution could only be met by a greater reliance on the productivity and marketing power of large corporations.

59. (A) is correct. In the 1920s, modern mass-production techniques were increasingly applied to new consumer-durable goods—automobiles, radios, washing machines, and telephones—permitting firms to make large profits while keeping prices affordable.

60. (B) is correct. Hoover fused faith in an old-fashioned individualism with a strong commitment to the progressive possibilities offered by efficiency and rationality.

61. (A) is correct. Massive unemployment across America became the most powerful sign of a deepening depression. By 1933, almost one quarter of American workers were without jobs.

62. (A) is correct. The Social Security Act of 1935 provided for old-age pensions and unemployment insurance. A payroll tax on workers and their employers created a fund from which retirees received monthly pensions after age 65.

63. (A) is correct. The "New Deal coalition" included traditional-minded white southern Democrats, big-city political machines, industrial workers of all races, trade unionists, and many Depression-hit farmers. Black voters in the North and West went Democratic in record numbers.

64. (A) is correct. The Atlantic Charter, drawn up before the U.S. had entered the war, stated noble objectives for the world after the defeat of fascism: national self-determination, no territorial aggrandizement, equal access of all peoples to raw materials and collaboration for the improvement of economic opportunities, freedom of the seas, disarmament, and "freedom from fear and want."

65. (A) is correct. The War Powers Act established a precedent for executive authority that would endure long after the war's end. The president gained the power to reorganize the federal government and create new agencies; to establish programs censoring all news and information abridging civil liberties; to seize property owned by foreigners; and even to award government contracts without competitive bidding.

66. (E) is correct. Stalin responded by halting all traffic to West Berlin, situated deep within the Soviet-occupied zone. In response, the United States air-lifted food and supplies.

67. (B) is correct. The new families who enjoyed postwar prosperity inaugurated a spending spree of trailblazing proportions. The baby boom and high rates of consumer spending encouraged a major change in the middle-class family.

68. (A) is correct. The revolution in American life wrought by the 1944 Servicemen's Readjustment Act, known as the GI Bill of Rights, extended beyond its impact on higher education. In addition to educational grants, the act provided returning veterans with low-interest mortgages and business loans, thus subsidizing the growth of the suburbs as well as postwar expansion of higher education.

69. (C) is correct. After the Soviet Union launched its first *Sputnik* satellite in the fall of 1957, American officials worried that the country might be lagging behind the Soviets in training scientists and engineers. The Eisenhower administration pledged to strengthen support for educating American students in mathematics, science, and technology. The National Defense Education Act (NDEA) of 1958 allocated $280 million in grants for such endeavors.

70. (A) is correct. Truman and his advisers walked a political tightrope on civil rights. They understood that black voters in several key northern states would be pivotal in the 1948 election. In July 1948, the president made his boldest move on behalf of civil rights, issuing an executive order barring segregation in the armed forces.

71. (E) is correct. In Mendez v. Westiminster, a 1947 California case, and in the 1948 Delgado case in Texas, the Supreme Court upheld lower-court rulings that declared segregation of Mexican Americans unconstitutional.

72. (A) is correct. In 1953, Congress passed House Concurrent Resolution 108, which allowed Congress to terminate a tribe as a political entity by passing legislation specific to that tribe. The leader of the termination forces, Senator Arthur Watkins of Utah, declared the new law meant that "the concept that the Indian people exist within the United States as independent nations has been rejected."

73. (D) is correct. By 1967, the Vietnam War had pushed aside such ambitions of working with liberal Democrats like Johnson. They now interpreted social injustice at home as the inevitable consequence of the president's dangerous and destructive foreign policies.

🔳 **74. (C) is correct.** The so-called sixties generation, the largest generation in American history, was also the best educated. By the late 1960s, nearly half of all young adults between 18 and 21 were enrolled in college.

🔳 **75. (A) is correct.** Between 1970 and 1982 the AFL-CIO lost nearly 30 percent of its membership. The only real growth took place among public employees, including teachers, civil service workers, and health professionals—all of them dependent on sagging public budgets.

🔳 **76. (A) is correct.** By freeing banks from congressional control, President Carter inadvertently encouraged bad investments, outright fraud, and a round of disastrous bank failures.

🔳 **77. (D) is correct.** Only 15 percent of men had no opinion on the Equal Rights Amendment, based on a 1975 Gallup Poll.

🔳 **78. (A) is correct.** Before coming president, George H.W. Bush had experience in international affairs, through his work as UN ambassador and envoy to China. He served as a two-term vice president under President Reagan and in the private sector was a leader in the Texas oil industry.

🔳 **79. (B) is correct.** In 1985, the Republican Congress had enacted, amid great fanfare, the Balance Budget and Emergency Deficit Reduction Act, more popularly known as Gramm-Rudman after its principal authors, Phil Gramm and Warren Rudman. The act mandated automatic spending cuts if the government failed to meet fixed deficit reduction goals leading to a balanced budget by 1991.

🔳 **80. (D) is correct.** Under George W. Bush's presidency the American economy continued to slow while budget deficits rose. The American dollar weakened against foreign currencies like the Euro and Chinese yuan.

Document-Based Question

Some argue that the United States is the product of an ongoing debate about the nature of liberty and equality, resulting in the continued expansion of democracy. Considering the changes the United States experienced from the Revolutionary War to the Civil War, do you agree or disagree with this assessment?

As Americans learned in the years following the American Revolution, democracy was not a static concept or practice. The principles established in the Declaration of Independence were difficult to translate into the practical mechanisms of power, and the new nation witnessed a number of controversies as its citizens struggle to apply their ideals to daily life. One of the earliest conflicts emerged during the Constitutional Convention in Philadelphia, when representatives debated the legitimacy of federal power over state power (**DOCUMENT 1**). Conflict over the power of the new state and its structure was also evident in Shay's Rebellion in Massachusetts. Despite the eventual suppression of the rebellion, some Americans like Thomas Jefferson, who recorded his response to the events to fellow founder James Madison, believed that rebellion was necessary to nurture democracy and crush the development of any potential tyranny (**DOCUMENT 2**). As the rebels that followed Daniel Shays had protested the nature of representation and power in Massachusetts, the new nation also struggled with the question of state representation in Congress in the debates that resulted in the Three-Fifths Compromise (**DOCUMENT 3**).

As the new nation worked out its system of representation, the challenges of world diplomacy propelled the federal government to issue restrictions on its citizens, especially noteworthy in the passage of the Alien and Sedition Acts (**DOCUMENT 4**). Though these acts were designed to increase national security, many realized that they challenged some of the fundamental rights guaranteed in the Constitution as part of American democracy. The question of Constitutional rights continued to be a subject of debate with the expansion of suffrage to all white males, which introduced a new definition of citizenship within a democracy (**DOCUMENT 5**). However, the expansion of the franchise to white males effectively underscored the fact that many were still left out of the democratic state. Native Americans, whose continued struggle to hold on to their native lands increased during the westward expansion of national boundaries, found that they held no real standing within the American system (**DOCUMENT 6**). Similarly, women and free African Americans were barred from voting, and slavery continued to present a challenge to many definitions of democracy (**DOCUMENTS 7 AND 8**). With the decision of the Supreme Court regarding the status of Dred Scott, a new interpretation of democracy was established, although it would not be unilaterally adopted and would, in fact, contribute to the political crisis leading to the Civil War (**DOCUMENT 9**).

AP United States History
Sample Practice Test 2

1. The people generally recognized as the first to develop a settled farming way of life in the southwest were the
   (A) Hohokam.
   (B) Skoaquik.
   (C) Arawaks.
   (D) Pimas and Papagos.
   (E) Mogollon.

2. Among the confederacies of the South, like the Cherokee, life was controlled by
   (A) the Great Sun.
   (B) both male and female members of matrilineal class.
   (C) high priests.
   (D) living in highly dispersed settlements to limit feuds.
   (E) the Longhouse Council of patrilineal clans.

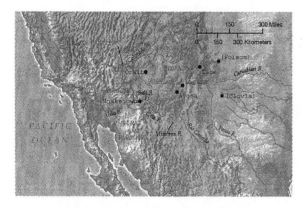

3. The map of the Southwestern Indians shows settlements in all of the following places EXCEPT
   (A) Taos.
   (B) Acoma.
   (C) Snaketown.
   (D) Laguna.
   (E) Moundville.

4. The Spanish monopoly of the New World was broken with the
   (A) signing of the Treaty of Torsedillas in 1494.
   (B) French successfully seizing Louisiana in 1564.
   (C) French defeat of the Spanish at St. Augustine in 1607.
   (D) English defeat of the Spanish Armada in 1588.
   (E) English defeat in the battle of Agincourt.

5. The most important legacy of the Roanoke expedition was
   (A) written accounts of the area and Indian peoples there.
   (B) the permanent military beachhead left there.
   (C) the mutually beneficial contacts with the area natives.
   (D) the discovery of the tobacco plant.
   (E) the intermarriage of the English settlers and certain Indian tribes.

6. The English settlers in southern New England were mainly interested in
   (A) trade.
   (B) land expansion.
   (C) gold and silver.
   (D) building missions for the Indians.
   (E) fishing and fur trading.

7. The southern part of early Carolina communities had a cultural character that was distinctly
   (A) English.
   (B) Spanish.
   (C) Dutch.
   (D) Scots-Irish.
   (E) West Indian.

8. Both Bacon's Rebellion and Culpeper's Rebellion showed conflict between these two communities:
   (A) Tidewater and frontier regions of Virginia and North Carolina.
   (B) Puritans and dissenters in Rhode Island and Massachusetts.
   (C) "Praying town" Indians and Covenant Chain Indians in New England.
   (D) slave traders and those who objected to slavery.
   (E) New York and New Jersey over the Hudson River boundary.

9. Which one of the following is <u>NOT</u> characteristic of the West African societies that many slaves were taken from to the New World?
   (A) polygamous marriage and family systems
   (B) sophisticated agricultural methods
   (C) elaborate trade networks
   (D) a few large ethnic groups
   (E) non-Christian religious practices

10. Most Africans were enslaved
    (A) by white kidnappers who invaded African territory.
    (B) by cooperation between European and African traders.
    (C) for committing criminal offenses against the tribe.
    (D) for violating religious taboos.
    (E) by the Arab states of North Africa.

11. English authorities made the Church of England the official state religion in
    (A) New England.
    (B) Pennsylvania.
    (C) Rhode Island.
    (D) the Chesapeake colonies.
    (E) New Jersey.

12. Social class in America was
    (A) non-existent.
    (B) based on land monopoly.
    (C) based on economic rank.
    (D) based on a meritocracy.
    (E) similar to European aristocracy.

13. In the eyes of the radical element in the British colonies, legislation like the Quebec Act set up a colonial government where
    (A) religious toleration was not practiced.
    (B) steps were taken toward full democracy.
    (C) the protection of individual liberties was paramount.
    (D) each colony basically governed itself.
    (E) colonists were denied representative self-government.

14. The British experience at Lexington and Concord foreshadowed a central difficulty with which they had to contend throughout the American Revolution. It was
    (A) a lack of readily available supplies.
    (B) fighting in the midst of an armed population.

    (C) Indian participation on the colonial side.
    (D) lack of knowledge of the countryside.
    (E) fighting against their fellow countrymen.

15. Which one of the following lists states that developed the most radically democratic constitutions?
    (A) Pennsylvania/Vermont
    (B) Maryland/South Carolina
    (C) New York/Massachusetts
    (D) New Hampshire/New Jersey
    (E) Maryland/New Jersey

16. Which one of the following is <u>NOT</u> a part of the declarations of rights in state constitutions?
    (A) trial by jury
    (B) the inherent rights of men
    (C) free speech
    (D) freedom of religion
    (E) voting

17. While not strategically significant, Washington revived morale by sneaking across the Delaware River to surprise the British at
    (A) Morristown.
    (B) Princeton.
    (C) Trenton.
    (D) White Plains.
    (E) Long Island.

18. Ratified in 1798, the Eleventh Amendment to the Constitution
    (A) declared that no state could be sued by citizens of another state.
    (B) declared that the Federal Government could not sue a state government.
    (C) created separate ballot for president and vice president.
    (D) established a system of federal courts.
    (E) spelled out the membership of the president's Cabinet.

19. To defend his National Bank's constitutionality, Hamilton proposed this argument:
    (A) delegated powers.
    (B) strict construction.
    (C) nullification.
    (D) northern merchants.
    (E) loose construction.

20. The Virginia and Kentucky Resolutions were an attempt to counter the Alien and Sedition Acts by defending
    (A) the rights of the states.
    (B) executive privilege.
    (C) freedom of the press.
    (D) implied powers.
    (E) political prisoners.

21. The United States entered the War of 1812 deeply divided along sectional lines. The sections most prowar were
    (A) Middle States and South.
    (B) West and South.
    (C) Middle States and New England.
    (D) West and New England.
    (E) Middle States and the West.

22. While the Treaty of Ghent that ended the War of 1812 was inconclusive on most issues, it did
    (A) specifically address the issue of British impressment of American sailors.
    (B) force the British to recognize the legitimacy of American neutral rights.
    (C) include a British agreement to vacate western posts.
    (D) exclude the French from further settlement and fort construction.
    (E) include provisions for a buffer state for neutral Indian peoples in the Northwest.

23. This particular event convinced Tecumseh that he needed to shift from a defensive strategy to active resistance to American westward expansion:
    (A) Louisiana Purchase.
    (B) Battle of Fallen Timbers.
    (C) Treaty of Fort Wayne.
    (D) *Chesapeake* and *Leopard* Incident.
    (E) Battle of Tippecanoe.

24. The most important export crops of the American colonial period were
    (A) cotton, sugar, and rice.
    (B) sugar, rice, and tobacco.
    (C) indigo, sugar, and sorghum.
    (D) cotton, tobacco, and rice.
    (E) tobacco, rice, and indigo.

25. The map of the United States at the time of the Missouri Compromise shows that
    (A) in 1820 there was more land area in the free states than in the slave.
    (B) the northern border of Missouri was at 36°30' north latitude.
    (C) the unorganized territory after 1820 was mostly south of 36°30'.
    (D) except for Missouri, slavery would not be allowed in the territories north of 36°30'.
    (E) slavery would be allowed in Kansas Territory.

26. Throughout the 1830s, southerners tightened these to protect the slave system:
    (A) manumission laws.
    (B) gag rules.
    (C) migrations.
    (D) black codes.
    (E) laws regulating slave marriages.

27. One of the most noteworthy features of the slave community in the American South was
    (A) its acceptance of white paternalism within its own social structure.
    (B) the slaves' belief that they could do better in America.
    (C) its refusal to incorporate Christian religious practices.
    (D) its animosity toward free African Americans.
    (E) the expanded kinship network that developed within it.

28. The "Trail of Tears" describes the removal of this group to Oklahoma:
    (A) Creeks.
    (B) Choctaws.
    (C) Iroquois.
    (D) Seminoles.
    (E) Cherokees.

29. The most prevalent themes of American writers and artists were the
    (A) presidential leaders and parties.
    (B) issues surrounding gender and democracy.
    (C) Pilgrims and Puritans.
    (D) battles of the Revolution.
    (E) wilderness and westward expansion.

30. The breakdown of the family work system may have had a liberating effect on
    (A) free African Americans.
    (B) Irish immigrants.
    (C) apprentices.
    (D) wage slaves.
    (E) farm women and children.

31. The religion that captured the attention of the new middle class in the early 1800s
    (A) emphasized an intellectual as opposed to emotional experience.
    (B) convinced its converts that original sin doomed all but an elite to damnation.
    (C) had its greatest impact on young males.
    (D) incorporated an enthusiastic evangelistic approach to religious practice.
    (E) promoted a narrow path to salvation.

32. The immediate impact of the abolitionist movement on the South was to
    (A) promote discussion on ending slavery.
    (B) stifle expressions of dissenting opinion.
    (C) embarrass the southern state legislatures.
    (D) force a loosening of restrictions on slaves.
    (E) close post offices that received abolitionist literature.

33. Most of the immigrants who came to the United States before the Civil War were from
    (A) Ireland and Germany.
    (B) England and Scotland.
    (C) Italy and Poland.
    (D) Africa and the West Indies.
    (E) Norway and Germany.

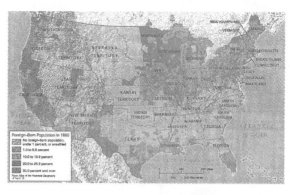

34. The map of the distribution of foreign-born residents in 1860 shows that states with some of the highest percentages of foreign-born workers included all of the following EXCEPT
    (A) Wisconsin.
    (B) California.
    (C) New Jersey.
    (D) Minnesota.
    (E) Michigan.

35. In Mexico, people of mixed blood (Indian and Spanish) were called
    (A) mulattos.
    (B) creoles.
    (C) iriknocks.
    (D) cajuns.
    (E) mestizos.

36. The Republic of Texas was not immediately annexed by the United States largely because of
    (A) the fact that Texas would have to be admitted as a slave state.
    (B) the fear of Mexican anger and opposition.
    (C) the opposition of Stephen F. Austin.
    (D) fear that there were too many outlaws residing in the republic.
    (E) the isolationist policies of the Democratic Party.

37. Which one of the following was NOT part of the Compromise of 1850?
    (A) California would be a free state.
    (B) New Mexico could be a slave state.
    (C) Slave trade ended in the District of Columbia.
    (D) Texas would cede land to New Mexico Territory.
    (E) a stronger fugitive slave law

38. Both the Kansas-Nebraska Act and the Dred Scott decision invalidated this agreement.
    (A) Tallmadge Amendment.
    (B) Compromise of 1850.
    (C) Three-fifths compromise.
    (D) Wilmot Proviso.
    (E) Missouri Compromise.

39. "Government girls" referred to women who were
    (A) nurses in both Union and Confederate armies.
    (B) hired by both governments to harvest crops.
    (C) wards of the government.
    (D) spies for the Confederacy.
    (E) workers in the Confederate bureaucracy.

40. Lincoln's action relative to Fort Sumter in April 1861 was to
    (A) send military supplies and naval reinforcement.
    (B) overwhelm the South from the outset.
    (C) do nothing and see what the South would do.
    (D) negotiate behind the scenes.
    (E) send a relief force with food only.

41. Johnson saw Reconstruction as the province of the
    (A) federal executive.
    (B) Congress.
    (C) individual states.
    (D) military.
    (E) Supreme Court.

42. The Radical Republican intention with the Tenure of Office Act was to limit the powers of
    (A) the planter Democrats.
    (B) the Supreme Court.
    (C) President Johnson.
    (D) Congress.
    (E) Lincoln admirers.

43. The Slaughterhouse cases, *U.S.* v. *Reese*, *U.S.* v. *Cruikshank*, and the Civil Rights Cases of 1883 all had the effect of
    (A) extending legal protection for African Americans.
    (B) limiting the ability of the Democratic Party to reestablish itself in the South.
    (C) restricting the protections of the Fourteenth and Fifteenth Amendments.

(D) ending the power of the Radical Republicans completely.
(E) enhancing southern access to public education.

44. To which state were the Nez Percé Tribe originally sent after surrendering?
    (A) Kansas
    (B) Michigan
    (C) Oregon
    (D) Oklahoma
    (E) Washington

45. The founder of the Mormons was
    (A) Brigham Young.
    (B) Henry Comstock.
    (C) Jedediah Smith.
    (D) Billy Sunday.
    (E) Joseph Smith.

46. The demise of the cattle barons was brought about largely because of
    (A) overgrazing.
    (B) scurvy.
    (C) cattle diseases.
    (D) cattle ingesting loco weed.
    (E) unionization by cowboys.

47. John D. Rockefeller's horizontal combination was so successful that he controlled this percent of the nation's oil refining by 1880:
    (A) 50.
    (B) 70.
    (C) 60.
    (D) 80.
    (E) 90.

48. This group of workers was most affected by the influx of immigrants in the late nineteenth century:
    (A) Chinese Americans.
    (B) middle-class Americans.
    (C) Irish Americans.
    (D) Native Americans.
    (E) African Americans.

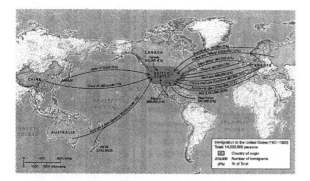

49. According to the chart on Immigration to the United States, 1901–1920, the greatest percentage of immigrants to the United States came from
(A) Italy and Austria-Hungary.
(B) Ireland and Germany.
(C) Japan and China.
(D) Mexico and the West Indies.
(E) Scandinavia and France.

50. Jim Crow laws were designed to foster
(A) black voter registration in the South.
(B) racial harmony.
(C) integration.
(D) limits on immigration.
(E) racial segregation.

51. Hawaii was annexed
(A) to protect American missionaries from cannibalism.
(B) for imperialistic reasons.
(C) for the coffee.
(D) to rid the island of the oppressive regime of King Kalakaua.
(E) to bring land reform to the Hawaiian peasants.

52. What is the significance of the Ludlow Massacre?
(A) It resulted in widespread demonstrations against John D. Rockefeller, Jr.
(B) It called for reform in the National Guards.
(C) It demonstrated how profitable mines operated when management and labor cooperated.
(D) It increased the wages for workers.
(E) It improved the living conditions for labor.

53. Social Darwinists held the view that racism toward African Americans was acceptable because
(A) with special treatment, African Americans would take jobs away from whites.
(B) that is just the way it is.
(C) African Americans were more advanced than whites and did not need special treatment.
(D) African Americans needed to fight their own battles for equality.
(E) they believed African Americans were predisposed to vice and crime; therefore, it was acceptable to hold racist views.

54. W.E.B. Du Bois represented the first effort to encourage African Americans to recognize
(A) African American culture is a source of communal strength and should be preserved.
(B) African Americans should seek to sublimate their culture to white culture.
(C) African Americans should only strive for manual work.
(D) African Americans should return to Africa.
(E) African Americans should remain in the South.

55. Why was the federal government more supportive of unions during WWI?
(A) A decline in union membership caused the government to fill the vacuum.
(B) It was not as concerned with labor issues because of the war.
(C) The government recognized past policies were unjust.
(D) Businesses asked the government to improve conditions for workers.
(E) Labor shortages required more attention to labor.

56. When the war broke out in Europe, Wilson declared that he would follow this policy towards both sides:
(A) neutrality.
(B) open door.
(C) dollar diplomacy.
(D) preparedness.
(E) zero tolerance.

57. Which one of the following was <u>NOT</u> one of the events from February 1917 to March of 1917 that prompted the United States to declare war on Germany?
(A) Germany resumes unrestricted submarine warfare.
(B) The Zimmerman note is discovered and revealed.
(C) Germany sinks seven U.S. merchant ships.
(D) German submarines sink the *Lusitania* and *Sussex*.
(E) Germany proposes an alliance with Mexico.

58. The Kellogg-Briand pact
(A) paved the way for the United States to join the League of Nations.
(B) renounced war but had no powers of enforcement.
(C) was an extension of the Big Stick policy.
(D) loaned funds to Germany so that war reparations could be paid.
(E) established ratios of naval tonnage for the major world powers.

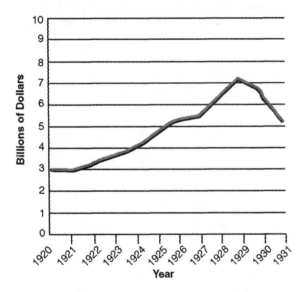

59. The graph of Consumer Debt, 1920–1931 shows that consumer debt
(A) rose steadily and rapidly throughout the 1920s.
(B) peaked in 1929 and then began a sharp decline.
(C) was higher in 1931 after the onset of the Great Depression than it had been in 1929.
(D) experienced its sharpest rises in the 1920s as people bought consumer goods after the war.
(E) tripled between 1920 and 1926.

60. Religious fundamentalism appealed to millions of Americans because it
(A) was a bulwark against the uncertainties they faced in a changing society.
(B) appealed to revelation, reason, and tradition.
(C) offered Christians a better place to worship.
(D) allowed for a more liberal interpretation of the Bible.
(E) allowed Church members to network with like-minded individuals.

61. The Public Works Administration or PWA was based on the principle of "priming the pump," which meant stimulating the economy through
(A) providing jobs and increasing consumer spending.
(B) forcing economic growth through government decree.
(C) making credit available to businesses, banks, and industries.
(D) encouraging small businesses and self-employment.
(E) setting prices at the 1909 to 1914 purchasing power average.

62. The Fair Labor Standards Act established this:
(A) federal minimum wage.
(B) credit card laws.
(C) public housing construction.
(D) closed shop.
(E) open shop.

63. Which of the following states was <u>LEAST</u> affected by the Dust Bowl?
(A) Colorado
(B) Oklahoma
(C) Texas
(D) Kansas
(E) Montana

64. The majority of African American soldiers served in this capacity in World War II:
(A) in construction and stevedore work.
(B) on the front lines.
(C) on naval vessels in the Pacific.
(D) on European foxholes.
(E) training other soldiers for combat.

65. The Potsdam Conference indicated what about the Grand Alliance?
    (A) It was more and more unified.
    (B) It was strong.
    (C) The alliance between the English and the Soviets was strong.
    (D) It was indicated that the Allies did not want to punish Germany.
    (E) It was fragile.

66. Women were encouraged to do the following in the 1950s:
    (A) quit their jobs and stay home.
    (B) balance work and family.
    (C) continue working in the defense industry.
    (D) stay at work so their family could remain middle class.
    (E) pursue a college degree.

67. The GI Bill underwrote these two items and caused a boom in both areas:
    (A) federal employment and defense spending.
    (B) college education and housing.
    (C) agricultural development and land ownership.
    (D) auto and television credit plans.
    (E) technical training and atomic energy jobs.

68. While the Federal Highway Act of 1956 helped both the automobile and construction industries, it hurt
    (A) mass transit systems.
    (B) the trucking industries.
    (C) urban center construction.
    (D) farming communities.
    (E) the satellite industry.

69. All of the following are associated with suburban life EXCEPT
    (A) reemphasis on religion.
    (B) the centrality of the automobile.
    (C) domesticity.
    (D) mass transit.
    (E) conformity to societal standards.

70. A symbolic first, Jackie Robinson broke the color barrier in
    (A) the Olympics.
    (B) the University of Alabama Law School.
    (C) Army Officer Corps.
    (D) Major League Baseball.
    (E) football.

71. The Greensboro sit-in established what phase in civil rights tactics?
    (A) working through the Congress and state houses
    (B) revolutionary
    (C) slow legal phase
    (D) violent resistance
    (E) activist phase

72. The new Immigration and Nationality Act of 1965
    (A) established a quota system that is still in place today.
    (B) limited the number of Asians that could enter the United States.
    (C) abolished national origin quotas.
    (D) enforced an alien land law.
    (E) allowed for confiscation of illegally held land.

73. Why did Johnson not want to inform the people about the realities of the Vietnam War?
    (A) He feared losing support for his domestic programs.
    (B) He was a devoted believer in executive privilege.
    (C) He was secretive by nature.
    (D) The Republicans undercut his war policies.
    (E) He feared public protest.

74. By the time of his death in 1968, Martin Luther King, Jr.
    (A) had called for a crusade against communism.
    (B) abandoned his nonviolent philosophy.
    (C) openly opposed the Vietnam War.
    (D) lost hope to bring about change.
    (E) had transferred control of the movement to younger leaders.

75. Why did the American public distrust Gerald Ford as president?
    (A) Because of his liberal record in Congress.
    (B) Because he could not solve the nation's economic problems.
    (C) Because he seemed clumsy and inarticulate.
    (D) Because he was too closely associated with Nixon.
    (E) Because he pardoned Nixon of possible federal crimes.

76. Political action and mobilization in the 1970s tended to concentrate
    (A) on mass demonstrations.
    (B) in communities.
    (C) on particular states.
    (D) on getting control of political parties.
    (E) in labor union groups.

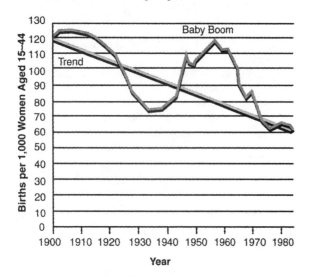

77. The graph showing the United States Birth Rate, 1930–1980 shows
    (A) the baby boom of the 1950s was unprecedented.
    (B) the peak of the baby boom came in 1970.
    (C) the increase in the birth rate did not begin until 1945.

    (D) the baby boom never reached the birth rate of 1901–1910.
    (E) by 1980, the birth rate was as high as in 1950.

78. After the Persian Gulf War,
    (A) Saddam Hussein punished the Iraqi Kurds.
    (B) trade sanctions limited Saddam's power.
    (C) Iraqi Shia were able to express themselves freely.
    (D) U.S. forces left Saudi Arabia immediately.
    (E) Saddam Hussein sought an alliance with Al Qaeda.

79. Clinton proposed health-care reform to
    (A) give the first lady more power.
    (B) provide more affordable care to more people.
    (C) establish a socialist system.
    (D) undermine the medical community in the United States.
    (E) create a health-care system based on the successful British model.

80. The insurgents in Iraq included all of the following EXCEPT
    (A) terrorists who used Iraq as a base before the war.
    (B) criminal elements.
    (C) members of the Baath Party.
    (D) Sunni Muslims who opposed the loss of their power.
    (E) foreign Islamist fighters.

Document-Based Questions

As the United States transformed from a largely rural, agricultural nation to a predominantly urban and industrial one in the late nineteenth and early twentieth century, many different political philosophies were advanced to address this change. Compare and contrast the competing ideologies that provided the basis for the different visions of government articulated during that era.

Use the following documents and your knowledge of the period to construct your essay.

DOCUMENT 1

Source: The People's Party Platform (1892)

We have witnessed for more than a quarter of a century the struggles of the two great political parties for power and plunder, while grievous wrongs have been inflicted upon the suffering people. We charge that the controlling influences dominating both these parties have permitted the existing dreadful conditions to develop without serious effort to prevent or restrain them. Neither do they now promise us any substantial reform. They have agreed together to ignore in the coming campaign every issue but one. They propose to drown the outcries of a plundered people with the uproar of a sham battle over the tariff, so that capitalists, corporations, national banks, rings, trusts, watered stock, the demonetization of silver, and the oppressions of the usurers may all be lost sight of. They propose to sacrifice our homes, lives and children on the altar of mammon; to destroy the multitude in order to secure corruption funds from the millionaires. . . .

We declare, therefore,-

First. That the union of the labor forces of the United States this day consummated shall be permanent and perpetual; may its spirit enter all hearts for the salvation of the republic and the uplifting of mankind!

Second. Wealth belongs to him who creates it, and every dollar taken from industry without an equivalent is robbery. "If any will not work, neither shall he eat." The interests of rural and civic labor are the same; their enemies are identical.

Third. We believe that the time has come when the railroad corporations will either own the people or the people must own the railroads; and, should the government enter upon the work of owning and managing all railroads, we should favor an amendment to the Constitution by which all persons engaged in the government service shall be placed under a civil service regulation of the most rigid character, so as to prevent the increase of the power of the national administration by the use of such additional government employees.

First, Money. We demand a national currency, safe, sound, and flexible, issued by the general government only, a full legal tender for all debts, public and private, and that, without the use of banking corporations, a just, equitable, and efficient means of distribution direct to the people, at a tax not to exceed two per cent per annum, to be provided as set forth in the sub-treasury plan of the Farmers' Alliance, or a better system; also, by payments in discharge of its obligations for public improvements.

(a) We demand free and unlimited coinage of silver and gold at the present legal ratio of sixteen to one.

(b) We demand that the amount of circulating medium be speedily increased to not less than fifty dollars per capita.

(c) We demand a graduated income tax.

DOCUMENT 2

Source: Eugene V. Debs, "The Outlook for Socialism in the United States" (1900)

The differences between the Republican and Democratic parties involve no issue, no principle in which the working class has any interest. . . .

Between these parties socialists have no choice, no preference. They are one in their opposition to socialism, that is to say, the emancipation of the working class from wage slavery, and every workingman who has intelligence enough to understand the interest of his class and the nature of the struggle in which it is involved will once and for all time sever his relations with them both; and recognizing the class struggle which is being waged between producing workers and nonproducing capitalists, cast his lot with the class-conscious, revolutionary Socialist Party, which is pledged to abolish the capitalist system, class rule and wage slavery-a party which does not compromise or fuse, but, preserving inviolate the principles which quickened it into life and now give it vitality and force, moves forward with dauntless determination to the goal of economic freedom.

The political trend is steadily toward socialism. The old parties are held together only by the cohesive power of spoils, and in spite of this they are steadily disintegrating. Again and again they have been tried with the same results, and thousands upon thousands, awake to their duplicity, are deserting them and turning toward socialism as the only refuge and security.

DOCUMENT 3

DOCUMENT 4

Source: Theodore Roosevelt, from The New Nationalism (1910)

It has become entirely clear that we must have government supervision of the capitalization, not only of the public service corporations, including, particularly, railways, but of all corporations doing an interstate business. I do not wish to see the nation forced into the ownership of the railways if it can possibly be avoided, and the only alternative is thoroughgoing and effective regulation, which shall be based on a full knowledge of all the facts, including a physical valuation of property. . . . Combinations in industry are the result of an imperative economic law which cannot be repealed by political legislation. The effort at prohibiting all combination has substantially failed. The way out lies, not in attempting to prevent such combinations, but in completely controlling them in the interest of the public welfare.

DOCUMENT 5

Source: Helen M. Todd, "Getting Out the Vote" (1911)

No words can better express the soul of the woman's movement, lying back of the practical cry of "Votes for Women," better than this sentence which had captured the attention of both Mother Jones and the hired girl, "Bread for all, and Roses too." Not at once; but woman is the mothering element in the world and her vote will go toward helping forward the time when life's Bread, which is home, shelter and security, and the Roses of life, music, education, nature and books, shall be the heritage of every child that is born in the country, in the government of which she has a voice.

There will be no prisons, no scaffolds, no children in factories, no girls driven on the street to earn their bread, in the day when there shall be "Bread for all, and Roses too."
To help to make such a civilization possible is the meaning of "Votes for Women."

DOCUMENT 6

Source: Warren G. Harding, Campaign Speech at Boston (1920)

This republic has its ample tasks. If we put an end to false economics which lure humanity to utter chaos, ours will be the commanding example of world leadership today. If we can prove a representative popular government under which a citizenship seeks what it may do for the government rather than what the government may do for individuals, we shall do more to make democracy safe for the world than all armed conflict ever recorded. The world needs to be reminded that all human ills are not curable by legislation, and that quantity of statutory enactment and excess of government offer no substitute for quality of citizenship. . . .

My best judgment of America's needs is to steady down, to get squarely on our feet, to make sure of the right path. Let's get out of the fevered delirium of war, with the hallucination that all the money in the world is to be made in the madness of war and the wildness of its aftermath. Let us stop to consider that tranquility at home is more precious than peace abroad, and that both our good fortune and our eminence are dependent on the normal forward stride of all the American people.

DOCUMENT 7

Source: Herbert Hoover, Speech at New York City (1932)

There is one thing I can say without any question of doubt-that is, that the spirit of liberalism is to create free men; it is not the regimentation of men under government. It is not the extension of bureaucracy. I have said in this city before now that you cannot extend the mastery of government over the daily life of a people without somewhere making it master of people's souls and thoughts. Expansion of government in business means that the government in order to protect itself from the political consequences of its errors or even its successes is driven irresistibly without peace to greater and greater control of the nation's press and platform. Free speech does not live many hours after free industry and free commerce die. It is a false liberalism that interprets itself into government operation of business. Every step in that direction poisons the very roots of liberalism. It poisons political equality, free speech, free press and equality of opportunity. It is the road not to liberty, but to less liberty. True liberalism is found not in striving to spread bureaucracy, but in striving to set bounds to it. It is found in an endeavor to extend cooperation between free men. True liberalism seeks all legitimate freedom first in the confident belief that without such freedom the pursuit of other blessings is in vain. Liberalism is a force truly of the spirit proceeding from the deep realization that economic freedom cannot be sacrificed if political freedom is to be preserved.

DOCUMENT 8

Source: FDR's First Inauguration Speech (1933)

This nation asks for action, and action now.

Our greatest primary task is to put people to work. This is no unsolvable problem if we face it wisely and courageously. It can be accomplished in part by direct recruiting by the government itself, treating the task as we would treat the emergency of a war, but at the same time, through this employment, accomplishing greatly needed projects to stimulate and reorganize the use of our natural resources.

Hand in hand with this, we must frankly recognize the overbalance of population in our industrial centers and, by engaging on a national scale in the redistribution, endeavor to provide a better use of the land for those best fitted for the land.

The task can be helped by definite efforts to raise the values of agricultural products and with this the power to purchase the output of our cities.

It can be helped by preventing realistically the tragedy of the growing loss, through foreclosure, of our small homes and our farms.

It can be helped by insistence that the Federal, State and local governments act forthwith on the demand that their cost be drastically reduced.

It can be helped by the unifying of relief activities which today are often scattered, uneconomical and unequal. It can be helped by national planning for and supervision of all forms of transportation and of communications and other utilities which have a definitely public character.

DOCUMENT 9

Multiple-Choice Questions

1. (E) is correct. Among the first to develop a settled farming way of life were a people known as the Mogollon, who farmed maize, beans, and squash, and constructed ingenious pit structures in permanent village sites along what is today the southern Arizona-New Mexico border.

2. (B) is correct. There were no ruling classes or kings, and leaders included women as well as men. Most peoples reckoned their descent matrilineally (back through generations of mothers), and after marriage, husbands left the homes of their mothers to reside with the families of their wives.

3. (E) is correct. Moundville is not on the map.

4. (D) is correct. In 1588, King Philip II of Spain sent a fleet of 130 ships carrying 30,000 men to invade the British Isles. Countered by captains such as Drake and Hawkins, who commanded smaller and more maneuverable ships, and frustrated by an ill-timed storm that the English chose to interpret as an act of divine intervention, the Spanish Armada foundered. The Spanish monopoly of the New World had been broken in the English Channel.

5. (A) is correct. Thomas Harriot and John White mapped the area, surveyed its commercial potential, and studied the Indian residents. Harriot's account of the New World provided the single most accurate description of North American Indians at the moment of their contact with Europeans.

6. (B) is correct. The principal concern of the English was not commerce, although the fur trade remained an important part of their economy, but the acquisition of Indian land for their growing settlements. The English believed they had the right to take what they thought of as "unused" lands—lands that were not enclosed.

7. (E) is correct. Most South Carolina settlers came from Barbados, a Caribbean colony the English had founded in 1627, which grew wealthy from the production of sugar. By the 1680s, the island had become overpopulated with English landowners and African slaves. Hundreds of Barbadians, both masters and slaves, relocated to South Carolina, lending that colony a distinctly West Indian character.

8. (A) is correct. The rebellions signaled a developing conflict between frontier districts and the more established coastal region. In the aftermath of these rebellions, colonial authorities in Virginia and North Carolina began to favor armed expansion into Indian territory, hoping to gain the support of backcountry men by enlarging the stock of available colonial land.

9. (D) is correct. In the sixteenth century, more than a hundred different peoples lived along the coast of West Africa, from Cape Verde south to Angola. In the north were the Wolofs, Madingos, Hausas, Ashantis, and Yorubas; to the south were the Ibos, Sekes, Bakongos and Mbundus.

10. (B) is correct. As the slave trade peaked in the middle of the eighteenth century, trading posts gave way to independent European and American traders who set up operations with the cooperation of local headmen or chiefs.

11. (D) is correct. English authorities made the Church of England the state religion in the Chesapeake colonies. Residents paid taxes to support the Church and were required to attend services. No other churches were allowed into Virginia and Maryland and dissenters were excluded or exiled.

12. (C) is correct. British North America celebrated social mobility: the class system was remarkably open and the entrance of newly successful planters, commercial farmers, and merchants into the upper ranks was not only possible but common.

13. (E) is correct. The British established an authoritarian and anti-republican royal government in Quebec. Furthermore, it established Catholicism as the state religion in

Quebec. The Act was a frightening preview of what imperial authorities might have in store for American colonists.

14. (B) is correct. As the British attempted to capture colonial supplies in Concord and retreat to Boston, they were outnumbered by approximately 4,000 Massachusetts militiamen defending their own community against outsiders. The engagement forecast what would become a central problem for the British: fighting an armed community defending itself.

15. (A) is correct. Pennsylvania instituted a radical democracy with a unicameral assembly, elected annually by all free male taxpayers. Delegates would be responsive to their constituent, sessions of assembly were open to the public, and there was no governor. For these reasons, Pennsylvania/Vermont is the best choice.

16. (E) is correct. Declaration of rights included trial by jury in criminal constitutions, "the free exercise of religion," freedom of speech and of the press, and the inherent rights of men.

17. (C) is correct. On Christmas night 1776, Washington defeated the Hessian forces in a surprise attack on their headquarters in Trenton, New Jersey.

18. (A) is correct. After the Supreme Court overthrew the common law principle that a sovereignty could not be sued without its consent, it supported the Constitution's grant of federal jurisdiction over disputes between a state and citizens of another state. In response, the Eleventh Amendment declared that no state could be used by citizens from another state.

19. (E) is correct. Hamilton reasoned that the Constitution "implied" the power to use whatever means were "necessary and proper" to carry out its enumerated power. This position was known as "loose constructionist" and stood in opposition to Jefferson's "strict constructionist" position that the powers of the federal government must be limited to those specifically enumerated in the Constitution.

20. (A) is correct. Madison and Jefferson co-authored the resolutions that declared the Constitution no more than a compact among the sovereign states and advocating the power of the states to "nullify" unconstitutional laws. The resolutions would later be used to justify the secession of the Southern states at the beginning of the Civil War.

21. (B) is correct. President James Madison yielded to the War Hawks' clamor for action in June 1812, and his declaration of war passed in the U.S. Senate by the close vote of 19 to 13, the House by 79 to 49. The vote was sectional, with New England and the Middle States in opposition and the West and South strongly prowar.

22. (C) is correct. Like the war itself, the Treaty of Ghent was inconclusive. The major issues of impressment and neutral rights were not mentioned, but the British did agree to evacuate their western posts, and late in the negotiations they abandoned their insistence on a buffer state for neutral Indian peoples in the Northwest.

23. (C) is correct. After the Treaty of Fort Wayne, in which the United States gained three million acres of Delaware and Potawatomi land in Indiana, Tecumseh decided on active resistance. Confronting William Henry Harrison, governor of Indiana Territory, directly, Tecumseh argued that the land belonged to the larger community of all the Indian peoples; no one tribe could give away the common property of all. He then warned that any surveyors or settlers who ventured into the three million acres would risk their lives.

24. (E) is correct. African American slaves grew the great export crops of the colonial period—tobacco, rice, and indigo—on which slave owners' fortunes were made, and their presence shaped southern society and culture.

25. (D) is correct. The Missouri Compromise stipulated that Missouri would enter the Union as a slave state but slavery would be prohibited in the Louisiana Territory north of 36°30'.

26. (D) is correct. Throughout the South in the 1830s, state legislatures tightened black codes—laws concerning free black people. Free African Americans could not carry firearms, could not purchase slaves, and were liable to the criminal penalties meted out to slaves. They could not testify against whites, hold office, vote, or serve in the militia.

27. (E) is correct. Parents made great efforts to teach their children the family history and to surround them with a supportive and protective kinship network. The emphasis on family and on kinship networks had an even more fundamental purpose: the kinship of the entire community represented a conscious rejection of white paternalism. The slaves' ability to structure a community that expressed these values was extraordinary.

28. **(E) is correct.** In 1838, resisting Cherokees were driven west to Oklahoma. A 7,000-man army escorting them watched thousands (perhaps a quarter of the 16,000 Cherokees) die along the way.

29. **(E) is correct.** James Fenimore Cooper's Leatherstocking novels achieved wide success in both American and Europe. Cooper's novels established the experience of westward expansion, of which the conquest of Indians was a vital part, as a serious and distinctive American literary theme.

30. **(E) is correct.** Although the breakdown of the family work system undoubtedly harmed independent urban artisans, it may have had a liberating effect on the women and the children of farm families. About a third of the Lowell women workers did not return to their farm homes, instead remaining in town and marrying urban men or continuing to do work. There is no doubt that working at Lowell provided these women with new options. Women and children who earned wages by doing out-work at home may have found their voices strengthened by evidence of their power and worth.

31. **(D) is correct.** Evangelism's stress on self-discipline and individual achievement helped them adjust to new business conditions. The enthusiasm and optimism in the face of evangelism aided what was often a profound personal transformation in the face of the markets stringent new demands.

32. **(B) is correct.** The South responded to the abolitionist movement by banning abolitionist literature and encouraging the harassment and abuse of anyone distributing it. Most serious, the majority of southern states reacted by toughening laws concerning emancipation, freedom of movement, and all aspects of slave behavior.

33. **(A) is correct.** Most of the immigrants to the United States during this period came from Ireland and Germany. Political unrest and poor economic conditions in Germany, and the catastrophic Potato Famine of 1845–1849 in Ireland were responsible for an enormous surge in immigration from those countries between 1845 and 1854.

34. **(C) is correct.** Less than 10.0 percent of New Jersey's 1860 population was foreign-born.

35. **(E) is correct.** In New Spain, *mestizo vaqueros* were renowned for their horsemanship. The Americanization of their name made "buckaroos" of the American cowboys to whom they later taught their skills.

36. **(A) is correct.** The United States refused to grant Texas statehood when it applied for admission to the Union in 1837. Petitions opposing the admission of a fourteenth slave state (against thirteen free states) poured into Congress. Congress debated and ultimately dropped the Texas application.

37. **(B) is correct.** The four-step compromise admitted California as a free state, allowed the residents of New Mexico and Utah territories to decide the slavery issue for themselves, ended the slave trade in the District of Columbia, and passed a new fugitive slave law.

38. **(E) is correct.** The Kansas-Nebraska Act's popular sovereignty position effectively repealed the Missouri Compromise of 1820 by allowing the possibility of slavery in the new territories. The *Dred Scott* decision declared the Missouri Compromise unconstitutional by asserting that the federal government had no right to interfere with the free movement of property throughout the territories.

39. **(E) is correct.** "Government girls" were a good part of the Confederate bureaucracy because of the need for military manpower.

40. **(E) is correct.** Both sides claimed Fort Sumter, a crucial fort in South Carolina. With the fort surrounded and dangerously low on supplies, Lincoln took cautious and careful action, notifying the governor of South Carolina that he was sending a relief force to the fort carrying only food and no military supplies. As the relief force neared Charlestown harbor, the Confederate general opened fire.

41. **(A) is correct.** Johnson defined Reconstruction as the province of the executive, not the legislative branch, and he planned to restore the Union as quickly as possible.

42. (C) is correct. Congress passed several laws aimed at limiting Johnson's power. One of these, the Tenure of Office Act, stipulated that any officeholder appointed by the president with the Senate's advice and consent could not be removed until the Senate had approved a successor.

43. (C) is correct. In *United States* v. *Reese* and *United States* v. *Cruikshank*, the Court restricted congressional power to enforce the Ku Klux Klan Act, thus restricting the powers of the Fourteenth and Fifteenth Amendments. Future prosecution would depend on the states, rather than on federal authorities.

44. (A) is correct. Promised they would be returned to Oregon, the Nez Percé were sent instead to disease-ridden bottomland near Fort Leavenworth in Kansas, and then to Oklahoma.

45. (E) is correct. The Mormons fled western New York in the 1830s for Illinois and Missouri, only to face greater persecution in the Midwest, when their founder, Joseph Smith, was murdered.

46. (A) is correct. High profits in the cattle industry attracted speculative capital and large companies. The industry collapsed in the 1880s due to overgrazing.

47. (E) is correct. By 1882 Standard Oil Company, founded by John D. Rockefeller, controlled more than 90 percent of the nation's oil-refining industry. Horizontal combination allowed the merger of Rockefeller's competitors in the same industry into his Standard Oil Company.

48. (E) is correct. The group of workers most affected by the influx of immigrants was the African Americans. African American men found themselves excluded from many fields. African American men were systematically driven from restaurant service and barred from new trades such as boilermaking, plumbing, electrical work, and paperhanging, which European immigrants secured for themselves.

49. (A) is correct. Over six million people immigrated from Italy and Austria-Hungary between 1901 and 1920, accounting for more than forty percent of the total immigrants during that period.

50. (E) is correct. Local and state governments codified racist ideology by passing discriminatory and segregationist legislation, which became known as Jim Crow laws.

51. (B) is correct. Hawaii was often viewed as a steppingstone to the vast Asian markets. In addition, American sugar planters had a great investment in the area.

52. (A) is correct. News of the Ludlow Massacre shocked millions and aroused widespread protests and demonstrations against the policies of Colorado Fuel and iron and its owner, John D. Rockefeller, Jr.

53. (E) is correct. The more virulent strains of racism held that blacks were a "degenerate" race predisposed to vice, crime, and disease and destined to lose the struggle for existence with whites. By portraying blacks as incapable of improvement, racial Darwinism justified a policy of repression and neglect towards African Americans.

54. (A) is correct. W.E.B. Du Bois argued that black people would always feel the tension between an African heritage and their desire to assimilate as Americans. *Souls* represented the first effort to embrace African American culture as a source of collective black strength and something worth preserving.

55. (E) is correct. As the demand for workers intensified, the federal government was forced to recognize that labor, like any other resource or commodity, would have to be more carefully tended to than in peacetime.

56. (A) is correct. President Wilson issued a formal proclamation of neutrality and urged citizens to be "impartial in thought as well as action."

57. (D) is correct. Germany sunk the *Lusitania* in May 1915 and sunk the *Sussex* in March 1916.

58. (B) is correct. In 1928, with great fanfare, the United States and 62 other nations signed the Pact which grandly and naively renounced war in principle.

59. (B) is correct. Consumer debt peaked in 1929 at over $7 billion before beginning a sharp decline.

60. (A) is correct. Fundamentalism was a religious creed and a cultural defense against the uncertainties of modern life for millions of Americans.

61. (A) is correct. "Priming the pump" meant providing jobs, thus stimulating the economy through increased consumer spending.

62. (A) is correct. The 1938 Fair Labor Standards Act established the first federal minimum wage and set a maximum workweek of 44 hours for all employees engaged in interstate commerce.

63. (E) is correct. The hardest-hit regions in the Dust Bowl were western Kansas, eastern Colorado, western Oklahoma, the Texas Panhandle, and eastern New Mexico.

64. (A) is correct. The army channeled black recruits into segregated, poorly equipped units, which were commanded by white officers. The majority served in the Signal, Engineer, and Quartermaster Corps, mainly in construction or stevedore work. Only toward the end of the war, when the shortage of infantry neared a crisis, were African-Americans permitted to rise to combat status.

65. (E) is correct. The negotiations at the Potsdam Conference lacked the spirited cooperation characteristic of the wartime meetings of Allied leaders. The Americans, British, and Soviet delegations had a huge agenda, including reparations, the future of Germany, and the status of other Axis powers such as Italy.

66. (A) is correct. Popular opinion and expert advice urged women to return to their homes. Eighty-six percent of the public disapproved of a woman supporting a man and saw something vaguely communistic about it.

67. (B) is correct. The G.I. Bill provided educational and employment benefits for men returning from war.

68. (A) is correct. The Federal Highway Act of 1956 gave another key boost to postwar growth, especially in the suburbs. But it also accelerated the decline of American mass transit and older cities. By1970, the nation possessed the world's best roads and one of its worst public transportation systems.

69. (D) is correct. Mass transit was not associated with suburban life. Rather the creation of better highways and the family automobiles of suburban life led to the decline in the American transportation system.

70. (D) is correct. In 1947, Jackie Robinson broke the color barrier in major league baseball, winning rookie-of-the-year honors with the Brooklyn Dodgers. Robinson's courage in the face of racial epithets from fans and players paved the way for the black baseball players who soon followed him to the big leagues.

71. (E) is correct. The Greensboro sit-in sent a shock wave throughout the South. During the next eighteen months 70,000 people—most of them black students, a few of them white allies—participated in sit-ins against segregation and marked the activist phase of the civil rights era.

72. (C) is correct. In 1965, Congress passed a new Immigration and Nationality Act, abolishing the national origins quotas that had been in place since the 1920s, and substituting overall hemispheric limits.

73. (A) is correct. Several advisers urged the president to inform the American people about his decisions in Vietnam, even to declare a state of national emergency. But Johnson feared he would lost momentum on domestic reform, including his antipoverty programs, if he drew attention to foreign policy.

74. (C) is correct. By 1968 the civil rights leadership stood firmly in opposition to the war, and Martin Luther King, Jr. had reached a turning point in his life. Despite the threats of investigation from the FBI, King abandoned his customary caution in criticizing U.S. policy in Vietnam.

75. (E) is correct. Replacing Nixon in August 1974, Gerald Ford reassured the public that "our long national nightmare is over"—then quickly pardoned Nixon for all the federal crimes he may have committed. The pardon reinforced public cynicism toward government and Ford in particular.

76. (B) is correct. By the end of the 1970s, evangelical Christians had become the backbone of the New Right and chief fund-raisers for key organizations such as the National Conservative Political Action Committee and the Moral Majority. These organizations gained their political support from within communities.

■ **77. (A) is correct.** Iraqi Kurds, who had supported the U.S. invasion in hopes it would topple Saddam, face violent reprisals, including gassing and chemical weapons, from the Iraqi army.

■ **78. (D) is correct.** The peak of the baby boom had a birth rate of nearly 120 births/1000 women. In 1910 the birth rate was nearly 125 births/1000 women.

■ **79. (B) is correct.** Clinton's biggest setback during his first term was in the area of health-care reform. Nearly 40 million Americans had no health insurance. Many simply could not afford it, and others were denied coverage by private insurers because of preexisting conditions such as AIDS and heart disease. His goal was to provide more affordable coverage to more people.

■ **80. (A) is correct.** A coordinated, heavily armed, and well-financed resistance to the American occupation gained strength in early 2004. It included elements of Sadaam's Baath party, foreign Islamist fighters, disaffected Sunni Muslims, and criminal gangs.

Document Based Question

As the United States transformed from a largely rural, agricultural nation to a predominantly urban and industrial one in the late nineteenth and early twentieth centuries, many different political philosophies were advanced to address this change. Compare and contrast the competing ideologies that provided the basis for the different visions of government articulated during that era.

Use the following documents and your knowledge of the period to construct your essay.

Increased urbanization and its problems, the spread of industry and the consolidation of commerce, and increased class differences were results of the shift from a rural agrarian society to an urban industrial one in the late nineteenth and early twentieth centuries. Such change was often greeted with fear and protest as much as it was welcomed, and many Americans struggled to redefine their institutions to keep pace with such change. The nature of government and its role in the new system was one of the greatest subjects of debate at this time, especially with regard to the relationship between government and business. Farmers resisted the growing power of industry, and united with others to form the alternative People's Party, also known as the Populist Party, and promoted their own vision of American government (**DOCUMENT 1**). Still others rejected the new system and called for its abolition and replacement with a Socialist system (**DOCUMENT 2**). The majority, however, seemed interested in maintaining the American political system, with modifications or reforms. President Theodore Roosevelt built upon the momentum of the Progressive movement to strengthen government's role in regulating industry (**DOCUMENTS 3 AND 4**). Other Progressive reformers, including African Americans and women, argued for an expansion of the franchise in order to introduce new elements into American political life (**DOCUMENT 5**). By the end of World War I, it was clear that Americans had still not reached a consensus regarding the exact powers of the federal government. Leading presidential candidates were especially divided. Warren Harding focused on the contributions of citizens over the exercise of federal power, while Herbert Hoover argued that challenges of the Great Depression could not be met with an expansion of governmental regulation over business without endangering personal liberty within a liberal state (**DOCUMENTS 6 AND 7**). Franklin Delano Roosevelt signaled a shift from this definition of government when he took office in 1933 and announced that he would seek a more active role for the federal government in meeting the crisis of the Depression (**DOCUMENT 8**). Under Roosevelt's New Deal, many programs were created to assist Americans in a time of national financial devastation (**DOCUMENT 9**). Though not without opposition, the increased role of the federal government has formed the basis of the American political system since that time.